The MCSE Windows 2000 Server Cram Sheet

This Cram Sheet provides the distilled, key facts about Exam 70-215, "Installing, Configuring, and Administering Microsoft Windows 2000 Server." Review these important points as the last thing you do before entering the test center. Pay close attention to those items you feel you need to review. A good exam strategy is to transfer all the facts you can recall from this cram sheet onto a piece of paper once you sit to take the exam.

INSTALLATION AND CONFIGURATION

1. Windows 2000 can be installed on the following types of partitions:
   - NTFS
   - FAT32
   - FAT16
2. Only the following operating systems can be upgraded to Windows 2000 Server:
   - Windows NT Server 4.0
   - Windows NT Server 3.51
3. `Winnt.exe` is used to perform an upgrade from a 16-bit operating system. Some common command-line switches are
   - `/s`—The source of the installation files.
   - `/u`—The unattended answer file.
   - `/udf`—The Uniqueness Database File (UDF).
4. `Winnt32.exe` is used to perform an upgrade from a 32-bit operating system. Some common command-line switches are
   - `/s`—The source of the installation files.
   - `/unattend`—The unattended answer file.
   - `/udf`—The Uniqueness Database File (UDF).
   - `/cmdcons`—Used to install the Recovery Console (after installation).
   - `/checkupgradeonly`—Used to verify that your computer can be upgraded to Windows 2000 Server.
5. Windows 2000 Server setup disks can be created using the MAKEBOOT (16-bit) or MAKEBT32 (32-Bit) utilities that are found in the BOOTDISK folder on the Windows 2000 Server CDROM.
6. Unattended answer files are used to provide input so the setup process can be automated. Answer files can be created manually using a text editor, or via the wizard in the Setup Manager utility.
7. Uniqueness Database Files are used to specify variations, such as different computer names. This is so that a common unattended answer file can be used.
8. The Sysprep utility is used to remove the computer name and unique Security Identifiers (SIDs) from a Windows 2000 installation, so that the disk can be duplicated using Ghost or a similar utility.
9. Slipstreaming is the process of applying Service Pack updates to a copy of Windows 2000 that is stored in a local folder or a network share. Subsequent installations performed from these files will automatically include all up-to-date files. Slipstreaming is performed by using the `-s` switch when installing the Service Pack.

NETWORK PROTOCOLS

1. TCP/IP is automatically installed with Windows 2000 when a network adapter is detected.
2. IP addresses can be assigned dynamically using a DHCP server or statically.
3. Clients use Automatic Private IP Addressing if they are enabled for DHCP but no DHCP server is available. DHCP clients will assign themselves an IP address in the range 169.254.0.1–169.254.255.254.
4. Windows 2000 supports the NWLink protocol, which is Microsoft's version of Novell's IPX/SPX protocol. NWLink is not installed by default but can be added through the Network and Dial-up Connections applet.
5. The frame type defines how IPX/SPX data is formatted. If only one frame type is present on the network, autodetect self-configures itself to match it. If multiple frame types are detected on the network, autodetect defaults to the first frame type it detects. NetWare servers 3.3 and later use the 802.2 frame type. NetWare servers earlier than 3.3 use the 802.3 frame type. You can manually configure NWLink for multiple frame types.

6. Client Service for NetWare (CSNW) is the Microsoft version of the NetWare client. It allows a Windows client to log on to and access NetWare servers.
7. Gateway Services for NetWare (GSNW) allows a Windows 2000 Server computer to act as a gateway through which other Windows clients can access file and print services on NetWare servers. In this case, only the Windows 2000 Server acting as a gateway has to have NWLink and Client Services for Netware (CSNW) installed. NWLink and CSNW are installed automatically with GSNW.
8. Network bindings determine the protocols and services available for a network adapter as well as the order in which they are used.
9. IP packet filters control the type of inbound traffic that is allowed to enter a computer and/or network. IP traffic can be filtered by protocol and destination port number.
10. Network Monitor can be used to capture and analyze network traffic.
11. IPSec is used to protect data sent between two hosts on a network.
12. IPSec supports two modes: tunneling mode and transport mode. In tunneling mode, only the IP header is encrypted.

STORAGE

1. The Distributed File System (Dfs) is installed by default in Windows 2000 Server. There are two types of Dfs roots:
   - *Standalone*—The root configuration information is stored on a single server.
   - *Domain*—The root configuration is stored in Active Directory. This makes it more fault-tolerant.
2. There can be only one Dfs root per server.
3. Windows 2000 supports the previous Windows file systems, but will install with NTFS 5.0 by default. NTFS 5.0 is required for the new file system features such as volumes and disk quotas.
4. Windows 2000 Basic disks are the same as the disks in previous versions of Windows NT. On each physical disk you can create a maximum of four primary partitions, or three primary partitions and one extended partition with multiple logical drives.
5. Windows 2000 Dynamic disks use volumes instead of partitions. An unlimited number of volumes can be configured on each physical disk. A Dynamic Volume can be extended at any time. The following types of volumes are supported in Windows 2000:
   - *Simple Volume*—The same as a basic partition. Disk space is used from only one physical disk.
   - *Spanned Volume*—A spanned volume can contain space from up to 32 physical disks. While you can add space non-destructively, there is no fault tolerance. If you lose a single disk, the entire volume is lost.
   - *Striped Volumes*—RAID 0, data is written across multiple disks in 64K stripes. Striped volumes have the fastest disk I/O performance. However they are not fault tolerant; if you lose one disk, you lose the entire volume.
   - *RAID 5 Volumes*—A RAID 5 volume can contain space from up to 32 physical disks. Data and parity information is written across multiple disks in 64K stripes. Fault tolerant, the parity information allows you to rebuild a failed physical disk.
6. Basic disks can be upgraded to dynamic disks at any time without data loss. You cannot revert a dynamic disk back to a basic disk without complete data loss on the volume.
7. Dynamic disks can only be read directly by Windows 2000, or by older clients when accessing a shared folder on a Windows 2000 computer over a network.
8. Disk Quotas allow you to specify how much disk space a user is allowed to use on any particular NTFS volume. You can specify disk quotas universally for all users of a volume or individually for specific users. Quotas are only supported on Windows 2000 volumes, which require NTFS 5.0. Disk quotas can only be applied to a volume, they cannot be applied to folders.

REMOTE ACCESS

1. Remote access allows users to dial into a server and access the network as though they were physically connected.
2. DCHP relay agent enables DHCP clients to obtain an IP address from a DHCP server on the network when they dial in.
3. Remote Access Policies determine who has permissions to dial in and the characteristics of the connection. Remote Access Policies consist of conditions, permissions, and profiles.
4. The default Remote Access Policy is to allow access to users who have dial-in permission enabled in their user account settings.
5. Multilink enables multiple phone lines to be combined into a single logical connection to increase available bandwidth.
6. The following protocols can be used for RAS authentication: PAP, SPAP, CHAP, MSCHAP, and EAP.
7. Windows 2000 supports two types of encryption: MPPE and IPSec.
8. VPNs are created using a tunneling protocol. A tunnel can be established using either PPTP or L2TP.

MCSE Windows® 2000 Server

Will Schmied

Lee Scales

MCSE Windows® 2000 Server: Exam 70-215

International Standard Book Number: 0-7897-2873-7

Library of Congress Catalog Card Number: 2003100814

Printed in the United States of America

First Printing: April 2003

06 05 04 03 4 3 2

Trademarks

All terms mentioned in this book that are known to be trademarks or service marks have been appropriately capitalized. Que Certification cannot attest to the accuracy of this information. Use of a term in this book should not be regarded as affecting the validity of any trademark or service mark.

Windows is a registered trademark of Microsoft Corporation.

Warning and Disclaimer

Every effort has been made to make this book as complete and as accurate as possible, but no warranty or fitness is implied. The information provided is on an "as is" basis. The authors and the publisher shall have neither liability nor responsibility to any person or entity with respect to any loss or damages arising from the information contained in this book or from the use of the CD or programs accompanying it.

Publisher
Paul Boger

Executive Editor
Jeff Riley

Development Editor
Steve Rowe

Managing Editor
Charlotte Clapp

Project Editor
Tonya Simpson

Production Editor
Benjamin Berg

Indexer
Ken Johnson

Proofreader
Tanya Hayes

Technical Editors
Ed Tetz
Jeff Dunkelberger

Team Coordinator
Pamalee Nelson

Multimedia Developer
Dan Scherf

Interior Designer
Gary Adair

Page Layout
Michelle Mitchell

Que Certification • 201 West 103rd Street • Indianapolis, Indiana 46290

A Note from Series Editor Ed Tittel

You know better than to trust your certification preparation to just anybody. That's why you, and more than two million others, have purchased an Exam Cram book. As Series Editor for the new and improved Exam Cram 2 series, I have worked with the staff at Que Certification to ensure you won't be disappointed. That's why we've taken the world's best-selling certification product—a finalist for "Best Study Guide" in a CertCities reader poll in 2002—and made it even better.

As a "Favorite Study Guide Author" finalist in a 2002 poll of CertCities readers, I know the value of good books. You'll be impressed with Que Certification's stringent review process, which ensures the books are high-quality, relevant, and technically accurate. Rest assured that at least a dozen industry experts—including the panel of certification experts at CramSession—have reviewed this material, helping us deliver an excellent solution to your exam preparation needs.

We've also added a preview edition of PrepLogic's powerful, full-featured test engine, which is trusted by certification students throughout the world.

As a 20-year-plus veteran of the computing industry and the original creator and editor of the Exam Cram series, I've brought my IT experience to bear on these books. During my tenure at Novell from 1989 to 1994, I worked with and around its excellent education and certification department. This experience helped push my writing and teaching activities heavily in the certification direction. Since then, I've worked on more than 70 certification-related books, and I write about certification topics for numerous Web sites and for *Certification* magazine.

In 1996, while studying for various MCP exams, I became frustrated with the huge, unwieldy study guides that were the only preparation tools available. As an experienced IT professional and former instructor, I wanted "nothing but the facts" necessary to prepare for the exams. From this impetus, Exam Cram emerged in 1997. It quickly became the best-selling computer book series since "*...For Dummies*," and the best-selling certification book series ever. By maintaining an intense focus on subject matter, tracking errata and updates quickly, and following the certification market closely, Exam Cram was able to establish the dominant position in cert prep books.

You will not be disappointed in your decision to purchase this book. If you are, please contact me at etittel@jump.net. All suggestions, ideas, input, or constructive criticism are welcome!

Ed Tittel

Contents at a Glance

Introduction xvii

Chapter 1 Microsoft Certification Exams 1

Chapter 2 Installing Windows 2000 Server 21

Chapter 3 Installing, Configuring, and Troubleshooting Access to Resources 67

Chapter 4 Configuring and Troubleshooting Hardware Devices and Drivers 111

Chapter 5 Managing, Monitoring, and Optimizing System Performance, Reliability, and Availability 141

Chapter 6 Managing, Configuring, and Troubleshooting Storage Use 181

Chapter 7 Configuring and Troubleshooting Windows 2000 Network Connections 215

Chapter 8 Implementing, Monitoring, and Troubleshooting Security 263

Chapter 9 Practice Test #1 299

Chapter 10 Answer Key to Practice Test #1 321

Chapter 11 Practice Test #2 331

Chapter 12 Answer Key to Practice Test #2 355

Appendix A Additional Resources 365

Appendix B Glossary 369

Appendix C What's on the CD 379

Appendix D Using the PrepLogic Practice Tests, Preview Edition Software 383

Index 391

Table of Contents

Introduction xvii

Self Assessment xxiii

Chapter 1
Microsoft Certification Exams 1

Introduction 2
Assessing Exam-Readiness 2
What to Expect at the Testing Center 3
Exam Layout and Design: New Case Study Format 4
- Multiple-Choice Question Format 5
- Build-List-and-Reorder Question Format 6
- Create-a-Tree Question Format 8
- Drag-and-Connect Question Format 9
- Select-and-Place Question Format 10

Microsoft's Testing Formats 12
Strategies for Different Testing Formats 14
- Case Study Exam Strategy 14
- Fixed-Length and Short-Form Exam Strategy 15
- Adaptive Exam Strategy 16

Question-Handling Strategies 17
Mastering the Inner Game 18
Additional Resources 19

Chapter 2
Installing Windows 2000 Server 21

Introduction 22
Windows 2000 Installation Preparation 22
- Hardware Compatibility 23
- Software Compatibility 24
- Disk Size and Partitions 25
- Current Operating System Upgradability 26

Performing Attended Installations of Windows 2000 Server 27
CD-ROM–Based Installation 28
Installing with the Setup Disks and a CD-ROM 35
Installing by Manually Invoking WINNT32.EXE 36
Installing by Manually Invoking WINNT.EXE 37
Performing Unattended Installations of Windows 2000 Server 37
Script-Based Unattended Installation Using Answer Files 38
Unattended Installations Using Disk Duplication 51
Performing Upgrade Installations from Windows NT 4.0 Server 53
Installing Windows 2000 Service Packs 55
Updating an Installation Source by Using Slipstreaming 55
Installing Service Packs 57
Troubleshooting Failed Installations 58
Practice Questions 60
Need to Know More? 66

Chapter 3
Installing, Configuring, and Troubleshooting Access to Resources ..67

Introduction 68
Install and Configure Network Services for Interoperability 68
NetWare Interoperability 68
File and Print Services for NetWare 72
Interoperability with Macintosh 72
Unix Interoperability 73
Monitor, Configure, Troubleshoot, and Control Access to Printers 73
Local Versus Remote Print Devices 75
Printing Environment Configuration and Security 77
Monitor, Configure, Troubleshoot, and Control Access to Files, Folders, and Shared Folders 79
The File Allocation Table (FAT) File System 79
The NT File System (NTFS) 79
Configure, Manage, and Troubleshoot a Standalone Distributed File System (Dfs) 81
Monitor, Configure, Troubleshoot, and Control Local Security on Files and Folders 86
Monitor, Configure, Troubleshoot, and Control Access to Files and Folders in a Shared Folder 90
Monitor, Configure, Troubleshoot, and Control Access to Files and Folders via Web Services 92

Monitor, Configure, Troubleshoot, and Control Access to Web Sites 95
Web Site Performance and Reliability Features in IIS 5.0 95
Web Site Security Features in IIS 5.0 96
IIS Security 98
Managing IIS Servers 99
Hosting Several Sites on One IIS 5.0 Server 100
Individual Site Management in IIS 5.0 101
Practice Questions 102
Need to Know More? 109

Chapter 4
Configuring and Troubleshooting Hardware Devices and Drivers 111

Introduction 112
Configuring Driver Signing Options 113
Configuring Driver Signing via Group Policy 115
Configuring Driver Signing Locally via the Control Panel 118
Working with Digitally Signed Drivers 119
Verifying Hardware Compatibility 120
The Hardware Compatibility List (HCL) 120
Windows 2000 Readiness Analyzer 121
Installing and Configuring Hardware Devices 122
Using the Add/Remove Hardware Wizard 124
Configuring Support for Legacy Hardware Devices 125
Updating Device Drivers 128
Troubleshooting Hardware Problems 130
Confirming Hardware Installation Status 130
Troubleshooting Hardware Installation Problems 132
Practice Questions 133
Need to Know More? 140

Chapter 5
Managing, Monitoring, and Optimizing System Performance, Reliability, and Availability 141

Introduction 142
Managing, Monitoring, and Optimizing System Performance 142
Task Manager 142
Monitoring System Resources 147
System Monitor 148
The Performance Logs and Alerts Snap-In 150

Optimizing System Resources 155
Optimizing Memory Usage 156
Optimizing the Disk Subsystem 157
Optimizing Processor Usage 158
Optimizing Network Access 159
Windows 2000 Backup 160
Types of Backups 161
System State Backups 163
Safe Mode 165
Recover System State Data by Using Directory Services Restore Mode 166
Recovery Console 170
Emergency Repair Disk (ERD) 172
Using the Emergency Repair Disk 174
Practice Questions 175
Need to Know More? 179

Chapter 6
Managing, Configuring, and Troubleshooting Storage Use 181

Introduction 182
Monitoring and Configuring Disks and Volumes 183
Viewing Disk Properties 184
Viewing Volume Health Status 185
Viewing and Configuring Volume Properties 186
Upgrading Basic Storage to Dynamic Storage 188
Creating New Partitions and Volumes 190
Formatting Volumes and Partitions 191
Deleting Volumes and Partitions 192
Extending Dynamic Volume Size 192
Assigning Drive Letters and Paths 193
Adding New Disks 193
Troubleshooting Disks and Volumes 193
Using the Disk Cleanup Utility 194
Using Check Disk 195
Defragmenting Disks 196
Configuring NTFS File and Folder Compression 197
Managing Disk Quotas 200
Recovering from Disk Failures 204
Recovering a Failed Mirrored Drive 204
Recovering a Failed RAID-5 Drive 205
Practice Questions 207
Need to Know More? 213

Chapter 7
Configuring and Troubleshooting Windows 2000 Network Connections . 215

Introduction 216
Installing, Configuring, and Troubleshooting Network Adapters and Drivers 216
General Network Adapter Properties 217
Advanced Network Adapter Properties 217
Driver Properties 218
Resources Properties 219
Power Management Properties 219
Troubleshooting Network Adapters 219
Installing, Configuring, and Troubleshooting Network Protocols 220
TCP/IP 222
NWLink 229
NetBEUI 230
Installing and Configuring Network Services 231
The Domain Name Service (DNS) 232
The Dynamic Host Control Protocol (DHCP) 233
The Windows Internet Naming Service 236
Troubleshooting TCP/IP 239
Internet Connection Sharing 240
Troubleshooting Internet Connection Sharing 243
Routing and Remote Access Service 244
Configuring Inbound Connections 245
Creating a Remote Access Policy and Profile 247
Virtual Private Networks (VPNs) 249
Terminal Services 250
Terminal Services Application Services Mode 254
Practice Questions 256
Need to Know More? 262

Chapter 8
Implementing, Monitoring, and Troubleshooting Security 263

Introduction 264
User Accounts and Groups 264
Domain Accounts 265
Local Accounts 267
Local Groups 268
The Local Users and Groups Snap-In 272
User Authentication 273

System Policies 274
Windows 2000 Group Policy 276
Local Computer Policy 278
Security Configuration Tool Set 285
Security Templates 285
Security Configuration and Analysis Tool 287
Encrypting File System (EFS) 289
Recovering an Encrypted File or Folder 291
Encryption Using the Cipher Command 292
Practice Questions 293
Need To Know More? 297

Chapter 9
Practice Test #1 299

Chapter 10
Answer Key to Practice Test #1 321

Chapter 11
Practice Test #2 331

Chapter 12
Answer Key to Practice Test #2 355

Appendix A
Additional Resources 365

Web Resources 366
Magazine Resources 367
Book Resources 367

Appendix B
Glossary 369

Appendix C
What's on the CD-ROM 379

PrepLogic Practice Tests, Preview Edition 380
Exclusive Electronic Version of Text 380
Easy Access to Online Pointers and References 381

Appendix D
Using the PrepLogic Practice Tests, Preview Edition Software 383

Exam Simulation 384
Question Quality 384
Interface Design 384
Effective Learning Environment 384
Software Requirements 385
Installing PrepLogic Practice Tests, Preview Edition 385
Removing PrepLogic Practice Tests, Preview Edition from Your Computer 385
Using PrepLogic Practice Tests, Preview Edition 386
Starting a Practice Test Mode Session 386
Starting a Flash Review Mode Session 387
Standard PrepLogic Practice Tests, Preview Edition Options 387
Time Remaining 388
Your Examination Score Report 388
Review Your Exam 389
Get More Exams 389
Contacting PrepLogic 389
Customer Service 389
Product Suggestions and Comments 389
License Agreement 390

Index 391

About the Authors

Will Schmied (BSET, MCSE, CWNA, MCSA, Security+, Network+, A+), consultant and author, is the principal partner of Area 51 Partners. Will holds a bachelor's degree in mechanical engineering technology from Old Dominion University. He currently resides in Newport News, Virginia with his wife, Allison; their children, Christopher, Austin, Andrea, and Hannah; and their two dogs, Peanut and Jay. You can visit Will at `www.area51partners.com` or `www.netserverworld.com`.

Lee Scales holds the MCSE+I (NT4) as well as the MCSE (Windows 2000) certifications and has been working in the computer industry for more than 20 years, including consulting engagements with several Fortune 100 companies. He is currently employed as a senior consultant with a Microsoft Gold Partner, where his duties include working with companies that are migrating to the Windows 2000 platform with Active Directory. In addition to his consulting duties, he has been developing courseware for the Windows platform for several years and has been a contributing/co-author to titles in the original *Exam Cram* and the *Windows Power Toolkit* series.

When not buried neck deep in a networking project, Lee enjoys camping, hunting, and fishing, especially in places where you can't plug in a laptop, and the cell phone doesn't work.

Acknowledgments

For Allison. Thank you for your love, your support, and most of all, your never-ending patience.—Will Schmied

Several people have helped with the development of this book and without them, it would not have been possible. First, a very special thanks to our series editor, Ed Tittel, for getting the *Exam Cram 2* series up and running and always finding writing projects for me. Thanks to my editor, Dawn Rader, a fellow Scorpio, for all her hard work in keeping me focused. In addition, thanks to my son, Davin, who was very understanding on those days when daddy couldn't come out and play.—Lee Scales

We Want to Hear from You!

As the reader of this book, *you* are our most important critic and commentator. We value your opinion and want to know what we're doing right, what we could do better, what areas you'd like to see us publish in, and any other words of wisdom you're willing to pass our way.

As an executive editor for Que, I welcome your comments. You can email or write me directly to let me know what you did or didn't like about this book—as well as what we can do to make our books better.

Please note that I cannot help you with technical problems related to the *topic* of this book. We do have a User Services group, however, where I will forward specific technical questions related to the book.

When you write, please be sure to include this book's title and author as well as your name, email address, and phone number. I will carefully review your comments and share them with the author and editors who worked on the book.

Email: feedback@quepublishing.com

Mail: Jeff Riley
Que Certification
201 West 103rd Street
Indianapolis, IN 46290 USA

For more information about this book or another Que title, visit our Web site at www.quepublishing.com. Type the ISBN (excluding hyphens) or the title of a book in the Search field to find the page you're looking for.

Introduction

Welcome to the *Exam Cram 2* series. The purpose of this book is to prepare you to take Microsoft certification exam 70-215, "Installing, Configuring, and Administering Windows 2000 Server."

Books in the *Exam Cram 2* series are designed to help you understand the material you will encounter on the exam. Their purpose is to cover the topics you are likely to encounter on the exam, but they do not teach you everything you need to know about a topic. The book contains as much information as possible about the exam.

The book begins by providing useful information about how to prepare for the exam and what to expect on your test day. To begin, we recommend that you take the self-assessment included in the book. This will help you to evaluate your current knowledge base against what is required for an MCSE candidate. This will help you determine where your training should begin, which may be some classroom training or reading one of the several study guides available.

It is also strongly recommended that you gain some hands-on experience with the technologies being covered on the exam. Again, this may be through some classroom training or by installing and configuring the software on a home system. In any case, nothing beats hands-on experience when it comes to learning essential exam topics.

Once you pass 70-215, you receive the status of Microsoft Certified Professional and demonstrate your efficiency and knowledge on the exam topics. Passing this exam can also earn you credit toward the following certifications:

- *Microsoft Certified Systems Engineer*—This is one of the core exams required to obtain MCSE status.
- *Microsoft Certified Database Administrator*—This exam can be used as one of the electives for the MCDBA certification.
- *Microsoft Certified Systems Administrator*—This exam can be used as one of the electives required to achieve MCSA status.

Taking a Certification Exam

This section gives information on exam pricing and registration processes.

Once you've fully prepared for an exam and feel that you ready for the next step, you'll need to register with a testing center to take the exam. To do so, contact either Prometric or Virtual University Enterprise using the following information:

- *Prometric*—You can register for an exam online at `www.prometric.com`. You can also register by phone at 1-800-775-3926 (within the United States and Canada). If outside these two countries, call 1-410-843-8000.
- *Virtual University Enterprise (VUE)*—You can register online at `www.vue.com` or call a local testing center. You can find local testing centers from the Web site.

You can register for an exam by contacting either of the parties previously listed. You must register at least one day in advance and any cancellations must be made by 7 a.m. the day before you are scheduled to take the test.

To make the registration process go smoother, make sure you have the following information handy, because you will be required to provide it during the registration process:

- Your name, organization, and mailing address.
- Microsoft Test I.D. In the United States, this will be your Social Security number. For those in Canada, this will be your Social Insurance number.
- The specific number of the exam you want to take.
- A method of payment. Credit card is usually the easiest method, although other arrangements can be made.

At this point, you will be given the date, time, and location of where you are to take the exam.

Arriving at the Exam Site

It is generally a good idea to arrive at the exam site at least 15 minutes before you are scheduled to take the test. Make sure you bring two pieces of identification with you, one of which must be a photo I.D., such as a driver's license. You must show the identification when you sign in.

In the Exam Room

Granted, you cannot mimic the pressures and environment of actually being in the exam room with a live exam in front of you, but this section does try to detail what being in the room is like.

After you've signed in for the exam, you'll be directed into a testing room. You will not be permitted to take anything into the testing room with you. You will be given a few blank pieces of paper and pen upon entering the room. This is where the facts on the cram sheet can be very handy. If you read over the distilled facts prior to the exam, this is a good time to write down as many of them as you can remember.

Once you complete the exam, your score will be tabulated and you will know immediately whether you passed or failed. If you need to retake the exam, you will have to contact VUE or Prometric to schedule a new test (and unfortunately this also means paying the price of another exam).

If you fail an exam, you can retake the test as soon as you are ready. If you fail the same exam a second time, you must wait at least 14 days before you will be allowed to reschedule.

How to Prepare for an Exam

All Microsoft exams have a set of objectives outlining the topics you need to understand in order to achieve exam success. This is a good place to start to give yourself a general idea of the topics you can expect to encounter and which ones you need to obtain study material for.

There is an abundance of resources available both online and in print that can be used to prepare for an exam. Microsoft's Web site is a good source of information pertaining to both the exam itself and in-depth coverage of exam topics. Due to the popularity of the MCSE certification, there are also a number of printed study guides and online resources. Some of the resources you may find useful include

- *The Windows 2000 product CD*—One of the best resources you can use when preparing for an exam is the Help included with the operating system. It usually covers different aspects of all the technologies included with the operating system.
- *The Microsoft Training and Certification Web site*—The Web site at `http://www.microsoft.com/traincert/default.asp` provides links to exam resources and outlines how an individual should prepare for an exam.

- *The InformIT Web site*—The Web site `http://www.informit.com/examcram2/index.asp` provides an abundance of information about certification exams and how to prepare for them.
- *Microsoft Training Kits*—Microsoft Press publishes study guides for the different certification exams, including exam 70-215. You can find more information about the training kit at `http://www.mspress.microsoft.com/findabook/list/series_ak.htm`.
- *Microsoft TechNet*—This monthly publication provides information on the latest technologies and topics, some of which pertain to the exam topics covered in 70-215.
- *Classroom Training*—For those who can afford the price of classroom training, many companies offer courses designed at preparing students to pass the exam.
- *The Exam Cram 2 Series*—The Exam Crams have always been a popular resource for exam preparation.

Notes on This Book's Organization

This section highlights all the different elements and pieces that will be found in your *Exam Cram 2*. Items such as exam alerts, tips, notes, practice questions, and so on will be explained here:

- *Terms You'll Need to Know*—Each chapter begins with a list of terms that you must learn and understand in order to fully grasp the content being covered; each of these terms is defined in the Glossary.
- *Techniques You'll Need to Master*—Following the important terms is a list of concepts/tools/techniques that need to be understood before attempting to take the exam.
- *Chapter Content*—The introductory paragraph will alert you to the topics that will be covered throughout the chapter. Following this a number of topics relating to the chapter title will be covered in detail.
- *Exam Alerts*—Concepts and topics that are likely to appear on the exam are highlighted in a special layout known as an Exam Alert. An Exam Alert appears within the chapter content like this:

Exam Alerts are included in each chapter to point your attention to a particular concept or topic that you are more than likely to encounter on the exam. So as you are working through the chapter, make sure you pay close attention to the topics addressed in the alerts. Exam Alerts can also be a good way of refreshing yourself with important information right before taking the exam, although the information is usually included in the Cram Sheet.

This is not to say that the general content within a chapter is not important. The Exam Alerts are there to flag the information that is more certain to appear in some scenario format.

- *Tips and Notes*—Throughout a chapter you may also find side tips and notes. The layout and purpose of each is as follows:

Tips are designed to give the reader some added piece of information pertaining to a topic being covered, such as an alternative or more efficient way of performing a certain task.

Notes are designed to alert you to a piece of information related to the topic being discussed.

- *Practice Questions and Answers*—The end of each chapter has a series of 10 questions designed to test your understanding of the topics covered throughout the chapter. Detailed explanations are provided for each of the 10 questions explaining both the correct and incorrect answers.
- *Need to Know More*—Each chapter ends with a listing of additional resources offering more details about the chapter topics.

Other elements of the book worth mentioning are the Sample Tests and Answer Keys found in Chapters 9 through 12. These questions cover all of the topics covered throughout the book. The questions can be used for review purposes and to determine exam readiness.

In addition to this, you'll also find a glossary of key terms used throughout the book and the appendixes listing additional resources that you may find valuable.

Last but not least, mention must be made about the Cram Sheet included with the book. The Cram Sheet distills all the important facts and topics covered and summarizes them in a few short pages. These are the facts that we feel should be memorized for the test. The Cram Sheet is the last thing you should review before going into the test. And once you enter the test room, the first thing you should do is transfer all the facts to paper.

How This Book Helps You

The topics in this book have been structured around the objectives outlined by Microsoft for Exam 70-215. This ensures that you are familiar with the topics that you'll encounter on the exam.

Some of the topics covered later in the book may require an understanding of topics covered in earlier chapters. Therefore, it's recommended that you read the book from start to finish for your initial reading. When it comes time to brushing up or reviewing certain topics, you can always use the index to go directly to specific sections while omitting others.

In preparing for Exam 70-215, we think you'll find this book a very useful reference to some of the most important topics and concepts of network infrastructure. It prepares you for the test day by outlining what you can expect. It covers all the important topics you can expect to find on the exam. Also, it provides many sample test questions to help you evaluate exam readiness and understanding of the material as well as familiarize you with the Microsoft testing format.

Self-Assessment

Based on recent statistics from Microsoft, as many as 400,000 individuals are at some stage of the certification process but haven't yet received an MCP or other Microsoft certification. We also know that three or four times that number may be considering whether or not to obtain a Microsoft certification of some kind. That's a huge audience!

The reason we included a self-assessment in this *Exam Cram 2* book is to help you evaluate your readiness to tackle MCSE certification. It should also help you understand what you need to know to master the topic of this book—namely, Exam 70-215, "Installing, Configuring, and Administering Microsoft Windows 2000 Server." But before you tackle this self-assessment, let's talk about concerns you may face when pursuing an MCSE, and what an ideal MCSE candidate might look like.

MCSEs in the Real World

In the next section, we describe an ideal MCSE candidate, knowing full well that only a few real candidates will meet this ideal. In fact, our description of that ideal candidate might seem downright scary. But take heart: Although the requirements to obtain an MCSE may seem formidable, they are by no means impossible to meet. However, be keenly aware that it does take time, involves some expense, and requires real effort to get through the process.

More than 200,000 MCSEs are already certified, so it's obviously an attainable goal. You can get all the real-world motivation you need from knowing that many others have gone before, so you will be able to follow in their footsteps. If you're willing to tackle the process seriously and do what it takes to obtain the necessary experience and knowledge, you can take—and pass—all the certification tests involved in obtaining an MCSE. In fact, we've designed the *Exam Cram 2* series to make it as easy on you as possible to prepare for these exams. But prepare you must!

The same, of course, is true for other Microsoft certifications, including

- MCSD, which is aimed at software developers and requires one specific exam, two more exams on client and distributed topics, plus a fourth elective exam drawn from a different, but limited, pool of options.
- Other Microsoft certifications, whose requirements range from one test (MCP) to several tests (MCP+SB, MCDBA).

The Ideal MCSE Candidate

Just to give you some idea of what an ideal MCSE candidate is like, here are some relevant statistics about the background and experience such an individual might have. Don't worry if you don't meet these qualifications, or don't come that close—this is a far from ideal world, and where you fall short is simply where you'll have more work to do.

- Academic or professional training in network theory, concepts, and operations. This includes everything from networking media and transmission techniques through network operating systems, services, and applications.
- Three-plus years of professional networking experience, including experience with Ethernet, token ring, modems, and other networking media. This must include installation, configuration, upgrade, and troubleshooting experience.
- Two-plus years in a networked environment that includes hands-on experience with Windows 2000 Server, Windows 2000 Professional, Windows NT Server, Windows NT Workstation, and Windows 95 or Windows 98. A solid understanding of each system's architecture, installation, configuration, maintenance, and troubleshooting is also essential.
- Knowledge of the various methods for installing Windows 2000, including manual and unattended installations.
- A thorough understanding of key networking protocols, addressing, and name resolution, including TCP/IP, IPX/SPX, and NetBEUI.
- A thorough understanding of NetBIOS naming, browsing, and file and print services.
- Familiarity with key Windows 2000–based TCP/IP-based services, including HTTP (Web servers), DHCP, WINS, and DNS, plus familiarity with one or more of the following: Internet Information Server (IIS), Index Server, and Proxy Server.

- An understanding of how to implement security for key network data in a Windows 2000 environment.
- Working knowledge of NetWare 3.x and 4.x, including IPX/SPX frame formats; NetWare file, print, and directory services; and both Novell and Microsoft client software. Working knowledge of Microsoft's Client Service For NetWare (CSNW), Gateway Service For NetWare (GSNW), the NetWare Migration Tool (NWCONV), and the NetWare Client For Windows (NT, 95, and 98) is essential.

Fundamentally, this boils down to a bachelor's degree in computer science, plus three years' experience working in a position involving network design, installation, configuration, and maintenance. We believe that well under half of all certification candidates meet these requirements, and that, in fact, most meet less than half of these requirements—at least, when they begin the certification process. But because all 200,000 people who already have been certified have survived this ordeal, you can survive it too—especially if you heed what our self-assessment can tell you about what you already know and what you need to learn.

Put Yourself to the Test

The following series of questions and observations is designed to help you figure out how much work you must do to pursue Microsoft certification and what kinds of resources you may consult on your quest. Be absolutely honest in your answers, or you'll end up wasting money on exams you're not yet ready to take. There are no right or wrong answers, only steps along the path to certification. Only you can decide where you really belong in the broad spectrum of aspiring candidates.

Two things should be clear from the outset, however:

- Even a modest background in computer science will be helpful.
- Hands-on experience with Microsoft products and technologies is an essential ingredient to certification success.

Educational Background

1. Have you ever taken any computer-related classes? [Yes or No]

   If Yes, proceed to question 2; if No, proceed to question 4.

2. Have you taken any classes on computer operating systems? [Yes or No]

If Yes, you will probably be able to handle Microsoft's architecture and system component discussions. If you're rusty, brush up on basic operating system concepts, especially virtual memory, multitasking regimes, user mode versus kernel mode operation, and general computer security topics.

If No, consider some basic reading in this area. We strongly recommend a good general operating systems book, such as *Operating System Concepts, 5th Edition*, by Abraham Silberschatz and Peter Baer Galvin (John Wiley & Sons, 1998, ISBN 0-471-36414-2). If this title doesn't appeal to you, check out reviews for other, similar titles at your favorite online bookstore.

3. Have you taken any networking concepts or technologies classes? [Yes or No]

   If Yes, you will probably be able to handle Microsoft's networking terminology, concepts, and technologies (brace yourself for frequent departures from normal usage). If you're rusty, brush up on basic networking concepts and terminology, especially networking media, transmission types, the OSI Reference Model, and networking technologies such as Ethernet, token ring, FDDI, and WAN links.

   If No, you might want to read one or two books in this topic area. The two best books that we know of are *Computer Networks, 3rd Edition*, by Andrew S. Tanenbaum (Prentice-Hall, 1996, ISBN 0-13-349945-6) and *Computer Networks and Internets, 2nd Edition*, by Douglas E. Comer (Prentice-Hall, 1998, ISBN 0-130-83617-6).

   Skip to the next section, "Hands-On Experience."

4. Have you done any reading on operating systems or networks? [Yes or No]

   If Yes, review the requirements stated in the first paragraphs after questions 2 and 3. If you meet those requirements, move on to the next section. If No, consult the recommended reading for both topics. A strong background will help you prepare for the Microsoft exams better than just about anything else.

Hands-On Experience

The most important key to success on all of the Microsoft tests is hands-on experience, especially with Windows 2000 Server and Professional, plus the many add-on services and BackOffice components around which so many of the Microsoft certification exams revolve. If we leave you with only one realization after taking this Self-Assessment, it should be that there's no substitute for time spent installing, configuring, and using the various Microsoft products upon which you'll be tested repeatedly and in depth.

5. Have you installed, configured, and worked with:

- Windows 2000 Server? [Yes or No]

  If Yes, make sure you understand basic concepts as covered in Exam 70-215. You should also study the TCP/IP interfaces, utilities, and services for Exam 70-216, plus implementing security features for Exam 70-220.

You can download objectives, practice exams, and other data about Microsoft exams from the Training and Certification page at **www.microsoft.com/traincert/**. Use the "Find an Exam" link to obtain specific exam info.

  If you haven't worked with Windows 2000 Server, TCP/IP, and IIS (or whatever product you choose for your final elective), you must obtain one or two machines and a copy of Windows 2000 Server. Then, learn the operating system, and do the same for TCP/IP and whatever other software components on which you'll also be tested.

  In fact, we recommend that you obtain two computers, each with a network interface, and set up a two-node network on which to practice. With decent Windows 2000-capable computers selling for about $500 to $600 apiece these days, this shouldn't be too much of a financial hardship. You may have to scrounge to come up with the necessary software, but if you scour the Microsoft Web site you can usually find low-cost options to obtain evaluation copies of most of the software that you'll need.

- Windows 2000 Professional? [Yes or No]

  If Yes, make sure you understand the concepts covered in Exam 70-210.

  If No, you will want to obtain a copy of Windows 2000 Professional and learn how to install, configure, and maintain it. You can use *MCSE Windows 2000 Professional Exam Cram 2* to guide your activities and studies, or work straight from Microsoft's test objectives if you prefer.

For any and all of these Microsoft exams, the Resource Kits for the topics involved are a good study resource. You can purchase softcover Resource Kits from Microsoft Press (search for them at **mspress.microsoft.com/**), but they also appear on the TechNet CDs (**www.microsoft.com/technet**). We believe that Resource Kits are among the best preparation tools available, along with the *Exam Crams* and *Exam Preps*, that you can use to get ready for Microsoft exams.

6. Have you installed, configured, used, and upgraded any specific Microsoft product that is not itself an operating system (for example, FrontPage 2000, SQL Server, and so on)? [Yes or No]

   If the answer is Yes, skip to the next section. If it's No, you must get some experience. Read on for suggestions on how to do this.

   Experience is a must with any Microsoft product exam, be it something as simple as FrontPage 2000 or as challenging as Exchange Server 5.5 or SQL Server 7.0. For trial copies of other software, search Microsoft's Web site using the name of the product as your search term. Also, search for bundles like "BackOffice" or "Small Business Server."

If you have the funds, or your employer will pay your way, consider taking a class at a Certified Training and Education Center (CTEC) or at an Authorized Academic Training Partner (AATP). In addition to classroom exposure to the topic of your choice, you get a copy of the software that is the focus of your course, along with a trial version of whatever operating system it needs (usually, NT Server), with the training materials for that class.

Before you even think about taking any Microsoft exam, make sure you've spent enough time with the related software to understand how it may be installed and configured, how to maintain such an installation, and how to troubleshoot that software when things go wrong. This will help you in the exam, and in real life!

Testing Your Exam-Readiness

Whether you attend a formal class on a specific topic to get ready for an exam or use written materials to study on your own, some preparation for the Microsoft certification exams is essential. At $100 a try, pass or fail, you want to do everything you can to pass on your first try. That's where studying comes in.

We have included two practice exams in this book, so if you don't score that well on the first test, you can study more and then tackle the second test. If you still don't hit a score of at least 70 percent after these tests, you'll want to investigate the other practice test resources we mention in this section.

For any given subject, consider taking a class if you've tackled self-study materials, taken the test, and failed anyway. The opportunity to interact with an instructor and fellow students can make all the difference in the world, if you can afford that privilège. For information about Microsoft classes, visit the Training and Certification page at www.microsoft.com/train_cert/ (use the "Find a Course" link).

If you can't afford to take a class, visit the Training and Certification page anyway, because it also includes pointers to free practice exams and to Microsoft Certified Professional Approved Study Guides and other self-study tools. And even if you can't afford to spend much at all, you should still invest in some low-cost practice exams from commercial vendors.

7. Have you taken a practice exam on your chosen test subject? [Yes or No]

   If Yes, and you scored 70 percent or better, you're probably ready to tackle the real thing. If your score isn't above that threshold, keep at it until you break that barrier.

   If No, obtain all the free and low-budget practice tests you can find (see the list above) and get to work. Keep at it until you can break the passing threshold comfortably.

When it comes to assessing your test readiness, there is no better way than to take a good-quality practice exam and pass with a score of 70 percent or better. When we're preparing ourselves, we shoot for 80-plus percent, just to leave room for the "weirdness factor" that sometimes shows up on Microsoft exams.

Assessing Readiness for Exam 70-215

In addition to the general exam-readiness information in the previous section, there are several things you can do to prepare for the Installing, Configuring, and Administering Microsoft Windows 2000 Server exam. As you're getting ready for Exam 70-215, visit the MCSE mailing list. Sign up at www.sunbelt-software.com (look for the "Subscribe to" button).

Microsoft exam mavens also recommend checking the Microsoft Knowledge Base (available on its own CD as part of the TechNet collection, or on the

Microsoft Web site at `support.microsoft.com/support/`) for "meaningful technical support issues" that relate to your exam's topics. Although we're not sure exactly what the quoted phrase means, we have also noticed some overlap between technical support questions on particular products and troubleshooting questions on the exams for those products.

Onward, Through the Fog!

Once you've assessed your readiness, undertaken the right background studies, obtained the hands-on experience that will help you understand the products and technologies at work, and reviewed the many sources of information to help you prepare for a test, you'll be ready to take a round of practice tests. When your scores come back positive enough to get you through the exam, you're ready to go after the real thing. If you follow our assessment regime, you'll not only know what you need to study, but when you're ready to make a test date at Sylvan or VUE. Good luck!

Microsoft Certification Exams

Terms you'll need to understand:

- ✓ Case study
- ✓ Multiple-choice question formats
- ✓ Build-list-and-reorder question format
- ✓ Create-a-tree question format
- ✓ Drag-and-connect question format
- ✓ Select-and-place question format
- ✓ Fixed-length tests
- ✓ Simulations
- ✓ Adaptive tests
- ✓ Short-form tests

Techniques you'll need to master:

- ✓ Assessing your exam-readiness
- ✓ Answering Microsoft's varying question types
- ✓ Altering your test strategy depending on the exam format
- ✓ Practicing (to make perfect)
- ✓ Making the best use of the testing software
- ✓ Budgeting your time
- ✓ Guessing (as a last resort)

Introduction

Exam-taking is not something that most people anticipate eagerly, no matter how well prepared they may be. In most cases, familiarity helps offset test anxiety. In plain English, this means you probably won't be as nervous when you take your fourth or fifth Microsoft certification exam as you'll be when you take your first one.

Whether it's your first exam or your tenth, however, understanding the details of taking the new exam (how much time to spend on questions, the environment you'll be in, and so on) and the new exam software will help you concentrate on the material rather than on the setting. Likewise, mastering a few basic exam-taking skills should help you recognize (and perhaps even outfox) some of the tricks and snares you're bound to find in some exam questions.

This chapter explains the exam environment and software and describes some proven exam-taking strategies that you can use to your advantage.

Assessing Exam-Readiness

We strongly recommend that you read through and take the Self-Assessment included with this book (it appears just before this chapter). This will help you compare your knowledge to the requirements for obtaining an MCSE or MCSA, and it will also help you identify parts of your background or experience that may need improvement, enhancement, or further learning. If you get the right set of basics under your belt, obtaining Microsoft certification will be that much easier.

After you've gone through the Self-Assessment, you can remedy those topical areas in which your background or experience may be lacking. You can also tackle subject matter for individual tests at the same time, so you can continue making progress while you're catching up in some areas.

After you've worked through an *Exam Cram 2*, have read the supplementary materials, and have taken the practice test, you'll have a pretty clear idea of when you should be ready to take the real exam. Although we strongly recommend that you keep practicing until your scores top the 75 percent mark, 80 percent is a better goal because it gives some margin for error when you are in an actual, stressful exam situation. Keep taking practice tests and studying the materials until you attain that score. You'll find more pointers on how to study and prepare in the Self-Assessment. But now, on to the exam itself.

What to Expect at the Testing Center

When you arrive at the testing center where you scheduled your exam, you must sign in with an exam coordinator and show two forms of identification, one of which must be a photo ID. After you've signed in and your time slot arrives, you'll be asked to deposit any books, bags, cell phones, or other items you brought with you. Then, you'll be escorted into a closed room.

All exams are completely closed-book. Although you are not permitted to take anything with you into the testing area, you are furnished with a blank sheet of paper and a pen (in some cases, an erasable plastic sheet and an erasable pen). Immediately before entering the testing center, try to memorize as much of the important material as you can, so you can write that information on the blank sheet as soon as you are seated in front of the computer. You can refer to this piece of paper during the test, but you'll have to surrender the sheet when you leave the room. Because your timer does not start until you begin the testing process, it is best to do this first while the information is still fresh in your mind.

You will have some time to compose yourself, write down information on the paper you're given, and take a sample orientation exam before you begin the real thing. We suggest you take the orientation test before taking your first exam (because the exams are generally identical in layout, behavior, and controls, you probably won't need to do this more than once).

Typically, the room has one to six computers, and each workstation is separated from the others by dividers. Most test rooms feature a wall with a large picture window or a closed-circuit video camera. This permits the exam coordinator to monitor the room, prevent exam-takers from talking to one another, and observe anything out of the ordinary. The exam coordinator will have preloaded the appropriate Microsoft certification exam (for this book, Exam 70-215), and you'll be permitted to start as soon as you're seated in front of the computer.

All Microsoft certification exams allow a certain maximum amount of time in which to complete your work (this time is indicated on the exam by an onscreen counter/clock, so you can check the time remaining whenever you like). All Microsoft certification exams are computer-generated. In addition to multiple choice, you'll encounter select and place (drag and drop), create a tree (categorization and prioritization), drag and connect, and build list and reorder (list prioritization) on most exams. The questions are constructed to check your mastery of basic facts and figures about Microsoft Windows 2000 network administration and to require you to evaluate one or more sets of circumstances or requirements. Often, you'll be asked to give more than one answer to a question. You may also be asked to select the best or most effective solution to a problem from a range of choices, all of which are technically correct. Taking the exam is quite an adventure, and it involves real thinking. This book shows you what to expect and how to deal with the potential problems, puzzles, and predicaments.

In the next section, you'll learn more about the format of Microsoft test questions and how to answer them.

Exam Layout and Design: New Case Study Format

The format of Microsoft exams can vary. For example, many exams consist of a series of case studies, with six types of questions regarding each presented case. Other exams may have the same six types of questions but no complex multi-question case studies.

For the Design exams, each case study presents a detailed problem that you must read and analyze. Figure 1.1 shows an example of what a case study looks like. You must select the different tabs in the case study to view the entire case.

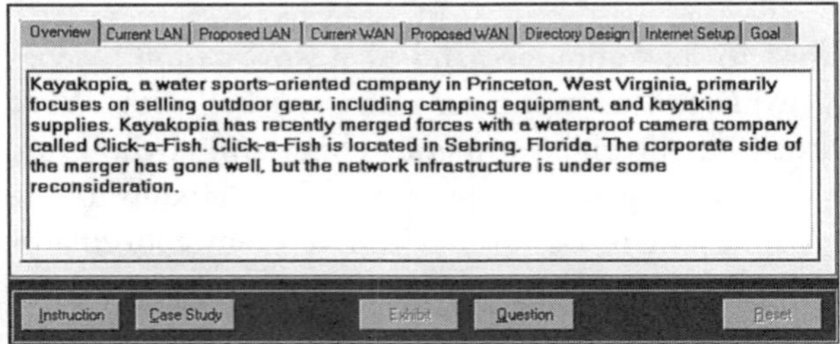

Figure 1.1 This is a typical case study.

Following each case study is a set of questions related to the case study. These questions can be one of six types (which are discussed next). Careful attention to detail provided in the case study is the key to success. You may want to read the questions first so that you know what to look for when reading the case study. Be prepared to toggle frequently between the case study and the questions as you work. Some of the case studies also include diagrams (called *exhibits*) that you'll need to examine closely to understand how to answer the questions.

After you complete a case study, you can review all of the questions and your answers. However, when you move on to the next case study, you cannot return to the previous case study and make any changes.

Following are the six types of question formats:

- Multiple-choice, single answer
- Multiple-choice, multiple answers
- Build list and reorder (list prioritization)
- Create a tree
- Drag and connect
- Select and place (drag and drop)

Exam formats can vary by test center location. You might want to call the test center to see if you can find out which type of test you'll encounter. Some exams will be offered in both forms on a random basis which cannot be pre-determined.

Multiple-Choice Question Format

Some exam questions require you to select a single answer, whereas others ask you to select multiple correct answers. The following multiple-choice question requires you to select a single correct answer. Following the question is a brief summary of each potential answer and why it is either right or wrong.

Question 1

You have three domains connected to an empty root domain under one contiguous domain name: **tutu.com**. This organization is formed into a forest arrangement with a secondary domain called **frog.com**. How many Schema Masters exist for this arrangement?

❍ A. 1

❍ B. 2

❍ C. 3

❍ D. 4

The correct answer is A, because only one Schema Master is necessary for a forest arrangement. The other answers (B, C, and D) are misleading because you are led to believe that Schema Masters may be in each domain, or that you should have one for each contiguous domain namespace.

This sample question format corresponds closely to the Microsoft Certification Exam format (of course, questions are not followed by answer keys on the exam). To select an answer, you position the cursor over the radio button next to the answer and click the mouse button to select the answer.

Let's examine a question where one or more answers are possible. This type of question provides check boxes rather than radio buttons for marking all appropriate selections.

Question 2

How can you seize FSMO roles? [Check all correct answers]

- ❑ A. The ntdsutil.exe utility
- ❑ B. The Replication Monitor
- ❑ C. The secedit.exe utility
- ❑ D. Active Directory Domains and FSMOs

Answers A and B are correct. You can seize FSMO roles from a server that is still running through the Replication Monitor, or in the case of a server failure, you can seize roles with the ntdsutil.exe utility. The secedit.exe utility is used to force group policies to be reloaded; therefore, answer C is incorrect. Active Directory Domains and FSMOs are a combination of truth and fiction; therefore, answer D is incorrect.

For this particular question, two answers are required. Microsoft sometimes gives partial credit for partially correct answers. For Question 2, you have to check the boxes next to answers A and B to obtain credit for a correct answer. Notice that picking the right answers also means knowing why the other answers are wrong.

Build-List-and-Reorder Question Format

Questions in the build-list-and-reorder format present two lists of items: one on the left and one on the right. To answer the question, you must move items from the list on the right to the list on the left. The final list must then be reordered into a specific order.

These questions are usually in the form, "From the following list of choices, pick the choices that answer the question. Arrange the list in a certain order." To give you practice with this type of question, some questions of this type are included in this study guide. Here's an example of how they appear in this book; for a sample of how they appear on the test, see Figure 1.2.

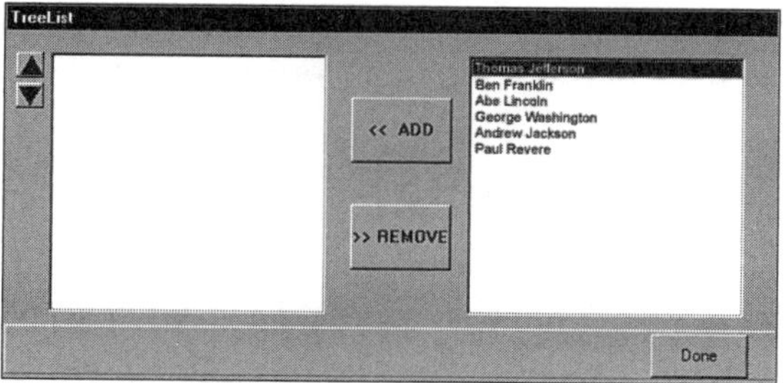

Figure 1.2 This is how build-list-and-reorder questions appear.

Question 3

From the following list of famous people, pick those that have been elected President of the United States. Arrange the list in the order in which they served.

- ❍ Thomas Jefferson
- ❍ Ben Franklin
- ❍ Abe Lincoln
- ❍ George Washington
- ❍ Andrew Jackson
- ❍ Paul Revere

The correct answer is

1. George Washington
2. Thomas Jefferson
3. Andrew Jackson
4. Abe Lincoln

On an actual exam, the entire list of famous people would initially appear in the list on the right. You would move the four correct answers to the list on the left and then reorder the list on the left. Notice that the answer to the question did not include all items from the initial list. However, this may not always be the case.

To move an item from the right list to the left list, first select the item by clicking on it and then clicking the Add button (left arrow). Once you move an item from one list to the other, you can move the item back by first selecting the item and then clicking the appropriate button (either the Add button or the Remove button). After items have been moved to the left list, you can reorder the list by selecting an item and clicking the up or down button.

Create-a-Tree Question Format

Questions in the create-a-tree format also present two lists: one on the left and one on the right. The list on the right consists of individual items, and the list on the left consists of nodes in a tree. To answer the question, you must move items from the list on the right to the appropriate node in the tree.

These questions are basically a matching exercise. Items from the list on the right are placed under the appropriate category in the list on the left. Here's an example of how they appear in this book; for a sample of how they appear on the test, see Figure 1.3.

Question 4

The calendar year is divided into four seasons:

- ❍ Winter
- ❍ Spring
- ❍ Summer
- ❍ Fall

Identify the season when each of the following holidays occurs:

- ❍ Christmas
- ❍ Fourth of July
- ❍ Labor Day
- ❍ Flag Day
- ❍ Memorial Day
- ❍ Washington's Birthday
- ❍ Thanksgiving
- ❍ Easter

The correct answer is

Winter

    Christmas
    Washington's Birthday

- Spring
    - Flag Day
    - Memorial Day
    - Easter
- Summer
    - Fourth of July
    - Labor Day
- Fall
    - Thanksgiving

In this case, all the items in the list were used. However, this may not always be the case.

To move an item from the right list to its appropriate location in the tree, you must first select the appropriate tree node by clicking on it. Then, you select the item to be moved and click the Add button. If one or more items have been added to a tree node, the node is displayed with a "+" icon to the left of the node name. You can click this icon to expand the node and view whatever was added. If any item has been added to the wrong tree node, you can remove it by selecting it and clicking the Remove button (see Figure 1.3).

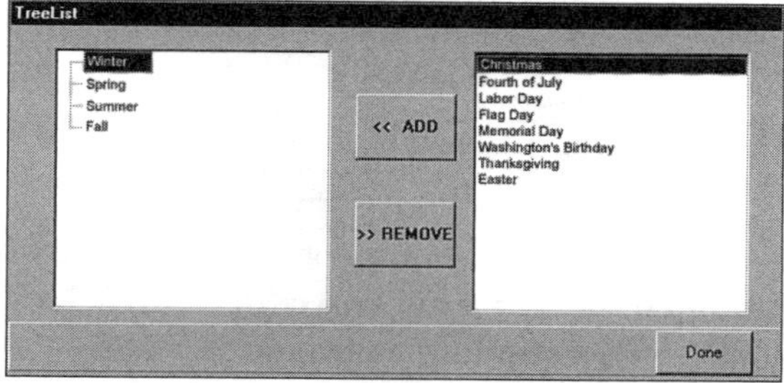

Figure 1.3 This is how create-a-tree questions appear.

Drag-and-Connect Question Format

Questions in the drag-and-connect format present a group of objects and a list of "connections." To answer the question, you must move the appropriate connections between the objects.

This type of question is best described using graphics. Here's an example.

Question 5

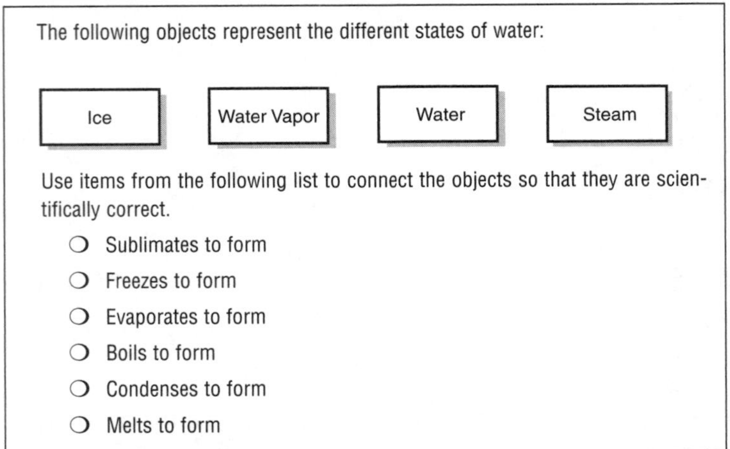

The following objects represent the different states of water:

Ice | Water Vapor | Water | Steam

Use items from the following list to connect the objects so that they are scientifically correct.

- ❍ Sublimates to form
- ❍ Freezes to form
- ❍ Evaporates to form
- ❍ Boils to form
- ❍ Condenses to form
- ❍ Melts to form

The correct answer is:

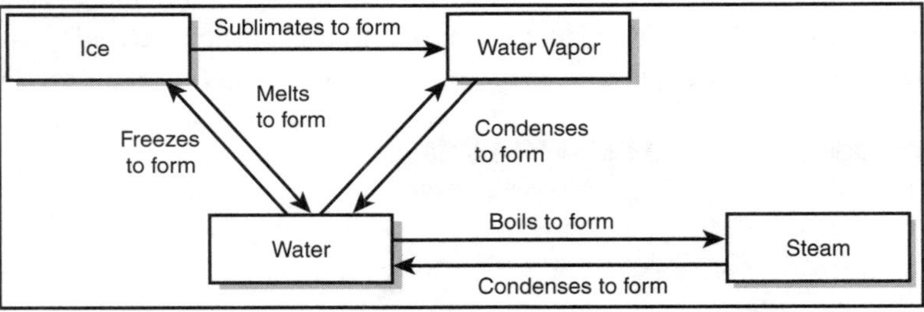

For this type of question, it's not necessary to use every object, but each connection can be used multiple times by dragging the answer to multiple locations. Dragging an answer away from its position removes it.

Select-and-Place Question Format

Questions in the select-and-place (drag-and-drop) format present a diagram with blank boxes and a list of labels that must be dragged to fill in the blank boxes. To answer the question, you must move the labels to their appropriate positions on the diagram.

This type of question is best described using graphics. Here's an example.

Question 6

Place the items in their proper order, by number, on the following flowchart. Some items may be used more than once, and some items may not be used at all.

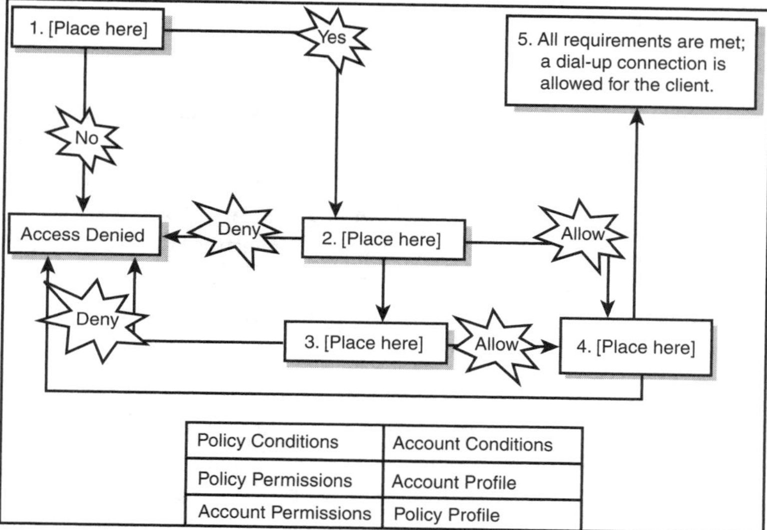

The correct answer is

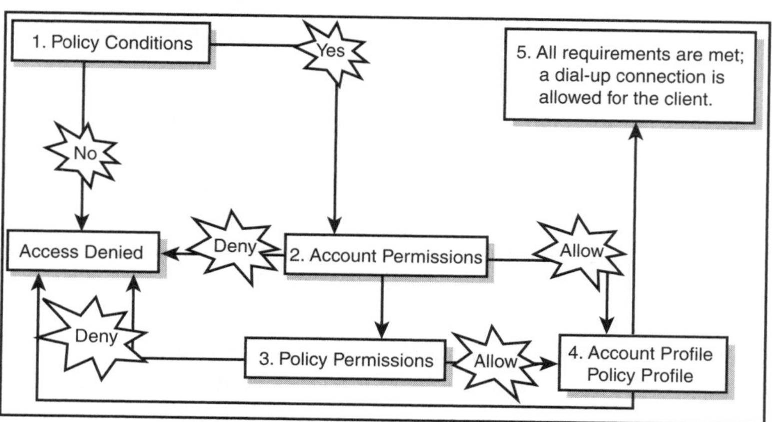

Microsoft's Testing Formats

Currently, Microsoft uses four different testing formats:

- Case study
- Fixed length
- Adaptive
- Short form

As mentioned earlier, the case study approach is used with many of the newer Microsoft exams. These exams consist of a set of case studies that you must first analyze to answer questions related to the case studies. Such exams include one or more case studies (tabbed topic areas), each of which is followed by 4 to 10 questions. The question types for exams will be multiple choice, build list and reorder, create a tree, drag and connect, and select and place. Depending on the test topic, some exams are totally case-based, whereas others are not at all.

Other Microsoft exams employ advanced testing capabilities that may not be immediately apparent. Although the questions that appear are primarily multiple-choice, the logic in *fixed-length tests*, which use a fixed sequence of questions, is more complex than that in older Microsoft tests. Some questions employ a sophisticated user interface (which Microsoft calls a *simulation*) to test your knowledge of particular software and systems in a simulated "live" environment that behaves just like the original. The Testing Innovations article at `www.microsoft.com/TRAINCERT/mcpexams/faq/innovations.asp` includes a downloadable series of demonstrations and samples.

For some exams, Microsoft has turned to a well-known technique, called *adaptive testing*, to establish a test-taker's level of knowledge and product competence. Adaptive exams look the same as fixed-length exams, but they determine the level of difficulty at which an individual test-taker can correctly answer questions. Test-takers with differing levels of knowledge or ability see different sets of questions; individuals with high levels of knowledge or ability are presented with a smaller set of more difficult questions, whereas individuals with lower levels of knowledge are presented with a larger set of easier questions. Two individuals may answer the same percentage of questions correctly, but the test-taker with a higher knowledge or ability level scores higher because his or her questions are weighted more heavily.

Also, lower-level test-takers may answer more questions than more-knowledgeable colleagues. This explains why adaptive tests use ranges of values to define the number of questions and the amount of time needed to complete the tests.

Adaptive tests work by evaluating the test-taker's most recent answer. A correct answer leads to a more difficult question (also raising the test software's estimate of the test-taker's knowledge and ability level). An incorrect answer leads to a less difficult question (also lowering the test software's estimate of the test-taker's knowledge and ability level). This process continues until the test targets the test-taker's true ability level. The exam ends when the test-taker's level of accuracy meets a statistically acceptable value (in other words, when his or her performance demonstrates an acceptable level of knowledge and ability) or when the maximum number of items has been presented (in which case, the test-taker is almost certain to fail).

Microsoft also introduced a short-form test for its most popular tests. This test consists of 25 to 30 questions, with a time limit of exactly 60 minutes. This type of exam is similar to a fixed-length test because it allows readers to jump ahead or return to earlier questions and to cycle through the questions until the test is done. Microsoft does not use adaptive logic in this test; it claims that statistical analysis of the question pool is such that the 25 to 30 questions delivered during a short-form exam conclusively measure a test-taker's knowledge of the subject matter in much the same way as an adaptive test. The short-form test is like a "greatest hits exam" (that is, the most important questions are covered) version of an adaptive exam on the same topic.

Some of the Microsoft exams may contain a combination of adaptive and fixed-length questions.

Because you won't know in which form the Microsoft exam may be, you should be prepared for an adaptive exam instead of a fixed-length or a short-form exam: The penalties for answering incorrectly are built into the test itself on an adaptive exam, whereas the layout remains the same for a fixed-length or short-form test, no matter how many questions you answer incorrectly.

The biggest difference between adaptive tests and fixed-length or short-form tests is that you can mark and revisit questions on fixed-length or short-form tests after you've read them. On an adaptive test, you must answer the question when it is presented and cannot go back to that question later.

Strategies for Different Testing Formats

Before you choose a test-taking strategy, you must determine what type of test it is: case studies, fixed length, short form, or adaptive.

- Case study tests consist of a tabbed window that allows you to navigate easily through the sections of the case.
- Fixed-length tests consist of 50 to 70 questions with a check box. You can return to these questions if you want.
- Short-form tests have 25 to 30 questions with a check box. You can return to these questions if you want.
- Adaptive tests are identified in the introductory material of the test. Questions have no check box and can be visited (and answered) only once.

Some tests contain a variety of testing formats. For example, a test may start with a set of adaptive questions, followed by fixed-length questions.

You'll be able to tell for sure if you are taking an adaptive, fixed-length, or short-form test by the first question. Fixed-length or short-form tests include a check box that allows you to mark the question for later review. Adaptive test questions include no such check box and can be visited (and answered) only once.

Case Study Exam Strategy

Most test-takers find that the case study type of exam is the most difficult to master. When it comes to studying for a case study test, your best bet is to approach each case study as a standalone test. The biggest challenge you'll encounter is that you'll feel that you won't have enough time to get through all of the cases that are presented.

Each case provides a lot of material that you'll need to read and study before you can effectively answer the questions that follow. The trick to taking a case study exam is to first scan the case study to get the highlights. Make sure you read the overview section of the case so that you understand the context of the problem at hand. Then, quickly move on and scan the questions.

As you are scanning the questions, make mental notes to yourself or notes on your paper so that you'll remember which sections of the case study you should focus on. Some case studies may provide a fair amount of extra information that you don't really need to answer the questions. The goal with this scanning approach is to avoid having to study and analyze material that is not completely relevant.

When studying a case, read the tabbed information carefully. It is important to answer each and every question. You will be able to toggle back and forth from case to questions, and from question to question within a case subsection. However, after you leave the case and move on, you may not be able to return to it. I suggest that you take notes while reading useful information to help you when you tackle the test questions. It's hard to go wrong with this strategy when taking any kind of Microsoft certification test.

Fixed-Length and Short-Form Exam Strategy

A well-known principle when taking fixed-length or short-form exams is first to read through the entire exam from start to finish. Answer only those questions that you feel absolutely sure you know. On subsequent passes, you can dive into more complex questions more deeply, knowing how many such questions you have left and the amount of time remaining.

There's at least one potential benefit to reading the exam over completely before answering the trickier questions: Sometimes, information supplied in later questions sheds more light on earlier questions. At other times, information you read in later questions may jog your memory about facts, figures, or behavior that helps you answer earlier questions. Either way, you'll come out ahead if you answer only those questions on the first pass that you're absolutely confident about.

Fortunately, the Microsoft exam software for fixed-length and short-form tests makes the multiple-visit approach easy to implement. At the top-left corner of each question is a check box that permits you to mark that question for a later visit.

Marking questions makes later review easier, but you can return to any question by clicking the Forward or Back button repeatedly.

Here are some question-handling strategies that apply to fixed-length and short-form tests. Use them if you have the chance:

- When returning to a question after your initial read-through, read every word again; otherwise, your mind can add or miss important details. Sometimes, revisiting a question after turning your attention elsewhere lets you see something you missed, but the strong tendency is to see what you've seen before. Try to avoid that tendency at all costs.

- If you return to a question more than twice, try to articulate to yourself what you don't understand about the question, why answers don't appear to make sense, or what appears to be missing. If you chew on the subject awhile, your subconscious may provide the missing details, or you may notice a "trick" that points to the right answer.

As you work your way through the exam, another counter that Microsoft provides comes in handy—the number of questions completed and questions outstanding. For fixed-length and short-form tests, it's wise to budget your time by making sure that you've completed roughly one-quarter of the questions one-quarter of the way through the exam period, and three-quarters of the questions three-quarters of the way through.

If you're not finished when only five minutes remain, use that time to guess your way through any remaining questions. Remember, guessing is always more valuable than not answering. Blank answers are always wrong, but a guess may turn out to be right. If you don't have a clue about any of the remaining questions, pick answers at random or choose all a's, b's, and so on. Questions left unanswered are counted as answered incorrectly, so a guess is better than nothing at all.

At the very end of your exam period, you're better off guessing than leaving questions unanswered.

Adaptive Exam Strategy

If there's one principle that applies to taking an adaptive test, it's "Get it right the first time." You cannot elect to skip a question and move on to the next one when taking an adaptive test, because the testing software uses your answer to the current question to select whatever question it plans to present next. You also cannot return to a question because the software gives you only one chance to answer the question. You can, however, take notes as you work through the test. Sometimes, information supplied in earlier questions may help you answer later questions.

Also, when you answer a question correctly, you are presented with a more difficult question next, to help the software gauge your level of skill and ability. When you answer a question incorrectly, you are presented with a less difficult question, and the software lowers its current estimate of your skill and ability. This continues until the program settles into a reasonably accurate estimate of what you know and can do.

The good news is that if you know the material, you'll probably finish most adaptive tests in 30 minutes or so. The bad news is that you must really know the material well to do your best on an adaptive test. That's because some questions are so convoluted, complex, or hard to follow that you're bound to miss one or two, at a minimum. Therefore, the more you know, the better you'll do on an adaptive test, even accounting for the occasionally strange or unfathomable questions that appear on these exams.

Because you can't always tell in advance if a test is fixed length, short form, adaptive, or a combination, you should prepare for the exam as if it were adaptive. That way, you will be prepared to pass, no matter what kind of test you take. If the test turns out to be fixed length or short form, remember the tips from the preceding section, which will help you improve on what you could do on an adaptive test.

If you encounter a question on an adaptive test that you can't answer, you must guess an answer quickly. (However, you may suffer for your guess on the next question if you guess correctly, because the software will give you a more difficult question next!)

Question-Handling Strategies

For those questions that have only one right answer, usually two or three of the answers will be obviously incorrect, and two of the answers will be plausible. Unless the answer leaps out at you (if it does, reread the question to look for a trick; sometimes those are the ones you're most likely to get wrong), begin the process of answering by eliminating those answers that are most obviously wrong.

At least one answer out of the possible choices for a question can usually be eliminated immediately because it matches one of these conditions:

- The answer does not apply to the situation.
- The answer describes a nonexistent issue, an invalid option, or an imaginary state.

After you eliminate all answers that are obviously wrong, you can apply your knowledge to eliminate further answers. Look for items that sound correct but refer to actions, commands, or features that are not present or not available in the situation that the question describes.

If you're still faced with a blind guess among two or more potentially correct answers, reread the question. Try to picture how each of the possible remaining answers would alter the situation. Be especially sensitive to terminology;

sometimes the choice of words ("remove" instead of "disable") can make the difference between a right answer and a wrong one.

You should guess at an answer only after you've exhausted your ability to eliminate answers and are still unclear about which of the remaining possibilities is correct. An unanswered question offers you no points, but guessing gives you at least some chance of getting a question right; just don't be too hasty when making a blind guess.

If you're taking a fixed-length or a short-form test, you can wait until the last round of reviewing marked questions (just as you're about to run out of time or unanswered questions) before you start making guesses. You will usually have the same option within each case study testlet (but once you leave a testlet, you may not be allowed to return to it). If you're taking an adaptive test, you'll have to guess to move on to the next question if you can't figure out an answer some other way. Either way, guessing should be your technique of last resort!

Numerous questions assume that the default behavior of a particular utility is in effect. If you know the defaults and understand what they mean, this knowledge will help you cut through many Gordian knots. Simple "final" actions may be critical as well. If a utility must be restarted before proposed changes take effect, a correct answer may require this step as well.

Mastering the Inner Game

In the final analysis, knowledge gives confidence, and confidence breeds success. If you study the materials in this book carefully and review all of the practice questions at the end of each chapter, you should become aware of those areas where additional learning and study are required. Knowing what you don't know also gives you confidence in what you do know, and allows you to concentrate your efforts in the most critical areas.

After you've worked your way through the book, take the practice exam in the back of the book. Taking this test provides a reality check and helps you identify areas to study further. Make sure you follow up and review materials related to the questions you miss on the practice exam before scheduling a real exam. Don't schedule your exam appointment until after you've thoroughly studied the material and feel comfortable with the whole scope of the practice exam. You should score 80 percent or better on the practice exam before proceeding to the real thing (otherwise, obtain some additional practice tests so you can keep trying until you hit this magic number).

If you take a practice exam and don't get at least 80 to 85 percent of the questions correct, keep practicing. Microsoft provides links to practice exam providers and also self-assessment exams at **www.microsoft.com/traincert/mcpexams/prepare/**.

Armed with the information in this book and with the determination to augment your knowledge, you should be able to pass the certification exam. However, you need to work at it, or you'll spend the exam fee more than once before you finally pass. If you prepare seriously, you should do well.

The next section covers other sources you can use to prepare for the Microsoft Certification Exams.

Additional Resources

A good source of information about Microsoft Certification Exams comes from Microsoft itself. Because its products and technologies—and the exams that go with them—change frequently, the best place to go for exam-related information is online.

If you haven't already visited the Microsoft Certified Professional site, do so right now. The MCP home page resides at `www.microsoft.com/traincert/default.asp` (see Figure 1.4).

This page may be replaced by something new and different by the time you read this, because things change regularly on the Microsoft site. Should this happen, please read the sidebar titled "Coping with Change on the Web."

Coping with Change on the Web

Sooner or later, all of the information we've shared with you about the Microsoft Certified Professional pages and the other Web-based resources mentioned throughout the rest of this book will go stale or be replaced by newer information. In some cases, the URLs you find here may lead you to their replacements; in other cases, the URLs will go nowhere, leaving you with the dreaded "404 File not found" error message. When that happens, don't give up.

There's always a way to find what you want on the Web if you're willing to invest some time and energy. Most large or complex Web sites (such as the Microsoft site) offer a search engine. On all of Microsoft's Web pages, a Search button appears along the top edge of the page. As long as you can get to the Microsoft site (it should stay at **www.microsoft.com** for a long time), use this tool to help you find what you need.

The more focused you can make a search request, the more likely the results will include information you can use. For example, you can search for the string

```
"training and certification"
```

to produce a lot of data about the subject in general, but if you're looking for the preparation guide for Exam 70-215, "Installing, Configuring, and Administering Microsoft Windows 2000 Server," you'll be more likely to get there quickly if you use a search string similar to the following:

```
"Exam 70-215" AND "preparation guide"
```

Likewise, if you want to find the Training and Certification downloads, try a search string such as this:

```
"training and certification" AND "download page"
```

Finally, feel free to use general search tools—such as **www.search.com**, **www.altavista.com**, and **www.excite.com**—to look for related information. Although Microsoft offers great information about its certification exams online, there are plenty of third-party sources of information and assistance that need not follow Microsoft's party line. Therefore, if you can't find something immediately, intensify your search.

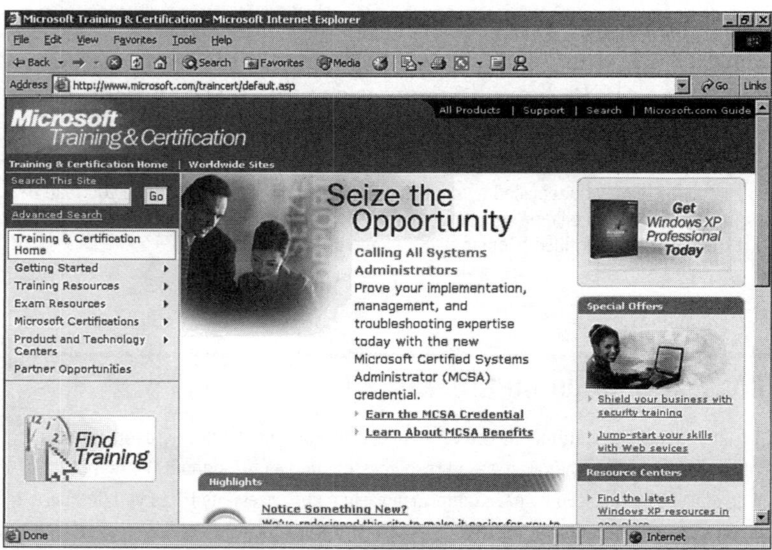

Figure 1.4 The Microsoft Certified Professional Training and Certification home page.

Installing Windows 2000 Server

Terms you'll need to understand:

✓ HCL
✓ System partition
✓ Boot partition
✓ Attended installation
✓ Unattended installation
✓ WINNT
✓ WINNT32
✓ MAKEBOOT
✓ MAKEBT32
✓ Answer file
✓ Uniqueness Database File (UDF)
✓ Setup Manager
✓ Sysprep
✓ Service Pack
✓ Slipstreaming

Techniques you'll need to master:

✓ Performing attended installations of Windows 2000 Server
✓ Performing unattended installations of Windows 2000 Server
✓ Upgrading Windows NT 4.0 to Windows 2000
✓ Creating setup disks
✓ Troubleshooting installation problems

Introduction

A good installation is essential to the proper operation of your Windows 2000 Server—this should come as no surprise to you. If you do not install Windows properly, you will spend a lot of time subsequent to installation repairing your configuration. Moreover, the more experience you have with installation, the more efficient you will want the process to be. To build your knowledge base, this chapter deals with a wide variety of attended and unattended installation methods. It addresses the pros and cons of the methods to ensure that you are doing the right thing at the right time.

The exam focuses on five main areas of installation:

- Attended installations
- Unattended installations
- Upgrade installations from Windows NT 4.0
- Applying Service Packs
- Troubleshooting installations

Each of these topics will be covered in detail in the following sections. Before you can actually get into the details surrounding Windows 2000 Server installation, you need to take a few moments and ensure you are prepared for the installation process.

Windows 2000 Installation Preparation

You need to take the following factors into consideration when installing Windows 2000 Server (as a clean installation or an upgrade installation):

- Hardware compatibility
- Software compatibility
- Disk sizes and partitions
- Whether the currently installed system can be upgraded

The following sections expand upon these topics. You must ensure that you are fully prepared in these areas before installing Windows 2000 Server.

Hardware Compatibility

Hardware compatibility is perhaps the most important of all requirements that you have to meet before attempting an installation. Windows 2000 has very strict hardware requirements. If you do not meet them, at best some of your components will not function properly and, at worst, the operating system will not install at all. Two hardware criteria are required to install and operate Windows 2000 Server:

- The components must meet the minimum requirements for installation (see Table 2.1).
- The components must be on the Hardware Compatibility List.

Table 2.1 Minimum Requirements for Windows 2000 Server Operating System Installation

Component	Published Minimums
Processor	Pentium 133MHz or better (also see Note)
RAM	256MB recommended minimum (128MB minimum supported)
Free disk space	2GB hard disk with a minimum of 1GB free; more is required when installing over the network

Minimum Hardware Requirements

The minimum hardware requirements refer to the processor type and speed, the amount of disk space, and the amount of memory available. In the past, Microsoft published only minimum installation requirements. For example, the minimum hardware required to install the operating system would be provided. However, Microsoft-published minimums now reflect the minimum hardware recommended to run servers in specific configurations. As a result, you may be able to install Windows 2000 Server with less than these minimum recommendations, but the servers you install will probably not function effectively in a production environment.

Support for running Windows 2000 on the HP Alpha processor has been discontinued because HP has decided it is no longer profitable to support this combination.

It is important to note that the minimum hardware requirements have increased dramatically since Windows NT 4.0 was released. If you are planning an upgrade of a Windows NT 4.0 Server to Windows 2000 Server, it is likely you may need to upgrade the server's hardware before attempting the upgrade. To keep up to date with any changes that may come out to the minimum requirements, be sure to visit http://www.microsoft.com/windows2000/server/evaluation/sysreqs/default.asp.

The Hardware Compatibility List (HCL)

The Hardware Compatibility List (HCL) is Microsoft's published list of Windows 2000–tested hardware components. Items that are listed in the HCL are guaranteed to function (at least to a bare minimum) with Windows 2000. If you want to ensure that all your hardware will function properly under Windows 2000, you should consult the current version of the HCL, which can be found on the Internet at http://www.microsoft.com/hwdq/hcl/search.asp.

Although many hardware products appear on the HCL (which means they have been tested and found to function with Windows 2000), not all products are listed. If the manufacturer has a driver available for the device that has been created for Windows 2000, the device should function properly. However, any problems with the driver or its effects on your server should be addressed to the manufacturer, not Microsoft.

Software Compatibility

In addition to confirming that your hardware is compatible with Windows 2000, you should also make sure your software is Windows 2000 compatible. Some applications that operated well under DOS, Windows 9*x*, or Windows NT 4.0 will no longer function (or function properly) under Windows 2000.

In the era of Windows NT 4.0 and Windows 9*x*, Microsoft published guidelines for the creation of software for these platforms. Although the guidelines were clear in terms of what the operating systems would allow developers to do, they often left loopholes that developers took advantage of to improve the performance of their applications. Microsoft has not changed their guidelines as much as they have closed up the loopholes. This means that software written to the old guidelines should still work on both old and new platforms. However, software written to take advantage of loopholes that existed in the old guidelines might not work on newer platforms, such as Windows 2000.

To check for software compatibility, you can do two things: First, you can consult the software compatibility Web site at http://www.microsoft.com/windows2000/server/howtobuy/upgrading/compat/search/software.asp. This Web site allows you to search for your software products based on manufacturer, product name, category, or key word(s). After the search, a list will be returned indicating the status of that software. The possible statuses are

- *Certified*—The application meets the standards in the Windows 2000 Application Specification and has passed compatibility tests conducted both by Microsoft and an independent testing organization.
- *Compatible*—The application has been deemed compatible with Windows 2000 and Microsoft will provide Windows 2000-related support with the application.
- *Caution*—The application may not function properly in Windows 2000. More research should be conducted before attempting to deploy this application on Windows 2000. Possible solutions include patches or upgrades.

Second, do not be dismayed (at least not yet) if you do not find your software product on the Web site. Contact the software vendor or test it yourself to see whether you can prove compatibility on your own. In many cases, software that is not on the Web site works just fine. Be aware, however, that if software is not on the list, it is not supported by Microsoft, which may create difficulties later. Some vendors do not want to spend the time and money involved to have their products certified for Windows 2000 even though they function properly, but caution is an approach that will always yield positive results.

Disk Size and Partitions

To install Windows 2000 Server on your computer, you have to have disk space—and a reasonable amount of extra space just to be safe. Table 2.1 showed that you need at least 1GB free on a hard disk that is at least 2GB in size. Furthermore, all of that free space must be on the same contiguous partition, so two 600MB empty partitions on a 3GB hard disk won't work.

If this is a typical Windows 2000 installation, you will usually want to install the operating system on the active partition (usually the C: drive), but this is not required. If you plan to dual-boot your Windows 2000 Server with another operating system, you must install Windows 2000 Server onto another partition. If you do this, Microsoft is going to use different terms to describe the partition from which your computer starts up and the one on which the Windows 2000 operating system files are stored, as defined in the following:

- *System partition*—This is the active partition; that is, the one from which your computer's BIOS begins the boot process. This partition is usually, but not always, the C: drive. This partition contains the Master Boot Record (MBR) and system files that allow Windows 2000 to take control of the boot process.
- *Boot partition*—This is the partition where the Windows 2000 operating system files are stored. These files are commonly found in a folder called WINNT. They are files that Windows 2000 uses to complete the start-up process and to run Windows 2000 after it is started.

In most cases, it is recommended that you install Windows 2000 on the same partition as you are booting from (the active partition). This would mean that the Boot and System partitions would be in the same location, which would be called the System/Boot partition. The only case where this would not be done is when you plan to dual-boot (or multiple boot) Windows 2000 with one or more other operating systems—a practice that is recommended only for test systems.

When you have decided on which partition to install Windows 2000, you may want to format it. You don't have to format it in advance because the installation process includes a utility to create new partitions as well as to format them. If you do choose to preformat the partition, you have the following format choices: NTFS, FAT16, and FAT32. These format types are discussed in detail in Chapter 3, "Installing, Configuring, and Troubleshooting Access to Resources." A quick summary of the available options is presented here:

- *NTFS*—Used only by Windows NT–based systems, such as Windows NT, Windows 2000, Windows XP, and Windows Server 2003. In Windows 2000, NTFS was upgraded to NTFS v5.
- *FAT16*—A fairly universal file format that is recognized by all Microsoft operating systems and several others as well. It is very inefficient and has a maximum volume size of 2GB.
- *FAT32*—An improved version of FAT16 that was introduced in Windows 95 OSR2. FAT32 is supported in all versions of Windows following Windows 95 OSR2.

Current Operating System Upgradability

In the event that you want to upgrade a machine running another operating system to Windows 2000, you have a number of paths you can follow. The working definition this book uses for *upgrade* is "the ability to install a new operating system without having to completely reconfigure the resulting system." Upgrades to Windows 2000 Server can be done directly from Windows NT Server 4.0 and Windows NT Server 3.51. Because of the new fluidity of domain controller roles, the current role of the server is not significant.

In the case of other operating systems (such as DOS, for example), you will have to choose whether to remove (or install over) the existing operating system or to dual-boot with it. *Dual-boot* means that you will choose which of the operating systems you will boot from at system startup and that all software will have to be installed separately for each operating system. Just as a quick reference, the following operating systems do not support a direct upgrade to Windows 2000 Server: MS-DOS, Windows 3.*x*, Windows 9*x*, Windows NT Server 3.51 with the Citrix software installed, or Microsoft BackOffice Small Business Server 4.0.

After taking the preceding steps, you will be ready to install Windows 2000 Server on your computer.

Performing Attended Installations of Windows 2000 Server

Attended installations of Windows 2000 Server are the most common installation performed, and thus will be our starting point for looking at installing Windows 2000 Server. Attended installations are those that are performed with a human sitting at the computer manually supplying required information (answers) during the course of the installation process. This is directly opposite of an *unattended installation*, which we will examine later in this chapter, which uses a script (an answer file) to provide the required installation information.

There are four ways to perform an attended installation:

- Boot from the Windows 2000 CD-ROM.
- Boot with a set of Windows 2000 setup disks and then install from the Windows 2000 CD-ROM.
- Boot to a current 32-bit operating system and manually invoke the setup routine using winnt32.exe.
- Boot to a current 16-bit operating system and manually invoke the setup routine using winnt.exe.

The end result will be the same no matter which method you use. In addition, the majority of the installation will follow the same steps, with only the installation initiation method varying.

If you want to fully repartition your hard drive, you must boot from the CD-ROM or setup boot disks; otherwise, you cannot delete the partition that has the temporary setup files.

CD-ROM–Based Installation

If you have a computer whose BIOS supports booting from a CD-ROM, you can install Windows 2000 Server without a previous operating system on your hard drive and without requiring network support. To do so, configure your computer to boot to the CD-ROM in the BIOS and then perform the following steps:

1. Insert the Windows 2000 CD-ROM into the drive and boot your computer. After you have confirmed that you want to boot to your CD-ROM, Setup will begin and start copying files. After a short time, you will see the Welcome to Setup screen, as shown in Figure 2.1, which prompts you to choose what Setup will do next.

Windows 2000 Server Setup
Welcome to Setup.
This portion of the Setup program prepares Microsoft(R) Windows 2000(TM) to run on your computer.
• To set up Windows 2000 now, press ENTER.
• To repair a Windows 2000 installation, press R.
• To quit Setup without installing Windows 2000, press F3.
ENTER=Continue R=Repair F3=Quit

Figure 2.1 Starting the Windows 2000 Server Setup.

2. As prompted in Figure 2.1, press Enter to start the setup of Windows 2000 Server.

3. Press F8 when the licensing agreement is displayed to continue on. You cannot install Windows 2000 without accepting the licensing agreement.

4. If your computer currently has no formatted volumes, you are presented with the screen shown in Figure 2.2. If you are prompted with this screen, press C to continue.

```
Windows 2000 Server Setup

  Setup has determined that your computer's startup hard disk is new
  or has been erased, or that your computer is running an operating
  system that is incompatible with Windows 2000.

  If the hard disk is new or has been erased, or if you want to discard
  its current contents, you can choose to continue Setup.

  If your computer is running an operating system that is incompatible
  with Windows 2000, continuing Setup may damage or destroy the existing
  operating system.

  •  To continue Setup, press C.
     CAUTION: Any data currently on your computer's startup hard disk
     will be lost.

  •  To quit Setup, press F3.

 C=Continue Setup  F3=Quit
```

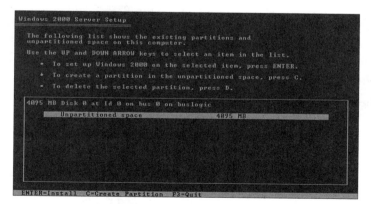

Figure 2.2 The new hard disk warning.

5. You are prompted to choose the partition (or to create a new one) on which Windows 2000 Server should be installed as shown in Figure 2.3. If you create a new partition, you see this screen after creation is complete. Select the partition onto which Windows 2000 Server will be installed and press Enter to continue.

```
Windows 2000 Server Setup

  The following list shows the existing partitions and
  unpartitioned space on this computer.

  Use the UP and DOWN ARROW keys to select an item in the list.

     •  To set up Windows 2000 on the selected item, press ENTER.

     •  To create a partition in the unpartitioned space, press C.

     •  To delete the selected partition, press D.

 4095 MB Disk 0 at Id 0 on bus 0 on buslogic
       Unpartitioned space                    4095 MB

 ENTER=Install  C=Create Partition  F3=Quit
```

Figure 2.3 Select a partition to install on or create a new one.

6. If the partition you chose was not already formatted, you will be prompted to format with either NTFS or FAT file system, as shown in Figure 2.4. If you format with the FAT file system and the partition is larger than 2GB, Setup formats it with FAT32; otherwise, it is formatted with FAT16. If the partition was already formatted, you see a

slightly different dialog that allows you to choose to leave the partition formatted as is, format it using either NTFS or FAT, or convert it from its existing format to NTFS (this preserves any data already on the partition). Make your selection and press Enter to continue.

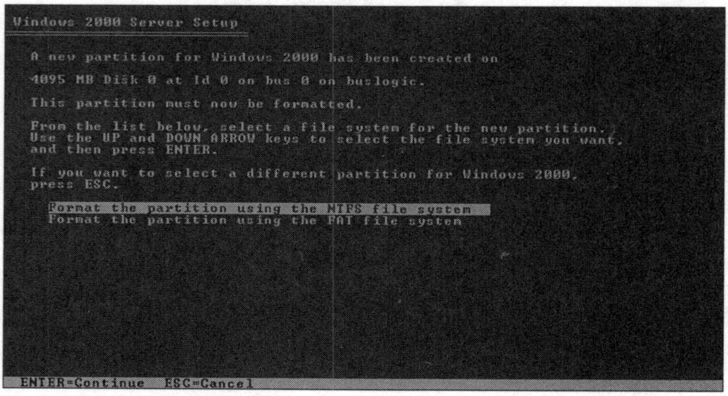

Figure 2.4 Format your partition.

7. Setup copies files onto the hard drive and reboots the system in preparation for the GUI part of the setup.

8. Once Setup has restarted your computer, you are presented with a screen prompting you to click Next to continue with system information gathering. You can click the Next button; however, if you do not do so after about 30 seconds, the device installation begins anyway. Setup spends some time locating and installing your system's hardware devices. Your screen may flicker during this process and the process may take several minutes, so be patient.

9. When the Regional Settings screen appears, as shown in Figure 2.5, you will have the option of changing the system and user locales (the computer's location that dictates how currency, numbers, and dates appear) and the keyboard layout. If you want, you can change either of these by clicking the Customize button for either (or both) and choosing a different country location. If you do not customize these settings, the locales will be set to English (United States), and the keyboard will be configured as US. Click Next to continue.

10. On the Personalize Your Software screen, enter your name and the name of your company or organization. You must supply an entry for the Name field. Setup cannot continue until you have typed something into the Name field. Click Next to continue.

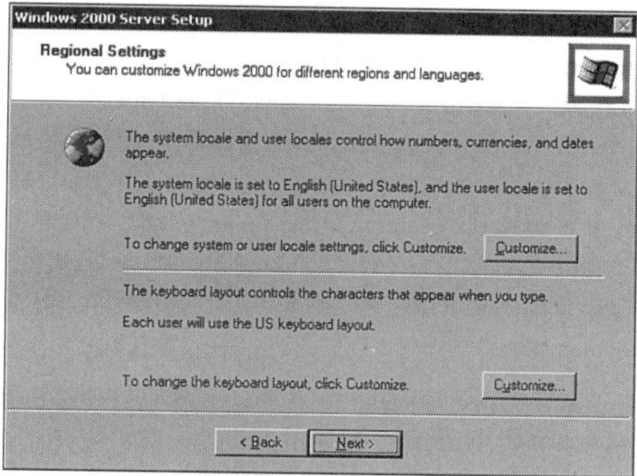

Figure 2.5 Selecting the regional settings and keyboard layout.

11. On the Your Product Key screen, enter the 25-character product key that is located on the CD case or certificate of authenticity for your Windows 2000 Server CD. Click Next to continue.
12. The Licensing Modes screen allows you to indicate what type of licenses you own for this server (see Figure 2.6). Your choices are Per Server and Per Seat. By default, Per Server is chosen with five Client Access Licenses (CALs) selected; however, you can change either of those settings.

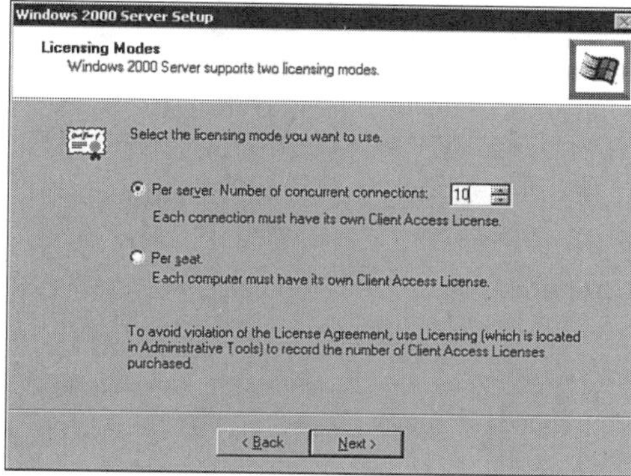

Figure 2.6 Select either Per Server (and the number of concurrent connections) or Per Seat licensing.

Licensing Options

To know what choice to make in the Licensing Modes screen, you must first understand the available licensing modes. Per Server mode is a connection-based licensing model. In it, you purchase one license for every connection made to a specific server. If you have 1 server and

10 users could possibly connect to it at any one time, you would purchase 10 CALs. If a single user makes a connection to two different servers at the same time, that user will be using a CAL on each of the servers at the same time. In other words, two licenses would be required for a single workstation. That scenario is where the Per Seat mode comes in. Per Seat licensing licenses a user to make connections to all servers. Instead of monitoring the total number of connections made, all that really matters is the number of users making those connections. If you have 5 servers and 25 users and each user could make a connection to each of the servers, you would need only 25 CALs with Per Seat licensing. With Per Server licensing, you would need 125 licenses to provide the same licensed access.

The rule on licensing is that if the number of possible connections made by your users is larger than the number of users you have, you should be looking at Per Seat licensing. In addition, Per Server is an effective model for use in organizations or departments with only one server. In cases where the same group of users is connecting to more than one server, it is usually best to consider Per Seat licensing. A simple way to remember these licensing concepts is as follows: Per Server = Any Seat (client) to one server and Per Seat = Any Seat (client) to any server.

13. The next screen is the Computer Name and Administrator Password dialog box as shown in Figure 2.7. Enter the computer name (as governed by your organization's naming conventions) and the password for the built-in Local Administrator account. By default, the computer name is generated from the first seven letters of the previously entered company name, followed by a hyphen and seven random alphanumeric characters. Ensure that your password conforms to good security standards; in other words, it should contain seven or more characters, include upper and lowercase characters, should be a combination of letters and numbers, and should not be any readily anticipated word or name from your personal or business life (like the name of your children, pets, or business) or any word from the dictionary. Having completed these fields, click Next to continue.

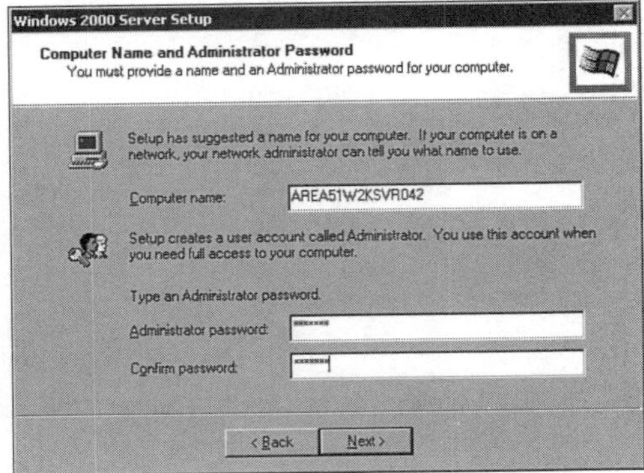

Figure 2.7 Enter a computer name and a password for the local Administrator account.

14. The next screen is the Windows 2000 Components screen, shown in Figure 2.8. You can select any optional components to install at this time. After making your selections, click Next to continue.

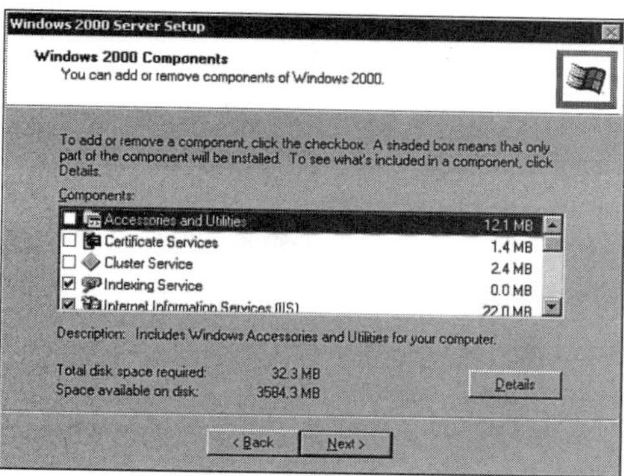

Figure 2.8 Select any optional Windows 2000 components to install at this time (these components can be added later if desired).

15. If you have a modem installed in your server, the Modem Dialing Information dialog box appears. You must provide at least a country of origin and an area code to proceed to the next screen. Click Next to continue.

16. In the Date and Time Settings dialog box, you are prompted for the current date and time as well as the time zone you are currently in (and whether you observe Daylight Savings Time in your location). Click Next to continue. At this point, networking settings are detected, and networking components are installed.

17. In the Networking Settings dialog box, you are prompted to configure the machine's networking components. If you choose *Typical* (the default), the Client for Microsoft Networks is installed, as is File and Print Sharing and TCP/IP with the DHCP (automatic address configuration) service enabled. If you choose *Custom*, you can manually add new clients (such as a NetWare client), services, or protocols (such as NWLink or NetBEUI). In addition, you can also manually configure TCP/IP to use static addressing. The options displayed differ depending on the options you chose during the network components section (for example, NetWare protocols are automatically added if Novell Services is selected).

18. In the Workgroup or Computer Domain screen, you can configure what kind of a network group this computer belongs to, as shown in

Figure 2.9. If you choose No, This Computer Is Not on a Network, you need to type the name of the this server's workgroup name in the text box provided. If this server is part of a domain, you need to provide this server's domain name. When you click Next, if you have decided to join a domain, you are prompted for the name and password of a user in that domain who has sufficient rights to create computer accounts (see following note). If you do not have this information available, to continue you have to make the computer a member of a workgroup, and then you can join the domain later.

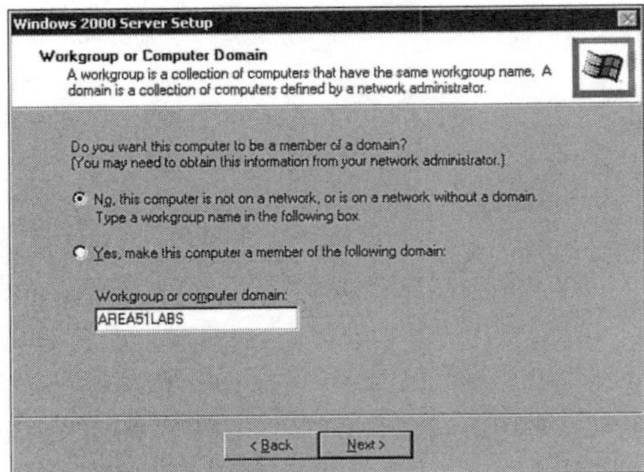

Figure 2.9 Choose the kind of network membership this server will have (Domain or Workgroup).

When a computer joins a domain it means that it becomes part of the domain structure. It also means that users logging in at the server's console will have the option of providing domain login credentials or local computer login credentials. To join a domain, either a computer account must exist in Active Directory or it must be created at the time the server is installed. This computer account is independent of any user and simply indicates that a specific (Windows 2000) computer will allow users to log in to the domain from it. This computer account provides authentication of the computer in the Active Directory. To create such an account, a user must have that right assigned to his user account.

19. After the domain membership has been established (if joining a domain) or after the previous step (if in a workgroup), the Installing Components dialog box appears, and Setup installs all the components that have been requested thus far in the process.

20. Finally, the Performing Final Tasks dialog box appears, and the final configuration of your server is completed. These steps may take a long time to complete, so be patient.

21. When the Completing the Windows 2000 Setup Wizard dialog box appears, remove the CD-ROM from your drive and click Finish to restart your server.

Installing with the Setup Disks and a CD-ROM

If you have a machine with no current operating system on it that will not boot from a CD-ROM, you must use the setup disk method. The Windows 2000 setup disks are a set of four disks that perform the actions carried out by booting from the Windows 2000 CD-ROM during the initial file copying process, before Setup actually begins. After you have made the disks, you boot from the first one and progress through all four, at which point you are prompted to insert the CD-ROM in the CD-ROM drive, and the installation continues from that point using the CD.

The disks are created using either MAKEBOOT.exe or MAKEBT32.exe, both of which are found in the BOOTDISK folder on your Windows 2000 Server CD-ROM. Both programs do the same thing, however, the "32" version is designed to be run under 32-bit operating systems, whereas the other is designed to be run under 16-bit operating systems, such as DOS and Windows 3.1.

The process to create the Windows 2000 setup disks is as follows:

1. From any operating system from which you can access a CD-ROM, navigate to the BOOTDISK folder on the Windows 2000 Server CD-ROM.
2. If you are using a 16-bit operating system, run MAKEBOOT.exe; if your are using a 32-bit operating system, run MAKEBT32.exe. See Figure 2.10 for an example.

```
C:\WINNT\System32\cmd.exe - makebt32
Microsoft Windows 2000 [Version 5.00.2195]
(C) Copyright 1985-1999 Microsoft Corp.

C:\>d:

D:\>cd bootdisk

D:\BOOTDISK>makebt32

*************************************************************
This program creates the Setup boot disks
for Microsoft Windows 2000.
To create these disks, you need to provide 4 blank,
formatted, high-density disks.

Please specify the floppy drive to copy the images to: a

Insert one of these disks into drive a:.  This disk
will become the Windows 2000 Setup Boot Disk.
Press any key when you are ready.
/  23% complete.
```

Figure 2.10 You can create a Setup disk set using the MAKEBOOT or MAKEBT32 utility.

3. When prompted, type the letter of your floppy drive.
4. Insert a blank disk (labeled *Windows 2000 Setup Boot Disk)* into the floppy drive and press Enter.

5. When prompted, insert another blank disk (labeled *Windows 2000 Setup Disk #2*) into the floppy drive and press Enter.
6. When prompted, insert a third blank disk (labeled *Windows 2000 Setup Disk #3*) into the floppy drive and press Enter.
7. When prompted, insert a fourth blank disk (labeled *Windows 2000 Setup Disk #4*) into the floppy drive and press Enter.
8. Remove the final disk and place them in a safe place for use later.

After you have created a set of setup disks, you can begin the process of installing Windows 2000 Server by performing the following steps:

1. Insert the disk labeled *Windows 2000 Setup Boot Disk* into your floppy drive and boot your computer.
2. When prompted, insert the disk labeled *Windows 2000 Server Setup Disk #2* and press Enter.
3. When prompted, insert the disk labeled *Windows 2000 Server Setup Disk #3* and press Enter.
4. When prompted, insert the disk labeled *Windows 2000 Server Setup Disk #4* and press Enter. Eventually you will see the screen shown previously in Figure 2.1.
5. Continue using the remaining installation steps (starting at Step 2) as detailed previously in the "CD-ROM–Based Installation" section.

Installing by Manually Invoking WINNT32.EXE

If a 32-bit Microsoft operating system is installed on the target installation computer, you can simply run setup.exe from the Windows 2000 Server CD-ROM after first booting the machine into the operating system that is already installed. If CD-ROM Autorun is enabled on your system, inserting the Windows 2000 Server CD-ROM into the drive also invokes setup.exe. Alternatively, you can invoke the program winnt32.exe, which is found on the CD-ROM in the I386 folder. In addition, if you have network connectivity, you can connect to a share point on another computer that has the Windows 2000 Server files on it, or in that computer's shared CD-ROM drive with the Windows 2000 Server CD in it, and run setup.exe or winnt32.exe from there. After you begin the Setup process, it progresses as previously discussed.

Installing by Manually Invoking WINNT.EXE

If you have MS-DOS or Windows 3.x installed on the target computer, you have two choices to complete the Windows 2000 installation. If you have a CD-ROM drive in that machine and the appropriate drivers to access it from DOS, you can use winnt.exe to begin the installation after first booting the machine into DOS. If you do not have access to a local CD-ROM but you have a networking client installed on the installation machine, you can connect to a network share to which the Windows 2000 Server CD has been copied, or connect to a computer's shared CD-ROM drive with the Windows 2000 Server CD in it, and use winnt.exe to begin the installation. To begin the installation from DOS, follow these steps.

1. At a DOS prompt, type `SMARTDRV` and press Enter. This loads the SmartDrive program, which greatly reduces the time it takes to copy files from the CD-ROM.
2. Insert your Windows 2000 CD into the CD-ROM drive and change to that drive letter using the DOS `CD` command.
3. Navigate to the I386 folder on the CD and type `WINNT`. This starts the Setup program.
4. When prompted, enter the location of the I386 directory you just navigated to and press Enter to continue. The file copying process commences.
5. When prompted, press Enter to reboot your computer to continue the setup process.
6. Continue using the remaining installation steps (starting at Step 8) as detailed previously in the "CD-ROM–Based Installation" section.

Although attended installations are common, there may be times when a number of similar servers need to be installed. To do that, an unattended installation is preferable. The next section describes that method of installation.

Performing Unattended Installations of Windows 2000 Server

Unattended installation methods allow for installation of Windows 2000 Server with little or no user intervention. They are beneficial when a number of similar servers need to be installed. When configured properly, unattended installations can be completely hands-off after the installation has begun.

For Windows 2000 Server, there are two methods of unattended installation:

- Installation from scripts
- Installation using disk images and third-party distribution software

Script-based installations are the most prevalent in real life and on the exam, thus this section provides in-depth coverage of the configuration and deployment of script-based installation. You also get an overview of disk duplication, but we do not cover it in depth because the exam does not do so.

Script-Based Unattended Installation Using Answer Files

The premise of the script-based installation is that the installation progresses like a normal attended installation, except that where a user would normally answer setup questions, a text file provides the answers instead. This text file is thus intuitively called an *answer file*. Once the installation has begun, if you have configured the answers properly, no intervention is required.

This list outlines the basic components of a script-based installation:

- *The I386 directory from the Windows 2000 CD-ROM*—This is generally copied into a server-based folder and shared (unattended installations are almost exclusively network based).
- *The WINNT.exe or WINNT32.exe programs*—WINNT is for DOS-based installations; WINNT32 is used for upgrades from 32-bit Windows operating systems.
- *An answer file providing the generic answers to setup questions*—This is typically a file with a .txt extension (although the extension does not matter), and is usually named UNATTEND.txt.
- *A uniqueness database file*—This file, which has a .udf extension, provides the answers to computer specific questions that will change from machine to machine (for example, the computer name or IP address).
- *A batch file or command line that invokes the unattended installation*—This file is used to launch the unattended installation using the answer file and UDB files created to perform the installation.

You can create the answer file using any text editor. However, a wizard is available to help you create this answer file and to ensure that you do not leave out crucial information. This wizard is called the Setup Manager Wizard.

Using the Setup Manager to Create Unattended Answer Files

The Setup Manager is part of the Windows 2000 Support Tools located in the \Support\Tools folder on the Windows 2000 CD-ROM. It is stored in a file called Deploy.cab and must be extracted from that .cab file before it will operate. Complete the following steps to extract the Setup Manager.

1. Navigate to the Support\Tools folder on your Windows 2000 CD-ROM and double-click the Deploy.cab file.
2. Select the setupmgr.exe, setupmgx.dll, and deptool.chm files; right-click one of them and choose Extract from the context menu as shown in Figure 2.11.

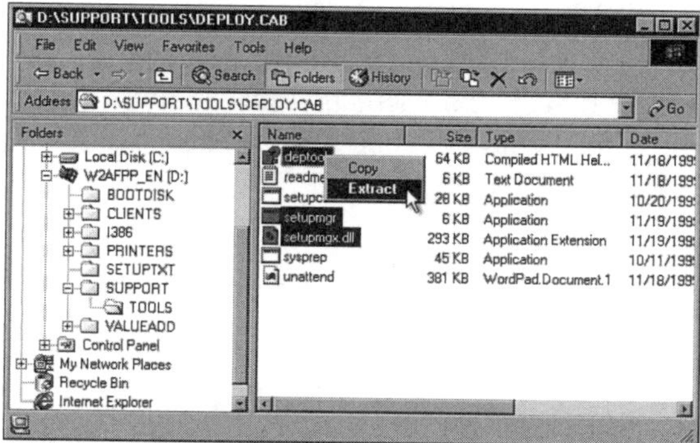

Figure 2.11 Extracting the Setup Manager files for use.

3. When the Browse for Folder dialog box appears, browse to the location to which you want to extract the Setup Manager files (it is recommended that you use *systemroot*\system32, but that is not required).
4. Create a shortcut to the setupmgr.exe file on the desktop and/or in the Start menu so that you can easily invoke it when required.

When the Setup Manager is extracted and accessible, you can use it to create an answer file as discussed in the following steps.

If you will be using the answer file to install multiple servers, you can use the combination of a single answer file and a single .udf file to avoid having to create an answer file for every machine you are going to install. This will be more apparent to you by the time you have finished the following steps.

1. Start the Setup Manager Wizard.
2. At the Welcome to the Windows 2000 Setup Manager Wizard screen click Next to continue.
3. At the New or Existing Answer File screen, choose whether you want to create a new answer file, have the current computer's settings be the defaults for the wizard, or modify an existing answer file. In this example, we want to create a new answer file. Click Next to continue.
4. At the Product to Install screen, choose the product that this answer file is designed to install. Your choices are Windows 2000 Unattended Install, Sysprep Install, and Remote Installation Services. Choose Windows 2000 Unattended Install and click Next.
5. At the Platform screen, choose the product (Windows 2000 Professional or Windows 2000 Server) for which you are creating this answer file. This example is for Windows 2000 Server. After making your selection, click Next to continue.
6. At the User Interaction Level screen shown in Figure 2.12, you will need to specify how much control the user will have over the installation process and how much interaction she will have. Your choices are fully described here:

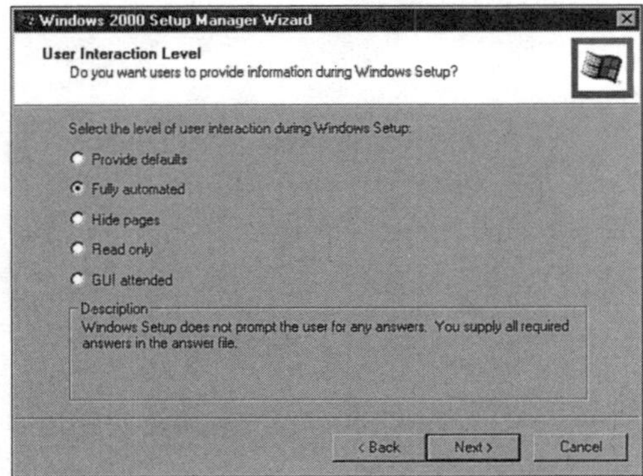

Figure 2.12 The User Interaction Level screen.

- *Provide Defaults*—The user will be prompted to review (and perhaps change) the information you provide. This gives the user a guide to follow but allows them to make changes in any area.
- *Fully Automated*—The user will see (perhaps only briefly) all the processes as they happen, but he or she will not be able to make any manual changes to the settings.
- *Hide Pages*—The user may be prompted for information, but only where you do not provide answers to questions. This is useful where you want some of the answers to be predefined but not all of them. This choice provides standardization in some areas and flexibility in others. In instances where all the information on a setup page has been provided, the user does not see the page.
- *Read Only*—You provide the answers to the questions, and the user will be prompted for information that you do not provide (just like the previous choice). However, pages that have been filled in will be displayed. Also, when pages are displayed, the user will be unable to modify those questions for which you provided answers.
- *GUI Attended*—The text-based setup is completely automated, but the GUI setup must be attended by a user who can answer the questions.

In this example, we assume you want to create a fully automated setup. Choose Fully Automated and click Next to continue.

7. At the License Agreement screen accept the licensing agreement by clicking the check box. Click Next to continue.
8. At the Customize the Software screen, enter your name and the organization name and click Next to continue.
9. If you selected Windows 2000 Server in step 5, the Licensing Mode screen will appear next. Select the licensing type and number of seats if you choose Per Server. Refer back to the "CD-ROM–Based Installation" section for a discussion on licensing options. Click Next to continue.
10. At the Computer Names screen, shown in Figure 2.13, enter the names of each of the computers on which you will perform the installation using this answer file. After you type each computer name, click the Add button. You can continue to do this until all your computer names have been added. You also have the option of importing the

names from a text file by clicking the Import button. Either of these options are used to create the UDB file that creates customized installations for each of the computers on which you are using this answer file. You can also simply allow Windows 2000 to automatically generate unique names for each machine by selecting the Automatically Generate Computer Names Based on Organization Name check box. This generates names as discussed previously in the attended installation section. Click Next to continue after you have added the required computer names.

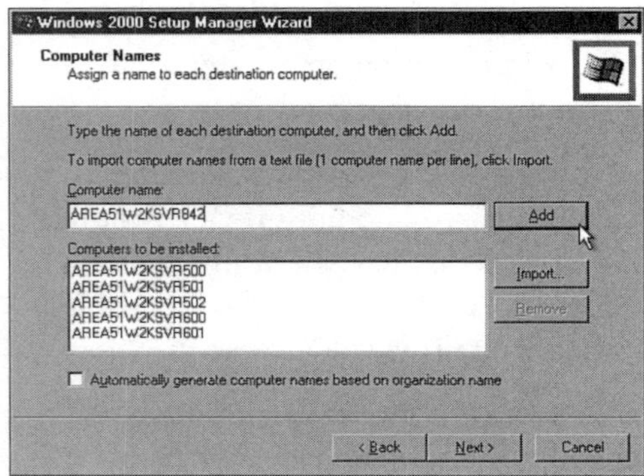

Figure 2.13 The Computer Names screen.

11. At the Administrator Password screen, provide a local administrator password for the computers you will be installing using this file. This password will be the same for each of the machines, so you may want to change them manually after the installation is complete. In addition to setting the password, you can also set the computer to automatically log on as the administrator. This option can be set to "auto" log on as many as 99 times before a user is prompted for a password. This feature not only allows for multiple automated logons as software is installed and the machine is restarted by the installation process, but it also allows for the security of passwords and manual logon once the allotted number of automatic occurrences is exceeded. Click the Next button when you are finished with this screen.

12. At the Display Settings screen, choose the Colors, Screen Area, and Refresh Frequency that is appropriate for the computers you will install with this script. If they are all the same and you want to choose specific settings, do so. If they are not all the same, you want to leave the settings as the default to ensure that you do not try to set any machines to values they cannot handle. When you are done, click Next to continue.

13. At the Network Settings screen, choose the type of network settings you want for each machine. If you choose Typical, each computer installed with this script will have the Microsoft Networking Client and TCP/IP with DHCP enabled. If you choose Custom, you will be prompted for the number of network adapters in each machine and you will be able to manually set networking properties (such as TCP/IP properties, additional clients, and so on) for each adapter. When you are done, click Next to continue.

14. At the Workgroup or Domain screen you can choose how these machines will participate in your network structure—whether in a workgroup or a domain. If you choose a domain, you enter the domain name and whether to create a computer account at installation time. If you wish to create a computer account, you need to provide the credentials of a user who is allowed to add computer accounts to Active Directory. When you are done, click Next to continue.

15. At the Time Zone screen, choose the time zone that the machines will be in and click Next. If you have machines in more than one time zone, consider making an answer file for each time zone.

16. At the Additional Settings screen, you can choose to add additional setup parameters to the basic answer file you are creating. If you choose Yes, proceed through the next seven steps. If you choose No, skip directly to step 24. After making your choice, click the Next button to continue.

17. The first additional setting is the Telephony screen. In it, you can choose location information for telephony configuration on the target machines. If you leave the settings at Do Not Specify This Setting, those settings are not put into the answer file and the user is prompted to enter this information upon the first login. Click Next to continue.

18. The second additional setting is the Regional Settings screen. Regional settings include such options as language settings, time locales, currency, numbers, and dates. Click Next to continue after making your selection.

19. The third additional setting is the Languages screen. Windows 2000 allows for the installation of support for more than just the primary language. You can choose which of the available languages you want to install automatically. Select as many languages as you require, and then click Next.

20. The fourth additional setting is the Browser and Shell Settings screen, shown in Figure 2.14. You can use the default settings, use an

autoconfiguration script (created by the IE Administration Kit), or specify proxy and default home page settings. Specify the settings appropriate to your environment by selecting a radio button. If you do not choose to use the default settings, you can customize the choice you made using the Settings buttons. When you finish, click Next to continue.

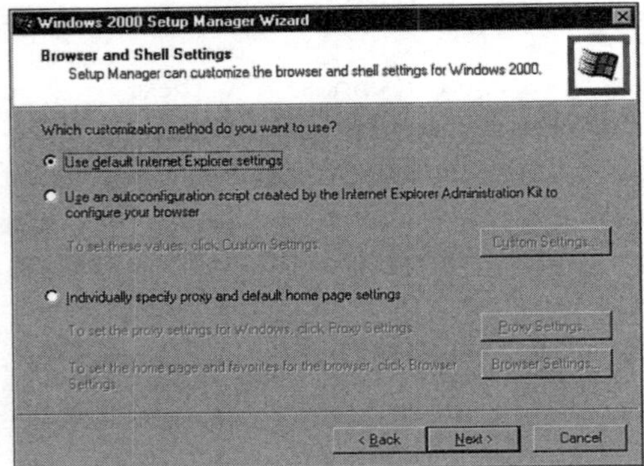

Figure 2.14 Customizing the browser and shell settings.

21. The fifth additional setting is the Installation Folder screen. In it, you can specify the location for the installation folder. You can install into the default location of WINNT, have the system create a unique name, or specify the folder name yourself. Click Next to continue.

22. The sixth additional setting is the Install Printers screen. Here you can configure which printers the destination machines should be connected to. The first time a user logs on to on of these computers the network printers you configure here will be attached, provided that the user login has access to the printers. Click Next to continue.

23. The final additional setting is the Run Once screen. On this screen, you can specify any commands you want to run after the installation has completed. These are most often setup files for installing software. You can use the Move Up and Move Down buttons to change the order in which these commands are executed. When you finish, click Next to continue.

24. On the Distribution Folder screen, you choose whether to create a distribution folder. A distribution folder is a network share that contains the files you need for the automated installation. If you do not choose to create a distribution folder, you have to provide the CD-ROM at each installation point. Follow steps 25–30 only if you choose to create

or modify a distribution folder by choosing Yes. Make your choice and click Next. If you chose No, skip to step 31.

25. If you choose to use a distribution folder, the Distribution Folder Name screen appears, prompting you for the path and share name of the folder you want to create or modify. Whether you choose to create or modify a distribution folder, you have to provide the path and the share name for it. Click Next to continue.

26. On the Provide Additional Mass Storage Drivers screen, you can provide the locations for drivers that need to be installed but are not part of the Windows 2000 Server driver set. This setting is used to install drivers for devices such as hardware RAID controllers. By specifying these drivers, you not only modify the script to install them, but you also modify the distribution folder to include these drivers. Click Next to continue.

27. On the Hardware Abstraction Layer screen, you can specify a new HAL to replace the default one. This is typically used by an OEM retailer who provides Windows 2000 Server with non-standard hardware that requires additional code not supplied in the Microsoft HAL. By using this setting, you can substitute your custom HAL when installing Windows 2000 Server on these non-standard client machines. Click Next to continue.

28. On the Additional Commands screen, you can specify the execution of additional setup or configuration routines. Because no user will be logged on when they run, these must be routines that can run in that state. If you were creating an integrated installation set that included hot fixes, this would be the place where you would want to call out a script executing the hot fixes and the Qchain.exe command. Click Next to continue.

29. On the OEM Branding screen, you can specify logos and backgrounds for the installation process. These are displayed while the automated installation is taking place. Click Next to continue.

30. On the Additional Files or Folders screen, you can indicate additional files or folders that are to be placed onto the target computers at installation time. This may be data, programs, or other special files that are required on the target computers. You can indicate where these files are to be placed by selecting a particular folder in the provided tree and then clicking the Add Files button. Click Next to continue.

31. On the Answer File Name screen, shown in Figure 2.15, you can indicate the name and path of the answer file to be created from the

responses you gave. This screen also indicates that if you specified more than one computer name (in step 10), a .udf file would be created. This .udf file (uniqueness database file) contains the computer-specific information for each machine you specified. The path you indicate must exist at this point; the wizard will not create it. When you are done, click Next to continue.

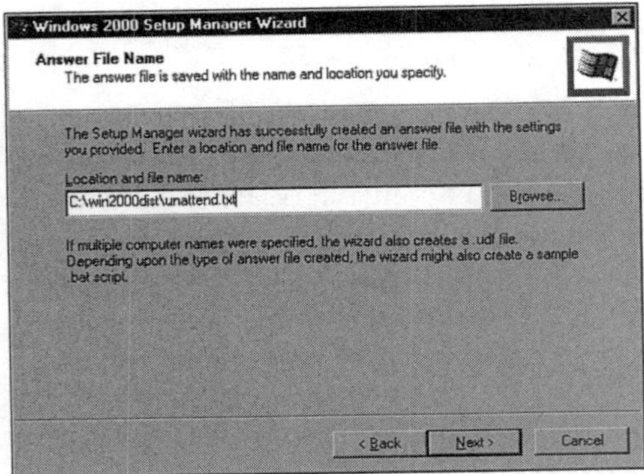

Figure 2.15 The Answer File Name screen.

32. On the Location of Setup Files screen, you indicate the location where the setup files are stored. This is used to create your distribution folder. You can specify the CD or a local or network location. Click Next to continue.

33. When the Setup Manager Wizard finishes copying files, click Next to continue.

34. When the Completing the Windows 2000 Setup Manager Wizard screen appears, note the files it has created. Click Finish to exit.

The following is a sample of an answer file (answer.txt), which could have been created using a text editor:

```
;SetupMgrTag
[Data]
  AutoPartition=1
  MsDosInitiated="0"
  UnattendedInstall="Yes"

[Unattended]
  UnattendMode=FullUnattended
  OemSkipEula=Yes
  OemPreinstall=Yes
  TargetPath=\WINNT

[GuiUnattended]
  AdminPassword=password
```

```
  OEMSkipRegional=1
  TimeZone=35
  OemSkipWelcome=1

[UserData]
  FullName="Authorized User"
  OrgName="Area 51 Partners"
  ComputerName=*

[LicenseFilePrintData]
  AutoMode=PerServer
  AutoUsers=100

[TapiLocation]
  CountryCode=1
  Dialing=Tone
  AreaCode=757
  LongDistanceAccess="9"

[SetupMgr]
  ComputerName0=AREA51W2KSVR500
  ComputerName1=AREA51W2KSVR501
  ComputerName2=AREA51W2KSVR502
  ComputerName3=AREA51W2KSVR600
  ComputerName4=AREA51W2KSVR601
  ComputerName5=AREA51W2KSVR842
  DistFolder=C:\win2000dist
  DistShare=win2000dist

[GuiRunOnce]
  Command0="rundll32 printui.dll,PrintUIEntry
➥/in /n \\AREA51W2KSVR042\HPLASERJET2200"
  Command1="rundll32 printui.dll,PrintUIEntry
➥/in /n \\AREA51W2KSVR042\HPLASERJET2200_2"

[Identification]
  JoinWorkgroup=AREA51LABS

[Networking]
  InstallDefaultComponents=Yes
```

If you study the preceding file, you will notice that the sections (headed by titles in square brackets) roughly correspond to the screens where you filled in answers in the Setup Manager Wizard.

Notice that the CD-key is not included in the answer file created by the Setup Manager. You can include the CD-key in your answer file to completely automate it by adding this line of code to the [UserData] heading:

```
ProductID=xxxxx-xxxxx-xxxxx-xxxxx-xxxxx
```

So, in the example answer file shown, the [UserData] section would look like this:

```
[UserData]
  ProductID=xxxxx-xxxxx-xxxxx-xxxxx-xxxxx
  FullName="Authorized User"
  OrgName="Area 51 Partners"
  ComputerName=*
```

The unattended.udf file was created because a number of computer names were entered in the wizard. The .udf file will look something like this:

```
;SetupMgrTag
[UniqueIds]
  AREA51W2KSVR500=UserData
  AREA51W2KSVR501=UserData
  AREA51W2KSVR502=UserData
  AREA51W2KSVR600=UserData
  AREA51W2KSVR601=UserData
  AREA51W2KSVR842=UserData

[AREA51W2KSVR500:UserData]
  ComputerName=AREA51W2KSVR500

[AREA51W2KSVR501:UserData]
  ComputerName=AREA51W2KSVR501

[AREA51W2KSVR502:UserData]
  ComputerName=AREA51W2KSVR502

[AREA51W2KSVR600:UserData]
  ComputerName=AREA51W2KSVR600

[AREA51W2KSVR601:UserData]
  ComputerName=AREA51W2KSVR601

[AREA51W2KSVR842:UserData]
  ComputerName=AREA51W2KSVR842
```

You *absolutely must know* the difference between an answer file and a .udf (uniqueness database file) and their functions before taking this exam.

The structure of a .udf file is like that shown previously. It begins with a set of computer names under the heading [Uniqueids]. What follows is a section for each computer, with the heading [computername:UserData], and under that is the unique variable name (such as ComputerName) and the value associated with that.

With the answer files created, your task is simply to invoke the setup routine, indicating which answer file to use. This task is covered as the first topic in the next section.

Installing Windows 2000 Server Using an Answer File

Unlike attended installation procedures, unattended installations do not use the Setup.exe program. Instead, they use either winnt.exe or winnt32.exe to complete the installation. Recall that winnt.exe is for 16-bit operating systems such as MS-DOS and Windows 3.*x*, while winnt32.exe is for 32-bit operating systems—Windows 95 and later.

Although you can use winnt.exe and winnt32.exe to initiate an attended installation, the true power of these programs lies in the fact that their behavior can be modified using various command-line switches as part of their execution syntax. Table 2.2 provides a brief explanation of the switches available for use with both winnt.exe and winnt32.exe.

Table 2.2 Switches for WINNT and WINNT32

WINNT	WINNT32	Function
/a	N/A	Enables accessibility options.
/e:*command*	**/cmd:*command***	Executes a command before the final phase of Setup.
/i:*inf_file*	N/A	Specifies the name of the setup information file.
/r:*folder*	**/copydir:*folder***	Specifies an optional folder to be installed in the system root directory.
/rx:*folder*	**/copysource:*folder***	Specifies an optional folder to be copied, used for installations, and then deleted when the installation is done.
/s:*path*	**/s:*path***	Specifies the location of the installation files for Windows 2000 Server. You can specify up to eight sources to speed up (and load balance) the file copy process. The first source must be valid or the installation will fail.
/t:*drive*	**/tempdrive:*drive***	Specifies the location that the temporary installation files can be copied to and the location where Windows 2000 will be installed (this becomes the Boot partition).
/u:*file*	**/unattend:[*num*]:[*file*]**	Specifies the location of the answer file for unattended installations and the number of seconds to wait between copying the files and restarting the computer.
/udf:*file*	**/udf:*id,file***	Specifies the location of the uniqueness database file for unattended installations. ID is the identifier within the UDF that defines the unique installation options for this computer.
N/A	**/cmdcons**	Specifies that files required for command-line repair console be installed.
N/A	**/debug level:*file***	Creates a log file when conditions of certain severity occur during installation. The default level is 2 (warning).

(continued)

Table 2.2 Switches for WINNT and WINNT32 *(continued)*

WINNT	WINNT32	Function
N/A	**/syspart:*drive***	Copies files to a hard drive and marks it as active. Used to begin installation to a hard drive, which will then be relocated to another machine (its permanent home).
N/A	**/checkupgradeonly**	Checks your computer to see if it can be upgraded to Windows 2000. This option does not actually perform an installation; instead, it creates a log file (winnt32.log for NT or upgrade.txt for Windows 9x), indicating the results of an upgrade.

You *absolutely must know* the switches for winnt.exe and winnt32.exe and their functions before taking this exam.

Having seen the previous table and the process for creating answer and .udf files, you are now ready for an example of how they would actually be used. Suppose you wanted to create a batch file for the installation of a server called AREA51W2KSVR601 from the sample answer file and .udf file shown earlier. Your batch file would look like this:

```
net use z: \\AREA51W2KSVR042\win2000dist

z:\winnt /s:q: /u:z:\answer.txt /udf: AREA51W2KSVR601,z:\answer.udf
```

This code supposes that the installation is being done from an MS-DOS machine with network connectivity. Also note that the share *win2000dist* on the server AREA51W2KSVR042 was the specified location used in previous examples for both the answer file and the distribution files—yours will vary slightly depending on where you choose to store the files.

Although creating unattended installations using scripts is a very popular method, many people have found other methods to be quicker and more efficient. The next section deals with disk duplication as an installation technique.

Unattended Installations Using Disk Duplication

Disk duplication, the process by which the entire hard drive of one machine is duplicated to the hard drive of another, is not a new concept. People have been doing it in one form or another for years, using third-party products. The idea that you can configure a machine completely (right down to all the application software you want), copy the information to a second disk, and then simply move the disk to a target machine is very appealing.

The following disk duplication process formalizes the steps for creating a duplicate hard drive and allows for automated setup using the Sysprep.exe program. Sysprep, like the Setup Manager, is a tool stored in the deploy.cab file. It is recommended that you extract the Sysprep files from this cabinet file into a folder called Sysprep, as outlined in the following steps.

1. From the Windows 2000 Server CD-ROM, navigate to the Support\Tools folder and double-click the Deploy.cab file.
2. Select the files sysprep.exe, setupcl.exe, and deptool.chm; right-click one of them and choose Extract from the context menu.
3. When the Browse for Folder dialog box appears, browse to the location to which you want to extract the Setup Manager files (it is recommended that you use *bootpartition*\sysprep, but it is not required).

The role of Sysprep.exe is to prepare a disk for duplication. Once the disk has been prepared, a third-party tool can be used to copy the duplicated drive onto other machines. Sysprep.exe, which is run from the Tools Management Console or from a command line, configures the disk image so that SIDs and other unique information are removed and ready to be re-created on the target machine. This ensures that no conflicts arise in interaction with other machines that have the same SID. The following steps describe the process to duplicate the *master computer* (the computer you are using as a model for your disk duplicates):

1. Install and configure Windows 2000 on the master computer.
2. Log on to the computer as Administrator.
3. Install and configure all applications on the master computer.
4. Run Sysprep.exe on the master computer to prepare that hard disk for duplication.

5. Use a disk-imaging tool on it to create an image of the master computer's hard drive. You need to use a third-party tool such as Norton's Ghost for this step.
6. Create a copy of the target drive using your third-party duplication tool. Place the duplicated disk into the target computer.

When the image has been transferred to a target machine, that machine is then restarted and a Mini-Setup Wizard is run to complete the setup on that computer. One of the problems in disk duplication in the past has occurred when the information on the target machine needed to be different from that on the source machine (for example, Security Identifiers—SIDs—and computer names). Sysprep takes care of that and they are modified when the target machine is restarted.

If you want to completely automate the process of creating new installations, you can have Sysprep create a Sysprep.inf file that provides answers to the setup routine that runs when the target machine is started after the disk image has been placed on it. This .inf file can make the installation completely automated (which is why this discussion falls under the topic of unattended installations).

Using Sysprep.exe

Table 2.3 outlines some additional parameters for Sysprep.exe that will allow you to control how it operates from a command line.

Table 2.3 Switches for Sysprep.exe

Switch	Function
-quiet	Runs the target computer's setup with no user interaction.
-pnp	Forces full Plug and Play device enumeration and installation during Mini-Setup. Use only when you need to detect and install legacy devices that are not Plug and Play compatible. Do not use the **-pnp** switch on computers that have all Plug and Play devices because you will increase the time required for first-run experience without providing any additional benefits.
-reboot	Restarts the configuration computer when Sysprep is complete rather than simply shutting it down. This will invoke the Setup program on the configuration computer and is used only when you want to verify that the setup program is going to function properly.
-nosidgen	Prevents the regeneration of SIDs on the target computer. This is useful when you are transferring the contents of one machine to another for the purposes of decommissioning the original. The new machine then becomes an exact duplicate of the first.

You *absolutely must know* the Sysprep switches and their functions before taking this exam.

If you want to completely automate the installation, you need to create a Sysprep.inf file. This file is similar in many ways to the answer file you created previously in this chapter and should be placed into a SYSPREP folder in the root of the hard disk that is being duplicated (on the source computer). You can create this file by using the Setup Manger Wizard and selecting that it is for a Sysprep installation. When the setup program runs on the target computer, it checks for this file and uses it if it's present.

Performing Upgrade Installations from Windows NT 4.0 Server

Due to its already large installed base, the possibility that you may need to upgrade a Windows NT Server 4.0 installation to Windows 2000 Server is quite likely. Fortunately, the upgrade of a Windows NT 4.0 member server to a Windows 2000 member server is very straightforward. A Windows 2000 member server can reside comfortably in a workgroup, a Windows NT 4.0 domain, or a Windows 2000 domain.

The following are two common ways of upgrading a Windows NT 4.0 Server to Windows 2000:

- Attended
- Unattended

You can use the setup program from a network share or from a local CD-ROM (attended), or you can use the WINNT32 program from a network share (unattended). To perform an attended upgrade of a Windows NT 4.0 member server, follow these steps:

1. From the Windows 2000 CD-ROM, run Setup.exe.
2. When asked if you want to upgrade to Windows 2000, click Yes to continue.
3. In the Welcome to Windows 2000 Setup Wizard screen shown in Figure 2.16, choose Upgrade to Windows 2000 (Recommended) and click Next.

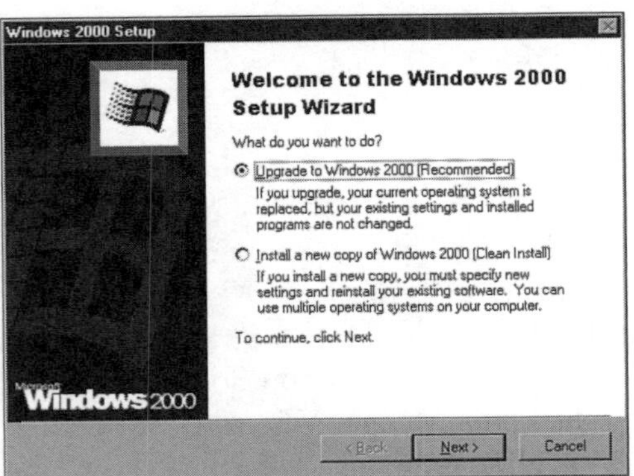

Figure 2.16 Starting the upgrade to Windows 2000.

4. In the License Agreement screen, choose I Accept This Agreement and click Next. Note that you must accept the licensing agreement to continue with the installation of Windows 2000 Server.
5. In the Report System Compatibility screen, you are informed about any services that might not function properly when the upgrade is complete. Possible problematic services are disabled by the Setup program. On this screen, you can see more details about the problems that might occur by clicking Details or you can export the report to a text file for detailed investigation later by clicking Save As. Click the Next button when you are satisfied that the areas identified will not pose major problems.
6. The setup program will copy source files from the CD onto the hard drive and then restart the computer.
7. After restarting, the server enters a text mode setup routine where it extracts and copies additional setup files from the local hard drive location created previously. When that extraction and copy process is complete, the server reboots again and enters the GUI portion of the setup process. If you decided to have the Boot partition converted to NTFS, the conversion takes place after the first reboot, and Windows 2000 reboots again before entering the GUI setup.
8. The setup process continues with the remaining installation steps as detailed previously in the "CD-ROM–Based Installation" section.

Unattended upgrades can also be performed using winnt32.exe from a network share. You have two primary options when installing in this way. First, you can use an answer file and a .udf file just like you would with a regular unattended installation. In this case, you can use the same wizard to help you create these files. Second, you could use winnt32.exe with the /unattend switch. This switch indicates that the installation is to progress without user input and that the answers to the setup questions are to be provided by looking at (and duplicating) the current Windows NT 4.0 configuration. For simple upgrades, such as member servers, this is the easiest method.

Installing Windows 2000 Service Packs

Microsoft upgrades software using Service Packs. A *Service Pack* is an executable that replaces one set of files with another newer and improved set of those files. In the case of an operating system (such as Windows NT 4.0), Service Packs have been a way to distribute bug fixes and fixes to security holes. However, beginning with NT 4.0's Service Pack 4, Microsoft began to release upgrades and additions to operating system functionality as well. For example, Service Pack 4 introduced the Microsoft Management Console to provide an integrated security interface.

With Windows 2000, however, Microsoft's plan is to release Service Packs on a regular schedule to fix bugs or security flaws. This plan of more regular updates is designed to keep the size of Service Packs to a manageable level. Only the most current Service Pack is required to be installed because each Service Pack contains all updates in the Service Packs that preceded it.

In many regards, Windows 2000 Service Packs are not very different from Windows NT 4.0 Service Packs. When they are released, the intent is to install the Service Pack on all Windows 2000 computers to implement any fixes included in them. This basic premise has not changed. However, one significant improvement has been made in the application of Service Packs: the concept called *slipstreaming*.

Updating an Installation Source by Using Slipstreaming

Before you can understand slipstreaming, a digression into Service Packs on Windows NT 4.0 is necessary. Under NT, if you installed a Service Pack, you had to ensure that if you made modifications to the operating system that involved reading files from the CD or a network share, you subsequently reinstalled the Service Pack. This was because the files found on the CD or in the network share were pre–Service Pack versions, and re-application was necessary to ensure that all components of the operating system were up to the current Service Pack.

Slipstreaming makes this unnecessary. With slipstreaming, changes from the Service Pack can be applied to the source files found on a local folder or network share (by using the `-s` switch when running update.exe for the Service Pack). This means that when you subsequently access those files, you will obtain the fixed versions of those files, not the old ones. This saves time because it means that the Service Packs are will be applied to any machine only once, even as additional services (and other operating system components) are installed in the future. In addition, this also means that new installations over the network will also automatically be up-to-date with the current Service Pack.

It must be noted that slipstreaming does not remove the need to install the Service Pack on each machine. What it does remove is the need to install the Service Pack on any subsequent fresh Windows 2000 installations and the need to install the Service Pack after making operating system changes.

In the standard Service Pack installation, two major things happen. First, the replacement files are copied into a backup directory so the installation can be reversed if necessary. Although this is an optional process prompted for by the Service Pack installation routine, it is always recommended that you use it. Second, the Service Pack replaces the operating system files that it finds installed on the target system with the new versions of those files.

The process to slipstream a Service Pack into an installation source is fairly simple and is outlined in the following steps. The procedure assumes that you do not currently have a network installation source, and thus it will be created as part of the process.

1. On a network share, create a new folder to hold the contents of the Windows 2000 CD-ROM, such as W2KFILES. Copy the entire contents of the Windows 2000 CD-ROM to this folder.

2. On a network share, create a second new folder to hold the contents of the Service Pack you are slipstreaming. Extract the Service Pack into this second folder by executing the command `W2KSP3 -x` at the command prompt. Of course if you are not using Service Pack 3 or your path needs to be entered, supply that information as well.

3. After the Service Pack verifies all files, you are asked to choose a location to extract them to, as shown in Figure 2.17. Choose the Service Pack folder you created earlier.

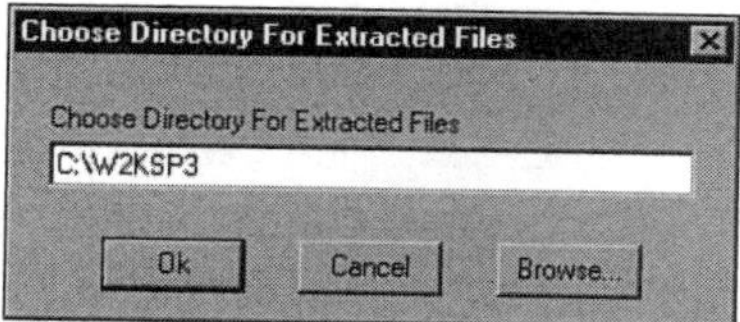

Figure 2.17 Choosing the location to extract Service Pack files to.

4. When the extraction is complete, click OK to close the extraction window.

5. The last step is to actually slipstream the Service Pack to the installation files. Assuming both of the folders are located on the C:\ volume, a sample command entered in the Run box would look like this: `C:\W2KSP3\I386\UPDATE\UPDATE.EXE -s:C:\W2KFILES\`. After entering the command a window will open and inform you of the Slipstream status.

6. When the integration is complete, click OK to close the integration window and complete the slipstream process.

Installing Service Packs

Installing Service Packs to individual computers is a simple task that is outlined below.

1. Install the Service Pack by running the update.exe file (found in the i386\update\ folder of the extracted Service Pack) or by simply double-clicking the Service Pack executable.

2. Back up the existing files by choosing that option in the Service Pack installation setup program.

3. Reboot your computer to allow the changes to take effect.

The update.exe command has some switches that can be used to modify its behavior. These switches are explained in Table 2.4.

Table 2.4 Update.exe Command-Line Switches

Switch	Description
-u	Runs the update in unattended mode
-f	Forces other applications to close upon computer shutdown
-n	Does not back up files for later Service Pack uninstallation

(continued)

Table 2.4 Update.exe Command-Line Switches (continued)	
Switch	**Description**
-o	Overwrites OEM files without prompting
-z	Does not reboot the computer when the Service Pack installation has completed
-q	Runs the installation in quiet mode, with no user interaction
-s:[directory]	Integrates the Service Pack files into the directory supplied

Troubleshooting Failed Installations

Unfortunately, sometimes installations of Windows 2000 Server fail. A variety of factors might cause this to happen. As a system administrator, you need to know as much about the causes for failure as possible to ensure a quick recovery from such a failure.

Believe it or not, most installation problems are caused by simple mistakes made by the installer not following the correct procedures. Granted, some failures are caused by faulty media. However, failures of media are the exception more than the rule. In general, if you follow the procedures outlined in this chapter, you will have successful installations.

If there is any question about any of your hardware or software being Windows 2000 compatible, it is recommended that you run the upgrade check tool, which is part of the winnt32.exe program. Executing `winnt32 /checkupgradeonly` from the Windows 2000 Server CD-ROM will generate a report telling you about possible issues. This report details hardware that may not work without new drivers and software that is not Windows 2000 compatible, that might not be Windows 2000 compatible, or that needs to be reinstalled after the upgrade. It also will identify system settings that will not function the way they used to or that will be disabled by the setup routine. If you have many servers, you are advised to run the upgrade check on a representative sample of your servers so you can anticipate problems and, using hardware and/or software upgrades, preempt them.

The most frequent reasons for failure are listed here:

- *Minimum hardware requirements are not met*—Windows 2000 Server has minimum hardware requirements that must be met for installation to be complete. If the processor is too slow, there is not sufficient RAM, or the amount of free disk space is insufficient, you will have to upgrade your server before installation can continue. This may be the case even when you are upgrading from Windows NT 4.0 because of the increased minimums in these areas.

- *Hardware is not on the HCL*—If hardware is not on the HCL, it may not be detected and installed properly. If the hardware is a network card, you might not be able to contact a domain controller or a network server, and the installation may fail. Check the Microsoft HCL Web site and run the upgrade check to see if there are going to be any HCL problems.
- *Media errors*—If there seems to be a problem with the Windows 2000 Server Installation CD-ROM, contact your software vendor to request a replacement.
- *Failure of dependency service to start*—At installation, this error is most often caused by an improperly configured network adapter. Make sure that the hardware is detected properly, and then manually change properties if required.
- *Inability to connect to the domain controller*—If you are joining a domain, you will have to contact a domain controller to create or check for a computer account. Ensure that the correct name has been given for the domain and that a domain controller can be contacted from your location.
- *Automated Installation fails*—Check the parameters you specified for the installation. If you got information incorrect or if you manually created or modified the answer file or .udf file, you might have introduced errors.

Practice Questions

Question 1

You are a hardware vendor who sells Windows operating systems with your products. You are creating scripted installations for your technicians to run on the machines they are configuring. You want to ensure that the text-based setup is completely automated but that the graphical portion prompts the owners of the machines for all their specific information. The dialog box shown in Figure 2.18 appears when you are using the Setup Manager to create your scripts. What option will you select to ensure that the scripts meet your specifications?

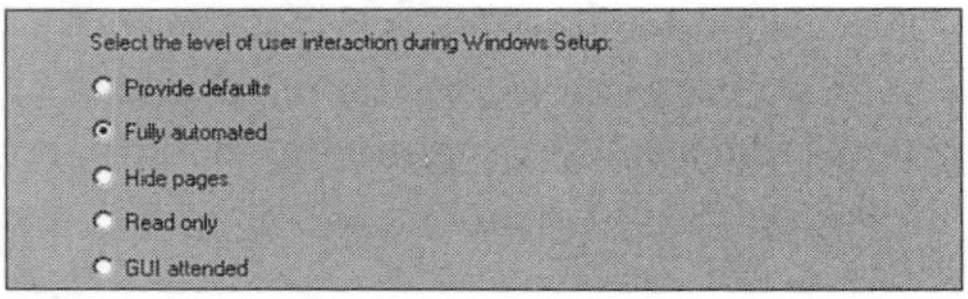

Select the level of user interaction during Windows Setup:

- Provide defaults
- Fully automated
- Hide pages
- Read only
- GUI attended

Figure 2.18

❍ A. Change to Provide Defaults.

❍ B. Change to Hide Pages.

❍ C. Change to Read Only.

❍ D. Change to GUI Attended.

Answer D is correct. The GUI Attended mode provides answers for the text-based part of the installation but prompts for all the GUI answers. The Provide Defaults option provides a guide for the user, but allows her to change the answers should she desire; therefore, answer A is incorrect. The Hide Pages option completely hides option pages where the answers have been provided; therefore, answer B is incorrect. The Read Only option allows the user to see answers you have supplied and prompts her for answers you have not provided; therefore, answer C is incorrect.

Question 2

Emma is a system administrator for a company that is currently implementing a Windows 2000 infrastructure. The company has five regional offices across North America (two in Canada and three in the United States), and they are all interconnected with T1 lines. Having set up a domain controller, she is about to configure 10 servers with identical hardware including 256MB RAM, two 18GB IDE hard drives, and dual PIII 600MHz processors. These servers, which will all end up in one of the five regional offices, are intended to perform a variety of functions including Web Service, File and Print Service, and Application Service.

Required Results:

Servers are all installed with Windows 2000 Server.

Optional Desired Results:

Servers are all to be installed with a minimum amount of effort at their destination sites.

Servers should be able to be configured by summer interns with a minimum of training or experience with Windows 2000 Server.

Servers end up as members of the domain.

Proposed Solution:

Emma will use Setup Manager to create an unattended text file and a uniqueness database file. These files will include configuration settings for completely setting up the machines, including adding them to the domain. The servers will be shipped to their permanent sites, and then a student working at each site will run a batch file that will begin the automated setup routine.

Which results will the proposed solution produce?

❍ A. The proposed solution produces the required result and all the optional results.

❍ B. The proposed solution produces the required result but only one of the optional results.

❍ C. The proposed solution produces the required result but only two of the optional results.

❍ D. The proposed solution does not produce the required result.

Answer A is correct. By configuring unattended installations using Setup Manager, Emma ensures that the software is installed and that the machines end up as domain members. In addition, because the unattended installation is invoked by a batch file, the summer student starting it does not need to know much about the installation process. Furthermore, because the configuration is simply running a batch file, it can be done with a minimum of effort at the destination site; therefore, answers B, C, and D are incorrect.

Question 3

Andrea is preparing to install Windows 2000 Server on three of her computers that are currently running Windows NT Server 4.0. She has a complete list of all installed hardware in each computer, but is not sure that it meets the requirements for Windows 2000. What online resource can Andrea best use to verify the compatibility of her currently installed hardware?

❍ A. She needs to visit each specific manufacturer's Web site to see whether the specific hardware has been certified for Windows 2000.

❍ B. She needs to visit the Windows Update Web site to see whether her hardware has been certified for Windows 2000.

❍ C. She needs to visit the Hardware Compatibility List Web site and search out her hardware to determine whether it has been certified for Windows 2000.

❍ D. She needs to visit the Web site of her server reseller to determine whether her hardware has been certified for Windows 2000.

Answer C is correct. The best way to ensure that all of her hardware has been certified for Windows 2000 would be for Andrea to search for it on the Windows HCL Web site. Only by finding it on the HCL can Andrea be certain that her hardware will function at a minimum acceptable level. Although manufacturers' Web sites and reseller Web sites may have this information, it is not a guarantee and you should not expect support from Microsoft for non-certified hardware; therefore, answers A and D are incorrect. Windows Update is used to update Windows software installations, not verify the compatibility of hardware; therefore, answer C is incorrect.

Question 4

Which of the following computers could be directly upgraded to Windows 2000 Server? (Choose all that apply)

❑ A. A Windows 98 client computer

❑ B. A Windows NT 4.0 IIS server

❑ C. A Windows NT 3.51 file and print server

❑ D. A Windows NT 3.51 Citrix server

Answers B and C are correct. The supported upgrade paths for Windows 2000 Server are from Windows NT Server 4.0 and Windows NT Server 3.51 (not running Citrix). Windows 9x and Windows NT Server 3.51 running Citrix are not directly upgradeable to Windows 2000 Server; therefore, answers A and D are incorrect.

Question 5

Christopher is an instructor at a Microsoft Certified Technical Education Center (CTEC). He teaches the Windows 2000 Professional and Windows 2000 Server classes, which run for three weeks each. At the end of each three-week period, he needs to wipe his 55 lab computers and restore them back to their original state. Which installation method might work best for Christopher?

❍ A. Perform an attended installation on each computer.

❍ B. Perform a RIS installation on each computer.

❍ C. Perform an unattended installation on each computer using an answer file.

❍ D. Replace them with new, prestaged computers.

Answer C is correct. Initiating unattended installations for his computers would be the best solution of the options provided. He could, for example, create a Sysprep image and use a third-party disk cloning application to restore the computers back to their original state. Alternatively, he could use a floppy disk containing a batch file, answer file, and .udf file to start the installation from the CD-ROM. Performing an attended installation on 55 computers every three weeks is not the best solution; therefore, answer A is incorrect. RIS cannot be used for Windows 2000 Server installation (it is not supported by Microsoft); therefore, answer B is incorrect. Replacing the computers with new, prestaged computers is too expensive and still not answer the problem of restoring the configuration back to the original state; therefore, answer D is incorrect.

Question 6

You have an older computer on which you would like to install Windows 2000 Server so you can use it in a lab environment. What is the absolute minimum amount of RAM that you must have to install Windows 2000 Server on this computer?

❍ A. 64MB

❍ B. 128MB

❍ C. 256MB

❍ D. 384MB

Answer B is correct. Although the recommended minimum is 256MB of installed RAM, the absolute minimum that you can install Windows 2000 Server with is 128MB; therefore, answers A, C, and D are incorrect. Do not, however, expect to get peak performance out of a computer running Windows 2000 Server on 128MB of RAM.

Question 7

You are preparing to install Windows 2000 Server on three file servers for your organization. What licensing mode would most make sense if your organization has 200 clients that can reasonably be expected to access all three servers at the same time?

❍ A. Per Seat

❍ B. Per Server

❍ C. Per Client

❍ D. Per Connection

Answer A is correct. Per Seat licensing makes sense in this situation because the total number of connections you can have, 600, is greater than the number of clients you have, 200. Per Server licensing only makes sense if you have small numbers of clients and large numbers of servers; therefore, answer B is incorrect. There is no such thing as Per Client and Per Connection for Windows 2000 Server licensing; therefore, answers C and D are incorrect.

Question 8

Hannah is preparing to create an answer file for the unattended installation of several new servers in her organization. Which of the following items can an answer file specify during the installation process? (Choose all that apply.)

❑ A. The servers should be SQL Server 2000 computers.

❑ B. The servers should use a specific networking configuration.

❑ C. The servers should be installed into a specific domain.

❑ D. The servers should use specific screen resolution and color depth settings.

Answers B, C, and D are correct. It is possible to specify the networking configuration, domain membership, and color settings (among many other options) in an answer file. You cannot specify that a newly installed server should perform a specific role until after the server has been installed and configured completely, including the installation of additional software; therefore, answer A is incorrect.

Question 9

You have several computers in your organization that you would like to upgrade to Windows 2000 Server. Which of the following file systems that are in use will support an installation of Windows 2000 Server? (Choose all that apply.)

- ❑ A. FAT12
- ❑ B. FAT16
- ❑ C. FAT32
- ❑ D. NTFS

Answers B, C, and D are correct. Windows 2000 Sever can be installed on FAT16, FAT32, and NTFS volumes. NTFS is the recommend file system as it enables security and management features of Windows 2000 not otherwise available (see Chapter 3). The FAT12 file system is the one used on floppy disks; therefore, answer A is incorrect.

Question 10

You have just completed a default installation of Windows 2000 Server. Where can you look on your computer's hard disk to see the Windows 2000 Server files?

- ❍ A. WINDOWS Folder
- ❍ B. WINDOWSNT Folder
- ❍ C. WINDOWS2000 Folder
- ❍ D. WINNT Folder

Answer D is correct. The default installation location of Windows 2000 is to the WINNT folder on the specified partition; therefore, answers A, B, and C are incorrect.

Need to Know More?

Russel, Charlie, et al. *Windows 2000 Server Administrator's Companion, 2nd Edition*. Microsoft Press, 2002. ISBN 0735617856.

Stanek, William R. *Windows 2000 Administrator's Pocket Companion*. Microsoft Press, 2000. ISBN 0735608318.

Windows 2000 Resource Kits online at `http://www.microsoft.com/windows2000/techinfo/reskit/en-us/default.asp`. Also available in print; ISBN 1572318082 (Windows 2000 Professional) and ISBN 1572318058 (Windows 2000 Server).

Windows 2000 Server Resource Kit: *Microsoft Windows 2000 Server Deployment Planning Guide*. Part 4: Windows 2000 Upgrade and Installation

Microsoft Windows 2000 Professional Resource Kit. Chapter 5: Customizing and Automating Installations

Installing, Configuring, and Troubleshooting Access to Resources

Terms you'll need to understand:

✓ NWLink
✓ File and Print Services for NetWare
✓ File Service for Macintosh
✓ File & Print Services for Unix
✓ Printer Driver
✓ Print Server
✓ Printer
✓ Print Device
✓ File Allocation Table (FAT)
✓ NT Files System (NTFS)
✓ Distributed File System (Dfs)
✓ File Replication System

Techniques you'll need to master:

✓ Implement NetWare, Macintosh, and Unix interoperability
✓ Configure and manage Print Services
✓ Control access to local files, folders, and shared folders
✓ Replicate folder structures using Dfs
✓ Implement WebDAV to access folders through a Web browser
✓ Manage IIS to control Web site access

Introduction

One of the primary reasons to have a network is to share resources between computers. In a network that contains Windows 2000 Server, it is typical that servers share or offer resources and clients access or use resources. As an MCSE, you should be well versed in the resources that a Windows 2000 Server system can offer. These include network services, printers, files, and interoperability with NetWare, Unix, and Macintosh. This chapter discusses the issues related to these subjects.

Install and Configure Network Services for Interoperability

In most modern networks, Windows 2000 Server is not the only network operating system present. In fact, it is more common to have hybrid networks than to have homogeneous networks. For an MCSE, this means you must understand how to support non-Windows systems on your network.

There are two goals to aim for when implementing interoperability on a network. The first is to grant non-Windows systems the ability to access Windows 2000 shared resources. The second is to grant Windows systems the ability to access non-Windows shared resources. Primarily, Windows 2000 interoperability is concerned with NetWare clients and servers. However, Unix and Macintosh interoperability is also addressed on the 70-215 exam.

NetWare Interoperability

NetWare has long been considered the primary competitor to Microsoft in the market of PC-based network operating systems. In an effort to prevent loss of market share, Microsoft has expended considerable effort to develop interoperability and migration tools. This allows existing NetWare shops to deploy Windows 2000 Servers without having to revamp their entire network. It also gives existing NetWare shops a reasonably smooth migration path if they elect to move over to Microsoft systems completely.

Installing NWLink

The foundation upon which Windows 2000-to-NetWare interoperability rests is a common protocol. Prior to NetWare 5, all NetWare systems used the Internetwork Packet Exchange/Sequenced Packet Exchange (IPX/SPX) protocol suite. Microsoft developed its own version of this suite, called

NWLink. Even though NetWare 5 and newer systems can use the Transmission Control Protocol/Internet Protocol (TCP/IP) suite, the interoperability tools for NetWare on Windows 2000 systems requires the use of NWLink (IPX/SPX).

NWLink can be installed manually and independently of any NetWare interoperability services. However, if you elect to install a NetWare interoperability service, the installation procedure will verify that NWLink is installed, or if not install it before installing the desired service.

Configuring the Frame Type

Once NWLink is installed, it must be configured. The real key as to whether configuration is actually necessary and what configuration is mandated depends on the NetWare servers that are installed in your network environment. Different versions of NetWare and the use of different network types (Ethernet or Token Ring for example) each use a different configuration setting. The primary configuration setting to be concerned with is the *frame type*.

If there is only a single frame type in use on your network, then once NWLink is installed, it automatically detects the frame type and self-configures. By default, NWLink is set to auto configure. However, if multiple frame types are in use, the auto detect and configure option is less than effective. Auto detect is able to detect and configure itself to use only a single frame type. Any other frame types in use on the network will be ignored. However, with manual frame type configuration, multiple frame types can be defined so all traffic can be accessed and understood.

Once NWLink is installed and the frame type configured, you have the ability to communicate with NetWare systems from your Windows 2000 systems. However, as you'll learn shortly, just a common protocol is not sufficient to provide true interoperability between these two network operating systems.

Adding the GSNW Service

The primary NetWare interoperability service for Windows 2000 Server is *Gateway Services for NetWare (GSNW)*. GSNW provides a connectivity service between Windows 2000 Server and NetWare. This service has two aspects. The first is that it provides the Windows 2000 Server system with the ability to interact with the NetWare server as a client. Thus, the Windows 2000 Server system can access the shared printers and files from the NetWare server. Installing the NetWare Client for Windows 2000 onto the Server provides the same services as Client Services for NetWare (CSNW) on a Windows 2000 Professional system.

The second aspect of this connectivity service is that the Windows 2000 Server can act as a gateway to allow Windows networking clients to access NetWare shared resources as if they were hosted by the Windows 2000 Server system.

GSNW is configured to use a single user account on the NetWare system. That one user account defines what printers and files the Windows 2000 Server itself or any Windows clients are able to access.

GSNW lets the Windows 2000 Server function as a true gateway, allowing client computers to connect using TCP/IP, which the Windows 2000 Server translates for communication with the NetWare server using NWLINK. This means that client computers are not required to load multiple protocols to communicate with both servers.

Because GSNW is a gateway service, it is designed for occasional use. If clients need regular or high-volume access to NetWare resources, it may be more efficient to install CSNW on each individual system.

To install and configure GSNW, the following actions must be taken on the NetWare system:

1. Create a user account (or several accounts) on the NetWare system to act or serve as the gateway access account(s). You could designate an existing account for this purpose as well. All resource accesses will be authenticated using this account.
2. Create a group called NTGATEWAY. Place all accounts created or designated in step 1 in this group.
3. Grant the NTGATEWAY group access to the resources you want to share with the Windows clients.

Because all users who access the NetWare server through the gateway connect with the same user ID, careful consideration is needed when assigning permissions on the NetWare server. Remember that permissions on the NetWare server can be configured for individual users or for the NTGATEWAY group.

Once the NetWare server is configured, install GSNW on the Windows 2000 Server system for the specific network connection that will be used to connect to the NetWare system. You must define either the Preferred Server name or the Tree and Context information. The Preferred Server name will be used if the NetWare system is version 3.x or higher and running bindery emulation. The Tree and Context information will be used if the NetWare system is version 4.a or 5.x running NDS (NetWare Directory Services).

Once GSNW is installed, it must be configured. You will create the virtual shares on the Windows 2000 Server system that map to resource shares on the NetWare system. To configure GSNW, follow these steps:

1. Open the GSNW applet from the Control Panel.
2. Click the Gateway button.
3. Mark the Enable Gateway checkbox.
4. Type in one of the NetWare account names that was made a member of the NTGATEWAY group on the NetWare system.
5. Provide the password for that account.
6. Click the Add button to create a virtual share mapping.
7. Type in a name that will be created on the Windows 2000 Server system as the share that Windows clients will access.
8. Type in the network path to the resource share on the NetWare system using a Universal Naming Convention (UNC) pathname (that is, //servername/sharename).
9. Select a drive letter to be mapped to the share. This drive letter is used by Windows 2000 to emulate a local drive, which is then shared with the network.
10. If desired, elect to restrict the number of simultaneous users of this share.
11. Click OK.
12. Repeat steps 6 through 11 for each resource share.
13. For each defined share, select it, then click Permissions.
14. Configure the user and group permissions for each share in the same manner you would configure a normal Windows 2000 share.
15. Click OK.
16. Click OK twice to save changes and close the GSNW applet.

Once GSNW is configured, clients will be able to see new shares in the list of available resources when they look at the Windows 2000 Server that is acting as the Gateway in My Network Places.

File and Print Services for NetWare

GSNW provides the ability for Windows systems to connect to NetWare resources. If you want NetWare systems to connect to Windows resources, you must employ the File and Print Services for NetWare tool. This service is installed on a Windows 2000 Server system and provides gateway services to NetWare clients running IPX/SPX.

File and Print Services for NetWare lets the Windows 2000 Server emulate a NetWare 3.12 server and supports many of the standard NetWare 3.x commands and utilities. Because File and Print Services for NetWare is not included with Windows 2000 (it must be purchased separately), it is not covered in detail on the exam. Consequently, there is little reason to cover it in more detail here.

Interoperability with Macintosh

In addition to NetWare systems, another computer system commonly found in organizations is Apple Macintosh. Microsoft provides four tools to support limited Macintosh interoperability.

The first of these tools is the *AppleTalk* protocol. AppleTalk is the proprietary protocol used by many Macintosh systems. However, just as with NetWare, newer versions of Macintosh systems rely on TCP/IP rather than their own protocol. In spite of this, the interoperability tools for Macintosh on Windows 2000 require the use of AppleTalk. AppleTalk can be installed manually before installing one of the other interoperability tools, or it will be installed automatically when you attempt to install one of the other two tools.

When the AppleTalk protocol is installed, it must be configured to interact with the network. Macintosh systems are logically segmented on a network into zones. AppleTalk on Windows 2000 can be configured to operate within any detected zone. However, the Windows 2000 AppleTalk implementation cannot be used to establish or define new zones.

The second tool is *File Server for Macintosh*. This service allows Windows 2000 to act as a file server for Macintosh clients. To use File Server for Macintosh, you must have an NTFS volume that can be used to host the Macintosh files. Once the File Server for Macintosh is installed, new Macintosh shared file volumes can be created through the Shared Folders section of the Computer Management tool. Each individual Macintosh volume can be assigned a password to limit access and a maximum simultaneous user limit.

Although Macintosh clients are able to connect to Windows 2000 Servers using plain-text passwords, this is not a secure method of authentication and is not recommended. To utilize secure, encrypted authentication, the Microsoft User Authentication Manager (UAM) must be installed on each Macintosh client.

The third tool is *Print Server for Macintosh*. As you might guess, this allows Macintosh clients to use Windows-hosted printers. However, it also allows Windows clients to print to Macintosh-hosted printers. Once Print Server for Macintosh is installed, you can map print shares for Windows clients by connecting to Macintosh printers shares from the server and sharing those printers to the Windows clients. In most cases, this requires the creation of a new port in the Add New Printer wizard set to AppleTalk Printing Devices.

Unix Interoperability

Support for Unix systems is still strong in numerous industries. Because of this, Microsoft has developed interoperability tools for Unix systems. Interacting with Unix systems takes place over the TCP/IP protocol. There are two Microsoft services that provide interoperability with Unix: *Print Services for Unix* and *Windows Services for Unix*.

Print Services for Unix allows Windows clients to print to Unix-hosted printers, and Unix systems to print to Windows-hosted printers. Once installed, Unix systems can connect to Windows printers just by linking to the printer share. To grant Windows clients access to Unix printers, you must create a Line Printer Remote (LPR) port via the Add New Printer Wizard that will redirect print jobs to the Unix-hosted printer.

Like File and Print Services for NetWare, Windows Services for Unix is not included with Windows 2000 and must be purchased and installed separately. Windows Services for NetWare provides functionality for Unix clients similar to what GSNW adds for NetWare. Also, like File and Print Services for NetWare, Windows Services for Unix is not covered in detail on the exam; the information provided in this section is sufficient for exam preparation.

Monitor, Configure, Troubleshoot, and Control Access to Printers

Printers are a commonly shared network resource used by clients throughout an organization. Understanding how to work with printers in a Windows

2000 Server-based network is a critical part of the 70-215 exam. At this point in your journey, you should already be very familiar with the printing capabilities of Windows 2000.

Before launching into the specifics of printer access, it's important to review the terminology around the components of the printing process. Some of the important terms are listed here:

- Print driver
- Printer
- Print server
- Print device

Beginning at the client computer, the first component of the printing process is the print driver. A *print driver* is essentially a file or group of files that is used by Windows 2000 to translate the print command into the print device's specific language. For example, when printing a document from Microsoft Word to an HP LaserJet 6, the print driver converts a print command from the format recognized by Word into the language used by the LaserJet.

From the print driver, the print job is sent to the printer. In Microsoft terms, the *printer* is a software interface that defines how the print job will reach the print device. This component is particularly important when dealing with networked printers, though it exists in all Microsoft configurations. In networked printing environments, the printer software is generally part of a print server. The print server is a computer that manages the flow of print jobs between the client computers and a shared print device. The *print device* is the physical hardware that produces the printed copy. Figure 3.1 diagrams the printing process from the client computer to the print device.

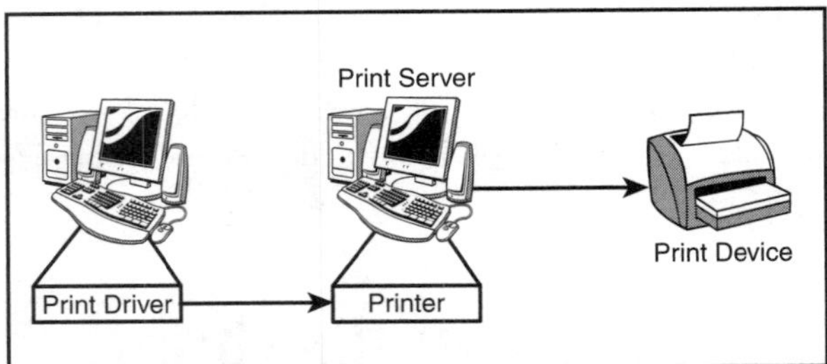

Figure 3.1 The printing process in the Windows 2000 Server environment.

Local Versus Remote Print Devices

There are two types of print devices: *local* and *remote*. The distinction as to whether a device is local or remote depends on where the print device's definition resides. There are actually two types of local print devices, those directly attached to the server, and those attached to the network, but managed by the server. Print device definitions managed by the Windows 2000 Server computer are local devices, whether they are physically attached to the server (a direct-attached device) or reside elsewhere on the network (a network-attached device). Network-attached devices require their own network adapters, which allows them to act as nodes on the network. Print devices managed by other computers on the network are considered remote devices.

The language used to define the Windows 2000 printing system can be very confusing (local printer vs. remote printer vs. network printer, for example). It's important to thoroughly understand the terms Microsoft uses to describe the print system when it comes time to take the exam. Many people are used to calling the physical printing hardware the printer. When it comes to Microsoft exams, it's important to remember that the printer is a software component that controls how print jobs reach their destination. The print device, on the other hand, is the equipment that sits on a desk and produces hard-copy documents. Put simply, when it comes to the exam, printer = software, print device = hardware.

Windows 2000 Server can act as a print server whether it is a member server or a domain controller. However, it is usually wise not to assign too many additional service-oriented tasks to domain controllers. *Service-oriented tasks* means printing services as well as to other functions, such as performance monitoring and application services. In essence, a Windows 2000 Server with shared printers acts as a print server. Before a print device can be shared, however, its definition must be created on the server. To do this, use the Add New Printer Wizard from the Printers folder in the Start menu. During this process, you are able to specify whether the new printer is a local print device or a network print device. The other options available during the Add New Printer Wizard process depend on whether you are creating a printer object for a local print device or a network print device.

In the Add New Printer Wizard, network print devices are those managed by other computers on the network. If you are setting up a Windows 2000 Server to manage the activity of a group of print devices, then all of those print devices must be defined as local.

If you are connecting to a local print device, you are given the opportunity to allow Windows 2000 to automatically detect and configure an attached print device. If you choose not to let Windows 2000 automatically detect the print device, then you must specify the port to which the print device is connected and then either choose the print driver from the list provided, or indicate that you have a driver on diskette from the print device's manufacturer. If the print device is directly attached to the print server, you can choose a local port (usually LPT1). If you are configuring the print server to manage a local network-attached print device, you must use the Create a New Port option when selecting the printer port and choose Standard TCP/IP Port. When you click Next to continue after opting to create the new port, the Add Standard TCP/IP Printer Port Wizard will be launched. To complete the wizard, the print device must be powered on and configured for TCP/IP. You are prompted to supply the print device's name or IP address and the port name. By default, the port name is created as "IP_" followed by the print device's IP address. However, this can be changed directly before continuing the wizard.

Once the port has been selected and the print driver has been identified, you are able to name the printer and indicate whether it should be the default printer for jobs on that system. For the most part, because print servers are seldom accessed locally, very little printing is actually done from the server computer itself; rather, print commands are executed from client computers connected to the print server. For this reason, the question of a whether to identify a default printer is a small one, but a system with printers defined must have a default printer identified. After naming the printer, you must specify whether the printer is to be shared on the network and if so, what the printer share name will be. Next, you are given the opportunity to provide detailed location information and comments regarding the printer. This information is helpful to end-users when they browse to find a printer through the Add New Printers Wizard and it is displayed in lists such as My Network Places. The last option you have is to print a test page to verify functionality. After clicking Next, you are presented with a summary of the new printer definition and can click Finish to complete the wizard.

When connecting to a network printer, on the other hand, the majority of these choices are made for you. After indicating you want to create a network print device object, you are asked to identify the printer, either by name or by Internet address. If you do not fill in a printer name and click Next, you can browse the network to locate the printer in question. After you select the printer, the only other question to be answered is whether it is to be the default printer for this computer.

In preparing for the exam, it is recommended that you run through the process of creating printer objects of various types. This can be done even without a print device attached to your local computer, as long as you remember to not allow Windows to autodetect the device. Although creating printer objects is not a large part of the exam, it is crucial you understand how they are created both for the test and for real-world application.

Printing Environment Configuration and Security

Like any Windows resource, the printing environment in Windows 2000 is highly secure and configurable. Access to printer objects is controlled in the same manner as access to objects such as files or folders; privileges are defined on a user and group basis. For printer objects, there are three basic permissions. The permissions given to users can be

- Print
- Manage documents
- Manage printer

Table 3.1 outlines what actions users can take within a Windows 2000 print environment based on the permission they were assigned.

Table 3.1 Printer-Specific Permissions

Permission	Print	Manage Documents	Manage Printer
Print documents	Y	Y	Y
Pause, restart, and cancel own documents	Y	Y	Y
Connect to a printer	Y	Y	Y
Control job settings for all documents	N	Y	Y
Pause, restart, and cancel all documents	N	Y	Y
Share a printer	N	N	Y
Change printer properties	N	N	Y
Delete printers	N	N	Y
Change printer permissions	N	N	Y

In addition to the three basic permissions outlined in Table 3.1, printer objects can be configured with more advanced settings. This configuration screen, called the Access Control Settings dialog box (see Figure 3.2), is accessed through the printer's properties page or by clicking Advanced on the Security tab. Using Access Control Settings to manage permissions allows you a finer level of granularity in your configurations. In addition, this utility is used to configure auditing for the object and manage the object's owner settings.

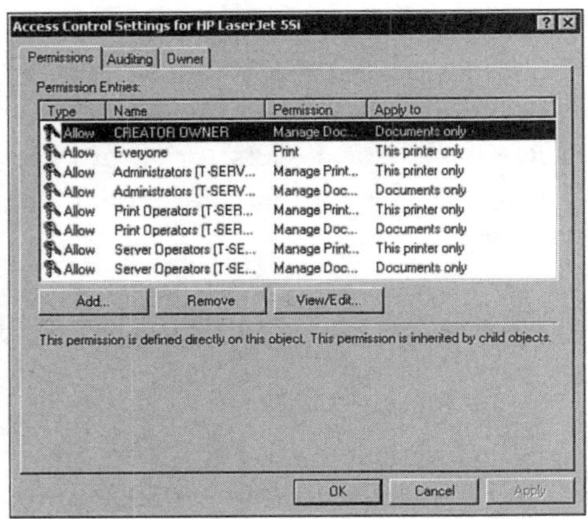

Figure 3.2 The Access Control Settings dialog box is used to manage Advanced security settings for printers in Windows 2000.

From a troubleshooting perspective, the best preparation for the test is extensive knowledge of how documents flow from the user's application to the physical print device. If only one user is experiencing problems printing, it is most likely a problem with the user's individual configuration or permissions assignment. To attempt to pin down a problem with a user's printing configuration, rely on the Print Test Page option in the print device's properties box. The test page is a good first step to identifying whether there are problems with the print driver, permission assignments, or the print server itself.

As you'll learn in greater detail in Chapter 5, "Managing, Monitoring, and Optimizing System Performance, Reliability, and Availability," Windows 2000 includes a Performance snap-in that is used to monitor system counters to gauge various aspects of system performance. To monitor print server performance, Windows 2000 includes the Print Queue performance object. This object allows you to monitor counters such as bytes printed per second and the number of errors generated.

Monitor, Configure, Troubleshoot, and Control Access to Files, Folders, and Shared Folders

Before discussing the ins and outs of file, folder, and shared folder access, it's important to understand the underlying file system functions and the differences between the file systems supported by Windows 2000. There are four file systems recognized by Windows 2000: Universal Disk Format (UDF), CD-ROM File System (CDFS), File Allocation Table (FAT), and the NT File System (NTFS). However, UDF and CDFS are read-only file systems and do not truly support detailed access controls. For this reason, this section and the Microsoft exam focus on the capabilities and features of the FAT and NTFS file systems.

The File Allocation Table (FAT) File System

The FAT file system is recognized by Windows 2000 to provide legacy support for earlier Windows operating systems. It was originally designed to support disks that were much smaller than the devices in use today. Consequently, it is not very efficient when handling large disks or files. Windows 2000 is able to read partitions formatted in two version of FAT, the 16-bit version (FAT16) supported by early versions of MS-DOS, and the 32-bit version (FAT32) first introduced with Windows 95 OEM Service Release 2 (OSR2).

Because FAT predates Windows NT and Windows 2000, it does not include support for security or enhanced partition features such as compression. From a practical perspective, the biggest difference between FAT16 and FAT32 is the maximum supported partition size. This is achieved by doubling the size of the File Allocation Table from 16 bits to 32 bits. For FAT16 partitions, the maximum size is 4GB. In theory, FAT32 partitions support a maximum size of 2,047GB. However, there is a 32GB limitation on creating FAT32 partitions in Windows 2000.

The NT File System (NTFS)

Introduced in 1993 with Windows NT 3.1, the *NT File System (NTFS)* is designed to provide a high performance, secure file system for Windows NT Servers. Windows 2000 includes the latest version of NTFS, 5.0, which is an improvement over the original version included with NT 3.1, but the differences between NTFS and FAT are even more dramatic.

One of the significant differences between FAT and NTFS is the recoverability and compression features of NTFS. To ensure data is consistently written to the volume, NTFS uses transaction logging and advanced recovery techniques. In the event of a failure, NTFS uses checkpoint and data logging information to automatically maintain the consistency of the data on the volume. NTFS also supports selective file, folder, and volume compression, which is not available on FAT volumes. The selectivity of the NTFS compression settings allows administrators the ability to pick and choose whether specific file system objects are compressed or not. Although data compression reduces the drive space required on the volume, it puts a greater burden the system's resources. Providing the option to compress entire volumes, folders, or individual files ensures that the drive space is used as efficiently as possible, while still maintaining timely file services. For additional information on compression, refer to Chapter 6, "Managing, Configuring, and Troubleshooting Storage Use."

In an effort to provide the fastest file services available, NTFS uses smaller clusters and has been designed to require fewer disk reads to find a file on the volume. NTFS version 5.0 also supports significantly larger volumes than FAT—up to 2 Terabytes on a single volume. NTFS volumes include highly configurable user and group options, including the use of disk quotas to limit the amount of drive space a user can consume. Perhaps more importantly, individual files, folders, and volumes can be secured at the user and group level. This is significantly more secure than the option available on FAT, which can only be secured for shared folders, and even then permissions are limited to three settings: Read, Change, and Full Control. Securing folders and files will be discussed in greater detail in the next few sections of this chapter.

Because NTFS offers such enormous improvements over the FAT file system, Microsoft recommends that all Windows 2000 volumes be formatted with NTFS. However, there are some situations where this is not possible. For example, most multiple-boot configurations require a FAT file system on the boot partition. If it is necessary to maintain a FAT volume on the server, it is important to understand the security implications of the configuration. As you'll learn later in the "Monitor, Configure, Troubleshoot, and Control Local Security on Files and Folders" section of this chapter, FAT partitions cannot be secured when they are accessed from the server console. This is an important consideration when making the determination to support a FAT partition on a Windows 2000 Server.

Configure, Manage, and Troubleshoot a Standalone Distributed File System (Dfs)

The *Distributed file system (Dfs)* is a new feature of Windows 2000. This item has been created to eliminate the confusion often experienced by end-users on large networks with multiple servers and extensive lists of shared folders. In other words, having to navigate for files through many folders found on many different servers is a cumbersome activity. Dfs functionality allows you to put these shared folders in one central location. This will improve the usability of your network for your end-users.

The Dfs service is installed automatically when Windows 2000 is set up on the server. When Dfs is implemented, it is configured to represent shared folders on multiple servers. The folders are shown in a hierarchical tree structure, as shown in Figure 3.3. The first shared folder in the tree acts as the *Dfs root* and is the shared folder end-users use to access all folders in the Dfs configuration. Once the Dfs root is created, shared folders on the network are tied to the Dfs root using Dfs links.

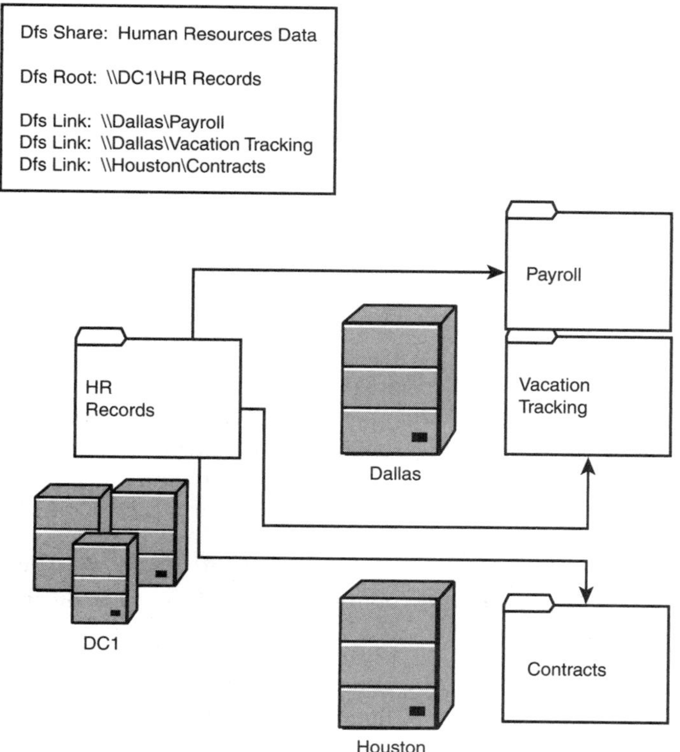

Figure 3.3 Dfs shares are made up of a Dfs root and related Dfs links to shared folders.

One of the biggest considerations when designing a Dfs implementation is that there can only be one Dfs root per server. This means you must carefully choose the servers to host Dfs root objects and design your Dfs configuration around the limitations of your network. Remember that the shares' security permissions ultimately control whether a user is granted access to the shares in the Dfs structure or their files.

Dfs management is handled through the Distributed File System MMC plug-in, which can be accessed through Administrative Tools in the Control Panel. To launch the New Dfs Root Wizard from this snap-in, click Action on the menu bar, then click New Dfs Root. After starting the wizard, the choice you must make is whether to create a domain or standalone Dfs root. A domain Dfs root must be administered through Active Directory, whereas a standalone Dfs root can operate independently of directory services; this distinction is discussed in more detail in the sections that follow. Figure 3.4 shows the next configuration screen in the New Dfs Root Wizard in which you identify the server to host the Dfs root. By default, the server from which you launched the wizard is listed.

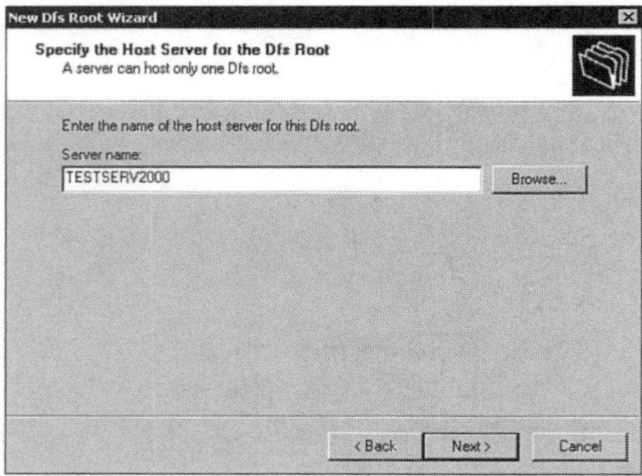

Figure 3.4 Identify the server to host the Dfs root.

If you are creating a Dfs root on another server, click Browse to search for the server on the network. After you've identified the server, click Next. You will be given the option of choosing an existing share on the server or creating a new share.

If you are creating a new share, you must identify the path to the share and the share name. To do this, of course, you must have sufficient permissions to create a share on the server.

Regardless of whether you are utilizing an existing share or creating a new one, be certain to review the security configuration for the share to verify the Dfs share users have the correct permission settings.

After clicking Next, you are presented with the Dfs root name, which by default is the name of the original share. It is also on this screen that you are able to add comments to the Dfs share's configuration. Click Next to proceed to the final screen of the wizard. Here, you are presented with the final configuration for the Dfs share, which outlines the share's configuration settings. Click Finish to complete the wizard.

On standalone Dfs roots, you cannot change the name of the root; it must be the same as the share. However, on domain Dfs roots, you are able to specify a root name that is different from the share name.

Standalone and Domain Dfs Types

There are two types of Dfs roots used in Windows 2000, *standalone* and *domain*. Domain Dfs roots are sometimes referred to as fault-tolerant Dfs roots because they use Active Directory services to distribute Dfs information to all servers in the tree. Standalone Dfs root information, on the other hand, is stored in the Registry on the hosting server. Because of this limitation, there is no backup for a standalone Dfs root. If the server hosting the Dfs root is unavailable, the information provided by the Dfs share is not accessible to users. Though it is possible to configure replicas of Dfs links associated with standalone Dfs roots on other servers, the files in the linked share must be synchronized manually, so it is not considered a truly fault-tolerant system. Standalone Dfs roots can be configured with one level of Dfs links and can reside on any supported file system. However, it is recommended that all Dfs links identify resources on NTFS volumes.

There are a few key differences between standalone Dfs roots and domain Dfs roots. Most evident is the fact that all Active Directory servers in the domain distribute information in response to requests from clients on the network. Because the information is stored as part of the Active Directory, it is replicated to every domain controller. This replication ensures that end-users are never without access to the information in the Dfs share. Because of their interaction with Active Directory, domain Dfs roots must be located on NTFS 5.0 partitions.

There is very little difference between creating a domain Dfs root and a standalone Dfs root, aside from selecting the option on the initial screen of the New Dfs Root Wizard. On the second screen of the wizard you are asked to choose the host domain for the Dfs root. After clicking Next, the configuration requirements are the same: Identify the host server, Identify the share, Name the Dfs root, and Add comments.

The differences are really seen after the Dfs root is created. As Figure 3.5 shows, right-clicking on a Dfs domain root presents a menu that includes "New Root Replica," which is not available for standalone roots. Selecting this option launches the same process for creating a Dfs root; the only difference is that is a replication of the original. Once the root replica has been created, you can enable Dfs replication between the roots. Because of the potentially high traffic volume, Dfs replication is disabled by default. To enable replication, right-click the Dfs root and select Replication Policy. You are then able to select each of the Dfs root replicas defined. Select at least two of the replicas and click Enable. Dfs root replication is handled by the File Replication Service discussed in the next section.

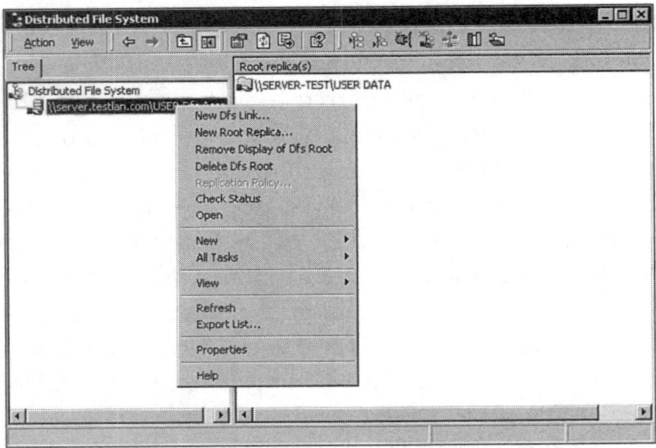

Figure 3.5 Select replication policy to synchronize files between replicas.

Dfs Links

As mentioned, Dfs links are created to tie share information from different servers into a single, easy to access location. Once the Dfs root has been created, you can create Dfs links to other shared folders. In the Dfs plug-in, select the Dfs root to which will host the Dfs link, then select New Dfs Link from the Action menu. When prompted, fill in the name to be assigned to the Dfs link, the shared folder information, and any comments regarding the link. If you are uncertain of the exact name and location of the shared folder, use the Browse button to search the network. When the Dfs links have been configured, they will look to the users like other folders normally found in the share.

File Replication Service (FRS)

The Windows 2000 *File Replication Service (FRS)* is included during installation and was designed to handle file replication traffic for domain controllers. It is included with all Windows 2000 Server installations, though it is configured for manual startup on standalone and member servers. When a server is configured as a domain controller, FRS is set to start automatically. Although FRS is originally set up for login script and policy replication, it is the foundation for Dfs root replication on domain roots. In fact, Dfs root replication will most likely take more FRS time than Active Directory file replication. To manage Dfs root replication, FRS uses the same structure as the Knowledge Consistency Checker (KCC) defined Active Directory file replication. When a user has changed a file in a Dfs root, the change is noted in the NTFS change log, which is monitored for changes to Dfs links. When the user closes the file, the changes are updated and FRS places the file in a staging area for scheduled replication.

Although Windows 2000 Servers use FRS for file replication, it is not used for Active Directory traffic. FRS on Windows 2000 domain controllers synchronizes SYSVOL contents among servers in the domain. SYSVOL stores login scripts and system policy files, and FRS ensures the most up-to-date files exist on each server. To do this, version files are maintained, which allows FRS to determine whether the most current updates have been distributed.

Among domain controllers, FRS automatically generates a replication ring. The Active Directory topology defines the path replication updates take from domain controller to domain controller, to ensure that all servers have up-to-date information. By using a ring topology, FRS is certain to have at least two paths from one domain controller to another in the event that a domain controller is down. Because Active Directory uses a multimaster replication scheme in which all domain controllers are equal, it is imperative that all Active Directory servers are completely up-to-date.

The replication scheme is configured into sites, which represent a group of connected computers. Because of the amount of traffic involved in replication, it's important that the networks supporting a site be reliable and relatively high-speed; Microsoft recommends network speeds of at least 512Kbps. Active Directory servers requiring synchronization over slower links, such as 56Kbps WAN lines, should be configured in separate sites. The KCC is responsible for generating and maintaining the replication ring among domain controllers within a site.

Replication between servers in the same site (intra-site replication) occurs every five minutes and is trigger-based, which means that the domain controller notifies its replication partners when it has changes to send, and when the replication partners are available, they send a request to the domain controller for the update. Intra-site replication traffic is not compressed. During the installation process, intra-site replication is automatically established between domain controllers on the same site.

Replication between sites (inter-site replication) takes place only at specific times (the default is three hours), unless there is an urgent need for replication. To ensure the best transmission speeds, the transport for inter-site replication is configurable and the data is compressed. Unfortunately, inter-site communication is not configured automatically. Urgent replication is triggered for inter-site connections when a user account has been locked out due to failed login attempts, when there is a change in the domain controller's Local Security Authority (LSA), and when there is a change in the relative identifier (RID) master role owner.

Monitor, Configure, Troubleshoot, and Control Local Security on Files and Folders

The Windows 2000 environment is exceptionally dynamic and allows for a wide variety of security configurations. The building blocks for implementing security on a Windows 2000 system, whether Server or Professional, are users and groups. Because creating and managing user and group accounts is a focus of the Installing, Configuring, and Administering Microsoft Windows 2000 Professional exam number 70-210, it is not covered on the Server exam. It is important, however, that you understand how users and groups are implemented in Windows 2000 before you tackle file and folder security.

There are two levels of security that can be implemented on a Windows 2000 system: *local security* and *share security*. Local security manages access for users who log on directly to the system: in other words, the user typing on the Server's keyboard. Share security (discussed in the next section) generally applies to users who are accessing the system's resources across the network.

To begin securing access to local files and folders, you must define which users are to log on to the server locally. This is done by using security policies, which are discussed in Chapter 8, "Implementing, Monitoring, and Troubleshooting Security." For the sake of discussion in this section, it's enough to understand that limiting local access to the server itself is key to controlling local access to files and folders.

Once the determination is made as to which users and groups will be allowed to access the server locally, securing the resources becomes a question of the drive partition's file system. As mentioned earlier, one of the most significant differences between the FAT and NTFS file systems is the number and variety of security settings available. Because the FAT file system is not inherently structured to provide security, it is not possible to control access to files and folders once the user has been granted access to the server console. FAT partitions can be secured when accessed remotely, however, which will be discussed in the next section.

NTFS Permissions

As mentioned, NTFS was designed to provide complete file-level security for file resources on Windows 2000 systems. It provides the ability to allow or deny specific access permissions to users and groups down to the individual files on the partition. It is preferable to use groups for any security configuration to provide for easier administration.

To provide the most secure configuration possible, denying a permission to a specific user or group overrides all other permissions. For example, if a folder's permission assignments dictate that the Accounting group be granted Full Control, but the permissions for a member of that group have been set to Deny for the Read permission, that member will not be able to see the folder or its contents. Because Deny overrides all other settings, it affects permission inheritance. It is often better not to specifically assign permissions to a user or group, rather than explicitly set deny permissions to restrict access.

One of the benefits of NTFS is that its security settings apply whether the user is accessing the resources locally or over the network. This is an important feature that ensures a user who accesses the server locally is not able to impact the server's operation. By securing access to the folders where system files are stored, or securing the files themselves, essential operating system files are protected from users deleting or modifying them. System files located on a FAT partition do not have this security, which means a user accessing the server locally can potentially render the server inoperable.

NTFS permissions are cumulative; in other words, the permissions assigned to a user are combined with the permissions assigned to any groups to which they are members to determine whether to grant the requested access to a resource. For the most part, access permissions are combined to allow access. For example, an Administrator may grant a group the Read and List Folder Contents permissions to a folder, then may grant specific users the Read, Write, and Modify permissions to files in that folder. When combined, the users will be able to review the contents of the folder, read the files, overwrite the files or change their attributes, and modify the contents of the file. Other members of the group, however, will only be allowed to view the contents of the folder and read the files.

Windows 2000 makes very little distinction between NTFS folder permissions and NTFS file permissions. In fact, there are few differences. The biggest difference is in the way Windows 2000 makes the determination on which permission to use. File permissions take precedence over folder permissions, which means that you can grant a group access to read a folder's contents, and then grant individual users permission to modify individual files in the folder. This ensures that the appropriate users are granted the highly secure, granular access to files they sometimes require. However, controlling security at the individual file level is very time consuming and is not recommended except in special circumstance. For the most part, utilizing NTFS security at the folder level is sufficient.

When determining whether to grant requests for files, Windows 2000 begins compiling security configuration settings at the root of the file tree. Progressing through the tree, permissions are inherited by the files and folders until the ultimate file is reached, unless inheritance has been disabled for a particular permission setting. When an NTFS object's security settings are modified, you can disable permission inheritance from parent objects. This means that the settings being specified will not be adjusted by other permissions higher in the tree. If you choose this setting, you are given the option of copying or removing the parent object's current settings.

The certification exam places significant focus on NTFS permission inheritance. You may have multiple questions that are nearly identical, but with one setting being different. It's important to understand how Windows 2000 will treat a particular resource request, based on the NTFS permissions settings.

Assigning Permissions

By default, the owner of a file or folder can assign permissions, as can Administrators. Figure 3.6 shows the Properties dialog box for a folder on an NTFS partition.

The Name window identifies the users or groups that currently have permissions assignments for the folder. The Permissions section indicates the permissions that have been allowed or denied for the highlighted user. If the selection has a black check mark, it has been defined on this folder. If it has a gray checkmark, the assignment has been inherited from the parent object.

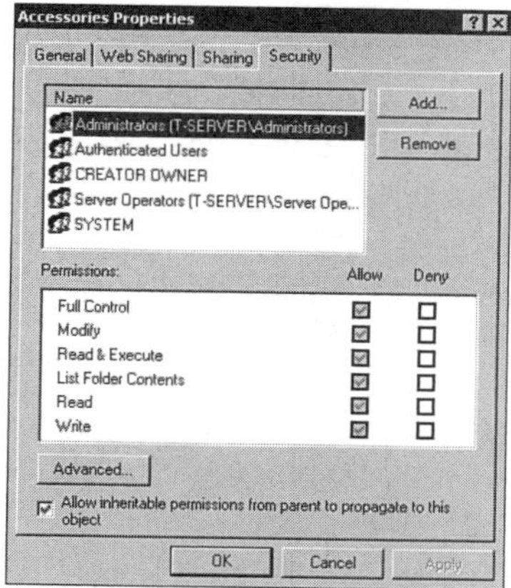

Figure 3.6 The Security tab is used to assign permissions for NTFS folders.

At the bottom of the dialog box, the Allow Inheritable Permissions from Parent to Propagate to This Object selection is used to specify the inheritance policy for the object. If you uncheck this selection, you are asked whether you want to copy the parent's permissions or remove them from the configuration. To add a user to the object's configuration settings, click Add. You will be presented with a list of users and groups on the server. Select the user or group, click Add, then click OK. Select the new permission assignments from the list provided or click Advanced to go to the Access Control Setting dialog box.

In addition to assigning more specific permissions, called *special commissions*, you can also manage auditing for the object as well as define the object's owner settings. Table 3.2 outlines the special and standard permissions available for an NTFS file or folders. Because standard permissions are actually combinations of special permissions, they are listed as such.

The standard folder permission List Folder Contents is not listed in the table. It is made up of the same permissions as Read & Execute, but is inherited differently, because it applies only to folders and is only inherited by folders. Whereas Read & Execute is inherited by both files and folders.

Table 3.2 NTFS File and Folder Permissions

Permission	Allows	Standard Permission
List Folder/ Read Data	Viewing folder contents (including subfolder names) and accessing data in files.	Read, Read & Execute, Modify, Full Control

(continued)

Table 3.2 NTFS File and Folder Permissions *(continued)*

Permission	Allows	Standard Permission
Read Attributes	Viewing of file and folder standard attributes (Read Only and Hidden, for example).	Read, Read & Execute, Modify, Full Control
Read Extended Attributes	Viewing of file and folder extended attributes, which vary by file and file type.	Read, Read & Execute, Modify, Full Control
Read Permissions	Viewing of file and folder permissions.	Read, Write, Read & Execute, Modify, Full Control
Create Files/ Read Data	Creating new files in the folder (folder) and modifying and overwriting existing files (file).	Write, Modify, Full Control
Create Folders/ Append Data	Creating new folders (folder) and appending data to the end of a file such as a database, but no other file modification, such as deleting or overwriting (file).	Write, Modify, Full Control
Write Attributes	Changing the file and folder attributes.	Write, Modify, Full Control
Write Extended Attributes	Changing the file and folder extended attributes.	Write, Modify, Full Control
Traverse Folder/ Execute File	Moving through folders where access has not been granted (folder) and running programs.	Read & Execute, Modify, Full Control
Delete	Deleting the specified file or folder.	Modify, Full Control
Delete Subfolders and Files	Deleting subfolders and files, even if the Delete permission has not been assigned to those subfolders or files.	Full Control
Change Permissions	Changing the file and folder permissions.	Full Control
Take Ownership	Taking ownership of the file or folder.	Full Control

Monitor, Configure, Troubleshoot, and Control Access to Files and Folders in a Shared Folder

As discussed earlier in the chapter, users gain access to file resources through shared folders on the server's partitions. When users attempt to gain access to the server remotely, through utilities such as My Network Places, they will be able to see the shared folders to which they have access.

The process of sharing folders is similar to the process for assigning NTFS permissions. By default, folders are not shared. The level of access granted to users is determined by their group membership. Figure 3.7 shows the Properties for a folder to be shared. Selecting the Share This Folder option seen in the folder's Properties dialog box enables you to specify the name of the share, add comments, as well as limit the number of users who are able to access the share at the same time.

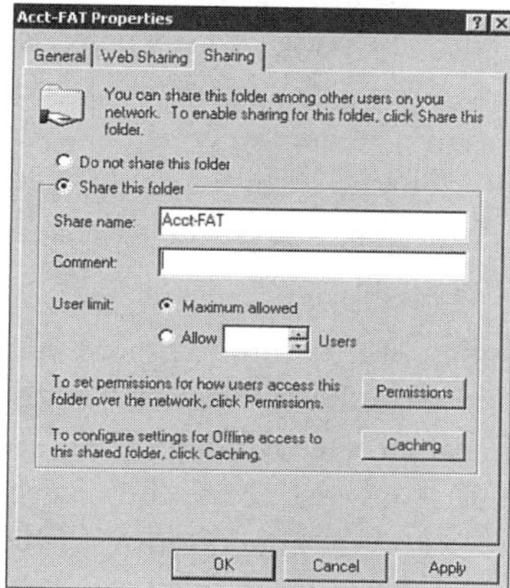

Figure 3.7 Share a folder to restrict access.

Clicking the Permissions tab gives you the opportunity to change the access settings for the shared folder. Note that the default setting is to allow the Everyone group Full Control to the shared folder. Remember that, as with NTFS permissions, an explicit Deny overrides all other permissions, including any that may be inherited from other group memberships. Shared folder permissions are significantly less comprehensive than NTFS permissions. Briefly, the permissions are

- *Read*—This permission lets the designated user or group view the files and subfolders present, as well as their attributes. Users are able to read the contents of the files and execute programs from the folder.
- *Change*—This permission allows users the ability to create subfolders within the shared folder, add files to the folder, modify the files (including changing their attributes), and do all the things allowed by the Read permission.

- *Full Control*—Gives users everything allowed under the Change permission, plus the ability to change file permissions and take ownership of files.

As with NTFS permissions, shared folder permissions are cumulative, unless a user is denied access in any of the groups to which they belong. The combination of their groups' permissions and their own will determine their total access level. Though they do not provide the most thorough security configuration, shared folders are the only way to secure network access to files and folders on FAT volumes. When the shared folder resides on an NTFS volume, it is preferable to configure the security settings either on the share or through the NTFS permissions, but not both. Because NTFS provides more thorough security options, it is generally the best choice to opt for NTFS permissions when possible. For this reason, the default configuration for share permissions (Everyone granted Full Control) is often acceptable. This limits the administrative effort required and makes it easier to ensure the correct permissions are granted to users and groups.

On a Windows 2000 Server in a domain, membersof the Administrators and Server Operators groups are able to share folders on any computer in the domain. On a standalone server, Power Users can create shares on the local partitions only. In a workgroup environment, Administrators and Power Users can create shares on the standalone server and on any Windows 2000 Professional computer which is a member of the group.

When volumes are created, Windows 2000 automatically creates special shares for administration. These shares are shown with a dollar sign ($) on the Sharing tab of the volume's properties page. For example, the root of the volume on the C drive is shared as C$. Administrative shares are also created for the system root folder, shared as Admin$, and the folder Windows 2000 users to store printer drivers, shared as Print$. All administrative shares are hidden and cannot be changed, but can be accessed by users on the network if they are granted appropriate access. By default, only Administrators are granted access to administrative shares.

Monitor, Configure, Troubleshoot, and Control Access to Files and Folders via Web Services

Windows 2000 includes Microsoft's Internet publishing product called Internet Information Services (IIS) version 5.0, which you'll learn more about in the next section. One of the new features of IIS allows you to grant access to network resources so that they can be accessed through a Web browser. This is possible because of an enhancement to HTTP, included in version 1.1, called WebDAV for Web distributed authoring and versioning. Using WebDAV and an HTTP/1.1-compliant Web browser, users with sufficient permissions are able to manipulate files and folders. This includes moving files to and from the WebDAV folder, changing the file's properties, and searching the WebDAV directory for content. Because WebDAV is integrated with both Windows 2000 and Internet Explorer 5, it includes security features from both products. This ensures that users who access the folders from the Internet are granted only the access desired by the administrator.

There are many different ways to establish a WebDAV site for users to access. For example, create a Web site in IIS specifically designated for WebDAV folder access, then create virtual directories for all folders you want to share through WebDAV. Once the Web site has been created, you can create the virtual directories either through IIS, or by choosing Web Sharing on the folder's Properties page, as shown in Figure 3.8.

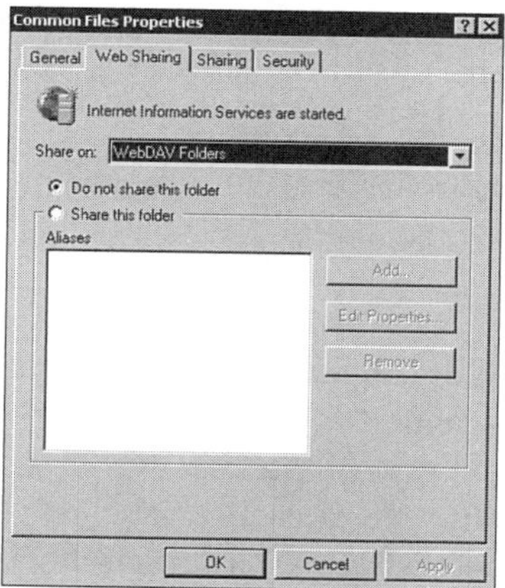

Figure 3.8 Share a folder for access via WebDAV.

To share a folder to the Web site, on the Web Sharing tab, select the Web site that will host the folder, then select Share this folder. You will be prompted for an alias for the share on the Web site, IIS access permissions for the folder, and application permissions. After you've made the appropriate selections, click OK to return to the folder properties, then OK again to continue.

Using the Web Sharing tab on a folder is a quick and familiar way to share folders for access via WebDAV. Once they are created, they are managed through the Internet Services Manager in Administrative Tools.

In fact, the Internet Services Manager is used to configure security for all Web sites, including WebDAV sites. Much like NTFS, IIS can configure security from the Web site level down to the individual files. The first four security settings dictate the authentication level required for users to access the resources. Selecting Anonymous will grant anyone access to the resource, which is not recommended for WebDAV implementations. The Basic authentication setting requires passwords to access the resources, but sends them in plain text. Although this is not the most secure option, it is the most widely supported because it is part of the HTTP standard. Integrated Windows authentication relies on the Windows security system, which encrypts and hashes passwords before sending them across the network, to validate user access and works well for intranet environments. Digest authentication is a secure method for validating user authentication through a browser and is the best option if the WebDAV data is to be shared over the Internet.

In addition to controlling the authentication method used on the Web site, IIS includes security permissions for the individual files and folders that make up the Web site. When the virtual folder is configured in the Internet Services Manager, the Local Path section is used to assign permissions. On the Home Directory tab of WebDAV Properties page you are able to configure the following:

- The location of the resource: as a resource on the local computer, a share located on another computer, or a redirection to a URL.
- The path to the resource.
- Which permissions to enable. If your Web site includes scripts such as ASP applications, the Script Source Access option will allow users to execute the scripts. Read lets users read or download the files, while Write allows users to place files in the WebDAV virtual directory. Directory browsing allows the user to view subdirectory listings if there are folders beneath the shared virtual folder. If this option is not selected and there are subfolders, they will be hidden from the users.
- Whether to log visits to the site.
- Whether to allow the Microsoft Indexing server to include the resource in a site index.
- The application name and starting point for applications launched from the site.
- The type of applications that can be launched from the site. None indicates that only static files can be accessed. Scripts Only dictates that only

scripts such as ASP applications can be launched. Scripts and Executables allows all types of applications to be launched.

- The extent to which the applications are separated from the server processes. This helps to minimize the impact of malicious code that may be uploaded to the site.

Because IIS is integrated closely with Windows 2000, the access it grants to users is controlled by the file system that hosts the Web site. The permissions chosen when creating the WebDAV virtual directory work with the file system to control how files within the folder are accessed by users. To simplify security administration for the virtual directory, it is recommended that you share the folder and keep the default share permissions (Full Control assigned to Everyone) in place, then utilize the more dynamic security settings available through IIS.

Monitor, Configure, Troubleshoot, and Control Access to Web Sites

As mentioned, Internet Information Services (IIS) version 5.0 is included as part of Windows 2000. IIS version 5.0 includes a number of improvements and features that are designed to provide highly secure, highly available Web services to users.

Web Site Performance and Reliability Features in IIS 5.0

As part of these improvements, IIS includes configuration options that are used to fine-tune Web site performance and increase service reliability. For example, IIS 5.0 has addressed an issue with servers running previous versions of IIS hosting multiple Web sites. When a server hosts multiple Web sites, each site requires a unique IP address to ensure that traffic is directed correctly. To do this, the server creates a protocol identifier called a *socket*, which is made up of the Web site's node address and the port number it is using.

Sockets are created when the server is started, and each socket requires a significant chunk of physical (non-paged) RAM. The number of sites a server could host is limited by the amount of memory that can be loaded on the system. IIS 5.0 has addressed this issue by allowing hosted sites that have different IP addresses, but are using the same socket, to share the sockets through socket pooling. This means that more sites could be hosted from a single server and that the performance of those sites would be better.

In addition, Microsoft has included *process throttling* and *bandwidth throttling* features in IIS 5.0. These are used to improve site performance. They allow administrators to specify the maximum percentage of a system's processor and network bandwidth that each site on the server is allowed to use. This helps to ensure that one site doesn't dominate the server's resources, resulting in poor performance for the other hosted sites. IIS 5.0's ability to host multiple sites has also improved. Each site on an IIS server is identified by a three-part address. This version is able to let sites share two of the three address parts to save resources and still ensure that the traffic is directed correctly.

Web Site Security Features in IIS 5.0

One of the biggest concerns for administrators today is having their Web site attacked. There are many ways that this can be done, and Microsoft has attempted to address them with IIS 5.0. One of the keys to this implementation of IIS is its ability to isolate the application from outside attack. Application protection is used to isolate each application process from the other processes in memory.

IIS 4.0 began to address these issues by allowing Web applications to be launched outside the IIS server process. In this configuration, if a Web application fails, it affects only the other applications launched in that environment. IIS 5.0 takes this further by pooling similar applications separately from the server service. Another significant improvement seen with IIS 5.0 is the way in which the service is restarted. Before this version of IIS, if there was a system failure, the computer would have to be restarted. In IIS 5.0, however, the service and all its components can be restarted without taking the server down.

IIS is installed by default during a new Windows 2000 Server installation and will be installed during an upgrade if an earlier version of IIS, Peer Web Services, or Personal Web Server is detected on the existing system. If IIS is not detected during an upgrade, however, it will not be installed.

IIS and its components can be installed and removed through the Add/Remove Windows Components Wizard in the Add/Remove Programs utility in Control Panel. If TCP/IP is not already installed before the installation, it will be installed automatically and configured to utilize DHCP for addressing. As part of the installation process, the Default Web Site, Administration Web site, Default SMTP Virtual Server, and Default FTP site are created.

Once installed, IIS can be managed through two versions of the same interface, each found in either Administrative Tools or in the Computer Management utility. When configuring IIS from the server console or from another Windows 2000 system, use the *Internet Information Services* utility in Administrative Tools. Like other MMC-based interfaces, the Internet Information Services tool can be used to remotely access and configure servers.

The same snap-in is included in the Computer Management utility under Services and Applications. It's important to note that earlier versions of the MMC utility were called Internet Services Manager. You may still see this name associated with IIS management, depending on the method used to install or upgrade the server.

As an alternative to the snap-in, IIS 5.0 includes support for securely accessing and managing the server across the Internet via a Web browser. Referred to as Internet Services Manager (HTML), it is a Web site that is automatically created when IIS is installed. You can launch the HTML version of the management tool from the snap-in by right-clicking on the Administration Web site link and selecting Browse. IIS 5.0 secures this site by randomly choosing a port number when it is created and by requiring authentication before granting access. To use the Internet Servers Manager (HTML) without launching it from the snap-in, you must have the port number assigned to the Administration Web site. Right-click on the site link and select Properties. Figure 3.9 shows the configuration properties for the Administration Web site on a newly created IIS server. To use Internet Services Manager (HTML) to manage the server, enter the Web site address and port in this format: http://<server address>:<port number>. You will be prompted to provide a login name and password.

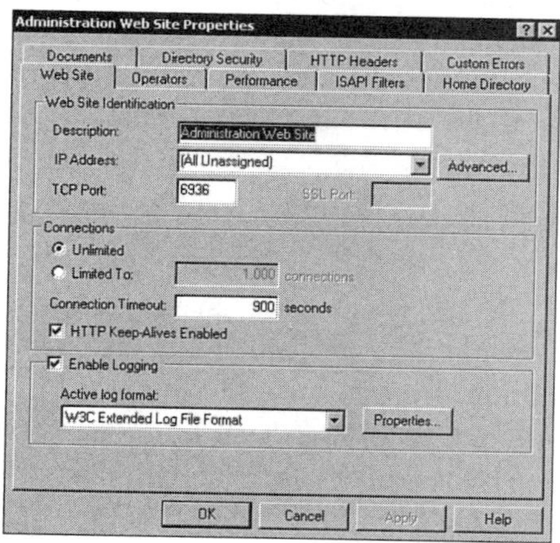

Figure 3.9 The Properties settings for the Administration Web site on an IIS server.

Although the Internet Information Services utility and the Internet Services Manager (HTML) Web site offer nearly identical functions, not all options are available through Internet Services Manager (HTML). For example, both interfaces allow you the ability to stop, start, pause, and resume individual sites, but only the Internet Information Services utility lets you stop and start IIS itself.

Among the other enhancements seen with IIS 5.0 are the ability to delegate administration tasks to other users, process accounting to ensure Web site scripts are not consuming processor time, custom error messages for the sites, enhanced command-line utilities to allow for greater site automation, support for the FTP Restart protocol which lets interrupted file transmissions resume the partial download rather than start over, and support for HTTP compression, which increases transmission speeds over the Internet. From an administration standpoint, it is easier than ever to back up and restore the IIS server's configuration; it's an option in both management tools. To back up a server's configuration, select the server in the Internet Information Services snap-in and select Backup/Restore Configuration from the Action menu. In the (HTML) version of the manager, the link is at the bottom of the main page. In addition, because IIS integrates closely with Windows 2000, it can utilize Dfs to synchronize files among servers.

IIS Security

Discussed briefly earlier in the chapter, IIS 5.0 includes comprehensive internal security capabilities to keep intruders away and keep the information on Internet sites secure. This security structure is based on an extensive list of industry-standard security protocols and authentication methods.

One of the most stringent standards IIS 5.0 adheres to is *Fortezza*, which satisfies the very strict Defense Messaging System security architecture. Fortezza employs cryptography that ensures message confidentiality, integrity, and authenticity, while controlling access to the messages, components, and systems. Note, however, that the Fortezza standards are only used when IIS 5.0 is implemented on a server and PCMCIA hardware and browser software are on the client computer.

IIS also supports *Secure Sockets Layer (SSL) 3.0*, which has been adopted as an industry standard for authentication over the Internet. SSL relies on certificates to provide the encryption algorithms. Transport Layer Security (TLS) is based on SSL, but it performs encryption at a lower level in the process, which improves performance, and in such a way that a programmer decrypting a message does not require the key code from the sender. It is expected to lay the groundwork for a truly secure public network. Public-Key

Cryptography Standard (PKCS) #7 and PKCS #10 are enhanced security protocols that are also supported by IIS 5. They define the format for encrypted data (digital signatures are a good example) and for requests for certificates made to certification authorities.

IIS 5.0 Authentication Methods

IIS has supported two primary authentication methods for some time, *Basic* and *Integrated Windows*. As mentioned in the WebDAV discussion earlier in the chapter, Basic Authentication dictates that users provide a user name and password to access a site, but this information is not encrypted for transmission. Because Basic Authentication is part of the original HTTP 1.0 standard, it is supported by most Web-enabled products, which almost ensures that the client device will be able to respond to the request for authentication information. However, because the password is not encrypted, it could potentially be intercepted during transmission and used to gain unauthorized access to the site.

Integrated Windows Authentication, previously Windows NT Challenge/ Response, uses NTLM to authenticate older browsers with IIS servers, and uses the industry standard Kerberos v5 for authentication with supported browsers. Integrated Windows Authentication should only be used if Anonymous access has been denied and the IIS server is not behind a proxy server.

Digest Authentication is a new process for ensuring secure transmission of the information between the client and server. It functions in much the same way as Basic Authentication, but the authentication credentials are passed through a one-way process called hashing. The result is a message digest (a hash) that masks the original text of the message. The server sends additional information with the password so that if it were intercepted it could not be used. Perhaps the biggest benefit, however, is that Digest Authentication is part of HTTP 1.1 and can be transmitted seamlessly across proxy servers.

Managing IIS Servers

As mentioned, IIS is managed through one of the Internet Information Services utilities, either the MMC snap-in or the HTML version. A Web or FTP site's configuration settings are accessed by selecting the site, then choosing Properties from the Action menu. The settings on the Home Directory tab, discussed in the earlier WebDAV section of this chapter, are of particular importance. Of note as well are the options available on the Directory Security tab, which is where the authentication control method is defined and IP address restrictions are enforced. Click *Edit* in the

"Anonymous access and authentication control" section to specify whether to allow anonymous access, and define the authentication method for the site—Basic, Digest, or Integrated Windows.

Virtual directories are used to link Web sites to folders outside the home directory. When a user accesses the Web site, the contents of the virtual directory are presented as though they were contained in the home directory. A virtual directory assigns an alias to the destination folder, allowing for a more secure Web site and easier administration. Virtual directories are more secure because the users cannot determine the actual location of the files in the virtual directory. Without virtual directories, moving files and folders that make up a Web site requires changing the URL links to the folders. Using virtual directories simplifies the process because it is no longer necessary to change the URL on the Web site, but merely to change the mapping between the alias and the folder.

Virtual directories are created through the Virtual Directory Creation Wizard, which is launched from the Internet Information Services snap-in by selecting the Web site, right-clicking and select New, and then selecting Virtual Directory. In Internet Services Manager (HTML), virtual directories are created through the IIS New Site Wizard. To launch the wizard, select the Web site, then click New in the left pane. Click Next, then select Virtual Directory from the list of options, then click Next again. Enter the alias for the virtual directory, click Next, and then enter the path for the virtual directory. Click Next, select the permissions to assign to the alias, and then click Finish.

Hosting Several Sites on One IIS 5.0 Server

IIS includes three features that allow hosting multiple sites on a single server: *port number assignment*, *multiple network adapters with separate IP addresses*, and *multiple IP address/domain name combinations assigned to a single network adapter using host header names*. The decision on which option to use depends on the server's hardware capabilities and the structure of the network. Even though the sites are hosted on the same server, they each have their own security configurations, which allows administrators greater flexibility in assigning management responsibility.

Although the properties for sites hosted on an IIS server can be configured individually, they are initially established based on the server's Master Properties values for the Web and FTP services. To configure the Master Properties for IIS, select the server in the Internet Information Services tool and choose properties. After sites have been established, their properties can be configured individually. Site components such as virtual directories or files can be configured to inherit the settings from the parent object. If a lower-level object is configured manually, updates made to the properties of the site will not be passed on to the component automatically; you will be prompted to choose whether to change the setting for the individual components affected.

Individual Site Management in IIS 5.0

Individual site management is assigned to a special group called Operators. By default, members of the local group Administrators are identified as Operators for IIS sites, but this can be changed for new sites at the Master Properties level, as well as within each of the individual site configurations. Although members of the Operators group have administrative control over their site, they cannot change settings that affect IIS functions or the Windows 2000 server itself.

Practice Questions

Question 1

You are responsible for managing the operation of an IIS 5.0 server. You must meet the following performance requirements:

You must limit the performance impact of one Web site on the server.

You must limit the network usage of two Web sites.

You must track access to the Web sites.

You must ensure users are allowed only to access files on the local server.

The proposed solution is to access the Default Web site's Properties page Home Directory tab, and select Log Visits and Index this Resource. On the same tab, you deselect Directory browsing.

Which of the following does the proposed solution provide? (Choose all that apply.)

❑ A. The proposed solution limits the performance impact of one Web site on the server.

❑ B. The proposed solution limits the network usage of two Web sites.

❑ C. The proposed solution tracks access to the Web sites.

❑ D. The proposed solution limits user access to those only on the local server.

Answers C and D are correct. Choosing the Log Visits selection tracks user access to the Web site. Selecting Directory Browsing limits the users access to sites outside the local server because the users are not allowed outside the directory hosting the Web site. Additional configuration settings are required to limit Web sites performance impact and network usage. Therefore, answers A and B are incorrect.

Question 2

NWLink is Microsoft's implementation of which of the following protocols?

❍ A. TCP/IP

❍ B. NetBEUI

❍ C. IPX/SPX

❍ D. Ethernet

Answer C is correct. IPX/SPX is the standard protocol for NetWare versions prior to NetWare 5, and is still supported by NetWare. To provide connectivity to NetWare resources, Microsoft developed their own version of the protocol called NWLink. TCP/IP is an industry standard protocol supported by Windows 2000 and has no Microsoft version. NetBEUI is a legacy protocol for Microsoft networking and has no ties to NWLink. Ethernet is an industry standard network type, not a protocol. Therefore answers A, B, and D are incorrect.

Question 3

Your Windows 2000 Server is configured with both FAT32 and NTFS volumes. You must configure the server to provide the most secure access possible to all files on the server and meet the following security requirements:

You must limit local access to change or delete files and folder all groups except Administrators.

You must track all failed file and folder access attempts.

You must allow members of the Accounting group complete access to the files in the Accounting and Payroll folders on the NTFS volume.

You must not allow remote access to the Everyone group to the Security Management folder on the FAT volume.

The proposed solution is to change the Security Policy settings. In the User Rights Assignments policies, change Log On Locally to include only Administrators. In the Audit Policy settings, change Audit Directory Security Access to Failure. On the Permissions for the Security Management folder, remove the Everyone group.

Which of the following does the proposed solution provide? (Choose all that apply.)

- ❑ A. The proposed solution limits local access to delete files and folders for all groups except Administrators.
- ❑ B. The proposed solution tracks all failed file and folder access attempts.
- ❑ C. The proposed solution allows members of the Accounting group complete access to the files in the Accounting and Payroll folders.
- ❑ D. The proposed solution restricts remote access for Everyone to the Security Management folder.

Answers A and D are correct. Because the server includes FAT and NTFS volumes, the only method for ensuring security is to limit local access to the server. Explicitly denying the Everyone group access to the share will ensure they are not able to access the Security Management folder. The security policy settings for Audit Directory Security apply to Active Directory components, not necessarily file and folder access. The proposed solution does not address the Accounting ad Payroll folders. Therefore, answers B and C are incorrect.

Question 4

Which of the following will not trigger an FRS inter-site update?

❍ A. Account lockout due to failed logon attempts.

❍ B. Change to the domain controller user policies.

❍ C. Change to the domain controller Local Security Authority.

❍ D. Change to the relative identifier master role owner.

Answers B is correct. Inter-site updates are strictly scheduled to reduce network traffic. However, there are three triggers that will initiate an inter-site update: account lockout due to failed logon attempts, change to the domain controller LSA, and change in the owner of the RID master.

Question 5

You are configuring access for client computers to access NetWare resources on your network. The services offered by the NetWare servers are required nearly as often as Windows 2000 services. In this environment, what is the best method for allowing Windows clients access to NetWare resources?

❍ A. Install GSNW on the Windows 2000 Server.

❍ B. Install CSNW on the Windows 2000 Server.

❍ C. Install GSNW on the Windows clients.

❍ D. Install CSNW on the Windows clients.

Answer D is correct. Although the Gateway Services for NetWare are intended to provide client access to NetWare resources through the Windows 2000 Server Gateway, it is intended to be a limited-use solution. If the clients require frequent access to NetWare resources, installing the Client Services for NetWare on the client systems is a better option. Installing CSNW on the server would not provide access for the Windows clients on the network. There is no GSNW for client computers. Therefore, answers A, B, and C are incorrect.

Question 6

You receive a phone call from a user on the network who is having problems printing. They have sent a document to the printer and have yet to receive their hard copy. You have the user double-click on the printer definition on their system and they see a large backlog of jobs waiting from various users on the network waiting to print. The user notes that their job is sixth in the queue behind jobs from other users. You ask the user to select the first job in the queue, then select Cancel from the Document menu. Unfortunately, the user receives a message they do not have sufficient rights to cancel this print job. Which of the following printer permissions must be assigned to the user to allow them to cancel the pending print job?

- ❍ A. Print
- ❍ B. Manage Documents
- ❍ C. Manage Printer
- ❍ D. Manage Server

Answer B is correct. The Manage Documents permission lets users manipulate their own print jobs, as well as other users' print jobs. Print allows users the ability to cancel their own jobs, but not other's print jobs; therefore, answer A is incorrect. Manage Printer allows the user to change the settings for the printer itself; therefore, answer C is incorrect. There is no printer permission setting called Manage Server; therefore, answer D is incorrect.

Question 7

The Corporate Policies and Procedures department has requested that shared folders be included on all Windows 2000 Servers to provide copies of the company's procedures to all employees. Policies pertaining to certain departments may be contained in individual folders on other servers. The proposed solution must meet the following requirements:

You must provide secure read-only access to the polices documents on the server.

You must ensure copies of the policies are available to all users at all times.

You must ensure departmental policies are accessible from the Policies folder.

Members of the Policies and Procedures department should have administrator access to the documents in the folders.

The proposed solution is to implement a Policies and Procedures folder on the NTFS volume of all servers. Members of the Policies and Procedures group are assigned Full Control NTFS permissions to the folders. Use Dfs to provide links from the Policies and Procedures folder to departmental policies folders on other servers.

Which of the following does the proposed solution provide? (Choose all that apply.)

- ❑ A. The proposed solution provides secure read-only access to the policies documents on the server.
- ❑ B. The proposed solution ensures copies of the policies are available to all users at all times.
- ❑ C. The proposed solution ensures departmental policies can be accessed from within the Policies folder.
- ❑ D. The proposed solution gives members of the Policies and Procedures group administrator access to the documents in the folders.

Answers C and D are correct. Utilizing Dfs to link departmental folders to the Policies folder ensures that they can easily be accessed from within the Policies folder. Setting NTFS Full Control for the Policies and Procedures group gives them administrative control over the files in the folders. Permissions for other groups are not specified in the solution and there is no provision for synchronizing files on different servers. Therefore, answers A and B are incorrect.

Question 8

You are establishing an intranet site for employee access to files and important company information. All client computers are running Windows 98 or Windows 2000 Professional. The proposed solution must meet the following security requirements:

You must use an authentication method that is supported by all clients.

You must use an encrypted authentication method.

You must ensure all requested are authenticated.

You must choose an authentication protocol that is part of the HTTP specification.

The proposed solution is to configure the Web site to allow anonymous access and also use Integrated Windows authentication.

Which of the following does the proposed solution provide? (Choose all that apply.)

- ❑ A. The proposed solution uses an authentication method supported by all clients.
- ❑ B. The proposed solution uses an encrypted authentication method.
- ❑ C. The proposed solution ensures all requests are authenticated.
- ❑ D. The proposed solution uses a protocol that is part of the HTTP specification.

Answers A and B are correct. Integrated Windows authentication is an encrypted authentication method supported by both Windows 98 and Windows 2000 Professional computers. The proposed solution does not require authentication because it allows anonymous access. Integrated Windows authentication is not part of the HTTP spec. Therefore, answers C and D are incorrect.

Question 9

You would like to limit the number of share names network users must remember to access their files each day. There are a wide variety of shared resources on multiple systems on the network, including Windows 2000 Professional systems, Windows 2000 Server systems configured as member servers, and standalone Windows 2000 Servers. Which of the following can be used to provide simplified access for users?

❍ A. Create a WebDAV folder to the root of the primary Windows 2000 Server.

❍ B. Create a domain Dfs root on the PDC and add links to the shared resources on then network.

❍ C. Create an FRS process to synchronize files across all servers on the network.

❍ D. Create a domain Dfs root on a standalone server and add links to the shared resources on the network.

Answer B is correct. A domain Dfs root with links to the shared network resources will bring all shares into a single location to simplify access for users. A WebDAV folder is used to access shared resources from a Web browser, but does not bring all shares together. Using FRS to synchronize files on all servers will not simplify access to network resources. A domain Dfs root cannot be created on a standalone server. Therefore, answers A, C, and D are incorrect.

Question 10

Which of the following services do not require an NTFS volume for operation? (Choose all that apply.)

❑ A. WebDAV folders

❑ B. File Services for Macintosh

❑ C. Domain-based Dfs

❑ D. IIS 5.0 Web sites

❑ E. Print Services for Unix

Answers A, D, and E are correct. File Services for Macintosh and Domain-based Dfs both require NTFS to operate. The other features listed can operate on either FAT or NTFS volumes. Therefore, answers B and C are incorrect.

Need to Know More?

MCSE Training Kit—Microsoft Windows 2000 Server (Second Edition), Microsoft Corporation, ISBN 0-7356-1767-8 (Second Edition)

Windows 2000 Resource Kits online at `http://www.microsoft.com/windows2000/techinfo/reskit/en-us/default.asp`. Also available in print; ISBN 1-5723-1808-2 (Windows 2000 Professional) and ISBN 1-5723-1805-8 (Windows 2000 Server).

For technical information on Windows 2000 Server and its components, including IIS 5.0, go to the Microsoft Technical Information Library at `http://www.microsoft.com/windows2000/techinfo/howitworks/default.asp`

Configuring and Troubleshooting Hardware Devices and Drivers

Terms you'll need to understand:

✓ Device Manager
✓ Driver Signing
✓ Digital Signature
✓ Driver
✓ Hardware Compatibility List (HCL)
✓ Plug and Play
✓ Windows 2000 Readiness Analyzer

Techniques you'll need to master:

✓ Configuring driver signing via Group Policy
✓ Configuring driver signing for a local computer
✓ Verifying hardware compatibility
✓ Using the Hardware Compatibility List (HCL)
✓ Installing Plug and Play hardware
✓ Manually installing non-Plug and Play hardware
✓ Updating device drivers
✓ Troubleshooting hardware installations

Introduction

Hardware installation, configuration, and support are tasks that many administrators take for granted. Perhaps the administrators have help desk personnel or junior administrators whose function it is to worry about such low-level issues. But what do you do if you don't have the luxury of having an entire group or department that manages your hardware? You then learn the value of knowing how Windows 2000 deals with hardware. Even if another group handles these issues for you, you still must have a firm grasp on hardware and how it interacts with Windows 2000. Most important, you need to be able to make all of your installed hardware interact properly, not only with other installed hardware, but also with Windows 2000. Many operating system problems that users experience start with the users themselves or the hardware that they are using. Knowing how to deal with hardware installation and configuration will help keep your users happy and your boss even happier. This chapter introduces you to the nuances of verifying, installing, and configuring hardware for your clients.

In the dark days of DOS and Windows 3.11, installing new hardware in a machine could actually turn out to be a major event. Plug and Play was just a dream on an engineer's scratch pad and getting sound technical support from most vendors was a rarity at best. The Microsoft Hardware Compatibility List (HCL) did not exist and thus you just had to hope more often than not that your new hardware would work properly when matched up with your old hardware and your operating system. Of course, there were always problems with custom applications that required specific hardware—but you get the point. When you got lucky, you were a godsend in your organization; when you were unlucky, you spent countless hours trying to figure out what went wrong. Oh the joy of it all....

Fortunately for us, these days have all but passed. In Windows 2000, with Plug and Play hardware, the installation and configuration of hardware devices has been simplified and improved substantially over all previous versions of Windows. The process for installing and configuring hardware has three basic steps:

- Set driver signing restrictions.
- Select the hardware to be installed and verify its compatibility.
- Install and configure the selected hardware.

There is, of course, more to this cycle than what is outlined here. These three steps are the core parts of managing hardware in Windows 2000. You may still find yourself facing the need to support legacy hardware devices that are not Plug and Play compliant, but Windows 2000 makes this an easy task compared to previous versions of Windows. We look at each of these items in greater detail in the following sections, plus a few other items of interest in the area of hardware installation and management.

Configuring Driver Signing Options

Realizing that poorly written drivers were often the cause of kernel stop errors (also known as the Blue Screen of Death) and other system problems, such as lockups and instability, Microsoft introduced *digital driver signing* in Windows 2000. Digitally signed device drivers are those that have been submitted to the Windows Hardware Quality Lab (WHQL) by vendors and subsequently subjected to compatibility tests administered by the WHQL. Drivers that complete the compatibility testing process successfully are approved by Microsoft and digitally signed. Due to this rigorous compatibility testing, digitally signed drivers can be counted on to be more robust and reliable. Driver files that have been digitally signed can be found on the Windows Update Web site and also on the Windows Hardware Compatibility List. Additionally, only digitally signed drivers are found on the Windows 2000 setup CD-ROM.

Driver signing, which is controlled from the System applet for standalone machines and via Group Policy for network machines, is important to ensure that your computers remain fully functional. By enforcing restrictions on the installation of unsigned drivers, you can prevent hardware conflicts and stop errors, both of which are common side effects of poorly written drivers. Poorly written drivers also tend to generate an unusually large number of CPU interrupts, thus interfering with all other operations.

The Windows Update Web site can be found at **http://windowsupdate.microsoft.com/**.

The Windows Hardware Compatibility List (HCL) can be found at **http://www.microsoft.com/hcl/default.asp**.

By digitally signing a file, in this case a driver file, one can be relatively certain that the file is trustworthy and authentic. In this way, digitally signing a driver file works in the same fashion as digitally signing your email message that you send to a co-worker. Because any type of computer file can be signed with a digital certificate signature, a means must exist to handle all of the different file formats. This is accomplished via a technique known as *catalog file signing*, in which digital signing information about files is available without any modification to the files themselves.

In catalog file signing, a CAT file is created for each driver or operating system file that is being signed. The CAT file includes a hash of the binary file. A *hash* is the result of a mathematical operation on some data (in this case, the binary file) that is sensitive to any changes made in the source data. Any change to the binary file can be detected because the hash procedure produces a different value. Other information, such as filename and version number, is also added to the file. A certificate from the publisher, along with a Microsoft digital signature, is included in the catalog file to complete the signing process. The relationship between the catalog file and the driver binary is contained in the information file (.inf) maintained by the system after the driver is installed.

The options available for configuring how to handle unsigned drivers include the following:

- *Ignore*—Directs the system to proceed with the installation even if it includes unsigned files. You have no protection from poorly written drivers when the Ignore option is selected. As a result, it is not recommended that you configure driver signing with the Ignore option due to the threat of viruses, Trojan horses, and so on.
- *Warn*—Notifies the user that files are not digitally signed and allows the user to decide whether to stop or proceed with the installation and whether to permit unsigned files to be installed. Driver signing is set to Warn by default; however, it is not recommended to keep this setting in a production environment.
- *Block*—Directs the system to refuse to install unsigned files. As a result, the installation stops, and none of the files in the driver package are installed. This is the recommended setting for a production environment, and it guarantees the highest level of protection for client machines against poorly written device drivers.

Be sure you know the three driver signing behaviors. This is an important feature of Windows 2000 that you can expect to be tested on.

As previously mentioned, you can configure driver signing from one of two locations depending on the configuration of your network and your preferences. Regardless of the location from which you choose to configure driver signing, you still have the same three choices available. The next section examines the process of configuring driver signing via Group Policy.

Configuring Driver Signing via Group Policy

If you have a Windows 2000 Active Directory domain, you should take advantage of Group Policy as often as possible. Using Group Policy Objects to configure your network and your computers gives you previously unavailable management abilities with very little overhead. Group Policy allows you to have granular control over the who, what, when, where, how, and why of configuring network settings. As an example of dealing with driver signing, assume that you work for a company that has the following departments:

- *Engineering*—These individuals are technically savvy and frequently need to install and configure new hardware devices. They have, however, in the past caused serious issues when installing hardware devices that shipped with poorly written device drivers. All Engineering client computers and user accounts are located in the Engineering organizational unit (OU).
- *Accounting*—The accountants rarely, if ever, need new hardware installed on their machines. In the event they need a new hardware device installed, it has been easy in the past to send out support personnel to install and configure the hardware device properly. All Accounting client computers and user accounts are located in the Accounting OU.
- *Developers*—The development team is responsible for all the software associated with the civil engineering equipment your company manufactures. The team also creates device drivers for this hardware and must install the device drivers on test machines to test and troubleshoot the hardware/software combination before shipping to customers. The developers have client computers spread out in two organizational units: their standard network machines are located in the Engineering OU, whereas their testing machines are located in the Developers OU. All user accounts are located in the Developers OU.

In this example, you are faced with three different types of clients and thus three different driver signing options you can configure via Group Policy for their respective OUs. In this case, you should consider configuring driver signing as follows:

- *Configure the Warn setting for the Engineering OU*—You want the Engineers to be able to install new hardware devices as required; however, you want them to be warned before installing unsigned drivers.
- *Configure the Block setting for the Accounting OU*—The Accountants infrequently add new hardware; therefore, it is safer to prevent them from

installing any new drivers that are not signed. Should they have an unsigned driver, you can address that on a case-by-case basis.

- *Configure the Ignore setting for the Developers OU*—The Developers are responsible for writing the drivers for your company's products. They have a distinct need to install drivers, unsigned or not, on their computers.

You might decide against setting driver signing to Ignore for the Developers. Driver signing policy options are a User Group Policy item, so the key item is the location of the user accounts. The location of the computer accounts is irrelevant in this case.

As you can see in the preceding example, you may need to configure different driver signing policies for different groups of users. Group Policy Objects (GPOs) applied to the applicable organizational units makes this an easy task. The process to configure driver signing via Group Policy is fairly simple and is outlined as follows:

1. Open the Active Directory Users and Computers snap-in by selecting Start, Programs, Administrative Tools, Active Directory Users and Computers.
2. Locate and right-click the OU for which you want to configure the Group Policy. From the context menu, select Properties.
3. Click the Group Policy tab and either click New to create a new GPO or click Edit to work with an existing GPO. Because it is recommended to create GPOs for specific tasks, we will create a new GPO for this purpose by clicking New and entering the name *Driver Signing Policies*. Click Edit to open the Group Policy window.
4. As shown in Figure 4.1, the Group Policy option we want to work with is located in the User Configuration, Administrative Templates, System node.
5. Double-click the Code signing for device drivers option, which opens the Code signing for device drivers Properties dialog box shown in Figure 4.2.
6. Select the Enabled option, and then select the appropriate behavior from the drop-down list. In this case, we enabled the Block configuration because this GPO is for the Accounting OU.

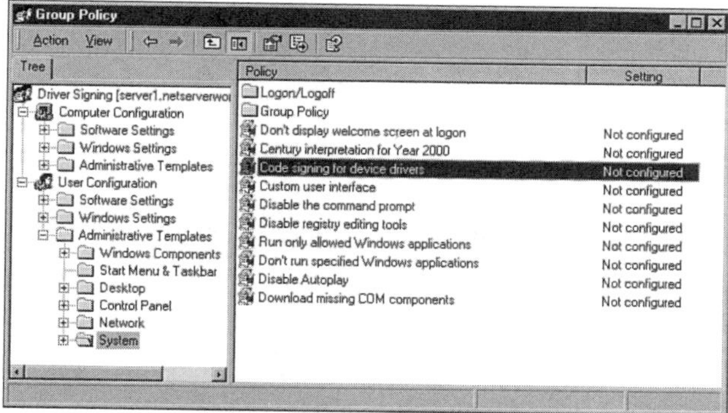

Figure 4.1 Locating the driver signing option.

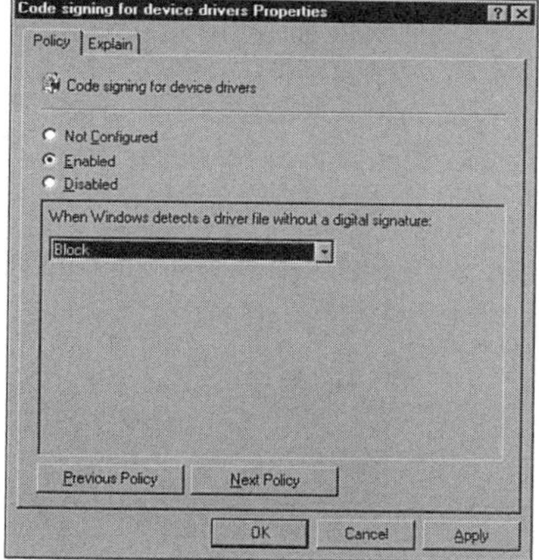

Figure 4.2 Configuring the driver signing options.

7. Click OK to close the Code signing for device drivers Properties dialog box. To close the Group Policy window, click the X in the upper-right corner of the window.

The Group Policy settings you configured will take effect as soon as Group Policy has been refreshed the next time users log on to the system. Now all users in the Accounting OU will be prevented from installing any device drivers that are not digitally signed.

Applying driver signing options via Group Policy is the quickest and easiest way to have them applied uniformly to a large number of users. However, if you only have a few computers to work with or need a specific computer configured in a certain manner, you can opt to configure driver signing from the Control Panel, which is discussed in the next section.

Although this exam (70-215) is not as in-depth about Group Policy as the 70-216 exam, you should still have a good understanding of the basic operations and functions of Group Policy.

Configuring Driver Signing Locally via the Control Panel

As an alternative to Group Policy–based driver signing, you can configure driver signing from the Control Panel locally on each machine. This is not a good approach for large networks, but it works well in small ones with few machines or peer-to-peer workgroups. The process to configure driver signing is as follows:

1. Open the System applet in the Control Panel by selecting Start, Settings, Control Panel, System, or by right-clicking the My Computer icon on the Desktop and clicking Properties from the shortcut menu.
2. Click the Hardware tab and click Driver Signing. The Driver Signing Options dialog box opens, as shown in Figure 4.3.

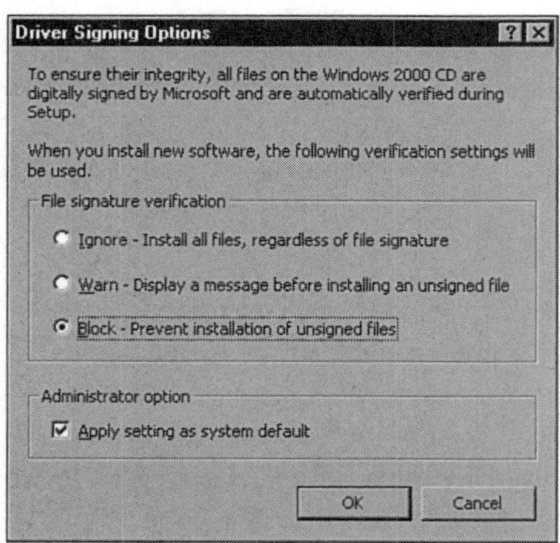

Figure 4.3 Configuring driver signing options from the Control Panel.

3. Make your selection from the three available choices (Ignore, Warn, or Block). When you are done, click OK twice to complete the process.

In just three easy steps you've now configured driver signing for a specific computer. Although this process is simple, you can see how you would quickly become overwhelmed if you had to perform this configuration on several hundred or even just several dozen computers.

If you are logged on with local Administrative privileges, selecting the Apply Settings as system default option applies the configured driver signing level for all users who log on to the computer. This option is not available to users without Administrative privileges, so don't worry about your users changing the setting after the fact! Users can adjust the settings to a strict control, such as from Warn to Block, but not to a more lenient setting, such as from Block to Allow.

Working with Digitally Signed Drivers

After you've set the driver signing options, you're pretty much done. Try to install an unsigned driver when you are configured for Warn, and you will get a warning dialog box similar to the one shown in Figure 4.4.

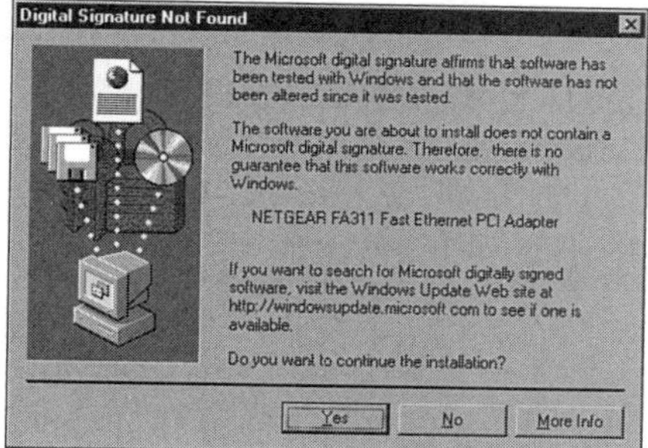

Figure 4.4 A warning dialog box appears when trying to install an unsigned driver.

If you are installing Windows 2000 across the network in an unattended setup, the default driver signing setting is Warn. See KB# Q236029 at **http://support.microsoft.com/default.aspx?scid=kb;EN-US;q236029** for help in changing the driver signing settings.

This section examined the concept of digital signatures and how you configure driver signing options for the installation of new device drivers on your computers. You've seen how to configure driver signing quickly and easily across an entire OU (domain or site) and also how to configure it on a computer-by-computer basis. The next section explores how you can ensure that your new hardware is ready for use with Windows 2000—before you install it.

Verifying Hardware Compatibility

With your driver signing policies firmly in place, you are ready to move on to the next step in the hardware installation process: verifying hardware compatibility with Windows 2000. It may seem like a trivial matter given that most hardware is Plug and Play compatible, but it is still important to make sure that the hardware you want to place into your Windows 2000 computer is recognized by Microsoft as a Windows 2000 compatible device. Before you purchase new hardware (or attempt to install Windows 2000 on a new machine), you should take the time to ensure that it is compatible with Windows 2000. This can be done in one of two ways:

- Check the Hardware Compatibility List (HCL). This is the preferred method to verify hardware compatibility as the HCL changes weekly and is updated as Microsoft certifies additional hardware items for use with Windows 2000.
- Run winnt32.exe with the /checkupgradeonly switch, which checks for compatibility with existing hardware before installing Windows 2000.

Command switches are somewhat difficult to remember, but are important to learn nonetheless. Doing so will make your day-to-day operations easier and improve your chances on passing this exam.

The Hardware Compatibility List (HCL)

The Hardware Compatibility List (HCL) is Microsoft's published list of hardware components that have been fully tested with Windows 2000. Items that are listed in the HCL are guaranteed to function with Windows 2000. If you want to ensure that all your hardware components will function properly under Windows 2000, you should consult the current version of the HCL, which can be found on the Internet at `http://www.microsoft.com/hcl/`.

Although thousands of products can be found on the HCL (meaning that the Microsoft WHQL has tested them and found them to function with Windows 2000), not every piece of hardware in existence is compatible. This is especially true if the hardware is either very old or very new. If the hardware manufacturer has a suitable Windows 2000 driver available for that device, it should function satisfactorily in Windows 2000. However, any future problems that you encounter with the device should be addressed to the hardware manufacturer, not Microsoft.

Once you're at the HCL Web site, finding your hardware is a fairly simple process. You just need to know what type of hardware you're looking for, such as video adapters, and search on that. Alternatively, if you know a model number, such as Matrox G450, then you can search for that specifically.

If you have two components that are both on the HCL, that doesn't necessarily mean that they have been tested together. That is, although each device is approved independently on the HCL, there may be conflicts between the devices that can cause errors.

The HCL for Windows 2000 DataCenter Server is located in a different location than the rest of the HCL. It can be found at **http://www.microsoft.com/windows2000/datacenter/hcl/**. Windows 2000 DataCenter is sold only by purchasing a packaged solution, which includes the hardware, DataCenter software, and the services to test and install the solution. It is sold only through approved vendors who can provide these capabilities. Details are available at **http://www.microsoft.com/windows2000/datacenter/howtobuy/purchasing/oems.asp**.

Windows 2000 Readiness Analyzer

Using the HCL is convenient for small amounts of hardware, but what do you do when you want to analyze the hardware contents of an entire computer? That's where the second method available to you comes into play. The *Windows 2000 Readiness Analyzer*, although arguably not as up-to-date as the HCL, can be used to determine the compatibility of hardware in an existing computer on which you want to install Windows 2000. The Windows 2000 Readiness Analyzer is run from the command prompt as follows:

1. Open a command prompt by typing `cmd` in the Run box (Start, Run), and then click OK.

2. From the command prompt, run the Readiness Analyzer by typing `X:\i386\winnt32 /checkupgradeonly` and pressing Enter, where *X* is the location of the Windows 2000 setup files.

3. The analysis output window appears when the Readiness Analyzer has finished. You can quickly determine if any incompatible hardware devices exist in the computer.

4. Should you need to, you can save the results of the Readiness Analyzer to a text file. Click Finish when you are done to close the Readiness Analyzer window.

During the installation of Windows 2000, an Upgrade report may be presented to you. This report provides information about hardware and other items that are incompatible with Windows 2000. More information can be found in KB# Q228213 at **http://support.microsoft.com/default.aspx?scid=kb;EN-US;q228213**.

The last major step to installing and configuring hardware devices in Windows 2000 is to actually install and configure the device. That is the topic of the next section.

Installing and Configuring Hardware Devices

If it seems like it's been a long process to finally get to the actual installation and configuration of your new hardware, take comfort in the fact that you are ready to perform the installation and configuration in a safe manner. All of the prep work that has been done up to this point will help ensure that your Windows 2000 computers function properly and have no hardware incompatibility issues in the future. We will now examine the installation and configuration of hardware in Windows 2000.

Windows 2000 includes many enhancements over previous versions of Windows that greatly simplify device management. Some of these include Advanced Power Management (APM), Advanced Configuration and Power Interface (ACPI), and Plug and Play (PnP).

Plug and Play is a combination of hardware and software that enables a computer to recognize and modify its hardware configuration changes with minimal intervention from the user. The hardware device that you are installing must support the Plug and Play specification to be automatically configured correctly. You will find that some older devices that predate Plug and Play will not be recognized, and thus require that you manually configure resource settings as discussed in the "Configuring Support for Legacy Hardware Devices" later in this chapter.

With Plug and Play, a user can add or remove a device dynamically without manual reconfiguration and without any intricate knowledge of the computer hardware. For example, you can have a laptop in a docking station that contains an Ethernet network connection and later use the same laptop connecting to the network using a built-in modem, without making any configuration changes.

With Plug and Play, you can make changes to the Windows 2000 computer's configuration with the assurance that all devices will work and the computer will reboot correctly after the changes are made. When you install a Plug and Play device, Windows 2000 automatically configures the device to allow it to function properly with the other devices already installed in your computer. Windows 2000 assigns system resources to the device including the following:

- Interrupt request (IRQ) number
- Direct memory access (DMA) channel
- Input/Output (I/O) port address
- Memory address range

Each resource must be unique or the device will not function properly. When the device you are installing is not Plug and Play compatible, Windows 2000 has no way of automatically configuring the device settings. You may have to manually configure the device driver or use the installation program provided by the manufacturer.

If you must manually configure a non–Plug and Play device, the resources assigned become fixed. This reduces the flexibility that Windows 2000 has for allocating resources to other devices. If too many resources are manually configured, Windows 2000 may not be able to install new Plug and Play devices.

Resource settings should be changed only if you are certain that the new settings do not conflict with any other hardware, or if the hardware manufacturer has supplied a specific set of resource settings with the device.

You can configure devices using the Add/Remove Hardware applet in the Control Panel or by using Device Manager, which is located in the Computer Management tool within the Administrative Tools folder in the Control Panel.

With most Plug and Play hardware, you simply connect the device to the computer, and Windows 2000 automatically configures the new settings. Devices and the drivers that control them can support Plug and Play. The possible combinations expand to the following four support scenarios:

- *Both the hardware and the driver support Plug and Play*—Full Plug and Play support is provided in this situation; this is the easiest combination and the most likely to have a successful installation.
- *The driver supports Plug and Play, but the hardware does not*—In this situation, Windows 2000 provides partial Plug and Play support. Windows 2000 does not automatically configure the device drivers, but Plug and

Play can manage resource allocations and interface to the power management systems.

- *The hardware supports Plug and Play, but the driver does not*—Windows 2000 does not support Plug and Play in this situation, and the device is treated as a legacy device. This device requires manual configuration of all resource settings.
- *Neither the hardware nor the driver support Plug and Play*—Windows 2000 does not provide any Plug and Play support for this hardware device. All resource settings must be configured manually.

Be sure to understand the difference between Plug and Play and non–Plug and Play compatible hardware. Know how installing each will affect your computer and what Windows 2000 does differently for each type.

For hardware that cannot be automatically identified, the Add/Remove Hardware Wizard provides a method of manually configuring the device resources or manually loading drivers. On the rare occasion that Windows 2000 does not automatically detect your Plug and Play hardware, you can manually initiate the Add/Remove Hardware Wizard if desired. Using the Add/Remove Hardware Wizard is discussed in some detail in the next section.

Using the Add/Remove Hardware Wizard

The *Add/Remove Hardware Wizard*, located in the Control Panel, is used to initiate automatic hardware installation of both Plug and Play and non-Plug and Play hardware devices. By following the steps that follow, you will initiate a search for a new Plug and Play hardware device. In the absence of any new hardware, you will be presented with a screen to add a new device or troubleshoot an existing device.

1. Click Start, Settings, Control Panel.
2. Double-click the Add/Remove Hardware icon to start the wizard.
3. Click Next to close the Welcome page.
4. Select Add/Troubleshoot a Device and click Next to start the wizard.

Windows 2000 searches for any new Plug and Play hardware and proceeds to install any that is found. If the wizard does not detect any new hardware installed in your computer, it displays a list of installed hardware for you to choose a device for troubleshooting (see Figure 4.5) or installation. The first entry on the hardware list is *Add a new device*, which provides you with an option to manually initiate the installation of a new hardware device.

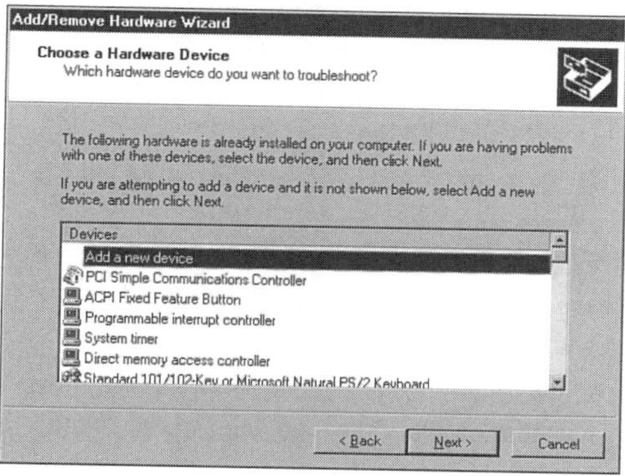

Figure 4.5 Installing or troubleshooting hardware.

Configuring Support for Legacy Hardware Devices

If you need to manually install a non-Plug and Play hardware device, you must understand the resources the hardware device expects to use. In most cases, you can readily locate the information about what resources the hardware device requires by reading the provided manufacturer's product documentation. Given this information, you must then determine how to best fit the new hardware device into your existing Windows 2000 system. Table 4.1 describes the resources available in a Windows 2000 computer system that hardware devices use to communicate with the operating system.

Table 4.1 Hardware Device Resources

Resources	Description
Interrupts	Hardware devices use interrupts to indicate to the processor that they need attention. The processor uses this interrupt request (IRQ) as a way of determining which device is looking for service and what type of attention it needs. Windows 2000 provides interrupt numbers 0 through 15 to devices (IRQ 1 is always assigned to the keyboard).

(continued)

Table 4.1 Hardware Device Resources *(continued)*

Resources	Description
Direct memory access (DMA)	DMAs are channels that allow the hardware device to access memory directly. This allows a device such as a disk drive or floppy drive to write information into memory without interrupting the processor. Windows 2000 provides DMA channels 0 through 7.
Input/Output (I/O) port	I/O ports are areas of memory that the device uses to communicate with Windows 2000. When the processor sees an IRQ request, it checks the I/O port address to retrieve additional information about what the device wants.
Memory	Many hardware devices have onboard memory or can reserve system memory for their use. Any reserved memory is not available for any other device or for Windows 2000.

Windows 2000 Shares Resources

Some resources that devices require must be specifically reserved for a single, specific device. Other resources can be shared between two or more devices, with Windows 2000 dynamically managing resources as required. Windows 2000 works with the computer's BIOS to share resources as follows.

The IRQ uses a Programmable Interrupt Controller (PIC) to request some service for the device. When a request is seen, the current operation is suspended and control is given to the device driver associated with the IRQ number (1–15). This resource therefore cannot be shared between devices.

The I/O port is a memory block used by the device to communicate the service it is requesting. This is tied to the IRQ number and therefore is dedicated to a device.

The DMA is a direct channel between the device and the computer's memory. The DMA controller supports a number of channels (usually seven) and they are shared between devices (one at a time).

A device memory block is a portion of system memory mapped to the internal memory of the device (usually). This is dedicated to the device and cannot be used by any other process, including Windows 2000.

Determining Available Resources

Once you know what resources your new hardware device requires, you can use *Device Manager* to display the resources available on your computer. To view the available resources list, double-click the System icon in the Control Panel and click the Hardware tab. Click the Device Manager button and select the Resources by Connection entry in the View menu. Figure 4.6 shows the Device Manager view of resources and their availability.

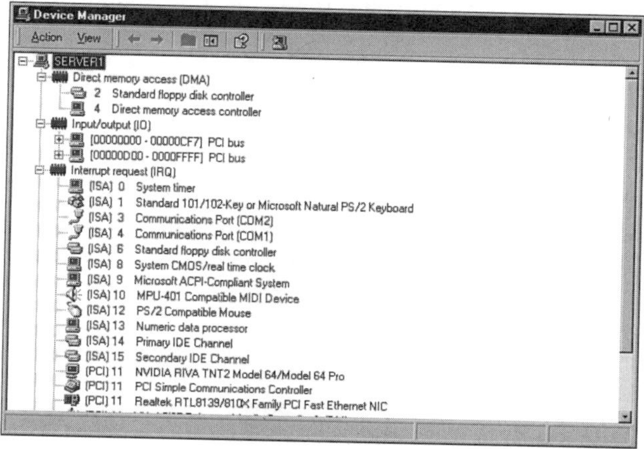

Figure 4.6 Hardware resources listed by connection in Device Manager.

Changing Resource Assignments

In the event that more than one hardware device in your computer requests the same resources, a conflict will occur. In some cases, these conflicts may only disable the affected devices and prevent you from using them. In other cases, your entire computer may become unstable or even cease to function properly. In any case, you must change one or more resource settings on the Resources tab in the device's Properties information. The following procedure allows you to modify a resource setting:

1. Click Start, Settings, Control Panel.
2. Double-click the System icon and then click the Hardware tab, or right-click the My Computer icon on the Desktop and click Properties from the shortcut menu.
3. Click the Device Manager button.
4. Expand the device type that you wish to change.
5. Right-click the specific device you wish to modify and select Properties from the context menu.
6. Click the Resources tab. If the Resources tab is not present, you will not be able to modify the device's resources.
7. Select the resource setting you wish to modify.

8. Clear the Use automatic settings check box if it is selected. If this box is dimmed, you will not be able to modify the device's resources.
9. Select the resource you wish to modify and then click the Change Setting button.
10. Change your resource settings as required and close the Properties dialog box when done.

After you complete this procedure, Windows 2000 uses the manually configured resource settings for the device. Remember, if this creates a resource conflict, you must solve it yourself—Windows 2000 cannot change any manually configured resource settings.

Changing Resources for Non–Plug and Play Devices

Changing the resources assigned to a non–Plug and Play device will not actually change the resources the device uses. This only instructs Windows 2000 what the device configuration is. You must consult the manufacturer's documentation as to what jumpers or software switches to set on the device to conform to the resource assignment you have told Windows 2000 to expect.

Updating Device Drivers

Hardware manufacturers like to keep loyal customers. One of the best ways to keep customers loyal is to continuously update and improve hardware drivers. Often times, drivers can be updated and improved to squeeze just a little bit more performance out of a device—drivers for video adapters and network adapters are updated more often than other types of devices for just this reason. Other times, a manufacturer may discover a bug or other coding error in a previously released driver and issue an updated driver in an effort to correct the problem. This can occur even in cases in which the driver has been certified by the WHQL.

Device drivers can be updated in several ways, including using a manufacturer's setup utility or by using Device Manager. In this section, we examine how to update device drivers via Device Manager.

1. Click Start, Settings, Control Panel.
2. Double-click the System icon, or right-click the My Computer icon on the Desktop and click Properties from the shortcut menu, and select the Hardware tab.

3. Click the Device Manager button.
4. Expand the device type that you wish to change.
5. Right-click the specific device you wish to modify and select Properties from the context menu.
6. Click the Driver tab, as shown in Figure 4.7.

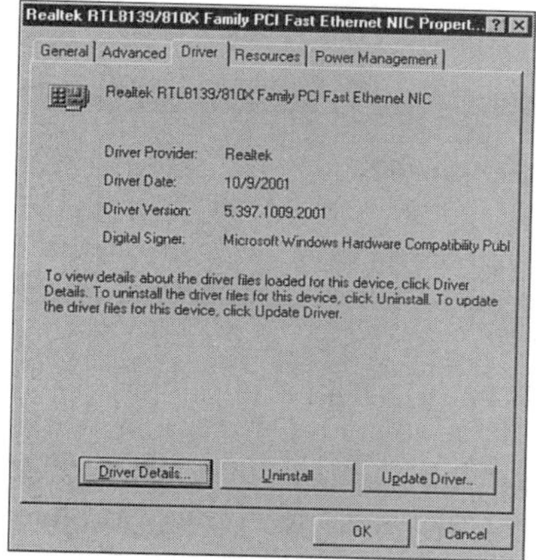

Figure 4.7 Working with device drivers.

7. Click the Update Driver button to start the Hardware Update Wizard.
8. Select either an automatic installation or a manual installation. The manual installation states that it is an advanced option, but in reality it is the best way to get to your updated driver file—assuming that you know where it is.
9. Follow through the rest of the steps in the Update Device Driver Wizard to install the updated device driver file on your computer.

The process to update drivers is very simple but very important. Expect to be tested on this in one way or another.

Troubleshooting Hardware Problems

Unfortunately, not every hardware installation goes according to plan—even with the great improvements that Windows 2000 brings to the table. Problems with hardware usually center around three things:

- Hardware that is not actually installed properly
- Hardware that is having a resource conflict
- Hardware that is not supported in Windows 2000

With the first two bullets listed previously, hardware that is not actually installed properly and hardware that is having a resource conflict, the problems associated with each bullet may often display the same symptoms. In either case, your starting point for gathering information, troubleshooting the problem, and subsequently correcting the problem is Device Manager. In the case in which hardware is not supported in Windows 2000, which often happens with old hardware, you may find it easier and safer to simply acquire a newer hardware device that performs the same or similar function and is Windows 2000 compatible.

If you have a hardware device that is Windows 2000 compatible but does not seem to function properly, the next section may help you glean some insight into the problem.

Confirming Hardware Installation Status

After you install new hardware, you can confirm that the device is installed and functioning properly by using Device Manager. You can also do this at any time after installation if you have a question about the device's status.

To start Device Manager, double-click the System icon in the Control Panel. Click the Hardware tab and then click the Device Manager button. This displays a list of installed hardware, as shown in Figure 4.8.

Expanding a device type node displays all of the devices of that type installed on the computer. The device icon indicates whether the device is functioning properly. You can use the information in Table 4.2 to determine the device status.

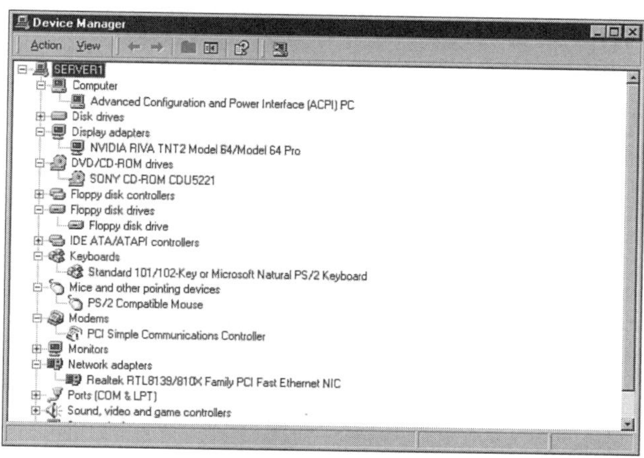

Figure 4.8 Installed devices listed by Device Manager.

Table 4.2 Device Manager Hardware Status

Device Icon	Device Status
Normal icon	The device is functioning normally.
Normal icon with a red X	The device has been disabled.
Normal icon with a yellow exclamation point	The device is not configured correctly or the device drivers are missing.
Yellow question mark with a red X	Windows 2000 has disabled the hardware due to resource conflicts. To correct this, right-click the device icon, click Properties, and set the resources manually according to what is available in the system.

Knowing how to interpret Device Manager output is critical to keeping your Windows 2000 computers running smoothly and just might be valuable for this exam as well!

You can access Device Manager from a number of places. It can be started using the Device Manager button from the Hardware tab in the System applet from the Control Panel. It can also be started from the Computer Management icon within the Administrative Tools folder in the Control Panel. Finally, it is available as a snap-in to the Microsoft Management Console (MMC).

Troubleshooting Hardware Installation Problems

If you determine that a hardware device is not functioning properly, as indicated by an icon detailed in Table 4.2 or by other observation, you can launch a hardware troubleshooting wizard to help you solve the problem. The hardware troubleshooter can be launched from the device's Properties page by clicking the Troubleshooter button on the General tab (see Figure 4.9). Each type of hardware launches a troubleshooting wizard specific to it; for example, starting the troubleshooting wizard from a mouse Properties page does not start the same troubleshooting wizard as one from a network adapter page.

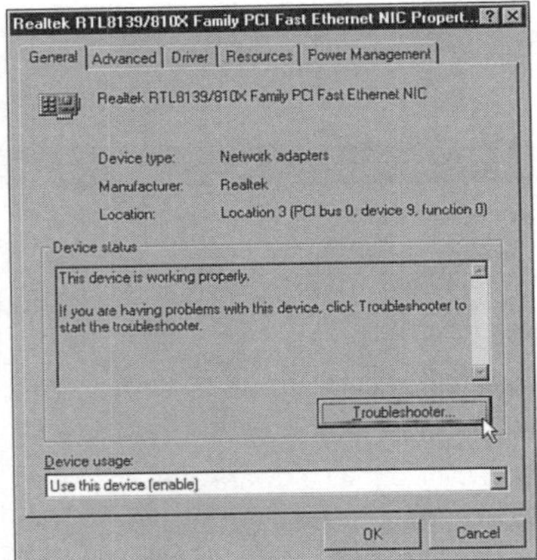

Figure 4.9 Launching the hardware troubleshooting wizard.

Practice Questions

Question 1

Christopher is the administrator of a medium-sized (about 500 machines) Windows 2000 network for an engineering firm. The previous administrator did a fairly good job of getting Windows 2000 rolled out in the organization, including breaking up each department into OUs. However, no matter what the administrator tried, one or two computers in the production department ceased to operate properly on a daily basis. You suspect the cause might be that the layout personnel have a tendency to experiment with new hardware. What can you do to help prevent future down time on these computers?

❍ A. On each machine, set the driver signing behavior to Block.

❍ B. From Active Directory Users and Computers, create a GPO and link it to the production department's OU. Configure driver signing in the GPO for Ignore.

❍ C. From Active Directory Users and Computers, create a GPO and link it to the production department's OU. Configure driver signing in the GPO to Block.

❍ D. Remove all user accounts in the production department's OU from the Users group to the Guest group.

Answer C is correct. The best option in this case is to create a GPO linked to the production department's OU and configure the driver signing behavior for Block. You are not told how many machines are part of the production department, but in a Windows 2000 Active Directory domain, you should always strive to apply policies via Group Policy Objects instead of manually configuring them. Thus, answer A is incorrect. Configuring a GPO with the Ignore option would not be an optimal solution because all drivers (signed or not) could then be installed. When the Block behavior is set, unsigned drivers cannot be installed. Thus, answer B is incorrect. Moving the users' accounts out of the Users group and into the Guest group would fix the problem but would likely cause additional, unnecessary problems. Thus, answer D is incorrect.

Question 2

Hannah works as a help desk support technician for a large organization. Recently, she received a phone call from a user who stated that his newly installed scanner wasn't working. When instructed to look at Device Manager, the user reported back that the icon next to the scanner looked normal except that it had a yellow exclamation point on it. What should Hannah have the user do to correct the most likely problem with the scanner?

❍ A. Manually assign resources for the device, because it is having a resource conflict with another device.

❍ B. Remove the device from the system and do not try to use it again. Devices that show this icon are incompatible with Windows 2000 and should not be used.

❍ C. Install the device drivers from the installation disks or from files downloaded from the manufacturer's Web site.

❍ D. Enable the device for use in the current hardware profile.

Answer C is correct. The best course of action is to install the device drivers either from the setup disks or from files downloaded from the manufacturer's Web site. Devices that display this icon are typically not enabled due to missing or corrupted drivers. Manually assigning resources to the device will not correct the situation and is not possible because the device is not currently using any resources. Thus, answer A is incorrect. Devices that are experiencing a resource conflict display the yellow question mark with a red X, and devices that are disabled show either a normal icon with a red X (disabled by the user) or a normal icon with a yellow exclamation point (disabled by Windows). In this case, the device is displaying a normal icon with a yellow exclamation point; thus answers B and D are incorrect.

Question 3

You are training a new help desk support worker. During the course of your discussions, the topic of digitally signed device drivers comes up. When asked about why digitally signed device drivers are important, what will you not tell your new employee because it is not true?

❍ A. Digitally signed device drivers have passed rigorous testing by the WHQL and therefore should provide a high degree of reliability.

❍ B. Digitally signed device drivers are protected against changes to the driver files since signing by the manufacturer.

❍ C. Digitally signed device drivers are the only type of driver files that are found on the Windows Update Web site or Windows 2000 CD-ROMs.

❍ D. Digitally signed device drivers can't be installed unless a certificate authority has been set up on your network.

Answer D is correct. The other three statements are true concerning digitally signed device drivers. Because the certificate used to sign the file is traceable to a third-party certificate authority, such as VeriSign, there is no need for any further certificate services to be in place. If you wanted to issue digitally signed drivers to your customers, you would need a certificate authority in place on your network, preferably with a root certificate issued by a third party. When a driver has been digitally signed, it has been certified to pass the rigorous testing done by the WHQL. Thus, answer A is incorrect. By digitally signing a driver file, it is protected against all changes since it was signed. Thus, answer B is incorrect. You will only find digitally signed drivers on the Windows Update Web site or the Windows 2000 CD-ROM, thus answer C is incorrect.

Question 4

Austin is using Device Manager to gather information about a particular server in his company. Which of the following items will he be able to gather information on using Device Manager? [Check all correct answers.]

❑ A. Resource settings for a specific device

❑ B. A list of all interrupts currently being used on the computer

❑ C. The status of a particular device, such as enabled or disabled

❑ D. Information about specific drivers installed for a particular device

Answers A, B, C, and D are correct. Using Device Manager, Austin will be able to gather all this information and more.

Question 5

Chris is an administrator for her organization. Two of her servers have hardware devices that recently have had updates issued for their drivers. Where can Chris go to install the updated device drivers?

- ❍ A. System Information
- ❍ B. Device Manager
- ❍ C. Add/Remove Programs applet of Control Panel
- ❍ D. Services MMC snap-in

Answer B is correct. Chris can install the new device drivers from Device Manager. To install the new drivers, she must right-click the device to be updated and select Properties. She then must click the Driver tab and click Update Driver. The System Information utility allows her to quickly determine many facts about your computer, but will not help her install an updated driver. Thus, answer A is incorrect. The Add/Remove Programs applet is used for installing programs and configuring Windows components, not for installing drivers. Thus, answer C is incorrect. The Services MMC snap-in is used to configure and control the services running on a computer, not to install drivers. Thus, answer D is incorrect.

Question 6

Andrea recently acquired a new modem for her Windows 2000 computer. The new modem is not Plug and Play compatible. How will Andrea go about installing the new hardware device on her computer?

- ❍ A. Use Device Manager to install the new hardware device.
- ❍ B. Use the Phone and Modem Options applet of the Control Panel.
- ❍ C. Install the device into the computer. Windows 2000 will detect and automatically install the device the next time it is started.
- ❍ D. Use the Add/Remove Hardware applet of the Control Panel.

Answer D is correct. Non-Plug and Play hardware must be added via the Add/Remove Hardware applet of the Control Panel. All drivers to be installed should be Windows 2000 compliant. Device Manager will not assist in installing new hardware directly. Thus, answer A is incorrect. The Phone and Modem Options applet of the Control Panel can be used to configure dialing rules and modem settings after a modem has been successfully installed. Thus, answer B is incorrect. Only Plug and Play hardware can be installed physically and have Windows 2000 automatically install and configure the device and drivers. Thus, answer C is incorrect.

Question 7

Which of the following driver signing behaviors will not prompt the user for action when installing new device drivers and could lead to system instabilities?

❍ A. Ignore

❍ B. Block

❍ C. Silent

❍ D. Quiet

Answer A is correct. When configured for Ignore, Windows 2000 ignores and silently installs all drivers regardless of their digital signature status. This could allow unsigned drivers to be installed on a computer and subsequently lead to problems such as lockups or instability. The Block behavior automatically blocks all unsigned drivers and does not display or prompt for feedback to the user. Thus, answer B is incorrect. Quiet and Silent are not valid driver signing behavior options. Thus, answers C and D are incorrect.

Question 8

Andrea noticed that her tape drive backup unit stopped responding last night when she tried to use it. When she asks you for help, you instruct her to open Device Manager and report to you the icon displayed next to the tape drive unit. She tells you that a yellow question mark with a red X is next to the device. What should you do to correct the problem?

❍ A. Manually assign system resource settings to the tape drive because it is obviously experiencing a conflict.

❍ B. Attempt to reinstall the device driver because it might have become corrupted.

❍ C. Enable the device because someone has manually disabled it.

❍ D. Replace the tape drive because it has become faulty.

Answer B is correct. In most cases, when a yellow question mark with a red X is displayed, there is a problem with the drivers. The drivers might not be installed or might be incorrectly configured. A resource conflict is indicated by normal icon with a yellow exclamation point, thus answer A is incorrect. A device that is manually disabled will have a normal icon with a red X, which is not the case. Thus, answer C is incorrect. A faulty tape drive would most likely not give any indication in Device Manager. Thus, answer D is incorrect.

Question 9

Jeff is the administrator of a Windows 2000 network. One of Jeff's critical file servers just experienced a sudden failure of its network adapter. While Jeff waits for the delivery of a new network adapter from the manufacturer, he takes the network adapter out of an old server sitting in storage and installs it in the critical file server. When Jeff restarts the server, he sees that the network adapter he just installed is not recognized by Windows 2000 as being Plug and Play. What must Jeff do to get the newly installed network adapter operating so he can get the file server back on the network?

❍ A. Jeff will not be able to get this adapter working because no non–Plug and Play devices are supported under Windows 2000.

❍ B. Jeff should download a BIOS upgrade for the adapter, which will make it Plug and Play compatible. Then he must restart the server.

❍ C. Jeff should go to the Internet, download a Windows 2000 compatible driver for the adapter, and manually install it through the Hardware Wizard.

❍ D. Jeff should go to the Internet, download a Windows 2000 compatible driver for the adapter, and manually install it through Device Manager.

Answer C is correct. Jeff needs a driver for this non–Plug and Play device. If he can obtain one, Windows 2000 will allow him to install it. When he gets the driver, he will go to the Hardware Wizard to install it. If he has time, it would be advisable for Jeff to check for this network card on the HCL to ensure that, although it's not Plug and Play compatible, Microsoft certifies it for reliable use with Windows 2000. Non–Plug and Play devices can still be used in Windows 2000; they require that an administrator configure their resources manually. Thus, answer A is incorrect. Flashing the BIOS on the network adapter will not make it Plug and Play compatible. Thus, answer B is incorrect. Although Device Manager allows you to do many things, you cannot use it to install non–Plug and Play devices. Thus, answer D is incorrect.

Question 10

Rick is the network administrator of a small Windows 2000 network consisting of 5 Windows 2000 servers and 45 Windows 2000 Professional clients. He is currently operating in a peer-to-peer workgroup. Every week, Rick must reinstall two or three of his Windows 2000 client computers due to sudden corruption and instability of the operating system. Rick is certain that the problems are created by users who are installing unsigned drivers for their hardware, thus creating instabilities and system failures. What can Rick do to prevent all unsigned drivers from being installed on his Windows 2000 clients, regardless of which user is logged in to the computer?

❍ A. Rick should configure a Group Policy Object that sets driver signing to Ignore, link it to the OU that houses his Windows 2000 Professional clients, and then refresh Group Policy on his network.

❍ B. Rick should log on to each computer using his administrative account and configure driver signing to Ignore. He should select to apply this setting to all users of the computer.

❍ C. Rick should log on to each computer using his administrative account and configure driver signing to Block. He should select to apply this setting to all users of the computer.

❍ D. Rick should remove all of his users from the Users group and make them members of the Guest group.

Answer C is correct. Because Rick's network is operating as a workgroup and not using Active Directory, Rick needs to configure the settings for driver signing locally on each computer from the System applet of the Control Panel. Rick does not have Active Directory on his network and configuring the Ignore setting would not accomplish the goal if he did have AD, thus answer A is incorrect. Configuring driver signing to Ignore does not prevent users from installing unsigned drivers. Thus, answer B is incorrect. Placing all users into the Guest group will cause more problems than it fixes, including severely hampering Rick's users from being able to carry out all of the normal daily tasks that they need to get done. Thus, answer D is incorrect.

Need to Know More?

Russel, Charlie, and Sharon Crawford. *Windows 2000 Server Administrator's Companion*, Microsoft Press, January, 2000, ISBN 1572318198.

Stanek, William R. *Windows 2000 Administrator's Pocket Companion*, Microsoft Press, January, 2000, ISBN 0735608318.

Windows 2000 Deployment Guide at `http://www.microsoft.com/windows2000/techinfo/reskit/dpg/default.asp`

Windows 2000 Resource Kits online at `http://www.microsoft.com/windows2000/techinfo/reskit/en-us/default.asp`. Also available in print; ISBN 1572318082 (Windows 2000 Professional) and ISBN 1572318058 (Windows 2000 Server).

Managing, Monitoring, and Optimizing System Performance, Reliability, and Availability

Terms you'll need to understand

✓ System Monitor

✓ Recovery Console

✓ Safe Mode

✓ System State

✓ Last Known Good Configuration

✓ Emergency Repair Disk (ERD)

✓ Performance MMC

Techniques you'll need to master

✓ Managing processes using Task Manager

✓ Starting, stopping, and assigning priorities to processes

✓ Monitoring system performance using the Performance tool

✓ Backing up and recovering user data using Windows 2000 Backup

✓ Backing up and recovering System State data

✓ Using Safe Mode

✓ Installing and using the Recovery Console

Introduction

Windows 2000 Server provides numerous tools to perform the common tasks of managing and monitoring the server. In addition, there are also a number of new tools that have been added to assist in system recovery. In this chapter, we look at the commonly used tools to manage your Windows 2000 Server, such as Task Manager and Performance Monitor. Then we explore some of the new system recovery features, including Safe Mode and the Recovery Console. These are areas that are very likely to be covered on the exam.

Managing, Monitoring, and Optimizing System Performance

A large part of the day-to-day tasks of an administrator is the management and monitoring of servers and the applications that are running on them. Let's start this section by looking at some of the utilities that are included in Windows 2000 to make the administrator's job easier. The system performance tools we discuss are as follows:

- Task Manager
- System Monitor
- Performance Logs and Alerts

Task Manager

The Task Manager utility is included in Windows 2000 to give the administrator a way to monitor and manage the state of currently running applications and processes. In addition, Task Manager also provides the administrator with a summarized view of the basic system resources that are in use.

Task Manager can be used to monitor the state of active applications, including a real-time view of the system resources assigned to each application. Task Manager also allows you to observe applications that have stopped responding and terminate them.

Task Manager can be started several ways, including

- Right-clicking the taskbar and clicking Task Manager on the shortcut menu.
- Pressing Ctrl+Shift+Esc.

➤ Pressing Ctrl+Alt+Del to open the Windows Security dialog box and clicking the Task Manager button.

The Task Manger window has three tabs: Applications, Processes, and Performance.

Applications Tab

The Applications tab, shown in Figure 5.1, displays a list of the currently active applications along with their status—either *Running* or *Not Responding*. The default status for a program is Running; however, there will be times when a program will temporarily display a status of Not Responding. This usually occurs when another program or programs have a higher priority and receive the bulk of the system resources or when an application crashes.

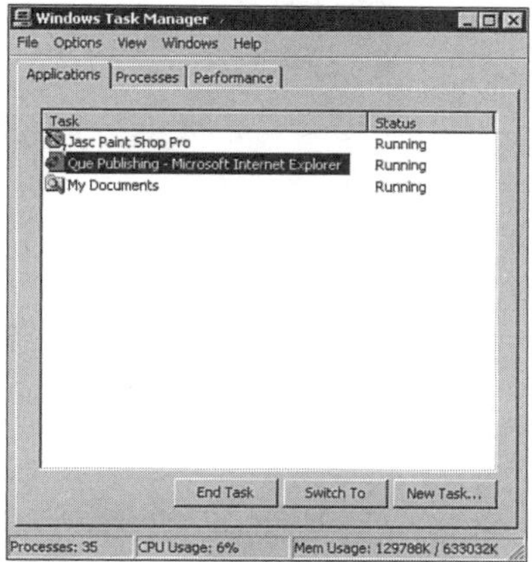

Figure 5.1 The Task Manager Applications tab showing running applications.

If the application that is not responding is not automatically restored to Running status after the other applications have completed, you probably need to manually terminate it. You can do this by right-clicking the application and selecting End Task from the shortcut menu, or clicking the End Task button at the bottom of the Task Manager window. Unfortunately, if the application has any files open, your data will not be saved. Task Manager also allows you to terminate running applications.

There are two methods to start applications using Task Manager:

➤ From the Task Manager menu, select File, New Task (Run).

➤ From the Task Manager Applications tab, click the New Task button in the lower-right corner of the window.

Using either method is identical to using the Run command from the Start menu.

Processes Tab

The Processes tab, shown in Figure 5.2, displays a list of the currently active processes along with the resources that they are using. The default resource columns displayed are CPU Time and Memory Usage. However, you can add additional columns, such as Page Faults, I/O Writes, and Peak Memory Usage, by selecting View, Set Columns from the Task Manager menu.

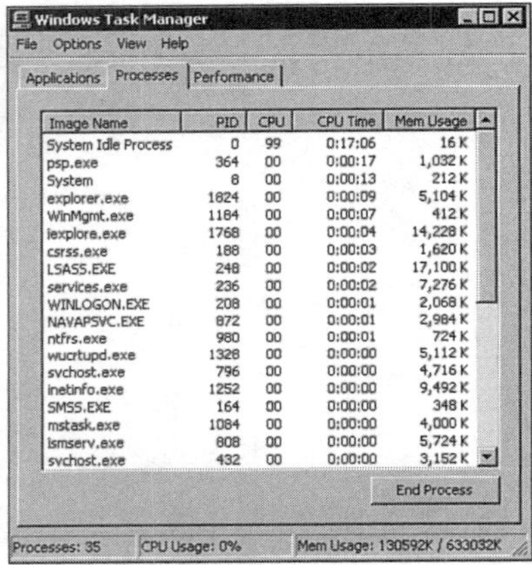

Figure 5.2 The Task Manager Processes tab showing processes sorted by CPU Time.

Using the Processes tab, you can immediately see which processes are using the majority of the system resources. In the default view, you can sort the processes by the following:

- Name (Image Name)
- Process ID (PID)
- CPU percentage used (CPU)
- CPU time used (CPU Time)
- Memory used (Mem Usage)

For example, to sort the processes by the amount of CPU time used, click the CPU Time column heading. This allows you to identify a process that is hogging resources and starving the other processes. This can indicate a process that is having a problem and needs to either be terminated or set to a lower priority.

Windows 2000 distributes processing time to applications using *priority levels*. Priority levels are assigned numbers from 0 to 31. Applications and non-critical operating system functions are assigned levels of 0 to 15, whereas real-time functions, such as the operating system kernel, are assigned levels of 16 to 31. The normal base priority is 8.

If a process is running at the base priority and a real-time process is started, the real-time process will receive more system resources than the process running at base priority. This can sometimes cause the application that the lower priority process is controlled by to show a status of Not Responding on the Task Manager Applications tab.

To keep a real-time process from starving a base process, you can manually increase the priority of a lower-priority process to a higher value. To do this, right-click the lower-priority process in the Processes tab of Task Manger, select Set Priority, and select a higher priority, as shown in Figure 5.3.

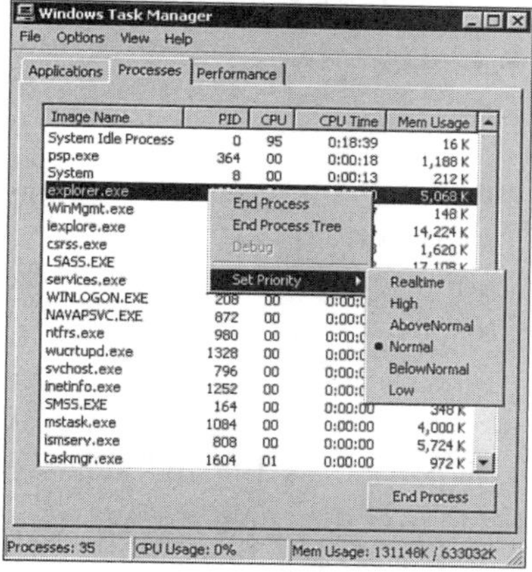

Figure 5.3 The Task Manager Processes tab showing how to change priorities.

Task Manager does not allow you to set a process to a specific number; it only allows you to set priority classes. The priority classes with their default priority numbers are as follows:

- *Realtime*—priority 24
- *High*—priority 13
- *AboveNormal*—priority 9
- *Normal*—priority 8
- *BelowNormal*—priority 7
- *Low*—priority 4

Only an administrator can assign the Realtime priority level to a process.

In some situations, a process must be terminated. You can either terminate a specific process or terminate the process and all other processes that are linked to it. To terminate a specific process, right-click the process entry, in the Processes tab of Task Manager, and select End Process. To terminate that process and any other process that it had started, select *End Process Tree*. For example, if you terminate the process for a word processing program, you can select End Process Tree to additionally terminate the spell checker or grammar processes that were started by the word processor process.

Not all processes can be terminated using Task Manager. The *Kill utility*, included in the Windows 2000 Server Resource Kit, will terminate most processes including services or system processes. Use it carefully, because terminating system processes can cause your server to become unstable.

On a multiprocessor server, there is an additional item on the shortcut menu of the Processes tab called *Set Affinity*. The Set Affinity command allows you to limit a process to a specific CPU. This option should be used with care, because it could potentially decrease the performance of the process.

Performance Tab

The Performance tab, shown in Figure 5.4, displays the CPU and memory usage for your server. The display includes graphs of the current usage, plus additional histograms showing recent usage. Below the graphs are numerical statistics for the CPU and memory usage.

The information shown here can give you a quick overview of the performance characteristics of your server. Any abnormalities that are displayed here indicate that you should investigate further using some of the other Windows 2000 Server utilities.

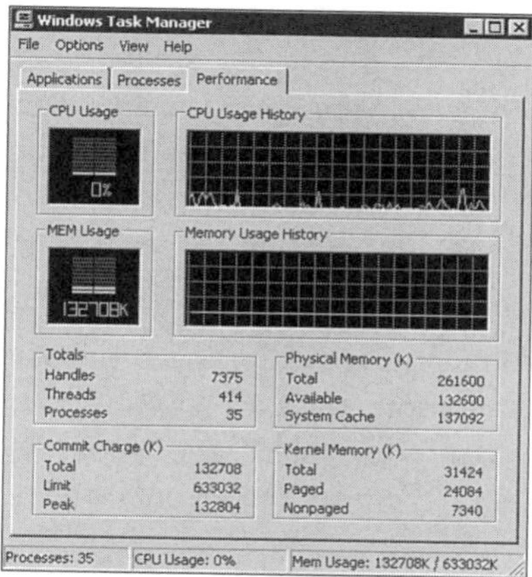

Figure 5.4 The Task Manager Performance tab showing server usage statistics.

Monitoring System Resources

Although Task Manager can give you a quick overview of system performance, there will be situations in which a more thorough investigation is needed. This is where the *Performance* tool comes in handy. The Performance tool is actually made up of two separate Microsoft Management Console (MMC) snap-ins: *System Monitor* and *Performance Logs and Alerts*. The Performance tool is started from the Windows 2000 Start menu. Select Start, Programs, Administrative Tools, Performance. As shown in Figure 5.5, the Performance tool opens with the System Monitor view displayed.

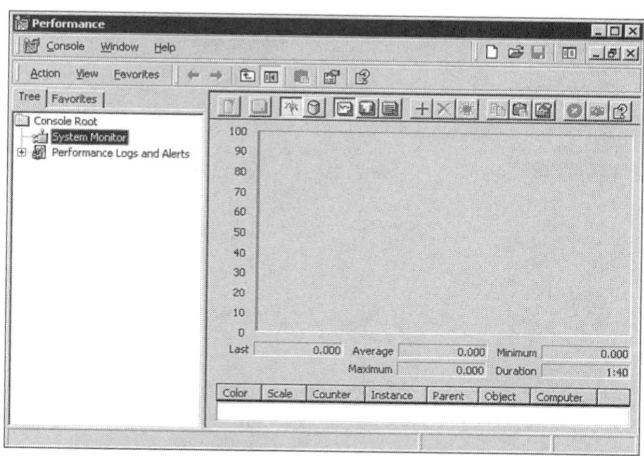

Figure 5.5 The Windows 2000 Performance tool showing the System Monitor view.

System Monitor

The System Monitor snap-in allows you to view real-time performance data contained in the counters from your domain controllers, member servers, or workstations on your network. In addition, System Monitor allows you to review performance data that is stored in a log file created with the Performance Logs and Alerts snap-in.

Windows 2000 is a modular, object-oriented operating system. Each subsystem within Windows 2000 is an object. For example, the CPU is an object, the memory is an object, the storage subsystem is an object, and so on. As your computer performs various tasks, each of these objects generate performance data.

Each object has several monitoring functions called *counters*. Each counter offers insight into a different aspect or function of the object. For example, the memory object has counters that measure % Committed Bytes In Use, Available Bytes, Page Faults/sec, and more. System Monitor takes the readings from these counters and presents the information to you in a human-readable format (numbers or graphs).

In addition, objects can be separated by *instance*. Instance is the terminology used to refer to multiple occurrences of the same type of object, such as in a multiprocessor server. A separate instance exists for each processor.

By default, System Monitor is started without any counters displayed. To add the counters to be monitored, click the "+" button on the System Monitor menu bar. This opens the Add Counters dialog box shown in Figure 5.6.

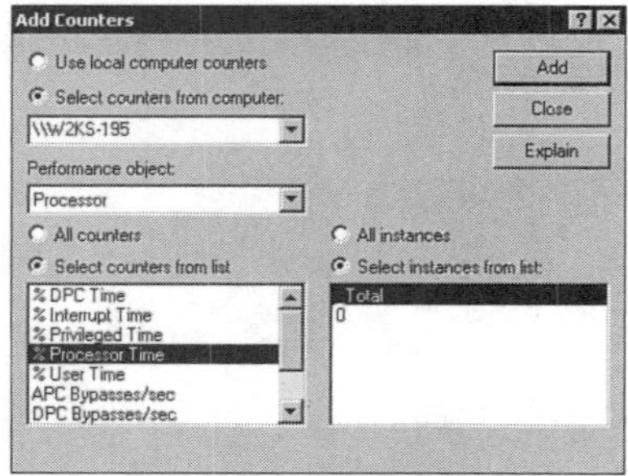

Figure 5.6 The Windows 2000 System Monitor showing the Add Counters dialog box.

In the Add Counters dialog box, you can make choices from several areas to customize your monitoring needs. The choices found on this dialog box are as follows:

- *Computer*—This option allows you to select whether to add counters from the local computer or any remote computer on your network. You add remote computers using their Universal Naming Convention (UNC) computer name.
- *Performance object*—This is a drop-down list that displays all of the objects that are available for monitoring.
- *Counters*—This option allows you to select either all counters or individual counters from a list. Hold down the Shift or Control key and click the mouse to select multiple items.
- *Instance*—If an object has multiple instances, for example, your server has multiple network cards, you can select each individual instance or all instances.

After selecting each counter, click the Add button to add the counter to the System Monitor display. For a description of each counter, highlight the counter and click the Explain button. When finished, click the Close button.

The number of objects that are available for monitoring will vary by system. Most server services and applications, such as DNS, DHCP, and mail servers, will install their own counters that can be used to monitor the performance of those functions.

Each counter can be displayed as a colored line in one of the graph views. Multiple counters from the same system or from remote systems can be viewed simultaneously. Figure 5.7 shows you an example of what one of the graph views, of which there are several, may look like on your system.

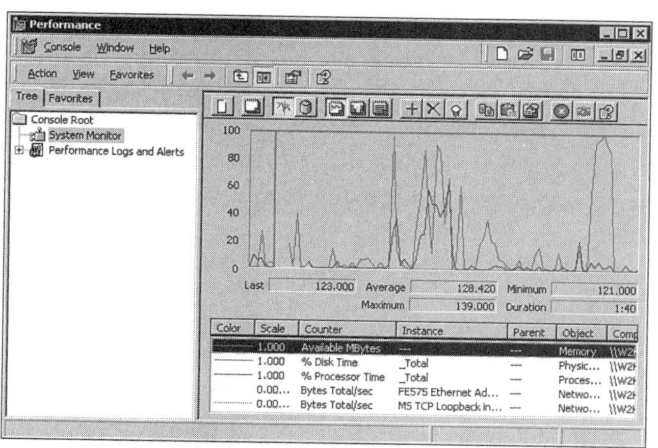

Figure 5.7 The Windows 2000 System Monitor showing server usage counters.

Of all the items you can monitor on a typical server, the objects that you need to monitor closely for performance issues are

- Memory
- Processor
- Physical disk
- Network

These counters provide instant insight into the overall performance on a system. When these counters get too high, it's a good indication of a need to upgrade the system or segment the network.

The Performance Logs and Alerts Snap-In

Although System Monitor provides far more system monitoring information than Task Manager, it still only provides a snapshot view of system performance. To perform a more thorough evaluation of system performance, you need to view the system statistics over a period of time. You can find these statistics in the Performance Logs and Alerts tool located underneath System Monitor in the Performance Tool MMC. The following two sections detail the logging and alert features you can use to capture performance data over an extended time period.

Performance Logs

The Performance Logs and Alerts MMC snap-in allows you to log performance data over a period of time and save it to a log file for later viewing. There are two logging options available: *Counter Logs* and *Trace Logs*. Counter Logs allow you to record data about hardware usage and the activity of system services from local or remote computers. You can configure logging to occur manually or automatically based on a defined schedule. Trace logs record data when certain activity, such as disk I/O or a page fault, occurs. When the event occurs, the provider sends the data to the log service.

The Trace Logs function is rarely used, because the logs can only be read by a custom-developed tool. It will probably not be covered on the exam.

The snap-in allows you to save log data in the following file formats:

- *Text File (CSV)*—Comma-delimited format, for import into spreadsheet or database programs.

- *Text File (TSV)*—Tab-delimited format, for import into spreadsheet or database programs.
- *Binary File*—This is the default for use with the System Monitor snap-in. Data is logged into this file until it reaches the maximum limit. The default maximum file size is 1MB, but this can be changed when you configure settings for the file from the Log Files tab of the Log properties dialog box by clicking the Configure button.
- *Binary Circular File*—Data is logged into this file until it reaches the maximum limit. Then the file is overwritten, starting at the beginning of the file. The default maximum file size is 1MB, but this can be changed when you configure settings for the file from the Log Files tab of the Log properties dialog box by clicking the Configure button.

By making the data available in so many common formats, you have the option of analyzing the data using the default Microsoft tools or importing it into the tool of your choice.

You should take a measurement of your system during its normal operation. By having a *baseline*, you have something to compare counters to when the system experiences problems. Having a baseline comparison provides a quick way to pinpoint problem areas.

The Performance utility allows you to log both on an object basis and a counter basis (see Figure 5.8). This means that you can configure a log to record all the data for an object instead of using individual counters. Therefore, after a log file is recorded, you can select any counter from an object to examine. After you determine what to record, you need to determine two time-related issues: *the measurement interval* and *the length of time to record the log file*. These issues are detailed as follows:

- The *measurement interval* determines how often a performance reading is taken. Too short an interval can produce spurious results and can cause additional workload on your system. Too long an interval might hide performance changes. Although most readings are insignificant, frequent readings can cause significant performance degradations.
- The *length of time over which a log file is recorded* should be long enough to capture all the normal operational activities. This typically means recording a log file for at least a week. A shorter time period might not offer you a complete picture of your system's normal weekly performance.

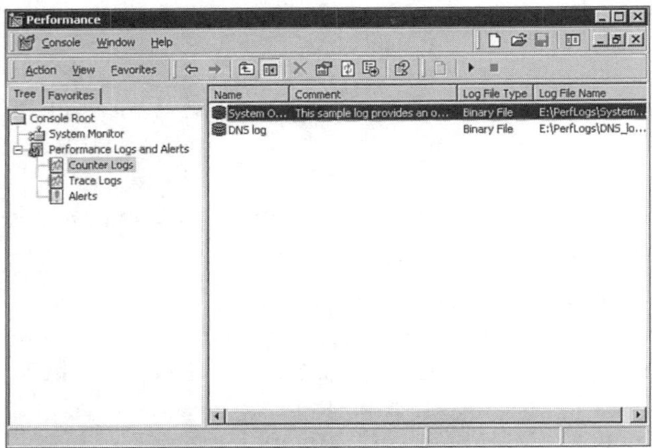

Figure 5.8 The Windows 2000 Performance Logs and Alerts showing Counter logs.

The sample log is defined with the following basic counters:

- Memory Pages/sec
- PhysicalDisk Average Disk Queue Length
- %Processor Time

To create a new counter log

1. Right-click Counter Logs in the left pane of the Performance Logs and Alerts snap-in and select New Log Settings.
2. In the New Log Settings dialog box, enter the name of the new log and click OK.
3. From the General tab of the log properties window, click the Add button.
4. Add the desired counters. The procedure is the same as adding counters to System Monitor.
5. Click the Log Files tab.
6. On the Log Files tab, enter the desired log file name, type, and location. Change the maximum log file size if desired. See Figure 5.9.

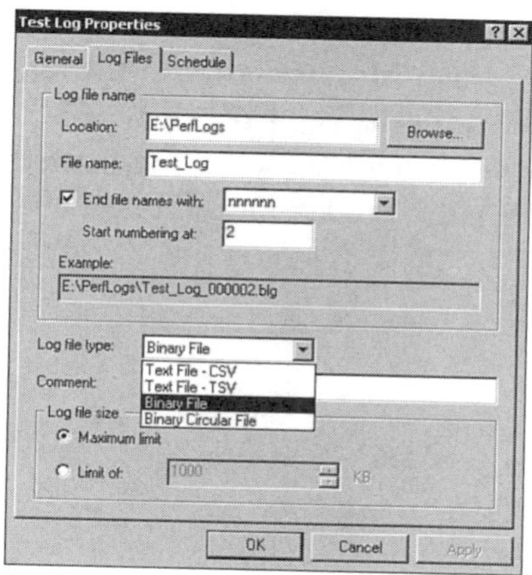

Figure 5.9 The Windows 2000 Performance Logs and Alerts snap-in showing Counter Log file configuration.

7. Click the Schedule tab. On the Schedule tab, you can select the start and stop times for logging or select to manually start and stop the log. See Figure 5.10.

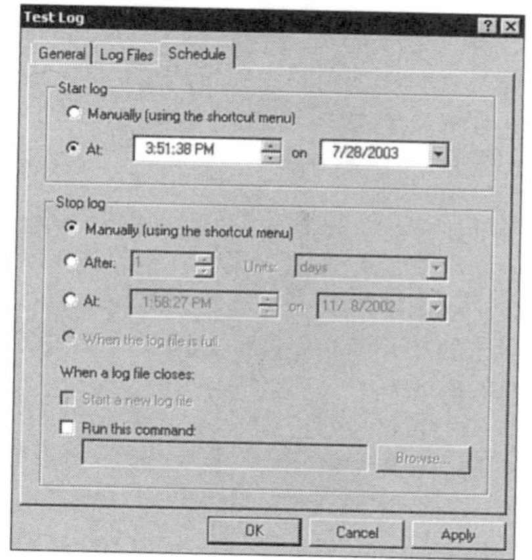

Figure 5.10 The Windows 2000 Performance Logs and Alerts showing Counter Log schedule.

8. Click OK to save the log.

If you selected to manually start the counter log, you can start it by right-clicking the log entry in the right pane of the Performance Logs and Alerts snap-in and selecting Start. The icon for the log will be green when running, red when stopped.

After you have recorded data in your log file, you can view it within System Monitor. To open your log file, select the System Monitor entry in the left pane of the MMC. Next, right-click anywhere in the right pane and select Properties. In the System Monitor Properties dialog box, select the Source tab. On the Source tab (see Figure 5.11), click the Browse button to browse for the log file.

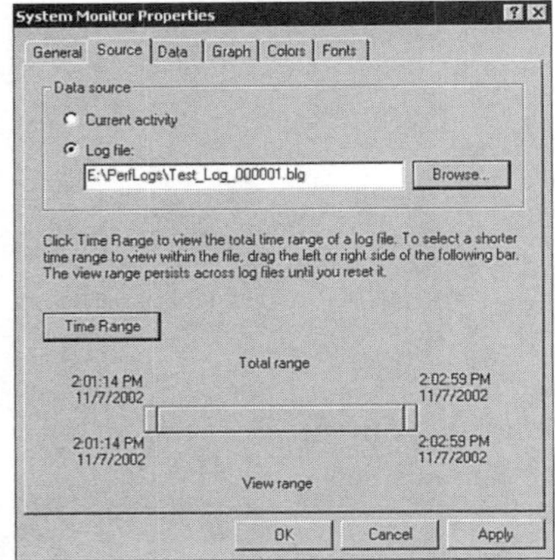

Figure 5.11 The System Monitor Properties dialog box showing the Source tab.

You can click the Time Range button to adjust the times that you want to view within the log file. Click OK when finished.

Performance Alerts

The Alerts container is used to define threshold alerts. These can be used with real-time measurements or with historical log files. An alert is issued when a specific counter crosses a defined threshold value. When this occurs, a trigger event is initiated.

Creating an Alert is similar to configuring a Counter Log. Right-click the Alerts entry in the left pane of the Performance Logs and Alerts snap-in and select New Alert Settings. In the New Alert Settings dialog box, enter a name for the alert. In the properties dialog box, you can select the desired counters and the value threshold. If you click the Action tab, shown in Figure 5.12, you can select the action to take when the threshold is reached.

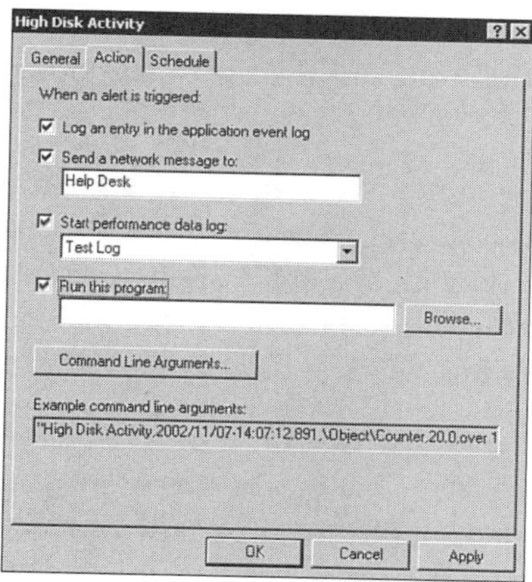

Figure 5.12 Alert properties showing the Action tab.

The options available are

- *Log an entry in the application event log*—If a threshold is reached, Windows 2000 will create an entry in this log and you can view it in the Application Event Log found in the Event Viewer.
- *Send a network message to*—This allows you to send a message to a user via the Messenger service.
- *Start performance data log*—This starts logging to a predefined Counter Log. This is useful if you are trying to see what happens to system performance when a specific event occurs.
- *Run this program*—This can be any program that can be run from a command line. For example, it might be a program that performs some type of system maintenance, such as compressing files.

Alerts are most often used to monitor systems in real-time. You can set an alert to notify you when a specific event occurs. Some of the conditions that you might want to configure an alert for are low disk space, swap file usage, and task queues for network cards and CPUs. Any of these items can point to a current or potential system problem.

Optimizing System Resources

Properly tuning and optimizing a server sometimes can appear to be more of an art than a science. In reality, this is an oversimplification because accurately measuring performance on a Windows system really requires a little art and a little science. In the final analysis, however, the best tuning and optimizing has far more to do with attention to detail than with any other skill.

Before you can optimize a server, you must understand its characteristics, including how it operates under a normal load, and what areas are stressed when the load increases. This has a lot to do with the application type and load of the server. For example, a Web server will react differently to a load condition than a server that is hosting Terminal Services.

The first step in optimization should be to establish a *baseline*. To establish a baseline for a server, you should log performance data for the server when it is under a normal load for an established period of time. You will typically want to log usually at least a day, and sometimes even a week or more. This will allow you to observe the various components of your server under "normal" load and stress circumstances. You should have a large enough sample so that you can observe all of the highs and lows and determine what figures are averages for your server.

After you establish this baseline, the next step is to observe your server under load, and identify any components that are limiting the overall performance of your server. As we mentioned earlier in this chapter, the main four components that cause the majority of the bottlenecks in a server are memory, disk, processor, and the network interface. The following four sections discuss optimizing resources associated with these vital server objects.

Optimizing Memory Usage

The Windows 2000 memory system uses a combination of physical memory and a swap file stored on the hard disk to provide space for the applications to run. Because accessing data from a hard disk is many times slower than accessing it from memory, you want to minimize the frequency that the server has to swap data to the hard drive. This can usually be accomplished simply by adding more physical memory.

Some counters to watch to monitor memory performance are

- *Memory: Pages Input/sec*—When this counter remains at a low value (2 or less), it indicates that all operations are occurring within physical RAM. This means that paging is not occurring and therefore is not the cause of the performance degradation.
- *Memory: Cache Faults/sec*—Indicates how frequently the system is unable to locate data in the cache and must search for it on disk. If this number grows steadily over time, your system is headed into constant thrashing.

This means every bit of information required by the system must be retrieved directly from the disk. This condition usually indicates an insufficient amount of RAM on your system. However, it can also be caused by running a combination of apps—such as a read-intensive application, typically a database that is performing a large number of queries—at the same time as an application that is using an excessive amount of memory. In this case, you can either schedule the applications to not run at the same time, or move one of them to another system.

- *Memory: Page Faults/sec*—Similar to cache faults, except that it also measures faults when a requested memory page is in use by another application. If this counter averages above 200 for low-end systems or above 600 for high-end systems, excess paging is occurring.
- *Memory: Available Bytes*—Indicates the amount of free memory available for use. If this number is less than 4MB, you do not have sufficient RAM on your system so the system performs excessive paging.
- *Paging File: % Usage Peak*—Indicates the level of paging file usage. If this number nears 100% during normal operations, the maximum size of your paging file is too small, and you probably need more RAM. If you have multiple drives with multiple paging files, be sure to view the Total instance of this counter.

Optimizing the Disk Subsystem

The disk subsystem can be a bottleneck, either directly or indirectly. If the access speed of the disk is slow, it will negatively affect the load time of applications and the read and write time of application data. In addition, because Windows 2000 relies on virtual memory, a slow disk subsystem will indirectly affect memory performance.

Some key performance counters for the disk subsystem are

- *PhysicalDisk: Avg. Disk Queue Length*—Tracks the number of system requests waiting for disk access. The number of queued requests should not exceed double the number of spindles in use. Most drives have only a single spindle, but RAID arrays have more (and Performance Monitor views RAID arrays as a single logical drive). A large number of waiting items indicates that a drive or an array is not operating fast enough to support the system's demands for input and output. When this occurs, you need a faster drive system.
- *PhysicalDisk: % Disk Time*—Represents the percentage of time that the disk is actively handling read and write requests. It is not uncommon for

this counter to regularly hit 100% on active servers. Sustained percentages of 90% or better, however, might indicate that a storage device is too slow. This usually is true when its Avg. Disk Queue Length counter is constantly above 2.

- *PhysicalDisk: Avg. Disk sec/Transfer*—Indicates the average time in seconds of a disk transfer.

Because the very act of recording storage performance data affects system performance, the disk counters on Windows systems are not enabled by default. Before you can monitor hard drive performance, you must turn on the counters that gather statistics for such devices. By default, in Windows 2000 the PhysicalDisk object is automatically enabled. However, the LogicalDisk object must be enabled manually. From the Run dialog box or a command prompt, the following command enables the LogicalDisk counters:

```
diskperf -y
```

After the command is entered, the system must be restarted for the command to take effect.

When recording a log file for the Disk objects, don't record the file to the same drive being measured. You are not recording accurate values because the act of reading the object and writing to the drive adds a significant amount of workload.

Optimizing Processor Usage

The processor is the heart of your server. Most operations in the server are controlled either directly or indirectly by the processor. Most processor bottlenecks are caused by multiple processes running at the same time, requiring more cycles than the processor can deliver efficiently. This can be alleviated by replacing the processor with a faster model or by adding an additional processor in a multiprocessor-capable server.

To identify problems with the processor, monitor the following counters:

- *Processor: % Processor Time*—Indicates the amount of time the CPU spends on non-idle work. It's common for this counter to reach 100% during application launches or kernel-intensive operations (such as SAM synchronization). If this counter remains above 80% for an extended period, however, you should suspect a CPU bottleneck. (There will be an instance of this counter for each processor in a multiprocessor system.)

- *Processor: % Total Processor Time*—Applies only to multiprocessor systems. This counter should be used the same way as the single CPU counter. If any value remains consistently higher than 80%, at least one of your CPUs is a bottleneck.
- *System: Processor Queue Length*—Indicates the number of threads waiting for processor time. A sustained value of 2 or higher for this counter indicates processor congestion. This counter is a snapshot of the time of measurement, not an average value over time.

Optimizing Network Access

Although not as common as a bottleneck, thanks to the preponderance of high-performance 100Mb NICs, there will still be those occasions on which the network card is a bottleneck. This is most likely to occur on Web servers or terminal servers.

To identify performance problems with the network interface, monitor the following counters:

- *Network Interface: Bytes Total/sec*—Indicates the rate at which data is sent to and received by a NIC (including framing characters). Compare this value with the expected capacity of the device. If the highest observed average is less than 75% of the expected value, communication errors or slowdowns might be occurring that limit the NIC's rated speed.
- *Network Interface: Current Bandwidth*—Estimates a NIC's current bandwidth, measured in bits per second (bps). This counter is useful only for NICs with variable bandwidth.
- *Network Interface: Output Queue Length*—Indicates the number of packets waiting to be transmitted by a NIC. If this averages above 2, you are experiencing delays.
- *Network Interface: Packets/sec*—Indicates the number of packets handled by a NIC. Watch this counter over a long interval of constant or normal activity. Sharp declines that occur while the Queue Length remains nonzero can indicate protocol-related or NIC-related problems.

Other network related counters that may be worth monitoring include protocol-specific objects, such as ICMP, IP, TCP, and UDP.

Be sure you understand these common performance counters and their meanings. In addition, know what ranges are normal and what values indicate that a specific hardware component needs to be upgraded.

Windows 2000 Backup

Windows 2000 provides a more advanced backup program than what was included with Windows NT. Windows 2000 Backup allows you to create backup jobs that you can run manually or schedule to run unattended. Unlike the previous NT Server version, NT Server 4, that could only back up to tape, you can now back up to disk, Zip drives, CD-R/RW, or any other media that is available via the Windows 2000 file system. In addition, you can use the backup program to make an Emergency Repair Disk (ERD).

To start the Windows 2000 Backup program, select Start, Programs, Accessories, System Tools, Backup. All of the backup and restore functions can be performed manually or via wizards. The Windows 2000 Backup dialog box is as shown in Figure 5.13.

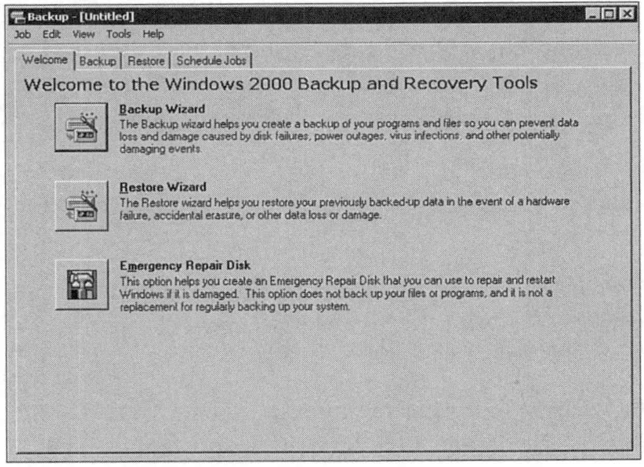

Figure 5.13 Welcome tab of the Backup program showing the buttons to start the Backup Wizard and Restore Wizard, and the Emergency Repair Disk tool.

To back up and restore a Windows 2000 server, you must be a member of the Administrators or the Backup Operators group. If you are not a member of these groups, you will only be able to back up the files that you are the owner of, or that you have one of the following permissions for:

- Read
- Read & Execute
- Modify
- Full Control

The backup utility allows you to back up a single file, a folder, a drive, or multiple drives. Although the Windows 2000 backup program will not back up files that are in use, many third-party backup programs are available that will: Refer to the "Need to Know More" section at the end of this chapter for additional information.

Types of Backups

There are five backup options in Windows 2000. Each type varies as to what is backed up and whether or not the archive bit is set. The archive bit is a file attribute that is turned on when a file is created or modified. It is cleared whenever a file is successfully backed up. It is used to let the backup software know what files need to be backed up based on whether the file has just been created or whether modifications to a previously backed up file have happened since the last backup.

Normal

A normal backup is used to back up all of the files and folders that you select, regardless of the setting of the archive bit. It then changes the archive bit of the files to show that they were backed up. The disadvantage of a normal backup is that it takes longer than some of the other backup types, because it backs up all of the files and folders. However, it does have the advantage of only requiring a single media (or set of media) for a full restore. To minimize backup time, the normal backup is typically used with incremental or differential backups.

For a typical weekly backup schedule and the differences in the media required for a full restore, consult Tables 5.1 and 5.2.

You should be familiar with the various types of backups, when each one should be used, and what data will be restored during a recovery procedure.

Table 5.1 Weekly Backup Schedule Using Normal and Incremental Backups

Day	Backup Type	Media Required for Full Restore
Monday	Normal	Monday
Tuesday	Incremental	Monday + Tuesday
Wednesday	Incremental	Monday + Tuesday + Wednesday
Thursday	Incremental	Monday + Tuesday + Wednesday + Thursday
Friday	Incremental	Monday + Tuesday + Wednesday + Thursday + Friday

Table 5.2 Weekly Backup Schedule Using Normal and Differential Backups

Day	Backup Type	Media Required for Full Restore
Monday	Normal	Monday
Tuesday	Differential	Monday + Tuesday
Wednesday	Differential	Monday + Wednesday
Thursday	Differential	Monday + Thursday
Friday	Differential	Monday + Friday

Copy

A copy backup is used to back up the desired files and folders. It does not read or change the archive bit. A copy backup is typically used to make an archival copy of data and does not interrupt your current backup set.

Daily

A daily backup is used to back up only the files and folders that have been created or modified on that day. It does not read or change the archive bit. A daily backup is typically used to make a quick snapshot of the daily activity; this is useful when you need to perform a task on the server and want to have a current backup available.

Differential

A differential backup is used to back up only the files and folders that have been created or modified since the last normal or incremental backup. It does not change the archive bit. However, it reads the archive bit to determine which files need to be backed up. A differential backup is typically used between instances of a normal backup. For example, if you perform a normal backup on Monday, you can perform differential backups the rest of the week. The differential backup will take longer and longer each day, because it will be backing up all of the files and folders that have been created and modified since the last normal backup. A differential backup has the advantage that it takes less time than a normal backup, but when you perform a full restore, it will require the media for both the normal backup and the differential backup.

Incremental

An incremental backup is used to back up only the files and folders that have been created or modified since the last normal or incremental backup. It reads the archive bit to determine which files need to be backed up. It then changes the archive bit of the files that were backed up so that the next time the backup program is run, the file will not be backed up again unless it was changed. An incremental backup is typically used between instances of a normal backup. Unlike the differential backup, the backup times typically do not get longer each day, because the incremental backup only backs up the files and folders that were modified since the last incremental backup. An incremental backup has the advantage of taking less time than a normal backup, but when you perform a full restore, it will require the media for the normal backup and all of the incremental backups that were performed since the normal backup, which is time consuming, depending on how many incremental backups you must restore.

System State Backups

All backups of a Windows 2000 server should include the System State data. For all Windows 2000 operating systems, the System State data includes

- Registry
- COM+ Class Registration Database
- System Boot Files

For Windows 2000 Server, the System State data also includes the *Certificate Services database* (if the server is operating as a certificate server). If the server is a domain controller, the System State data also includes *Active Directory services* database and the *SYSVOL directory*. Due to their interdependencies, these components cannot be backed up or restored separately.

It is important to back up the System State data for each server and domain controller. The System State backup from one server or domain controller cannot be restored to a different server or domain controller.

There are two types of System State backup/restores, *Local* and *Remote*. A Local backup/restore is used when the backup media is hosted on the server that is being restored. A Remote restore is performed when the backup media is located on another machine. The Windows 2000 Backup program is only capable of backing up and restoring the System State data on the server that is hosting the backup media.

To back up System State data on a Windows 2000 server, from the Backup tab in the Windows 2000 Backup program, select the System State check box, as shown in Figure 5.14.

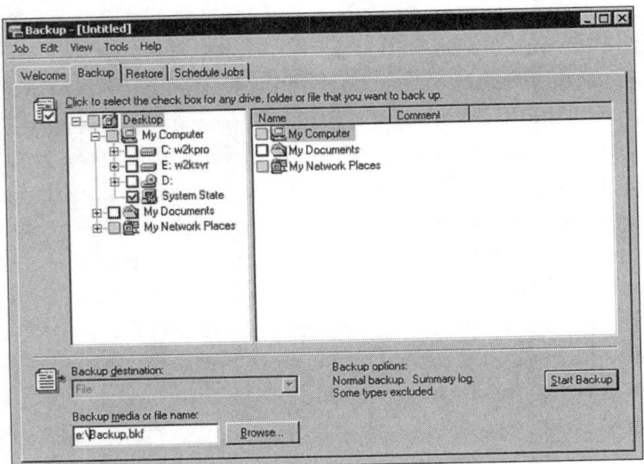

Figure 5.14 Backup tab of the Backup program showing the System State data check box selected.

The System State data can be backed up separately or as part of a complete server backup. To restore the System State data on a Windows 2000 Server (not a domain controller), perform the following steps:

1. Start the Windows 2000 Backup program by selecting Start, Programs, Accessories, System Tools, Backup.
2. Select the Restore tab.
3. Select the desired media.
4. Select the System State check box.
5. Click the Start Restore button.
6. After the restore completes, restart the server.

For information on how to restore System State data on a domain controller, see the section titled "Recover System State data by Using Directory Services Restore Mode" later in this chapter.

Safe Mode

Windows 2000 includes an option called *Safe Mode*. This is a recovery tool that was carried over from the Windows 9x product line that allows you to start your system with a minimal set of device drivers and services loaded.

Safe Mode is useful for those situations in which you load a new driver or software program or make a configuration change that results in an inability to start your system. You can use Safe Mode to start your system and remove the driver or software that is causing the problem.

To get into Safe Mode, restart your server and press F8 on the boot menu screen when you see the prompt, "Please Select The Operating System To Start." The following options are available on the Windows 2000 Advanced Options menu (as shown in Figure 5.15):

- *Safe Mode*—This option starts Windows 2000 with the basic drivers for the mouse, video, monitor, mass storage, and keyboard.
- *Safe Mode with Networking*—This option starts Windows 2000 with the basic drivers, plus the network drivers.
- *Safe Mode with Command Prompt*—This option starts Windows 2000 with the basic drivers and opens a command window instead of the desktop.
- *Enable Boot Logging*—This option starts Windows 2000 normally, but logs a list of all device drivers, services, and their status that the system attempts to load to %systemroot%\ntblog.txt. This is a good option to select to diagnose system startup problems.
- *Enable VGA Mode*—This option starts Windows 2000 normally, but forces it to load the basic VGA driver. This option is useful for recovering from the installation of a bad video driver.
- *Last Known Good Configuration*—The option starts Windows 2000 with the contents of the Registry from the last time that the user logged on to the system. This is helpful when recovering from a configuration error. When this option is selected, any configuration changes made after the last logon will be lost.
- *Directory Services Restore Mode*—This option is used to restore the Active Directory database and SYSVOL on a domain controller. It will only be listed on a domain controller.

- *Debugging Mode*—This options starts Windows 2000 normally, but sends debugging information over a serial cable to another computer. This option is for software developers.
- *Boot Normally*—This option bypasses the menu options and starts Windows 2000 without any modifications.

```
Windows 2000 Advanced Options Menu
Please select an option:

    Safe Mode
    Safe Mode with Networking
    Safe Mode with Command Prompt

    Enable Boot Logging
    Enable VGA Mode
    Last Known Good Configuration
    Directory Services Restore Mode (Windows 2000 domain controllers only)
    Debugging Mode

    Boot Normally
    Return to OS Choices Menu

Use ↑ and ↓ to move the highlight to your choice.
Press Enter to choose.
```

Figure 5.15 Windows 2000 Advanced Options menu showing Safe Mode option selected.

If your startup problem does not appear when you start the system in Safe Mode, you can eliminate the default settings and minimum device drivers as problems. Using Safe Mode, you can diagnose the problem and remove the faulty driver, or restore the proper configuration.

If your server will not start properly using Safe Mode, you might have to boot to the Recovery Console, or restore your system files using the Emergency Repair Disk (ERD).

Recover System State Data by Using Directory Services Restore Mode

On a domain controller, the Active Directory files are restored as part of the System State. The System State on a domain controller consists of

- Active Directory (NTDS)
- The boot files
- The COM+ Class Registration database

- The Registry
- The system volume (SYSVOL)

The individual components cannot be backed up or restored separately; they can only be handled as a unit.

When a single domain controller fails, and the other domain controllers are still operational, it can be repaired and the data restored using a current backup tape. After Active Directory is restored, the domain controller will replicate with the other domain controllers to synchronize any changes that were made on the other domain controllers since the backup tape was created. This process is called a *non-authoritative restore*.

Windows 2000 assigns an Update Sequence Number (USN) to each object created in Active Directory. This allows Active Directory to track updates and prevents it from replicating objects that have not changed. When you perform a normal file restore of the Active Directory, all the data that is restored is considered "old" data and will not be replicated to the other domain controllers. This data is considered to be *non-authoritative* because it is considered to be old and out of date because the objects have lower USNs. All of the objects contained in the other copies of Active Directory on the other domain controllers that have higher USNs than the objects in the restored data will be replicated to the restored domain controller so that all copies of Active Directory will be consistent. A non-authoritative restore is the default restore mode for Active Directory and is used most often.

However, in specific circumstances, it will be necessary to perform an authoritative restore. When performing an authoritative restore, the USNs on the objects in the copy of the Active Directory database that is restored to the domain controller are reset to a number higher than the current USNs so that all of the data that is restored is no longer considered old data. This allows the objects in the restore job to overwrite newer objects on the other domain controllers.

When Active Directory is in a corrupted state on all of the domain controllers, it will be necessary to restore AD from tape and force the replication of the restored data to all of the other domain controllers. This type of operation is called an *authoritative restore*. An authoritative restore will cause the data that is restored from tape to overwrite the corrupted data that is stored on all of the domain controllers. This is accomplished by changing the USNs on all of the objects in the AD database to a higher number so that they are considered to be authoritative, and will overwrite the lower numbered objects.

An authoritative restore cannot be performed while a domain controller is online—the domain controller must be restarted into Directory Services Restore Mode, which is an option available in Safe Mode. To perform an authoritative restore, perform the following steps:

1. Reboot the server.
2. From the boot menu, when you see the message, "Please Select The Operating System To Start," press the F8 key.
3. From the Advanced Options menu, select Directory Services Restore Mode. Press Enter.
4. On the Windows 2000 Boot menu, select the operating system to start and press Enter.
5. The server will boot into Directory Services Repair Mode. From the Windows 2000 logon screen, log on using the Directory Services Administrator password. This is not the normal Administrator password. This is the password that was entered during the DCPROMO procedure.
6. Start the Windows 2000 Backup program by selecting Start, Programs, Accessories, System Tools, Backup.
7. Select the Restore tab.
8. Select the desired media.
9. Select the System State check box.
10. Click the Start Restore button.
11. When the Confirm Restore dialog box appears, click the Advanced button.
12. From the Advanced Restore Options dialog box shown in Figure 5.16, select the When Restoring Replicated Data Sets, Mark the Restored Data as the Primary Data for All Replicas check box, and click the OK button.
13. Click the OK button in the Confirm Restore dialog box.
14. After the restore completes, restart the server.

An authoritative restore is used most often in situations where an Active Directory object such as a user, group, or organizational unit (OU) has been accidentally deleted and needs to be restored.

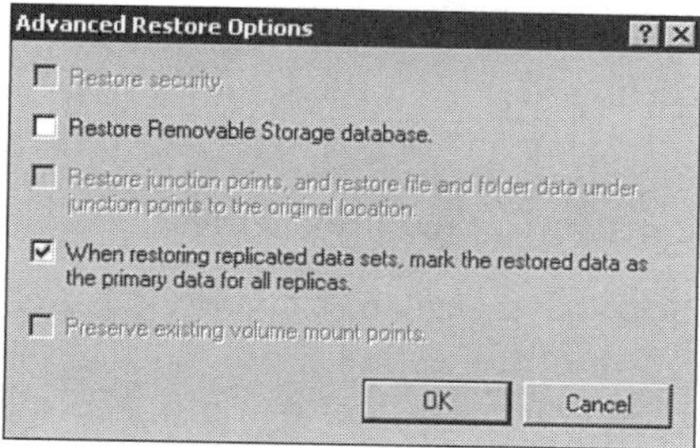

Figure 5.16 Advanced Restore Options dialog box showing authoritative restore selection.

If an Active Directory object is accidentally deleted, it is possible to restore the object from a backup tape by performing a partial authoritative restore. This is accomplished by restoring from the last backup before the object was deleted. The procedure to perform the restore is very similar to the full Active Directory authoritative restore that was shown in the previous section.

When performing a partial authoritative restore, it is very important to only restore the specific item that needs to be restored. If the entire Active Directory is restored, you could inadvertently overwrite newer objects. For example, the naming context of Active Directory contains the passwords for all of the computer accounts and trust relationships. These passwords are automatically changed approximately every seven days. If the existing values are overwritten by the restore, and the passwords have been renegotiated because that backup was created, the computer accounts will be locked out of the domain and the trust relationships will be dropped. For more information see article Q216243, "Impact of Authoritative Restore on Trusts and Computer Accounts" in the Microsoft Knowledge Base.

To restore a deleted Active Directory object:

1. Perform steps 1 through 10 of the previous procedure to restore the AD database from tape.
2. When the Confirm Restore dialog box appears, click OK.
3. After the restore has completed, reboot the domain controller. From the boot menu, when you see the message, "Please Select The Operating System To Start," press the F8 key.
4. From the Advanced Options menu, select Directory Services Restore Mode. Press Enter.
5. On the Windows 2000 Boot menu, select the operating system to start and press Enter.
6. The server will boot into Directory Services Repair Mode. From the Windows 2000 logon screen, log on using the Directory Services

Administrator password. This is not the normal Administrator password. This is the password that was entered during the DCPROMO procedure.

7. Open a command window and type **ntdsutil**, then press Enter.
8. At the command prompt, type **authoritative restore**, then press Enter.

To restore an object, you will need to know its common name (CN), the organization unit (OU), and the domain (DC) that the object was located in. For example, to restore the ABC St. Louis User OU, in the abc.com domain, you would enter the following command:

```
Restore Subtree "OU=ABC St. Louis User,DC=abc,DC=com"
```

This command restores all of the objects that have been deleted in the ABC St. Louis User OU since the backup tape was created.

To restore a user, the command would be

```
Restore Subtree "CN=JDoe,OU=ABC St. Louis User,DC=ABC,DC=com"
```

To restore a printer, the command would be

```
Restore Subtree"CN=DeskJet 3rdfloor,OU=ABC St. Louis User,DC=abc,DC=com"
```

After the command has completed, enter **quit** and reboot the domain controller. The domain controller will now replicate the restored Active Directory object to the other domain controllers.

The following are the default Active Directory folders shown in the root of the Active Directory Users and Computers MMC:

- Users
- Builtin
- Computers

These folders are actually containers and not Organizational Units. When referencing these containers, you have to use the CN= attribute and *not* the OU=.

Recovery Console

For those situations in which the tools and methods available via Safe Mode are not enough to recover from a server failure, Microsoft has provided an additional tool called the Recovery Console. The Recovery Console is a DOS-like command-line interface in which you can perform a limited set of commands and start and stop system services. Unlike booting from a DOS disk, the Recovery Console allows you access to files on an NTFS formatted volume.

The Recovery Console is not installed by default; you must install it manually after you have installed Windows 2000. To install the Recovery Console:

1. Load the Windows 2000 CD-ROM.
2. Open a command prompt, access the Windows 2000 CD-ROM, and enter the `\i386\winnt32 \cmdcons` command.
3. Click the Yes button when the Setup window appears.
4. When the setup procedure completes, restart the server.

The Recovery Console option is added to the Windows 2000 Boot menu as shown in Figure 5.17.

Please select the operating system to start:
Microsoft Windows 2000 Server -SP2
Microsoft Windows 2000 Recovery Console -SP2
Use ↑ and ↓ to move the highlight to your choice.
Press Enter to choose.
For troubleshooting and advanced startup options for Windows 2000, press F8.

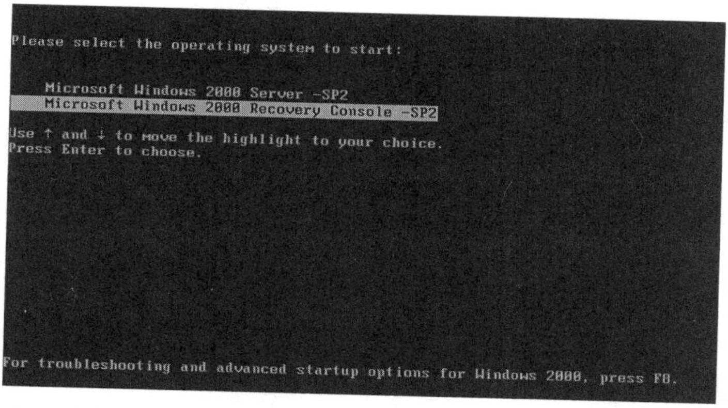

Figure 5.17 Windows 2000 Boot menu showing the addition of the Recovery Console.

If your system fails and you don't have the Recovery Console installed, or if you are having startup problems, you can run it from the Windows 2000 CD-ROM or the startup floppies. To run the Recovery Console from a CD-ROM or a floppy, perform the following steps:

1. Insert the desired media and start the server.
2. In the Windows 2000 Setup procedure, select the option to repair the operating system. Select Recovery Console as your repair method.
3. Follow the instructions to log on to the Recovery Console.

After you start the Recovery Console, either from media or by starting from the hard disk, you will be prompted for the operating system number to log on to and the Administrator password, as shown in Figure 5.18. This is not the domain or local Administrator password, but is the Directory Services Restore Mode password that you were prompted to create during the Dcpromo procedure that you used to install Active Directory.

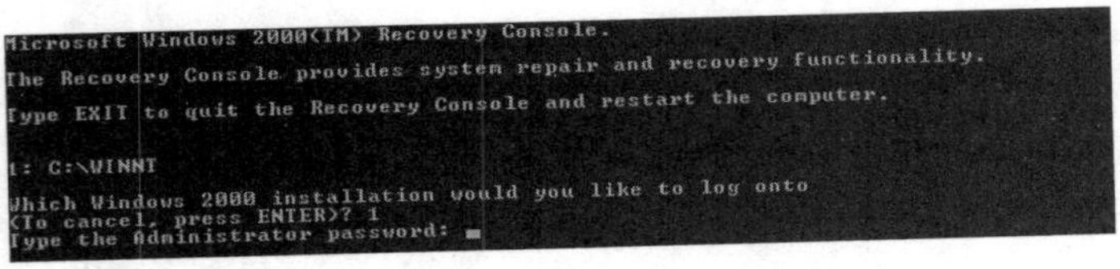

```
Microsoft Windows 2000(TM) Recovery Console.
The Recovery Console provides system repair and recovery functionality.
Type EXIT to quit the Recovery Console and restart the computer.

1: C:\WINNT
Which Windows 2000 installation would you like to log onto
(To cancel, press ENTER)? 1
Type the Administrator password:
```

Figure 5.18 Windows 2000 Recovery Console showing the logon screen.

After you log on, the following commands are available:

- Attrib
- Batch
- CD
- Chdir
- Chkdsk
- CLS
- Copy
- Del
- Delete
- Dir
- Disable
- Diskpart
- Enable
- Exit
- Expand
- Fixboot
- Fixmbr
- Format
- Help
- Listsvc
- Logon
- Map
- MD
- Mkdir
- More
- RD
- Ren
- Rename
- Rmdir
- Systemroot
- Type

As you can see, the Recovery Console allows you to perform a variety of tasks, such as formatting a drive; copying, deleting, or renaming files; and starting and stopping services. However, there are some limitations:

- You only have access to %systemroot% and its subfolders, the root partitions of %systemdrive%, any other partitions, floppy drives, and CD-ROMs.
- You cannot copy a file from the hard disk to a floppy, but you can copy a file from a floppy, a CD-ROM, or another hard disk to your hard disk.

Emergency Repair Disk (ERD)

If the previous methods of recovery have failed, you can try to repair your system files using the *Emergency Repair Disk*. Unlike the previous versions of

Windows NT, a Windows 2000 ERD does not contain the Registry files. A Windows 2000 ERD contains the following:

- Basic system files
- The partition boot sector
- The startup environment

A Windows 2000 ERD must be created while your system is fully operational. To create a Windows 2000 ERD, perform the following steps:

1. Start the Windows 2000 Backup program by selecting Start, Programs, Accessories, System Tools, Backup.
2. In the initial Backup Wizard screen, or from the Tools menu, select the Emergency Repair Disk option.
3. Insert a blank floppy disk into drive A:, select the option to back up the Registry in the repair directory, and then click OK (see Figure 5.19).
4. Click the OK button when the disk has been created.

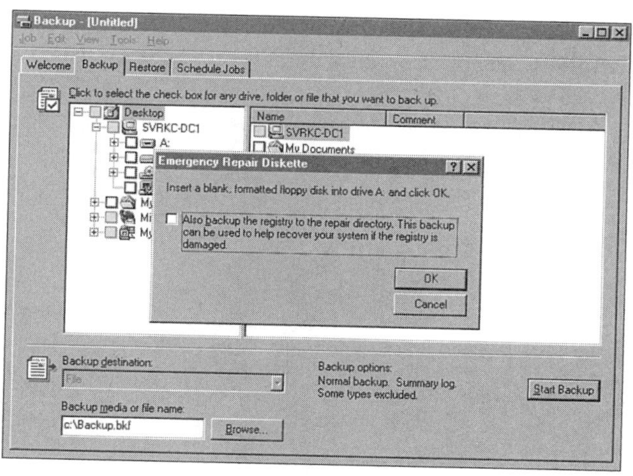

Figure 5.19 Windows 2000 Backup showing the creation of the Emergency Repair Disk.

The Registry option does not save the Registry files on the disk—they are saved in the %systemroot%\Repair\Regback folder on your computer. Just like in previous versions of Windows, you should make a new ERD after you make changes to your system, such as adding new hardware, installing a service pack, or other major configuration changes.

Using the Emergency Repair Disk

To repair your system using the ERD, you must start from the Windows 2000 CD-ROM or the four startup floppies. During the setup process, select the Repair option. When prompted for the type of repair, you have the option of selecting a *Manual Repair* or a *Fast Repair*. If you select the Manual Repair option, you will be presented with the following options:

➤ *Inspect Startup Environment*—This option inspects the files in the system partition to make sure that they are not missing or corrupted. If necessary, the files are copied from the Windows 2000 CD-ROM.

➤ *Verify Windows 2000 System Files*—This option verifies the system files by comparing them bit by bit with the files on the Windows 2000 CD-ROM. If there is a difference, you are asked whether or not to replace it.

➤ *Inspect Boot Sector*—The option inspects the boot sector and attempts to repair it, if necessary.

If you select the Fast Repair option, it automatically performs the three previous tasks and also inspects and attempts to repair the Registry. If it cannot repair the Registry, it will copy the saved Registry files from the %systemroot%\Repair\Regback folder that were saved when you created the ERD.

You should be familiar with the various recovery methods for Windows 2000, and when and how to use each one.

Practice Questions

Question 1

Which of the following tools allow you to see how much memory is being used by your applications? [Check all that apply.]

- ❑ A. System Monitor
- ❑ B. Performance Logs and Alerts
- ❑ C. Task Manager
- ❑ D. Performance Monitor

Answers A and C are correct. Both Task Manager and System Monitor allow you to see the current performance of you applications. The Performance Logs and Alerts snap-in only allows you to log data and create alerts. The Performance Monitor is the utility used in previous versions of Windows. Therefore, answers B and D are incorrect.

Question 2

Which of the following system views are available using Task Manager? [Check all that apply.]

- ❑ A. Applications
- ❑ B. Processes
- ❑ C. Network Performance
- ❑ D. Disk Activity

Answers A and B are correct. Task Manager provides three views, Applications, Processes, and Performance.

Question 3

Which of the following performance measurements are available from the Task Manager? [Check all that apply.]

- ❑ A. Disk I/O
- ❑ B. Memory Usage
- ❑ C. CPU Time
- ❑ D. Page Faults

Answers B, C, and D are correct. Task Manager provides the memory usage and CPU time as default measurements. Page faults and many other measurements can be selected by selecting View, Select Columns on the menu bar.

Question 4

If you are having performance problems with your server, which devices should you monitor closely? [Check all that apply.]

- ❑ A. Memory
- ❑ B. Video
- ❑ C. Application load time
- ❑ D. Processor

Answers A and D are correct. Although video performance might be important on a workstation, on a server the big four are memory, processor, physical disk, and network. Answer C is incorrect because application load time is not a device.

Question 5

Which of the following utilities allows you to view real-time performance data? [Check all that apply.]

- ❑ A. System Monitor
- ❑ B. Performance Logs and Alerts
- ❑ C. Task Manager
- ❑ D. Performance Monitor

Answers A and C are correct. The Performance Logs and Alerts snap-in only allows you to log data and create alerts. The Performance Monitor is the utility used in previous versions of Windows. Therefore, answers B and D are incorrect. Both Task Manager and System Monitor allow you to see the real-time performance of you applications.

Question 6

Members of which of the following groups are permitted to backup a Windows 2000 server? [Check all that apply.]

- ❑ A. Server Operators
- ❑ B. Power Users
- ❑ C. Account Operators
- ❑ D. Administrators
- ❑ E. Backup Operators

Answers D and E are correct. The Server Operators, Power Users, and Account Operators do not have the proper file-level permissions to backup files. Therefore, answers A, B, and C are incorrect.

Question 7

Which program is used to create a Windows 2000 Emergency Repair Disk?

- ❍ A. Rdisk
- ❍ B. MakeERD
- ❍ C. Windows 2000 Backup
- ❍ D. ERDclone

Answer C is correct. In Windows 2000, the Emergency Repair Disk is created using the Windows 2000 Backup program. Answer A is incorrect because Rdisk was the program used in previous versions of Windows. Answers B and D are incorrect because MakeERD and ERDClone are not Windows 2000 utilities.

Question 8

Which of the following is not a valid Windows 2000 backup type?

- ❍ A. Copy
- ❍ B. Differential
- ❍ C. Incremental
- ❍ D. Dump
- ❍ E. Normal

Answer D is correct. Although SQL server uses Dumps as backups, Windows 2000 does not.

Question 9

Which of the following is not a component of a System State backup on a Windows 2000 Member server?

❍ A. COM+ Class Registration database

❍ B. Registry

❍ C. System boot files

❍ D. SYSVOL folder

Answer D is correct. The SYSVOL folder is only present on a domain controller, not a member server.

Question 10

How is the Recovery Console installed?

❍ A. During the initial Windows 2000 setup

❍ B. Using the rconsole command

❍ C. Using the winnt32 /cmdcons command

❍ D. Using the instrecv command

Answer C is correct. The Recovery Console folder is installed from the command line after the initial Windows 2000 installation. Rconsole is a NetWare utility.

Need to Know More?

Shilmover, Barry and Stu Sjouwerman, *Windows 2000 Power Toolkit*, New Riders, Indianapolis, IN, 2001. ISBN 0-7357-1061-9. This book is a valuable resource for reference material on the Performance Tool and the various counters.

Search TechNet on the Internet at `http://www.microsoft.com/technet` or the TechNet CD for information on Performance Tool, System Monitor, objects, counters, System State, backup, authoritative restore, Recovery Console, and Safe Mode.

Search `http://www.cnet.com` for additional information and reviews on performance tools and utilities.

For additional information, refer to the Microsoft Windows 2000 online help. To access, select Help from the Start menu. Terms and technologies to search for include Performance Tool, System Monitor, objects, counters, System State, backup, authoritative restore, Recovery Console, and Safe Mode.

Managing, Configuring, and Troubleshooting Storage Use

Terms you'll need to understand:

- ✓ Basic disk
- ✓ Dynamic disk
- ✓ Partition
- ✓ NTFS compression
- ✓ Disk Defragmenter utility
- ✓ Check Disk utility
- ✓ Disk Management console

Techniques you'll need to master:

- ✓ Performing basic disk and volume management with the Disk Management console
- ✓ Performing maintenance and repairs on disks and volumes
- ✓ Defragmenting disks and volumes
- ✓ Using the Disk Cleanup tool to remove unnecessary files from your computer
- ✓ Configuring and managing disk quotas
- ✓ Configuring and managing NTFS file and folder compression
- ✓ Troubleshooting and repairing problems with disks and volumes

Introduction

You've probably heard the saying "The more things change, the more they stay the same" a hundred times—maybe even more. This statement couldn't be more true than when it comes to managing your computer's hard drives. Windows 2000 is light years ahead of its predecessors, Windows 9x and Windows NT, but you will still find yourself needing to effectively manage and monitor your hard drives.

Windows 2000 provides an extremely useful GUI tool for performing the majority of management tasks on your computer's hard drives and volumes: the *Disk Management* utility. Disk Management can be accessed in several ways, the easiest of which is via the Computer Management console (Start, Programs, Administrative Tools, Computer Management), as shown in Figure 6.1.

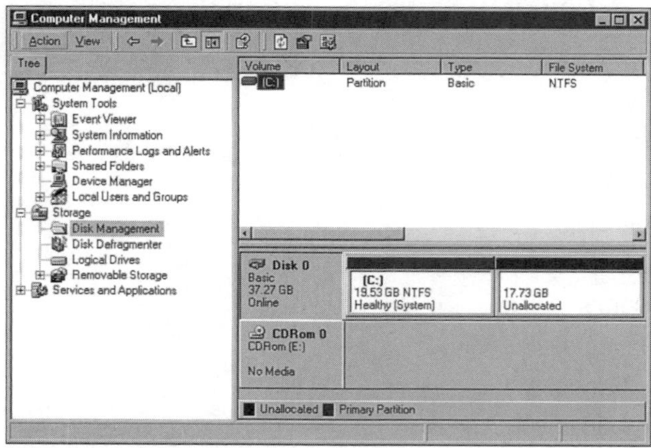

Figure 6.1 The Disk Management utility—storage management console.

The Disk Management utility provides the following information to you at a glance:

- Volumes installed and recognized by the computer
- The file system in use, such as FAT32 or NTFS
- The type of disk, such as basic or dynamic
- The health status of each volume
- The status of each volume, such as system partition, and so on
- The total size and free space on each volume

Although the Disk Management utility provides many of the tools you'll need, you should also master usage of the *Disk Defragmenter* tool (also located in the Computer Management console) and the Properties page for each of your computer's volumes. Together, these three management tools provide you with a wealth of capability and control that have been previously unavailable so easily right out of the box.

Monitoring and Configuring Disks and Volumes

The bulk of your hard disk and volume management tasks will be performed with the Disk Management utility, as shown in Figure 6.1. From here, you can perform the following tasks:

- Determine disk and volume information, such as size, file system, and other pertinent information
- Determine disk health status
- Upgrade basic storage to dynamic storage
- Create new partitions and volumes
- Format partitions and volumes
- Delete partitions and volumes
- Extend the size of dynamic volumes
- Assign and change drive letters or paths to hard drives and removable storage drives
- Add new physical disks

Although you will most commonly access the Disk Management utility from the Computer Management console, you can access Disk Management in any one of the following three ways, depending on your preferences:

- On the command line, enter **`diskmgmt.msc`**.
- On the command line, enter **`MMC`**. In the empty console, add the Disk Management snap-in. This can be useful for creating powerful, customized MMC consoles for a variety of management tasks.
- From within the Computer Management console, click Disk Management.

Viewing Disk Properties

You can quickly determine the properties of each physical disk in your computer by right-clicking the disk in question (see Figure 6.2) in the bottom area of the Disk Management window and selecting Properties from the shortcut menu.

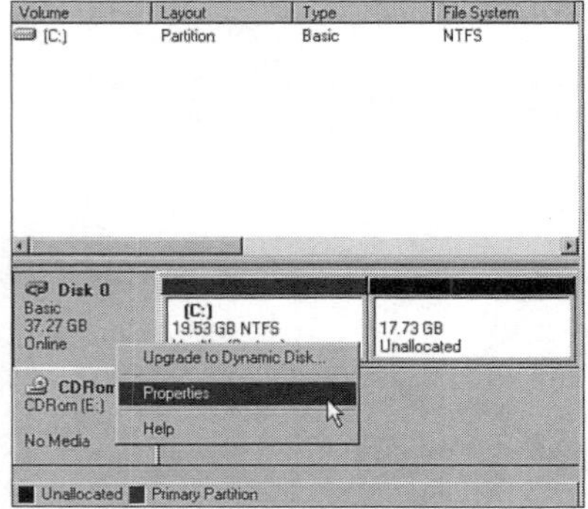

Figure 6.2 Getting to the Disk Properties dialog box.

As shown in Figure 6.3, the Disk Properties dialog box shows you the following information about your disks:

- The disk number, such as 0 or 1
- The type of disk, such as Basic or Dynamic
- The status of the disk, such as online or offline
- The total capacity of the disk
- The unallocated (non-partitioned) space remaining on the disk
- The device type, such as IDE or SCSI
- The vendor of the hard disk, such as Western Digital or IBM
- The adapter channel, such as primary IDE or secondary IDE
- The volumes located on the physical disk, such as E and F

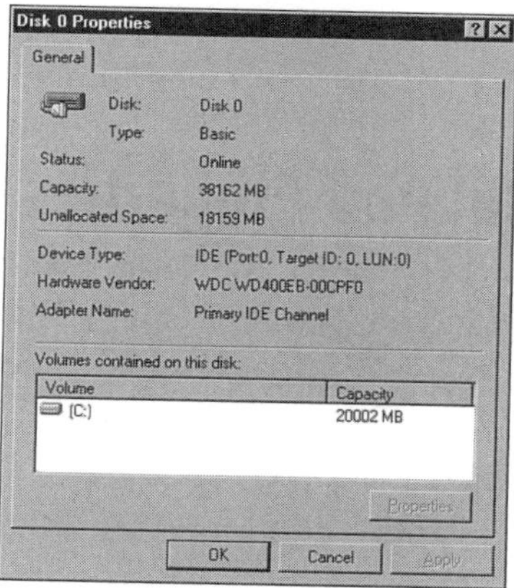

Figure 6.3 The Disk Properties dialog box.

Viewing Volume Health Status

The health status of each volume is provided in the volume properties pane under the volume size (see Figure 6.1) in Disk Management. One of the following statuses are displayed in this area:

- *Online*—The disk is operating normally with no known problems.
- *Online (errors)*—Only used for dynamic disks, this status indicates that I/O errors have been detected on the disk.
- *Offline*—Only used for dynamic disks, this status indicates that the disk is not accessible due to any number of possible problems or errors.
- *Foreign*—Only used for dynamic disks, this status indicates that a dynamic disk was removed from another Windows 2000 computer and placed into this Windows 2000 computer, but has not yet been imported into this computer.
- *Unreadable*—The disk is not accessible and may have experienced hardware failure, corruption, or I/O errors. The disk's copy of the system's disk configuration database may be corrupt, thus causing this status indication.
- *Unrecognized*—This disk is not recognized, such as a disk that was taken from a Unix system.
- *No Media*—Used only for removable media drives. The status will change to Online when a readable media is inserted into the drive.

Correcting problems with drives is discussed further in the "Recovering from Disk Failures" section later in this chapter.

Viewing and Configuring Volume Properties

To gather information about a specific volume, right-click the desired volume in the lower pane of the Disk Management window and select Properties from the shortcut menu. Note in Figure 6.4 that Disk 0 in the lower pane was right-clicked.

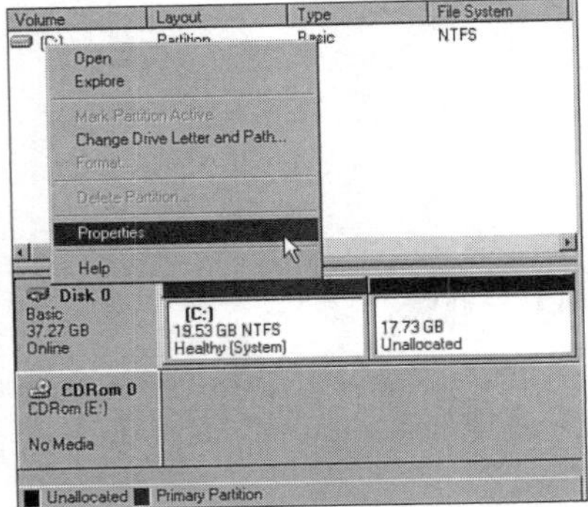

Figure 6.4 Getting to the volume properties dialog box.

As shown in Figure 6.5, the volume's Properties dialog box shows you the following information about your volumes (from the General tab):

- The volume label, which is the local name of the volume
- The type of volume, such as local disk (basic storage) or simple, spanned, or striped (dynamic storage)
- The file system in use, such as FAT32 or NTFS
- The amount of space in use on the volume
- The amount of space remaining available for use on the volume
- The total capacity of the volume
- Whether or not the volume has been configured for volume-level NTFS file and folder compression
- Whether or not the volume has been configured for indexing by the Indexing Service

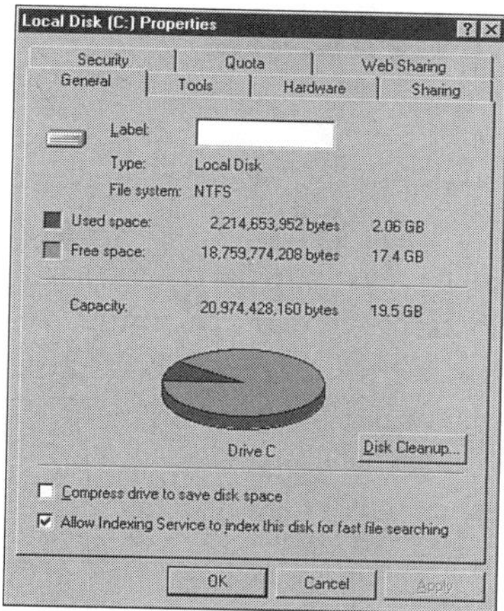

Figure 6.5 A volume's Properties dialog box.

If you click the *Disk Cleanup* button, the Disk Cleanup utility starts, which is discussed in the "Troubleshooting Disks and Volumes" section of this chapter. The Tools tab is also covered in the troubleshooting section.

By switching to the Hardware tab of the volume's Properties dialog box, you can quickly get a summary of all installed storage devices in your computer. To open a troubleshooting wizard for a particular device, select it and click the *Troubleshoot* button. To view a device's properties, select the device and click the Properties button. The device's Properties dialog box opens, just the same as if you had accessed it through the Device Manager. (See Chapter 4 for more information on Device Manager.)

The *Sharing tab* of the volume's Properties dialog box allows you to configure sharing of a volume for use by network clients across the network. Working with shared folders is discussed in Chapter 3. The Security tab allows you to configure the NTFS permissions for the root of the volume; NTFS permissions are also discussed in Chapter 3.

The *Quota tab* allows you to configure and enforce disk usage quotas for your users. Working with disk quotas will be discussed later in this chapter in the "Managing Disk Quotas" section.

The last tab in the volume's Properties dialog box is the *Web Sharing tab*. If you have IIS installed on your computer, you will see this tab. Working with IIS and Web Sharing is discussed in Chapter 3.

Upgrading Basic Storage to Dynamic Storage

Should you want to take advantage of the capabilities offered by dynamic disks in Windows 2000, you must upgrade your basic disk to a *dynamic disk*. The upgrade is done on an entire physical disk, not just one particular partition. A dynamic disk is a hard disk that can only house dynamic volumes created through the Disk Management administrative tool. Dynamic disks do not include partitions or logical drives, and they cannot be accessed by DOS. A basic disk is a standard hard disk.

The types of volumes offered to you as dynamic storage disks include the following:

- *Mirrored volumes*—A mirrored volume is a fault tolerant disk configuration in which data is written to two hard disks, rather than one, so that if one disk fails then the data remains accessible. Mirrored volumes work only on a Windows 2000 Server.
- *Simple volumes*—Simple volumes are essentially the same as a basic storage partition; disk space is only used from one physical disk.
- *Spanned volumes*—Spanned volumes can take disk space from two to thirty-two physical disks to create one large apparently contiguous volume. Spanned volumes offer you no fault tolerance, thus if one disk should fail the entire set is lost. The advantage of spanned volumes is that you can quickly add more storage to a spanned volume if it is running low.
- *Striped volumes*—Striped volumes write data to multiple disks in 64KB sequential stripes, using two to thirty-two physical disks. The first stripe is written to the first disk, the second stripe is written to the second disk, and so forth. Striped volumes, also known as RAID-0, provide no fault tolerance. The advantage provided by striped volumes lies in the overall disk I/O performance increase of the computer as the total disk I/O is split among all of the disks in the volume—striping writes to all disks so that data is added to all disks at the same rate.
- *RAID-5 volumes*—RAID-5 volumes provide fault-tolerant data storage using two to thirty-two physical disks of the same size. The total volume capacity will be equal to that provided by the number of physical disks minus one. Data is written sequentially across each physical disk and contains both data and parity information. The parity information from the set is used to rebuild the set should one disk fail, thus providing fault tolerance. RAID-5 volumes in Windows 2000 cannot sustain the loss of more than one disk in the set while still providing fault tolerance.

Basic disks can be upgraded to dynamic disks at any time without data loss, provided that you meet all of the following requirements. You cannot revert a dynamic disk back to a basic disk without complete data loss on the volume.

- Master Boot Record (MBR) disks must have at least 1MB of free space available at the end of the disk for the dynamic disk database to be created.
- Dynamic storage cannot be used on removable media such as Zip disks.
- Hard drives on portable computers cannot be converted to dynamic storage. Because most portable computers contain only one hard drive, there is no benefit to be realized by upgrading to a dynamic disk.
- The sector size on the hard disk must be no larger than 512 bytes in order for the conversion to be able to take place. Use the `fsutil fsinfo ntfsinfo x:` command to determine the sector size, where *x*: is the volume in question.

Dynamic disks can be used by only one operating system. If you plan on multibooting your computer, do not upgrade your basic disks to dynamic disks.

To upgrade a basic disk to a dynamic disk, follow these steps:

1. In the lower pane of Disk Management, right-click the disk that you want to upgrade and select Upgrade to Dynamic Disk from the shortcut menu (see Figure 6.2).
2. Select the disk that you want to upgrade from the provided list and click OK.
3. When the Disks to Upgrade dialog box appears, click Upgrade to continue.
4. A warning dialog box opens, informing you that dynamic disks cannot be used by any previous version of Windows 2000. Click Yes to proceed.
5. Another warning dialog box opens, notifying you that any file systems existing on the disk will be dismounted as part of the upgrade process. Click Yes to proceed—this is your last chance to abort the process.
6. Click OK when the dialog box appears notifying you that a restart is required to complete the process. After the computer restarts, the disk upgrade will be complete.

Note that there must be at least 1MB of unpartitioned space on drive to upgrade to a dynamic disk. Also, the dynamic disk option is not available for laptop systems.

Creating New Partitions and Volumes

Should you happen to have any unallocated (free) space on one of your disks (see Figure 6.1), you can create a new partition or volume in that space. To create a new partition out of free space on a basic disk, perform the following steps:

1. Right-click an area of free (unallocated) space (see Figure 6.1) on a disk and select Create Partition.
2. Dismiss the opening page by clicking Next.
3. Select the type of partition (see Figure 6.6) and click Next to continue.

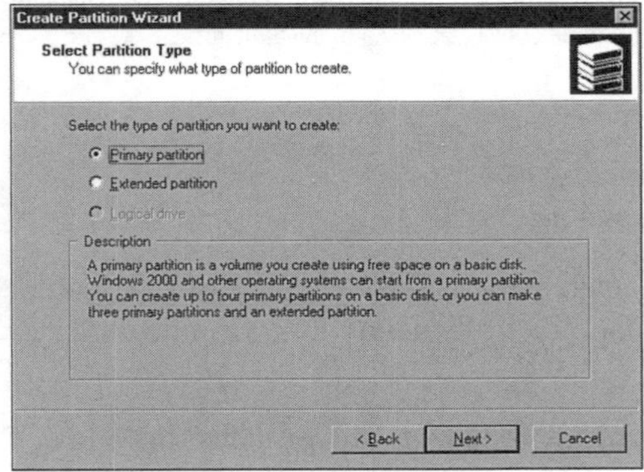

Figure 6.6 Selecting the partition type.

4. Specify the size of the partition and click Next.
5. Specify the drive letter or the mount location, as shown in Figure 6.7, and click Next.
6. Choose your partition formatting and name selections and click Next.
7. Click Finish to complete the wizard.

Creating a new dynamic volume follows the same basic process as does creating new basic disk partitions, with the exception that when creating a dynamic volume you can choose from one of the available volume types, as previously mentioned. You are also given the opportunity to select the total size of the volume to be created in the case of a spanned volume. Figure 6.8 shows a server that is utilizing dynamic disks. Note how the C: volume is divided across two different hard disks in a mirrored volume.

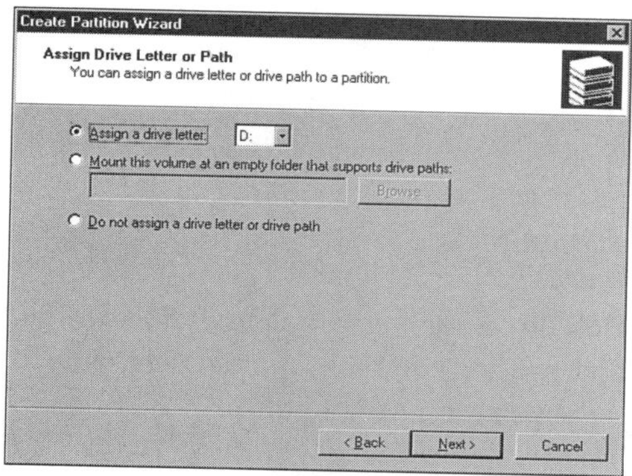

Figure 6.7 Selecting the drive letter or mount point.

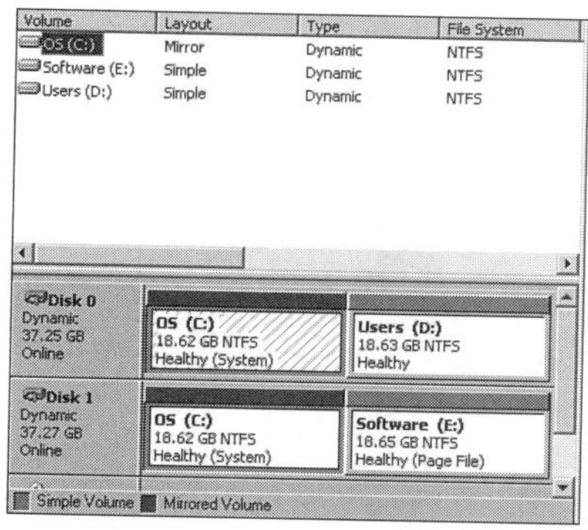

Figure 6.8 Computer using dynamic disks.

Formatting Volumes and Partitions

To format a volume or partition, follow these steps:

1. Right-click the volume or partition that you want to format and select Format from the shortcut menu.
2. Provide the required information, as shown in Figure 6.9, and click OK.

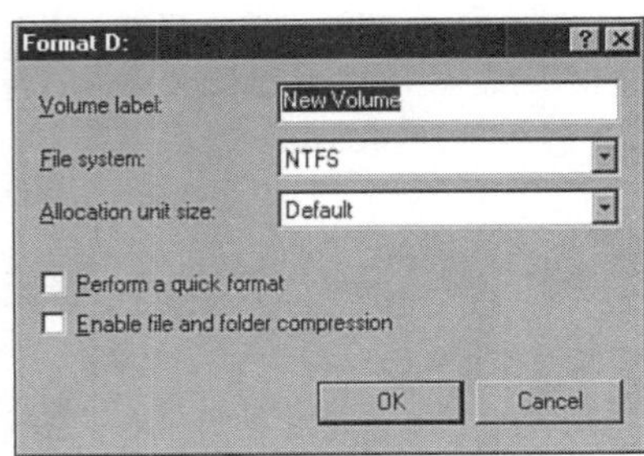

Figure 6.9 Selecting formatting options.

3. Acknowledge the warning dialog box notifying you that all data will be lost by clicking OK. The format process commences and takes some time depending on the size of the partition or volume.

Windows 2000 is self-preserving in that it will not allow you to format the system partition from within the GUI.

Deleting Volumes and Partitions

To format or delete a partition, follow these steps:

1. Right-click the volume or partition that you want to format and select Delete Partition or Delete Volume from the shortcut menu.
2. Acknowledge the warning dialog box notifying you that all data will be lost by clicking Yes.

As with formatting a volume or partition, Windows 2000 is self-preserving in that it will not allow you to delete the system partition from within the GUI.

Extending Dynamic Volume Size

Dynamic volumes that were not created from basic disks can be resized after their creation to add (extend) more space. To extend a dynamic volume, right-click the dynamic volume of concern and select Extend volume from the shortcut menu. Simply follow the screen prompts to resize your dynamic volume.

Assigning Drive Letters and Paths

To change the drive letter or path, right-click the volume and select Change Drive Letter and Path from the shortcut menu. The Change Drive Letter and Paths dialog box opens, as shown in Figure 6.10.

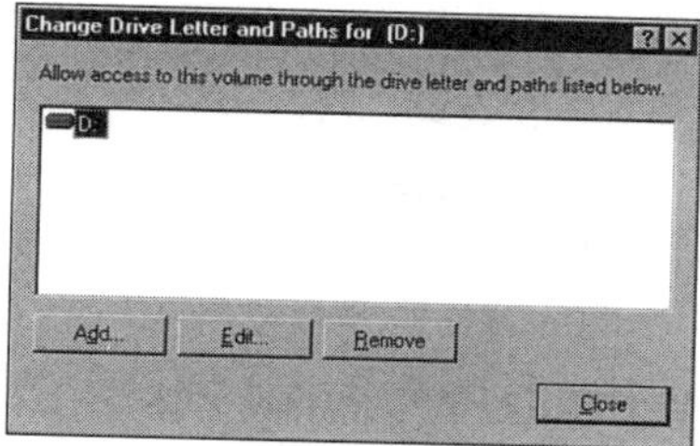

Figure 6.10 Changing the drive letter or path assignment.

A mounted drive functions the same as any other drive, but is assigned a name rather than a drive letter. To mount the drive as an NTFS folder path, ensure that the path specified exists and is empty, and click the Add button. To change the drive letter assigned, click the Edit button. To remove a drive letter or path, select it and click the Remove button.

Adding New Disks

Adding new disks is a simple process. The only thing that may make adding a new disk different than adding any other type of hardware device (see Chapter 4 for more information on installing hardware in Windows 2000) is if your computer supports hot swapping. If your computer does support hot swapping, you can click Action, Rescan Disks after inserting the disk and Disk Management should show it. If your computer does not support hot swapping, the disk should appear in Disk Management on the subsequent restart of the computer.

Troubleshooting Disks and Volumes

Windows 2000 comes with three fairly robust, built-in tools that you can use to perform basic troubleshooting, cleanup, and repair. They are

- *Disk Cleanup*—The utility that removes temporary files and other "dead wood" that may be on your computer's disks.
- *Check Disk*—The utility that checks the file and folder structure of your hard disk. You can also have Check Disk check the physical structure of your hard disk. Check Disk can perform repairs as required.

- *Disk Defragmenter*—The utility that defragments your hard disks by moving all pieces of each file into a continuous section on the hard disk.

We will examine each of these tools in the following sections.

Using the Disk Cleanup Utility

The Disk Cleanup utility can remove temporary files, installation logs, Recycle Bin items, and other "dead wood" that accumulates on your volumes over time. You can start the Disk Cleanup utility in three different ways depending on your needs:

- On the General tab of the volume's Properties dialog box (see Figure 6.5), click the Disk Cleanup button.
- From the Start menu, click Programs, Accessories, System Tools, Disk Cleanup.
- On the command line, enter `cleanmgr /d x`, where *x* represents the volume to be cleaned. The /d switch is not mandatory, but specifies the volume to be cleaned.

Starting Disk Cleanup from the General tab of the volume's Properties dialog box yields the Disk Cleanup dialog box, as shown in Figure 6.11, after the cleanup scan has completed.

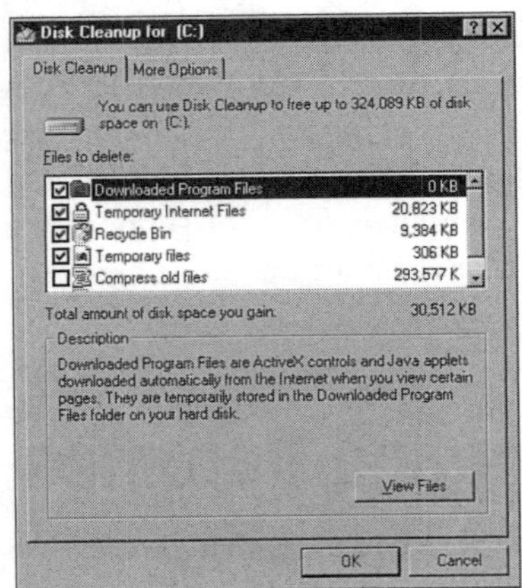

Figure 6.11 Selecting items to be cleaned.

Select the items you want to clean and/or compress and click OK. When prompted, click Yes to confirm your selections and start the cleanup process.

The Disk Cleanup utility can be configured for scheduled cleaning by using the Scheduled Tasks Wizard located in the Control Panel.

Using Check Disk

The Check Disk utility can be used to check the file and folder structure of your hard disks as well as checking the physical structure of your hard disks. Check Disk can also be configured to automatically correct errors that are located. Check disk can be launched by using one of the following methods:

- In the Tools tab of the volume's Properties dialog box, click the Check Now button.
- On a command line, enter `chkdsk`.

  When started from the command line, the `chkdsk` command has the following syntax:

  ```
  chkdsk [volume[[path]filename]]] [/F] [/V] [/R]
    [/X] [/I] [/C] [/L[:size]]
  ```

  Table 6.1 presents the available options for use with the chkdsk command.

Table 6.1 Chkdsk Options

Switch	Description
Volume	Specifies the drive letter, mount point, or volume letter.
file name	Specifies the files to check for fragmentation (FAT only).
/F	Specifies that errors are to be fixed if found on the disk.
/V	Specifies that cleanup messages are to be displayed.
/R	Locates bad sectors and recovers any readable information. Requires the /F switch.
/L:size	Specifies the log size to be created.
/X	Specifies that the selected volume is to be dismounted if required. Requires the /F switch.
/I	Specifies that less vigorous checking of index entries is to be performed.
/C	Specifies that checking of cycles within the folder structure is to be skipped.

Figure 6.12 shows the Windows 2000 Check Disk configuration options when started from the GUI. Note that the requirement for rebooting is the same for both GUI and command-line checkdisks. If you are scanning (that is, not fixing errors) the system/boot partition, then you can leave the system

running, but if you want to fix errors or recover bad sectors, then you have to do it on the next reboot. If you are checking partitions other than system/boot, then you should not have to reboot.

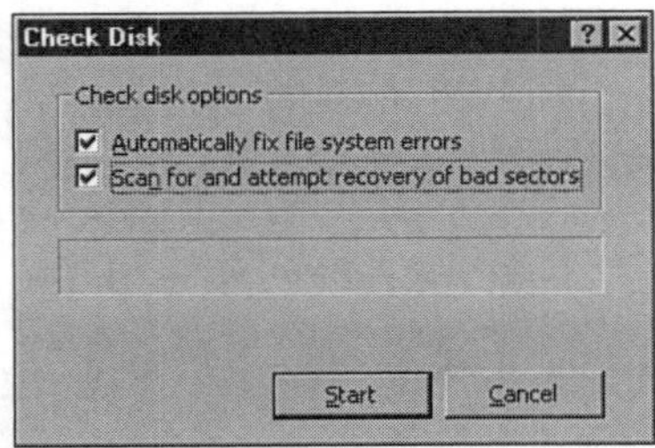

Figure 6.12 Configuring disk scan properties.

Defragmenting Disks

It was once thought that the NTFS file system could not become fragmented. Windows NT 4.0 brought this belief to the forefront due to the fact that it did not ship with a built-in defragmentation utility. Unfortunately, it was soon discovered that NTFS becomes fragmented just as FAT and FAT32 do, thus the Disk Defragmenter tool was reintroduced with Windows 2000. Windows 2000 includes a "light" version of Executive Software's Diskeeper for performing disk defragmentation.

Fragmentation occurs when the operating system saves a file to the first available space on the hard disk, instead of placing it neatly into an available space or the amount of space remaining. Over time, fragmentation can slow down or degrade disk performance. It's a good idea to analyze your drives for fragmentation once a month.

You can access the Disk Defragmenter utility from any one of the following five methods:

- On the Tools tab of the volume's Properties dialog box, click the Defragment Now button.
- From the Start menu, click Programs, Accessories, System Tools, Disk Defragmenter.
- From within the Computer Management console, click Disk Defragmenter, as shown in Figure 6.13.

- On the command line, enter **`dfrg.msc`**.
- On the command line, enter **`MMC`**. In the empty console, add the Disk Defragmenter snap-in. This can be useful for creating powerful, customized MMC consoles for a variety of management tasks.

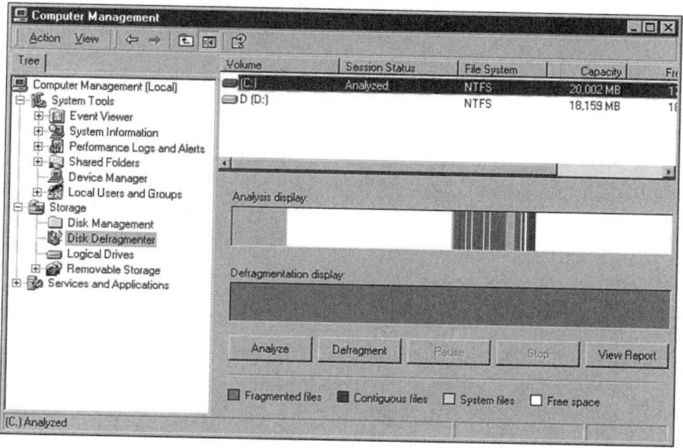

Figure 6.13 Disk Defragmenter in the Computer Management console.

No matter which way you start Disk Defragmenter, your options are the same. To analyze a volume, click the Analyze button. You can defragment a volume, with or without first analyzing it, by clicking the Defragment button. The View Report button will show the analysis report again. You can pause or stop a running defragmentation.

The Disk Defragmenter utility can be configured for scheduled cleaning by using the Scheduled Tasks Wizard located in the Control Panel.

Check out the full version of Diskeeper at **http://www.executivesoftware.com/diskeeper/diskeeper.asp**.

Configuring NTFS File and Folder Compression

Native file and folder compression is one of the many benefits of using the NTFS 5.0 file system. The compression algorithm used by NTFS is a lossless one, which results in no data loss during the compression or decompression routine. Unfortunately, this capability comes at a price—NTFS compression and EFS encryption are mutually exclusive. That is, you cannot both compress and encrypt a file or folder at the same time. See Chapter 8 for more information about EFS encryption in Windows 2000; also see Chapter 3 for additional information on file compression.

You can manage compression from the command line by running the `compact` command or from the Windows GUI in the applicable disk, folder, or file Properties dialog box. The following steps outline how to enable NTFS compression on a folder on your computer from within Windows.

1. In the Properties dialog box for the folder, click the Advanced button to open the Advanced Attributes dialog box (see Figure 6.14).

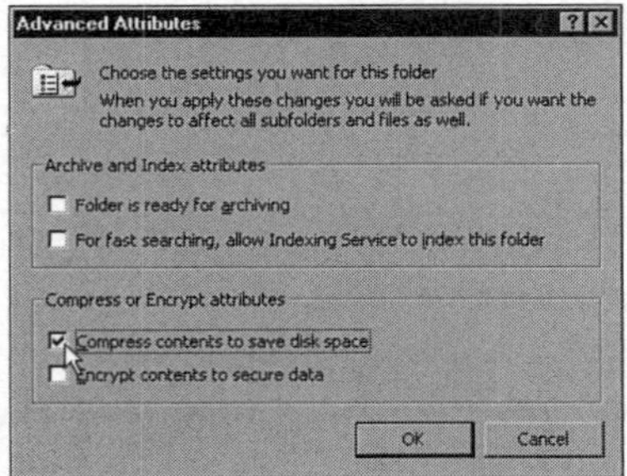

Figure 6.14 Configuring compression and/or encryption.

2. Select the Compress contents to save disk space option and click OK.
3. Click OK again to close the Properties dialog box.
4. You might be presented with a dialog box asking you whether you want to apply the changes to just the selected folder, or to the selected folder, subfolder, and all files. Make your selection and click OK one last time to complete the process.

If you enabled compression, you will be able to see this folder (and any files and folders in the folder) displayed in blue text in Windows Explorer (see Figure 6.15). To enable this option from within Windows Explorer, click Tools, Folder Options and click the View tab. Select the Display Compressed Files and Folders with Alternate Color option.

If you want to manage NTFS compression from the command line, you can do so by using the `compact` command, which has the following syntax:

```
compact [{/c¦/u}] [/s[:dir]] [/a] [/i] [/f]
       [/q] [FileName[...]]
```

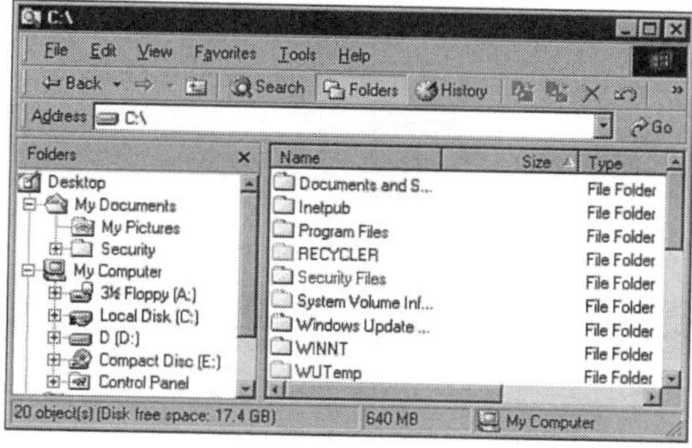

Figure 6.15 Compressed folder displayed in blue text.

Table 6.2 presents the available options for use with the `compact` command.

Table 6.2 compact Command Options

Switch	Description
/c	Specifies that the directory or file is to be compressed.
/u	Specifies that the directory or file is to be decompressed.
/s	Specifies that the compression action is to be performed on all subdirectories of the specified directory.
/a	Specifies the display of hidden or system files.
/i	Specifies that errors are to be ignored during the compression process.
/f	Specifies that the compression operation is to be forced on the specified directory or file. This is useful in cases in which a directory is only partly compressed.
/q	Specifies that only the most essential information is to be reported.
filename	Specifies the file or directory. You can use multiple file names and wildcard characters (* and ?).

The possible outcomes of moving or copying NTFS compressed files or folders are as follows:

- Moving an uncompressed file or folder to another folder on the same NTFS volume results in the file or folder remaining uncompressed, regardless of the compression state of the target folder.
- Moving a compressed file or folder to another folder results in the file or folder remaining compressed after the move, regardless of the compression state of the target folder.
- Copying a file to a folder causes the file to take on the compression state of the target folder.

- Overwriting a file of the same name causes the copied file to take on the compression state of the target file, regardless of the compression state of the target folder.
- Copying a file from a FAT folder to an NTFS folder results in the file taking on the compression state of the target folder.
- Copying a file from an NTFS folder to a FAT folder results in all NTFS-specific properties being lost, so the file will be uncompressed.

Managing Disk Quotas

In previous versions of Windows, you had no control over how much space your users used on your hard disks. In Windows 2000, this has changed, thanks to the *disk quotas* capability. Disk quotas allow you to specify how much disk space a user is allowed to use on any particular NTFS volume. You must be using NTFS 5.0 for this feature to be available. You can specify disk quotas universally for all users of a volume or individually for specific users. The following points of concern apply to disk quotas:

- As previously stated, you can only implement disk quotas on Windows 2000 NTFS 5.0 volumes.
- Disk quotas can only be applied at the root level of the volume, not to specific folders.
- Disk usage is based on all files that the user creates, copies, or takes ownership of.
- Disk quotas are based on the actual file size, not the compressed file size.
- Disk quotas affect the free size that an installed application will see during the installation process.
- Disk quotas will not be applied to any users accessing data on a Windows 2000 disk from Windows NT 4.0 (with the required Service Packs installed).

To configure disk quotas, open the volume's root properties by right-clicking a volume and selecting Properties from the shortcut menu. Click the Quota tab (see Figure 6.16) to configure disk quotas for that volume.

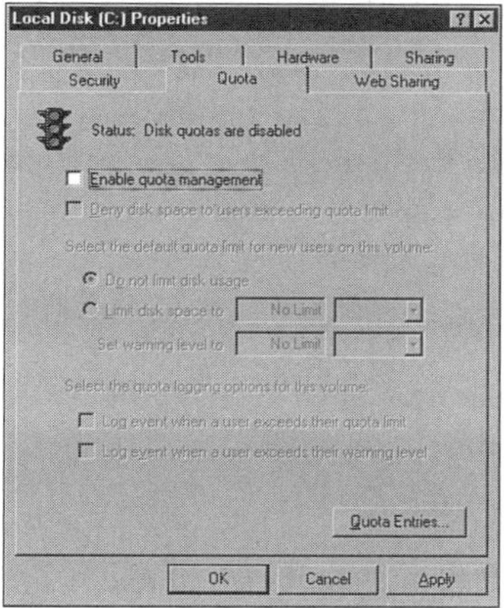

Figure 6.16 Managing disk quotas.

The first thing you should notice is the Status indicator, which visually indicates the status of disk quota applications on the volume. The disk quota traffic light has the following indications:

- *Green light*—Disk quotas are enabled on the volume.
- *Yellow light*—Disk quotas are currently inactive on the volume due to quota information being rebuilt.
- *Red light*—Disk quotas are not enabled on the volume (this is the default).

Table 6.3 outlines each of the disk quota options found in the dialog box in Figure 6.16.

Table 6.3 Disk Quota Configuration Options

Option	Description
Enable quota management	Enables quota management when checked.
Deny disk space to users exceeding quota limit	Denies additional disk space usage by users when they have exceeded their assigned quota limit.
Do not limit disk usage	Automatically assigns unlimited quota to new users on the volume.
Limit disk space to	Automatically assigns the configured quota limit to new users on the volume.
Log event when a user exceeds their quota limit	Generates an event log entry when a user's usage has exceeded the quota limit.
Log event when a user exceeds their warning level	Generates an event log entry when a user's usage has exceeded the warning level.

Notice that in Table 6.3, the phrase *new user* was used when discussing the application of quota limits on the volume. In Windows 2000, disk quota settings are only *automatically* applied to users who have yet to use any space on the volume. Thus you can see that it is best to implement disk quotas from the very beginning so that any user using disk space on that volume will automatically be subjected to the disk quota limitations.

To enable disk quotas for new users on a volume, follow these steps:

1. Open the Properties dialog box of the volume you want to configure the quota settings for. Click the Quota tab.
2. Select the Enable Quota Management check box.
3. Select the Deny Disk Space to Users Exceeding Quota Limit check box to prevent users from being allowed to exceed their quota setting.
4. Select Limit Disk Space, and configure the Limit level and Warning level to something such as 10MB and 8MB, respectively.
5. Click Apply to apply the quota control settings.
6. If you already have data on the disk, a dialog box will open informing you that the disk must be rescanned. Click OK to acknowledge this information.

As mentioned previously, disk quota settings will not be automatically applied to users who have already started using disk space on that volume. You need to manually configure the disk quota for these users. You may also find the need to configure disk quotas for other users who have special needs or issues, such as a user in the graphic design department who has the legitimate need to store several hundred megabytes of graphics files. The user in the human resources department who routinely downloads MP3s to the file server, however, needs to have a much stricter quota put in place.

If a user already has data on the drive, then a quota entry is automatically created for that user when the drive is scanned after enabling quotas. This may take several minutes if the drive has a lot of data on it. Users are all considered to be new users for the quota system, so they get the default quota settings.

No matter what reason you have for creating user disk quotas manually, the process is the same and performed as follows:

1. Open the Properties dialog box of the volume you want to configure the quota settings for. Click the Quota tab.
2. Click the Quota Entries button to open the window shown in Figure 6.17. You can see the status of each of your users who currently has a quota enforced on their disk usage.

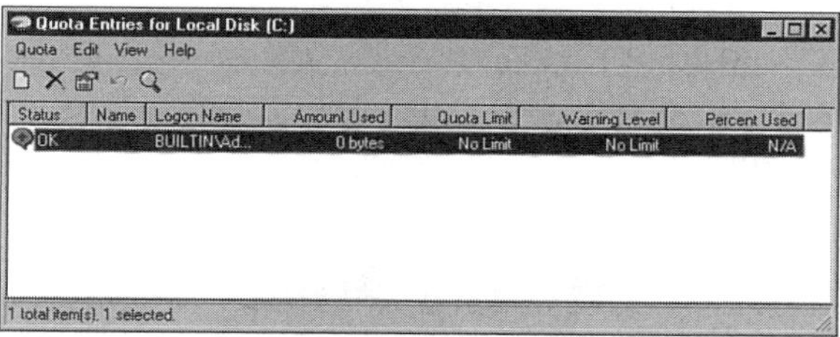

Figure 6.17 The Quota Entries window.

3. To create a new quota entry (for a user who is not listed), click Quota, New Quota Entry.
4. Select the user or users to whom to apply the new quota.
5. Configure the desired quota settings and click OK.
6. To edit the quota settings of an existing (listed) user, double-click the user and modify the settings as desired. Click OK when done.

You can monitor each user's disk usage as well through the Quota Entries window shown in Figure 6.17. The following information is available to you through this window:

- The Quota status. A green arrow in the dialog bubble is OK, an exclamation point in a yellow triangle indicates that the warning limit has been exceeded, and an exclamation point in a red circle indicates that the usage limit has been exceeded.
- The name and logon name of each user with a disk quota entry.
- The amount of disk space each user has used.
- The quota entry setting for each user.
- The warning entry setting for each user.
- The percentage of disk space each user has used relative to their configured quota entry setting.

Recovering from Disk Failures

Unfortunately, hard disks can and do fail. This alone is a very solid reason for ensuring that you have a well thought-out and practiced disaster recovery plan in place (see Chapter 5 for more information on using the Windows Backup utility). If your data was on a basic storage disk or a simple, spanned, or striped dynamic volume, you will have no other choice but to replace the disk and restore the data from the last backup. If you experience failure of a disk in a mirrored volume or a RAID-5 array, fault tolerance is in place and you will be able to recover your data.

Recovering a Failed Mirrored Drive

Should one of the drives in a mirrored set happen to fail, you will be provided with a graphical indication in Disk Management. The process to repair the mirror depends on whether or not the disk that failed was part of a mirrored set that contained the system or boot partition.

If the failed disk did not contain the system or boot partition (only data), you can restore the mirror by following these steps:

1. From within Disk Management, right-click the failed mirrored volume and select Remove Mirror from the shortcut menu.
2. In the Remove Mirror dialog box, select the disk that is to be removed and click Remove Mirror.
3. Confirm that you want to remove the mirror by clicking OK when prompted with a dialog box.
4. Power down the computer, replace the hard disk, and restart the computer.
5. Create a new mirrored volume using the previous mirrored disk and the replacement disk.

If the failed disk contained the system or boot partition, then you can restore the mirror by following these steps:

1. Determine which mirrored disk failed. If the secondary disk failed (the disk that contains the mirrored data), you can replace it as outlined previously. If the primary disk failed (the disk that contains the original data), you must proceed with these steps.

2. Create a Windows 2000 boot floppy that contains a copy of the boot.ini file pointing to the secondary disk in the mirrored set.
3. If you have another Windows 2000 computer available, copy the ntldr, ntdetect.com, and boot.ini files from it to a blank, formatted 3-1/2 inch floppy disk. You need to edit the boot.ini file as shown in Step 5 to reflect the location of your secondary drive.
4. If you do not have another Windows 2000 computer available, copy the ntdetect.com file from the I386 folder on a Windows 2000 Setup CD-ROM to a blank, formatted 3-1/2 inch floppy. You also need to expand the NTLDR file from this same location by entering the following command from the command line: `expand Ntldr._ Ntldr`.
5. Finally, create a boot.ini that looks something like this that points to the secondary drive in your broken mirror (for more help on working with ARC paths, see `http://support.microsoft.com/default.aspx?scid=kb;en-us;Q102873`):

```
[boot loader]
timeout=30
default=multi(0)disk(0)rdisk(0)partition(1)\WINNT
[operating systems]
multi(0)disk(0)rdisk(0)partition(1)
\WINNT="Microsoft Windows 2000 Server" /fastdetect
```

6. Use your boot disk to start your Windows 2000 computer.
7. Remove and re-create the mirror as discussed in the previous procedure.

Recovering a Failed RAID-5 Drive

Recovering from a disk failure in a RAID-5 array is a fairly simple process thanks to the fault tolerance provided by the array. Remember that RAID-5 arrays can only provide fault tolerance for one failed disk, so be sure to replace the failed disk as soon as possible. While the disk is failed and not replaced, you will still be able to use the RAID-5 array; however, I/O performance will be severely degraded as the missing data will have to be re-created from the parity information. Again, you should replace a failed disk in a RAID-5 array as soon as you can by performing the following steps:

1. Power down the server, if necessary. Replace the failed disk. Restart the server, if necessary. If the disk is hot swappable, rescan the disks.
2. In Disk Management, right-click the failed RAID-5 set (it will be marked as Failed Redundancy) and select Repair Volume from the shortcut menu.
3. When prompted, select the new disk you installed and click OK to begin the rebuilding process.

Practice Questions

Question 1

In Windows 2000, which of the following types of disk configurations can you create on a Windows 2000 Professional computer? [Choose all that apply.]

- ❑ A. Mirrored volume
- ❑ B. RAID-5 array
- ❑ C. Spanned volume
- ❑ D. Primary partition

Answers A, C, and D are correct. On a Windows 2000 Professional computer, you can create primary, extended, and logical partitions on a basic disk. You can also create mirrored, spanned, striped, and simple volumes on a dynamic disk. Windows 2000 Professional does not support RAID-5 or fault-tolerant arrays, thus answer B is incorrect.

Question 2

Dawn configured a RAID-5 array on one of her Windows 2000 Servers that consists of seven 80GB SCSI hard disks. What amount of this space is required for use by the parity information?

- ❍ A. 60GB
- ❍ B. 80GB
- ❍ C. 120GB
- ❍ D. 132GB

Answer B is correct. RAID-5 arrays require all disks to have the same capacity. The parity information requires the capacity of one of the disks in the array, thus if Dawn uses seven 80GB disks to construct a RAID-5 array, she will have 480GB available for storage and 80GB used for the parity information. Thus, answers A, C, and D are incorrect.

Question 3

Andrea is the administrator in charge of your organization's Windows 2000/SQL 2000 servers. Last night, one of her SQL servers experienced a failure of one of the hard disks in its RAID-5 array. What must Andrea do to get the SQL server back into operation at full capability? [Choose all that apply.]

- ❑ A. Edit the boot.ini file to reflect the location of the boot partition.
- ❑ B. Replace the failed disk.
- ❑ C. Perform a restoration of data from the most recent backup set.
- ❑ D. Use Disk Management to repair the RAID-5 array.

Answers B and D are correct. Andrea needs only to replace the failed hard disk and then use the Disk Management utility to rebuild the RAID-5 array. Editing of the boot.ini file is only required when the primary disk in a mirrored set fails, thus answer A is incorrect. Because RAID-5 arrays are fault tolerant, no restoration of data using Windows Backup will be required. The parity information will be used by Windows 2000 to rebuild the data on the failed disk, thus answer C is incorrect.

Question 4

Christopher is a user in the advertising department of your organization. He routinely creates large files using desktop publishing applications. Today, when attempting to save a new catalog for an upcoming sales event, he was denied access to the disk he saves his files on with an out of space error. You configured disk quotas for all users to prevent misuse of disk space. What can you do to quickly remedy the situation and allow Christopher (and Christopher only) more disk space?

- ❍ A. Change the disk quota settings for the organizational unit (OU) that Christopher belongs to with the Group Policy Editor.
- ❍ B. Change the disk quota settings for Christopher from his user account properties in Active Directory Users and Computers.
- ❍ C. Move Christopher's home directory to another file server without disk quotas in place.
- ❍ D. Change the disk quota settings for Christopher in the Quota Entries window.

Answer D is correct. Disk quota settings can be configured manually for a variety of reasons from the Quota Entries window. Disk quotas are not controlled in Group Policy, thus answer A is incorrect. Disk quotas are not controlled in the user properties in Active Directory Users and Computer either, thus answer B is incorrect. Moving Christopher's home directory to another server will fix the problem, but is not the best (easiest) solution, thus answer C is incorrect.

Question 5

Hannah is the administrator responsible for the Windows 2000 file servers in your organization. She wants to use file and folder compression on her file servers, but does not see the option to enable it. What is the most likely cause of this problem?

- ❍ A. Hannah does not have the NTFS file system on her file servers.
- ❍ B. Hannah is not a member of the Enterprise Admins group.
- ❍ C. Hannah is not using a RAID-5 array on her file servers.
- ❍ D. Hannah is using disk quotas on her file servers.

Answer A is correct. Use of the NTFS file and folder compression feature requires the NTFS file system to be in place on the disks to be used. Being a member of the Enterprise Admins group is not required to enable compression, thus answer B is incorrect. The use of a RAID-5 array is not required for usage of file and folder compression, thus answer C is incorrect. The usage of disk quotas on a server does not affect the use of file and folder compression, thus answer D is incorrect. Disk quotas are, however, based on uncompressed file sizes.

Question 6

Austin is the administrator in your organization that is responsible for the Windows 2000 backup servers. All of Austin's backup servers are running Windows 2000 Server with a two-disk mirrored set. The morning following a power outage in your building, Austin reports to you that the primary disk in one of his mirrored sets failed. What will you tell Austin to do to correct the problem in the quickest manner? [Choose all that apply.]

- ❑ A. Edit the boot.ini file on the secondary disk to reflect the location of the boot partition.
- ❑ B. Replace the failed disk.
- ❑ C. Perform a restoration of data from the most recent backup set.
- ❑ D. Create a Windows 2000 boot disk and ensure that the boot.ini file on it points to the secondary disk.

Answers B and D are correct. Austin needs to create a Windows 2000 boot disk that has the boot.ini file pointing to the secondary disk in the mirror. After restarting Windows 2000 and breaking the mirror, Austin needs to replace the disk, restart Windows, and re-create the mirror. There is no boot.ini file on a secondary mirrored disk, thus answer A is incorrect. No data restoration should be required as the secondary mirrored disk has the data intact, thus answer C is incorrect.

Question 7

Jeff is the IIS server administrator for your organization. He currently has all of his IIS servers running with RAID-5 arrays that use hot-swappable hard disks. This morning he discovered that one of his IIS servers had a disk failure on one of its RAID-5 array disks. Jeff installed a new hard disk in the IIS server. What does he need to do now to get Windows 2000 to recognize the new disk?

- ❍ A. Restart the IIS server.
- ❍ B. Open Disk Management and rescan his disks.
- ❍ C. Use the Add/Remove Hardware Wizard.
- ❍ D. Create a new RAID-5 array.

Answer B is correct. Using the rescan disks command in Disk Management will allow his newly installed disk to be recognized by Windows. After this, he can rebuild the existing RAID-5 array. Restarting the IIS server will cause the new disk to be recognized, but it is not recommended or required in the case of hot-swappable disks, thus answer A is incorrect. Using the Add/Remove Hardware Wizard is not required in this case, thus answer C is incorrect. Creating a new RAID-5 array is not required, thus answer D is incorrect.

Question 8

Joe is a member of your graphic art department. He frequently stores large files on his Windows 2000 Professional computer while he is still editing them. He would like to implement some form of fault tolerance for his data. Joe currently has two 60GB hard disks installed in his computer. What should you do to Joe's computer to implement fault tolerance with the least administrative effort?

- ❍ A. Upgrade his Windows 2000 Professional computer to Windows 2000 Server and create a mirrored volume for him.
- ❍ B. Upgrade his basic disks to dynamic disks and create a mirrored set from them.
- ❍ C. Install a SCSI controller card and three SCSI external hard disks. Create a RAID-5 array from these external hard disks.
- ❍ D. Create a RAID-5 array on his computer using the two installed 60GB disks.

Answer A is correct. The easiest course of action would be to upgrade Joe's basic disks to dynamic disks and then create a mirrored set out of them. Windows 2000 Professional does not support mirrored sets; therefore, answer B is incorrect. Installing a SCSI controller card and three external SCSI hard disks for a RAID-5 array will solve the problem as well, but is not the least amount of effort, thus answer C is incorrect. You cannot create a RAID-5 array on a Windows 2000 Professional computer, nor can you create one with less than three disks, thus answer D is incorrect.

Question 9

Rick is a user in the administrative department of your organization. Rick complains to you today that he is out of disk space to save his files. Upon further investigation, you find that he has completely used his disk quota allowance of 200MB, with more than 175MB being used by MP3 files that you suspect he has downloaded from the Internet. You do not want Rick to be able to fill your file servers with MP3s. What should you do to put a stop to this problem with the least administrative effort?

- ❍ A. Move Rick's user account into the Guest group.
- ❍ B. Manually configure Rick's quota settings from the Quota Entries window.
- ❍ C. Manually configure Rick's quota settings from the properties dialog box of his user account in Active Directory Users and Computers.
- ❍ D. Remove Rick's computer from the network.

Answer B is correct. The easiest way to correct this problem without preventing Rick from being able to accomplish his assigned work will be to manually configure the quota settings for his account from the Quota Entries window. Moving Rick's user account into the Guest group will most likely cause more problems than it fixes and will not fix this particular problem, thus answer A is incorrect. Disk quota settings are not configured from Active Directory Users and Computers, thus answer C is incorrect. Removing Rick's computer from the network, while tempting, will most likely prevent him from being able to accomplish his assigned work, thus answer D is incorrect.

Question 10

Chris is attempting to configure disk quotas for her Windows 2000 file server. All user documents are stored in a shared folder named "Users," which is located in the root of Volume C on the server. When she opens the Properties page for the Users folder, she does not see a tab for disk quotas. What is the most likely reason?

- ❍ A. Disk quotas must be enabled at the root of the volume, not at a folder level.
- ❍ B. Only Domain Admins can enable disk quotas.
- ❍ C. Disk quotas can only be enabled on NTFS 5.0 volumes.
- ❍ D. Disk quotas must be enabled using a local Administrator account, not a domain-based Administrator account.

Answer A is correct. Chris is attempting to place a disk quota on a subfolder instead of the volume root, thus she will not see the Quota tab of the Properties dialog box. Chris needs to enable the quotas on the entire volume (C, in this case). You do not need to be a member of the Domain Admins group to enable disk quotas, thus answer B is incorrect. Although it is true that disk quotas can only be enabled on an NTFS 5.0 volume, the problem is that Chris is attempting to enable a quota on a folder on the volume, not on the volume itself. Therefore, answer C is incorrect in this case. You do not have to log on with a local Administrator account to enable disk quotas, you only need to have Administrative privileges, thus answer D is incorrect.

Need to Know More?

Russel, Charlie and Sharon Crawford, *Windows 2000 Server Administrator's Companion*, Microsoft Press, 2000. ISBN 1572318198

Stanek, William R., *Windows 2000 Administrator's Pocket Consultant*, Microsoft Press, 2000. ISBN 0735608318

`http://www.microsoft.com/windows2000/techinfo/reskit/en-us/default.asp` is the source for Windows 2000 Resource Kits. Also available in print: ISBN 1572318082 (Windows 2000 Professional) and ISBN 1572318058 (Windows 2000 Server).

Configuring and Troubleshooting Windows 2000 Network Connections

Terms you'll need to understand:

- ✓ Network adapter
- ✓ TCP/IP
- ✓ Binding
- ✓ Protocol
- ✓ Client
- ✓ Service
- ✓ Remote access policy
- ✓ Internet Connection Sharing
- ✓ DNS
- ✓ WINS
- ✓ Virtual Private Network
- ✓ Terminal Services

Techniques you'll need to master:

- ✓ Installing and configuring network adapters
- ✓ Installing and configuring network protocols
- ✓ Configuring DHCP, DNS, WINS, and ICS
- ✓ Configuring Terminal Services

Introduction

This chapter covers a lot of ground, starting at the bottom of the pyramid, so to speak, and working our way up. We first look at some simple yet very critical items, such as installing network adapters, configuring network protocols, and configuring network services. These topics make up the bottom levels of our networking pyramid. As we move through the chapter, we examine more complex subjects, such as sharing connection access, configuring for Remote Access and Virtual Private Networking, and Terminal Services. Because many networks often have an improperly configured network adapter, we start first with that topic.

Installing, Configuring, and Troubleshooting Network Adapters and Drivers

Installing a network adapter into your Windows 2000 computer should be one of the easiest tasks you ever have to perform. Chapter 4, "Configuring and Troubleshooting Hardware Devices and Drivers," covered hardware installation and configuration in some detail, so if you need a refresher on installing your network adapter, see Chapter 4.

After you have the network adapter and drivers properly installed, you need to configure the network adapter driver. Each network adapter allows different levels of configuration options; some network adapters allow more configurable options than others. Figure 7.1 displays the network adapter properties shown in the Device Manager for a typical AMD network adapter.

It's important to note that not all network adapters have the same properties nor the same properties tabs. In the following sections, we examine each tab of the network adapter properties page shown in Figure 7.1 and discuss the typical network adapter configuration options available to you.

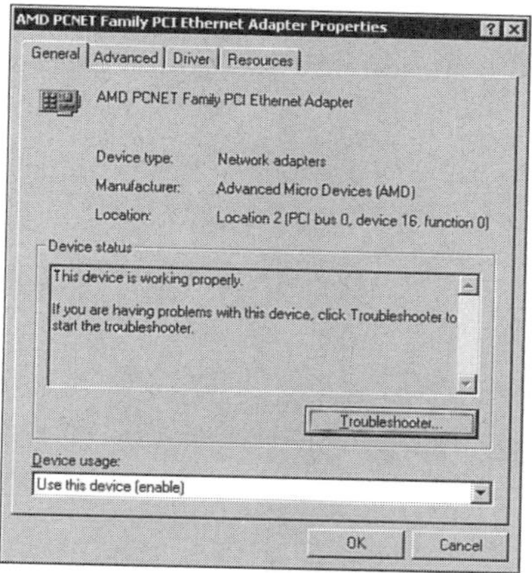

Figure 7.1 The network adapter properties page.

General Network Adapter Properties

From the General tab, seen in Figure 7.1, you can gather some basic information about the network adapter, such as the type of network adapter you have, the manufacturer, and the physical location within your computer. You can also determine whether the device is functioning properly.

If the device is functioning improperly, you can opt to start the Hardware Troubleshooter by clicking the Troubleshooter button. Lastly, you can manually disable and enable the network adapter by using the Device usage drop-down.

Advanced Network Adapter Properties

On the Advanced tab, shown in Figure 7.2, you can configure some of the deeper options that your network adapter may support.

Bear in mind that each network adapter will have different options listed on the Advanced tab. Therefore, if you don't see what's listed in Figure 7.2, it's not necessarily a problem as long as your drivers are up to date and properly installed.

By selecting a value from the list on the left side, you can configure its options in the right side of the page. The most common item you may want to consider configuring manually is that for speed (Link Speed/Duplex Mode in our example). You should configure the adapter to the maximum speed supported by the network adapter and your network infrastructure. In most cases this should be configured to 100MBps full duplex, but your network conditions may vary.

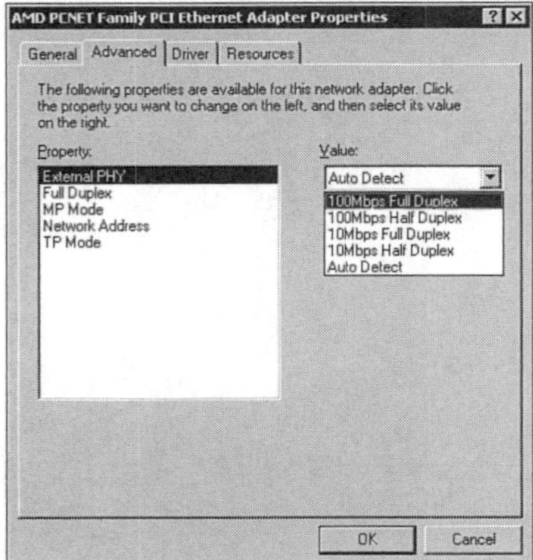

Figure 7.2 Configuring the network adapter's advanced options.

Driver Properties

On the Driver tab, you can get more detailed information on the currently installed driver. The following is some of the information that is available to you:

- Driver provider
- Driver date
- Driver version
- Digital signer

Each item in this list can be used to help discover or prevent driver-related problems with the hardware installed on your network. Refer to Chapter 4 if you need to refresh on the importance of digital signatures.

By clicking the Driver Details button, you can gain very detailed information on each file that makes up the driver file set. Clicking the Uninstall button allows you to actually uninstall the network adapter itself, which is a useful first step to try when you begin experiencing hardware problems. Clicking the Update Driver button allows you to update the installed driver file set as discussed previously in Chapter 4.

Resources Properties

The Resources tab contains a listing of the computer resources that the network adapter is currently using. You may or may not be able to manually configure these resources; however, in most cases, you should leave them alone and let Windows 2000 do the resource management work for you. Chapter 4 covered hardware resources in great detail.

Power Management Properties

The Power Management tab may or may not be present on your particular network adapter. If it is, you typically have two options for configuring power management behavior for the network adapter. The Allow This Device to Bring the Computer out of Standby option can be selected to allow the network adapter to bring the computer out of standby—a popular function with Wake-ON LAN (WOL) capable network devices. The WOL cable must be connected to the network adapter and the WOL plug must be connected to the computer's mainboard for this function to work properly. This is not recommended for use on portable computers, because this process periodically wakes up a computer in standby to check the network connection, which can have an adverse impact on battery life. You can select the Allow Computer to Turn Off This Device to Save Power option to allow Windows to manage the network adapter's state to save power. This option should be selected on portable computers to maximize battery lifetime.

Troubleshooting Network Adapters

More often than not, network adapters work fine for many years. When they do act up, however, it is a critical situation that you want to correct as soon as possible. Without a functioning network adapter, the network does not serve much purpose. Table 7.1 outlines some of the more common issues that plague network adapters and serves as a starting point for your troubleshooting efforts.

Table 7.1 Common Network Adapter Problems

Problem	Solution
The network adapter is not on the Windows 2000 HCL.	Replace the adapter with a similar, but HCL supported, network adapter.
The network adapter driver is outdated.	Attempt to update the driver from the network adapter's Properties page (in Device Manager). If unsuccessful, seek out a new driver from the vendor.

(continued)

Table 7.1 Common Network Adapter Problems *(continued)*

Problem	Solution
The hardware is not functioning.	Replace the network adapter with a known good one. Verify that the network adapter is not functioning by placing the defective adapter into one or more other machines to test it.
The network adapter is not automatically installed by Windows 2000.	You must initiate a manual installation of the network adapter by using the Add/Remove Hardware Wizard. Ensure that you have set any resource settings on the adapter as required. Also ensure that you have recorded all required resource settings so that you can manually configure them in Windows.
Network adapter installed, but communications do not succeed.	Ensure that you have the required networking protocols installed and configured as detailed in the next section of this chapter.
Network adapter installed, but communications do not succeed.	Ensure that you have all the required network services installed and configured properly on your network as detailed later in this chapter. Services typically include DNS and DHCP, but might include others.
Network adapter installed, but causing computer to behave erratically.	Remove the network adapter from the Device Manager. A Safe Mode startup may be required. This is usually a case of incompatible drivers: Seek out compatible drivers or replace the network adapter with a different type.

Installing, Configuring, and Troubleshooting Network Protocols

After getting your network adapter installed and configured to your liking, your next step is to install and configure the required network protocols. Think of network protocols as a language. If you were speaking to a friend in English and he replied back to you in German (and assuming that you didn't understand German), you would not know what was being said. Just the same, a computer that requires the AppleTalk protocol would not be able to effectively communicate with a computer using the TCP/IP protocol for communications.

Windows 2000 is a radical departure from all previous versions of the Windows operating system in that it is designed from the ground up to use the TCP/IP network protocol for all network communications. In fact, it is now possible (and recommended) to run an entire Windows network using TCP/IP only, because all versions of Windows include support for TCP/IP. Before you can actually begin communication between computers, you must install and configure the required network protocols.

Installing network protocols is a very simple process and is done as follows:

1. Open the network adapter properties by selecting it from the Network Connections window, right-clicking on it, and selecting Properties. The window shown in Figure 7.3 opens.

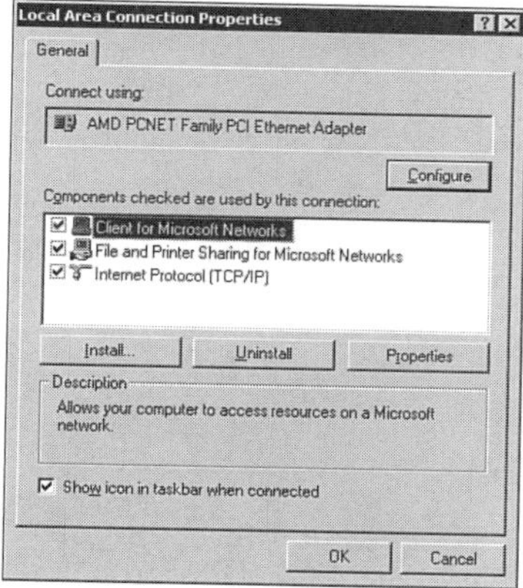

Figure 7.3 The Local Area Connection properties window.

2. Click on the Install button to open the Select Network Component Type dialog box as shown in Figure 7.4.

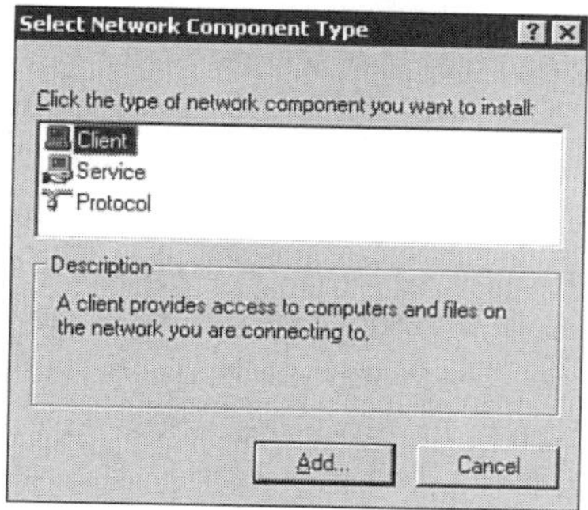

Figure 7.4 Installing a new network protocol.

3. You have the option of installing Clients, Services, or Protocols from the dialog box shown in Figure 7.4. Other options, such as the Client Service for NetWare or the Client for Microsoft Networks, appear under the Client listing. The Service listing includes things like the QoS (Quality of Service) Packet Scheduler or the Service Advertising Protocol. Finally, under Protocols, are the network communications protocols that we are interested in, such as AppleTalk, IPX/SPX, and TCP/IP (see Figure 7.5). Click Protocols and then select the protocol you wish to install on your computer.

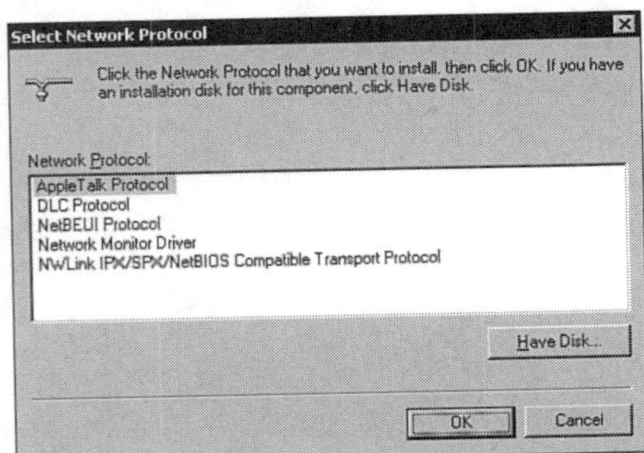

Figure 7.5 Selecting the protocol to be installed.

TCP/IP

By default, all Windows 2000 installations include the TCP/IP protocol, but you may need to reinstall or configure it later. To that end, we examine the configuration of TCP/IP here.

To begin the configuration of any protocol, select it from the network adapter properties page (refer to Figure 7.3) and click Properties. The Internet Protocol (TCP/IP) Properties window opens, as shown in Figure 7.6.

IP addresses are 32-bit (4 octet) numbers that uniquely identify a computer on a network. The first part of each IP address is used to identify the network the computer is on and the last part of the IP address is used to identify the computer itself. Consider the case of a house's street address such as 325 Peachtree Road. The street address can be considered to be two parts, the first part being the street name (Peachtree Road) and the last part being the house number (325). IP addresses function in the same way, but are slightly more complicated.

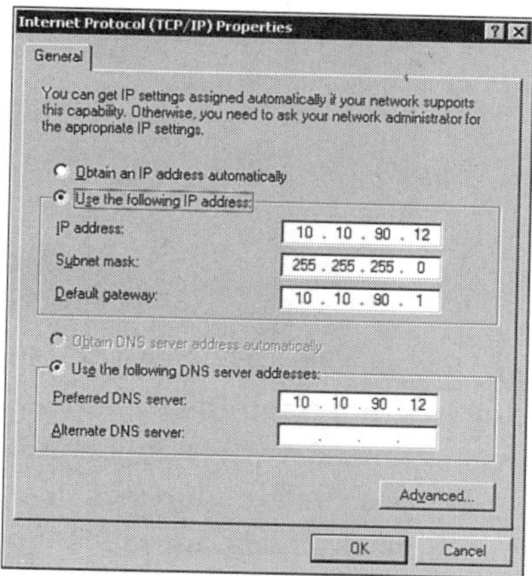

Figure 7.6 The TCP/IP properties page showing manually configured settings.

There are five classes of IP address: Not surprisingly they are called Class A, B, C, D, and E. Table 7.2 outlines the key points of the classes of public IP addresses (A, B, and C), which are usable by your system. Class D addresses are multicast addresses and Class E addresses are experimental addresses reserved for future use; neither Class D or E addresses is for public use.

Table 7.2 Public IP Address Classes

Network Class	Address Range for Network Address	Number of Networks	Number of Host Nodes	Default Subnet Mask
A	1–126	126	16,777,214	255.0.0.0
B	128–191	16,384	65,534	255.255.0.0
C	192–223	2,097,152	254	255.255.255.0

In the default Class A IP address of 45.234.67.122, the first octet only (45 in this case) identifies the network and the remaining three octets (234.67.122) identify a specific host on that network. A host is any device that requires or uses an IP address, including managed hubs, printers, and so on. If this were a default Class B IP address of 145.234.67.122, then the first two octets (145.234 in this case) would identify the network and the remaining two octets would identify the host. In a default Class C IP address of 215.234.67.122, the first three octets would identify the network address, with the remaining octet left to identify the host. When we say "default," we are referring to the default subnet masks as outlined in Table 7.2. It is possible, and very commonplace, for the subnet mask to be non-default. That is beyond the realm of this exam, however.

In each address range, there exists a range of *private IP addresses* that are specified for usage only on a private network. They are as follows:

- *Class A*—10.0.0.0–10.255.255.255
- *Class B*—172.16.0.0–172.31.255.255
- *Class C*—192.168.0.0–192.168.255.255

Private IP addresses are sometimes referred to as *non-routable addresses*. This is because the addresses are not routed to the Internet by an Internet service provider (ISP). The name is misleading because these networks can be routed within private networks and Intranets. To conserve IP addresses, most companies use private IP addresses within their network, and use some type of proxy or firewall to translate the private address to a public address when a internal user is going out to the Internet. This is also a good security measure, because outsiders have no easy way of knowing the IP addresses of computers in your organization.

IP address 127.0.0.1 is reserved as the loopback address for testing the configuration of the network card. Any other addresses in the 127 range are considered invalid or are not supported by some TCP/IP implementations.

A feature that was first used in Windows 98 and has now been brought over to Windows 2000 is *Auto Private IP Addressing (APIPA)*. APIPA automatically supplies an IP address to your network adapter if you don't specify a static IP address and your computer is unable to contact a DHCP server. The APIPA service queries the network to find out what APIPA addresses are in use, and then it attempts to assign your computer a unique IP address in the 169.254.0.0–169.254.255.255 range. APIPA does not assign a default gateway, or the address of a Domain Name Service (DNS) or Windows Internet Naming Service (WINS) server, so your computer is usually not able to contact other computers with normally assigned IP addresses, or access the Internet or other networks through your router.

General TCP/IP Properties

By default, Windows 2000 configures your computer as a DHCP client, which gives your workstation an automatic TCP/IP address. This is all well and good in about 90 percent of the cases, but what about the other 10 percent of the time when you are dealing with a server that requires a static IP address, or have a network without a DHCP server? In cases such as these, or for any other reason, you can very easily manually configure your TCP/IP settings. Click the alternate set of radio buttons to enable manual entry of IP addresses and other IP-related items. For example, you must supply the computer's IP address, subnet mask (Windows 2000 automatically suggests a default subnet mask based on the IP address you enter), default gateway IP address, and a primary DNS server IP address (you can also configure additional DNS servers to use if the primary server is offline).

Should you need to enter some very specific TCP/IP configuration options, you can do so by clicking the Advanced button seen in Figure 7.6. The Advanced TCP/IP Settings window, shown in Figure 7.7, opens with four available tabs: IP Settings, DNS, WINS, and Options. Each of these is described in greater detail in the following sections.

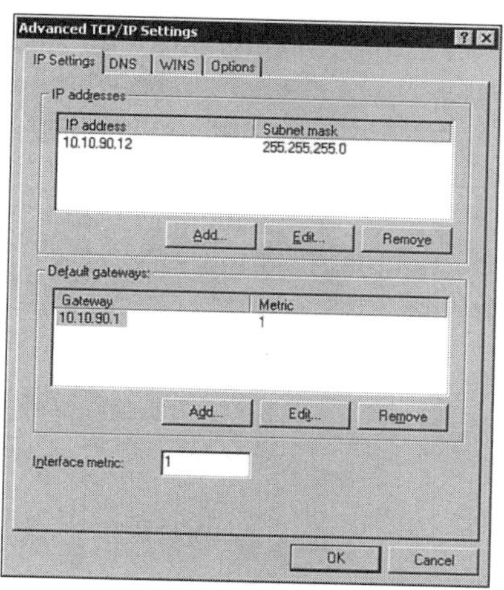

Figure 7.7 The Advanced TCP/IP Settings page.

The IP Settings Properties

From the IP Settings page, you can manually configure additional IP addresses and subnet masks, additional gateways, and the metric (link cost) for each gateway configured. The link cost is the number of hops between routers.

Multiple IP addresses may need to be configured on the server for a variety of reasons. One such reason is when you have multiple IP subnets in use on your network and the computer must use a different IP address to communicate on each of these logical IP networks. Gateways are routers that forward IP packets to destinations beyond the boundaries of the local network. It is possible in larger networks that you may have multiple gateways passing traffic out off the network. The metric, as stated previously, indicates the cost of the route that could be used to pass traffic, the least costly route is chosen automatically. You can specify the cost of each of the configured default gateways as you desire, thus indicating to Windows the order in which they are to be used to route packets.

DNS Properties

Domain name servers have been in use on the Internet for many years. DNS resolves numerical IP addresses into more user-friendly host names. Prior to DNS, HOSTS files were used for name resolution, but as the Internet quickly grew in size and popularity, maintaining HOSTS files became impossible. When the Internet community realized there was a need for a more manageable, scalable, and efficient name resolution system, DNS was created.

From the DNS Properties tab (see Figure 7.8), you can configure advanced DNS options such as adding more DNS servers to the computer's list of DNS servers, as well as specifying domain suffixes for unqualified names and instructing Windows to register or not register this connections address in DNS.

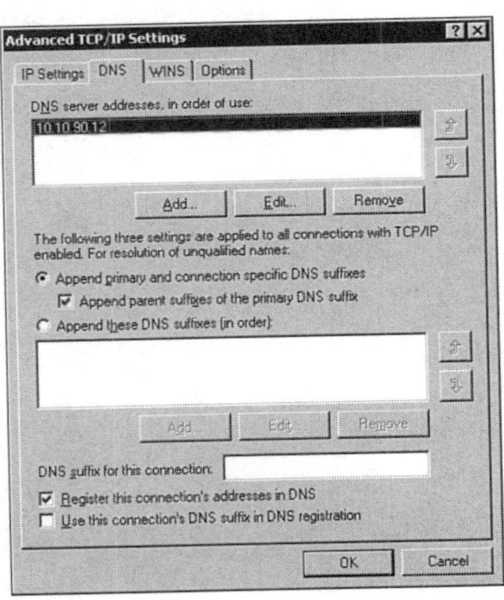

Figure 7.8 The DNS properties page.

WINS Properties

WINS provides a dynamic database to register NetBIOS names and resolve them to IP addresses. Clients can dynamically register their NetBIOS names with a WINS server and query the WINS server when they need to resolve a NetBIOS name to an IP address.

From the WINS Properties tab (see Figure 7.9), you can configure WINS options, such as adding more WINS servers to the computer's list of WINS servers as well as specifying whether to import an LMHOSTS file.

An LMHOSTS file is a flat file database that contains the mapping of computer Network Basic Input/Output System (NetBIOS) names to IP addresses. A sample LMHOSTS file is stored in the %systemroot%\system32\drivers\etc folder. LMHOSTS files are generally used for NetBIOS name resolution when you don't have a WINS server.

The following options are available for NetBIOS configuration:

- Enable NetBIOS over TCP/IP
- Disable NetBIOS over TCP/IP
- Use NetBIOS setting from the DHCP server

These options are used to select whether or not the computer is configured to use the NetBIOS protocol, or to allow the DHCP server to supply the NetBIOS setting.

In previous versions of Windows, the NetBIOS Application Programming Interface (API) and the NetBIOS Enhanced User Interface (NetBEUI) protocol, with or without WINS servers, was the primary name resolution method. Pre-Windows 2000 clients still require the presence of WINS and NetBIOS. In a completely Windows 2000 Active Directory network, NetBIOS support is rarely necessary.

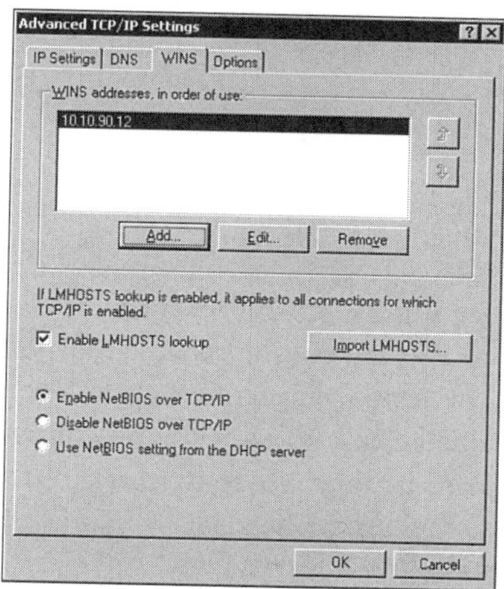

Figure 7.9 The WINS Properties page.

Options Properties

The Options tab lets you configure two of the more advanced TCP/IP options: *TCP/IP Filtering* and *IP Security*. Both of these options are used to increase the security of your computer by allowing you to control what incoming traffic is accepted.

TCP/IP packet filtering allows you to specify, by adapter, whether communication is allowed, secured, or blocked, according to the IP address ranges, IP protocols, or even specific TCP and UDP ports. As shown in Figure 7.10, when TCP/IP filtering is turned on, it is turned on for all network adapters. However, you can configure each adapter with separate settings via each adapter's properties page. Note, however, that the Windows 2000 Server Routing and Remote Access Service (RRAS) provides much more advanced filtering capabilities and should be used in place of TCP/IP filtering.

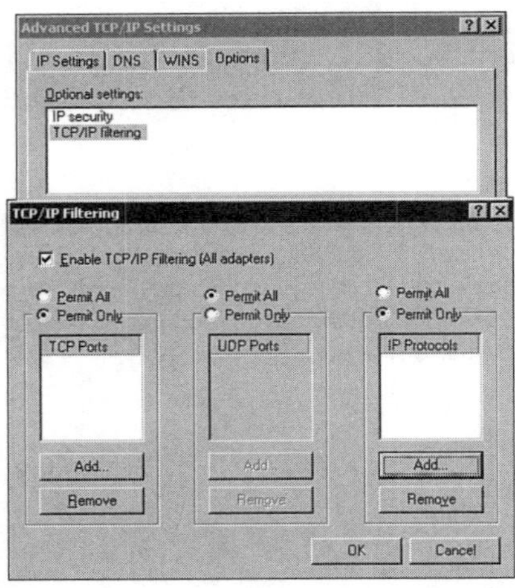

Figure 7.10 The TCP/IP Filtering Properties page.

The second option is IP Security (IPSec), see Figure 7.11. IPSec provides for secure communications between computers. You can configure an IPSec policy as part of the local or domain security policy to assign encryption levels and private or shared keys. In addition, IPSec can automatically be configured for you by applying a security template to your computer. For more information on security policy and security templates, see Chapter 8, "Implementing, Monitoring, and Troubleshooting Security."

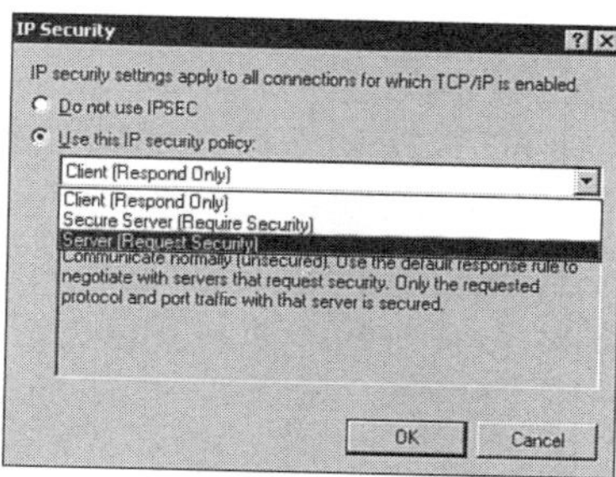

Figure 7.11 The IP Security Properties page.

If you're not using a predefined security policy, you can use the options page to control what types of traffic are allowed in and out of your computer. The following options are available:

- *Client (Respond Only)*—This option allows your Windows 2000 server to communicate normally with the computers on your network. However it uses IPSec to communicate to any computers that require IPSec secured communications.
- *Secure Server (Require Security)*—This option requires that all traffic in and out of your Windows 2000 server must be secured.
- *Server (Request Security)*—With this option turned on, your Windows 2000 server requests that any client that communicates with it uses secure communications. However, if the client is unable to do so, it will allow unsecured communications.

NWLink

NWLink is the Microsoft version of Novell's Internetwork Packet Exchange/Sequenced Packet Exchange (IPX/SPX) protocol. Although more efficient and easier to configure than TCP/IP, generally you will find that it is only used on Novell NetWare networks.

NWLink is installed like any other protocol by selecting the Install button from the Local Area Connection Properties page (refer to Figures 7.3 through 7.5) of your network adapter. From the Select Network Protocol dialog, just select NWLink and click OK. NWLink is automatically installed.

For most environments, the default settings are sufficient and no other configuration is required. However, the following configuration settings can be configured by highlighting the NWLink entry and clicking the Properties button in the Local Area Connections Properties dialog box:

- *Frame Type*—The default is for NWLink to use auto frame type detection, and this is appropriate for most situations. However, if it needs to be changed, select the Manual frame type detection option, click the Add button in the NWLink Properties dialog box, and select the desired frame type from the drop-down, as shown in Figure 7.12.
- *Network number*—This number identifies the network in which the computer is installed. All computers on the network must have the same number. This is automatically detected with the frame type. If the frame type is manually configured, the network number must be as well.
- *Internal network number*—This is a unique number that the administrator assigns to identify a server.

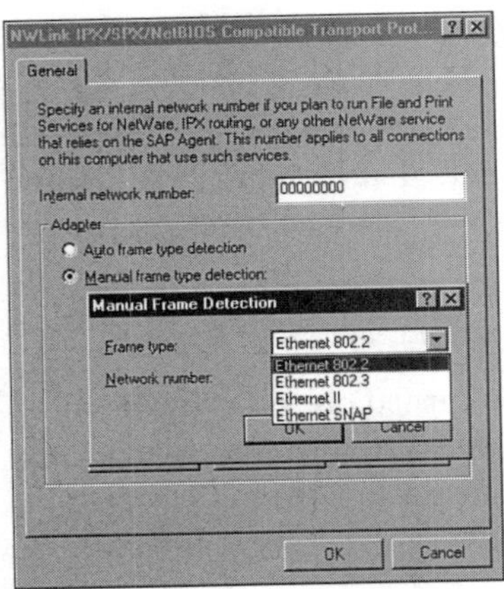

Figure 7.12 NWLink, selecting Frame Type.

NetBEUI

NetBEUI is a legacy protocol that was used on Microsoft networks before TCP/IP was available. NetBEUI is only suitable for small networks because it is not routable. There is basically no configuration involved; just give the computer a unique name.

NetBEUI is installed like any other protocol by selecting the Install button from the Local Area Connection Properties page (refer to Figures 7.3–7.5) of your network adapter. From the Select Network Protocol dialog, just select NetBEUI and click OK. NetBEUI will be automatically installed and configured.

There is absolutely no reason to install NetBEUI. If any applications or downlevel Windows clients require NetBEUI support, you can just configure the network adapters on all of your computers to support NetBIOS over TCP/IP. For details, see the previous section that covers the network adapter WINS Properties tab.

Installing and Configuring Network Services

Now that we have seen how to configure some of the client services that are common to all Windows 2000 computers, let's take a brief look at the network services that we configured our network card to use. All of the services we are going to look at can only be installed on a Windows 2000 Server or Advanced Server computer; they cannot be installed on Windows 2000 Professional.

All the network services that we are going to be discussing can be installed using the following procedure:

1. Select Start, Settings, Control Panel, Add/Remove Programs, Add/Remove Windows Components.
2. From the Windows Component Wizard dialog, select Networking Services and click the Details button.
3. This opens the Networking Services dialog as shown in Figure 7.13. From here you can select DNS, DHCP, WINS and several other network services.

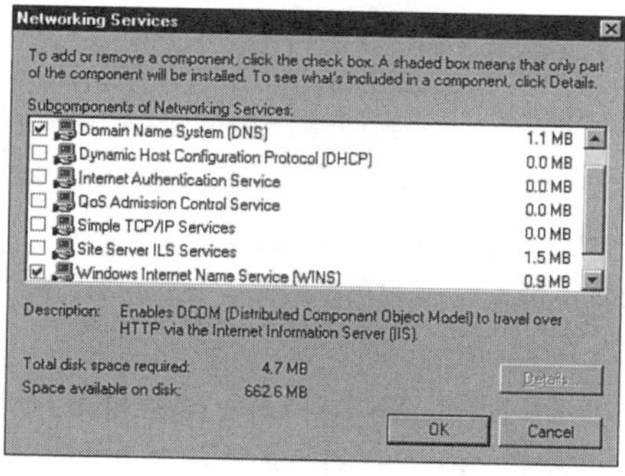

Figure 7.13 The Networking Services installation dialog.

The Domain Name Service (DNS)

The Domain Name Service is an Internet standard TCP/IP name service. DNS allows client machines to resolve, or locate, TCP/IP devices (servers, workstations, routers, and so on) within the LAN, and Internet hosts beyond the LAN. Although humans are comfortable with names, computers require numbers, so DNS is necessary to handle this resolution. For example, it is the responsibility of DNS to translate the user-friendly name `http://www.quepublishing.com/` into the computer-friendly IP address 165.193.123.44.

Windows 2000 uses DNS as the locator service for Active Directory (AD), and AD cannot be installed without a DNS server present and operational. Windows 2000 computers query DNS at boot time to find the closest domain controller. Servers use DNS to create a replication topology to facilitate directory updates.

DNS replaces Windows Internet Naming Service (WINS) as the default name resolution mechanism in Windows 2000. However, WINS is still required for support of downlevel Windows 9x and NT 4.0 clients, and certain software applications.

The shift to DNS as the primary lookup method provides a Windows 2000 environment with significant added functionality in its ability to locate and share addressing information across an organization and to provide support for an open industry standard. Windows 2000 also supports a number of innovations to the DNS environment, one of which is support for Dynamic DNS (DDNS), as described in RFC 2136, which allows Windows 2000 to dynamically register with DNS servers listed in the TCP/IP properties.

Windows 2000 DNS also supports integrating the DNS database with Active Directory. This integration allows for DNS zone information to be maintained and distributed using the Active Directory replication technology already in place. This feature brings significant benefits to DNS, including

- *No single point of failure*—Windows 2000 Active Directory uses multiple-master replication. Therefore, updates can be submitted to any participating DNS server.
- *Efficient replication*—All Active Directory replication is on a per-property basis. For example, a user object has many properties associated with it—first name, last name, email address, phone extension, and so on. If one of these properties is changed, Active Directory replicates only that individual property, not the entire user object. This results in significantly smaller replication traffic across the network. Rather than an

entire zone file being replicated every time a record changes, as would happen in traditional DNS, the integration of Microsoft DNS with Active Directory means that only the affected record is replicated to other DNS servers.

- *Dynamic Registration*—All computers that receive a leased IP address are automatically entered into the DNS database, and are removed when the lease expires.

ADS replication can be scheduled or compressed to save WAN bandwidth. Also, even without ADS, DNS attempts incremental updates by default, thus replicating only changes rather than the entire zone file. If that fails due to servers that don't support incremental updates, it transfers the entire file.

You install DNS using the procedure that was discussed in the previous section. After installation, open the DNS MMC, as shown in Figure 7.14, and allow the wizard that appears automatically to step you through creating the forward and reverse lookup zones necessary for a proper DNS infrastructure.

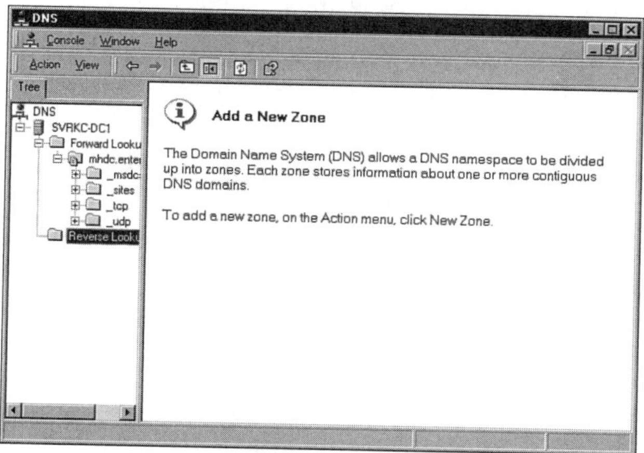

Figure 7.14 The DNS MMC, using the wizard to create a zone.

The Dynamic Host Control Protocol (DHCP)

Dynamic Host Configuration Protocol (DHCP) is a TCP/IP standard designed to provide client machines with IP addresses dynamically at boot time. The client has use of this IP address for a predetermined amount of time, called a *lease-duration*. Before the lease expires, the client reconnects to the DHCP server and renews the lease. This process frees administrators from maintaining static IP addresses, and ensures consistency of IP configuration across the LAN.

Once a client receives an IP address from a DHCP server, a renewal process occurs as the lease approaches expiration. After 50 percent of the configured lease duration has elapsed, the client attempts to contact the DHCP server. The client that's requesting to renew its IP address broadcasts a DHCPREQUEST message. The DHCP server, if available, responds with a DHCPACK, granting the client's request to renew the IP address. Also, information about other DHCP options is included in this reply. If any information has changed since the client first obtained its lease, the client updates its configuration accordingly.

If the server from which the client originally leased the IP address does not respond, the client again attempts to renew the IP address when 87.5 percent of the lease duration has elapsed. At this point, the client attempts to renew its current lease with any available DHCP server. If a server responds with a DHCP offer message (DHCPOFFER) to update the current client lease, the client can renew its lease based on the offering and continue operation.

If the lease expires and no server has been contacted, the client must immediately discontinue using its leased IP address. The client then follows the same process used during its initial start up operation to obtain an IP address.

You install DHCP using the procedure that was discussed in the previous section. After installation, open the DHCP MMC, as shown in Figure 7.15, and right-click on the server name and select New Scope. This opens the New Scope Wizard. Scopes determine the pool of IP addresses from which a DHCP server can assign IP addresses. Every DHCP server must be configured with at least one scope.

Follow the wizard's prompts and configure the following:

- *Scope Name*—This should be something descriptive.
- *IP Address Range*—This is the starting and ending IP addresses of the range of IPs that you want to distribute to clients. The subnet mask is also entered here.
- *Add Exclusions*—If you are going to manually assign any static IP addresses that are included in the previously defined range of IP addresses, you should exclude them here. This prevents DHCP from leasing an IP address that is earmarked for use on a specific device. If this specification is not made for the static addresses, an IP address conflict occurs, causing one or more computers to not function.

➤ *Lease Duration*—This is the length of time that the IP address is be leased to a client. The client has the opportunity to renew the lease before it expires. The default is eight days; it should be suitable for most environments.

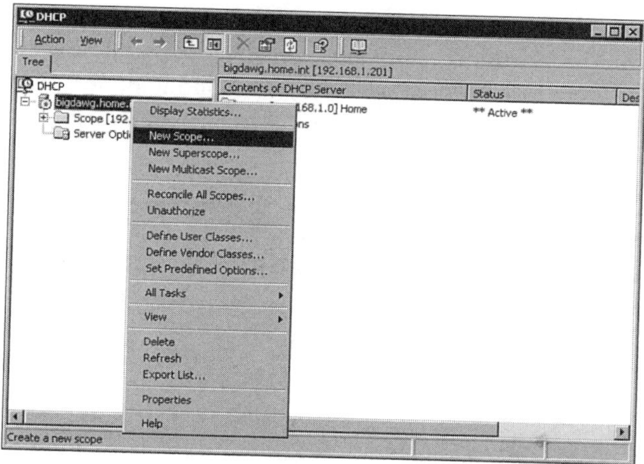

Figure 7.15 The DHCP MMC, using the wizard to create a scope.

At this time, the wizard gives you the opportunity to configure the DHCP options. When a computer receives an IP address from the DHCP service, it can also receive other optional TCP/IP configuration settings, such as

➤ WINS Server Address

➤ DNS Server Address

➤ Gateway Address

➤ Time Server Address

➤ WINS/NBT Node Type

These settings can be configured using the wizard, or can be configured later by right-clicking Scope Options and selecting Configure Options.

Before a DHCP server can service client requests, it must be authorized. This is accomplished by right-clicking the scope name and selecting Authorize. This is a step that is very important in the real world, so you could reasonably expect to see some reference to it on the exam.

Additionally, DHCP in Windows 2000 has been extended to provide additional services beyond traditional IP address assignment. First, Windows

2000 DHCP is integrated with DNS, providing dynamic name-to-IP mapping. This allows the DHCP server to automatically register a computer in DNS when it issues it an IP address, and de-register it when the IP address lease expires. Second, Windows 2000 DHCP supports Remote Installation Service (RIS), providing auto configuration of Windows 2000 Professional workstations by pressing F12 during power-on self-test (POST). Using DHCP and RIS, a pristine workstation can receive an IP address and be configured with Windows 2000 Professional and other productivity software without an administrator being present.

The Windows Internet Naming Service

Each computer has an DNS host name and a NetBIOS computer name. Unless specifically configured otherwise, these names are the same. Windows Internet Naming Service (WINS) provides NetBIOS name-to-IP address resolution. The WINS service provides for NetBIOS names what DNS provides for host names.

You install WINS using the procedure that was discussed in the beginning of this section. Compared to some of the other services, there is relatively little configuration involved for WINS. The only recommended task is to configure the WINS database to be backed up periodically.

This is accomplished by right-clicking the server name in the WINS MMC and selecting Properties. From the General tab, as shown in Figure 7.16, enter the path where you want the database to be backed up to. This cannot be a network drive; it must be on the local computer. The database is backed up every three hours. In addition, you can select the Back Up Database During Server Shutdown option, which automatically backs up the database whenever the server is shut down or rebooted, or the WINS service is stopped.

You can also configure replication of the WINS database to other servers through the use of push and pull partners. A push partner reports changes to the database to other servers. A pull partner is a server that requests a replica of the database from the push partner. To configure general replication parameters from the WINS console, perform the following steps on both push and pull partners:

1. Expand the view for the server by clicking the plus sign next to it.
2. Right-click Replication Partners and select Properties from the pop-up menu.

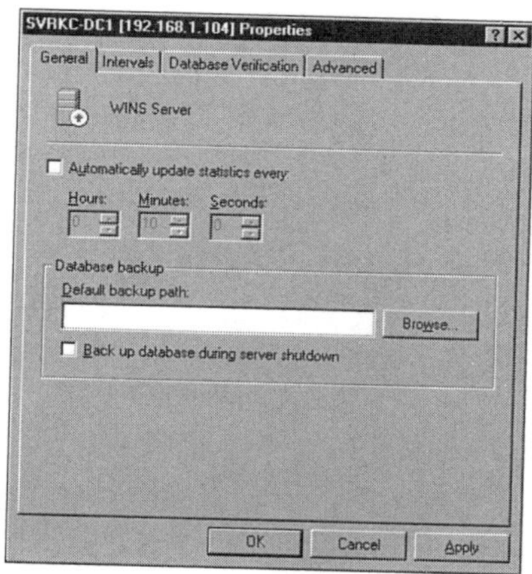

Figure 7.16 The WINS server Properties page, showing the database backup selection on the General tab.

3. From the General tab, select or deselect Replicate Only with Partners. Selecting this option guarantees that WINS information is replicated only with designated replication partners. Deselecting this option allows you to manually replicate WINS information with any WINS server on the network.

4. Static mappings are created for non-WINS clients on the network, which allows their computer names to be registered in WINS. If multiple computers may use the same IP addresses, you may want WINS to overwrite existing entries with information from new registrations. To do this, select Overwrite Unique Static Mappings At This Server.

To configure a push partner, perform the following steps from the WINS console:

1. Expand the view for the server by clicking the plus sign next to it.

2. Right-click Replication Partners and select Properties from the pop-up menu.

3. Select the Push Replication tab.

4. To configure when the push should take place, select At Service Startup or When Address Changes, or both.

5. The Number of Changes in Version ID Before Replication filed specifies the number of registrations and changes that must take place before pull partners are notified, which activates database replication.

This counter is for local changes only and doesn't count changes pulled from other partners. If this field is set to zero, no push replication takes place.

6. The default selection for persistent connections is enabled; if you do not want to keep the default setting, clear the Use Persistent Connections for Push Replication Partners check box. Click OK.

To configure a pull partner, perform the following steps from the WINS console:

1. Expand the view for the server by clicking the plus sign next to it.
2. Right-click Replication Partners and select Properties from the pop-up menu.
3. Click the Pull Replication tab.
4. Configure start time for when replication should begin.
5. Next, set the Replication Interval for when scheduled replication should occur, such as every 60 minutes.
6. Set the number of times a pull partner should retry the connection to a push partner in the event of a failed connection in the Number of Retries field.
7. The default setting for pull replication is to start when the WINS server starts. To change this, clear the Start Pull Replication at Service Startup check box. When it's cleared, pull replication starts only at the specified Start Time.
8. The default selection for persistent connections is enabled; if you do not want to keep the default setting, clear the Use Persistent Connections for Pull Replication Partners check box. Click OK.

To configure push and pull replication partners, perform the following steps:

1. Expand the view for the server by clicking the plus sign next to it.
2. Right-click Replication Partners and select New Replication Partner from the pop-up menu.
3. Either type in the IP address or name of the server, or click the Browse button to find the partner on the network.
4. Click OK.

With the exception of Advanced Server clusters, WINS is not required for Windows 2000 Server and Professional. However, it is necessary for coexistence with downlevel clients such as Windows 9x or NT 4, and certain software applications.

Troubleshooting TCP/IP

Even though TCP/IP is a mature technology, and you will rarely have problems, you should be able to perform some basic troubleshooting. For example, if a newly installed computer is unable to communicate with the other computers on the network or access the Internet, you should first verify that the TCP/IP settings are properly configured. This can most easily be accomplished using the `ipconfig` command line utility.

Just open a command prompt and type `ipconfig /all`, and you should see something similar to the output shown in Figure 7.17.

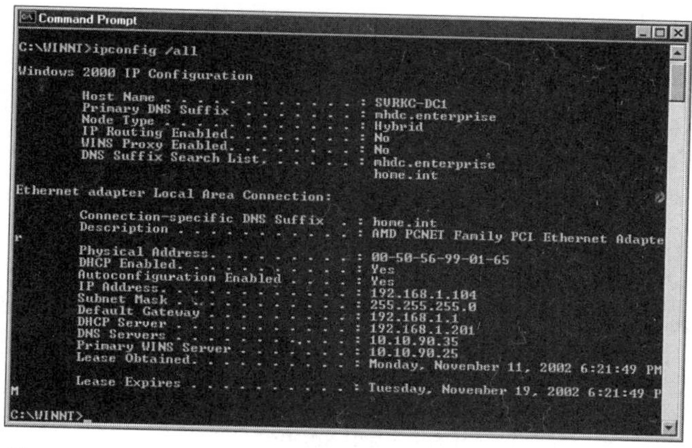

Figure 7.17 Output from running the **ipconfig /all** command.

Some things to check:

- Make sure that all the configuration settings are correct. It's easy to make a typo that keeps your computer from communicating.
- Make sure that the IP address doesn't start with 169.254: This would be an APIPA address, meaning that the computer was unable to get an IP address from a DHCP server, or that you forgot to configure a static address.
- Confirm that you are using the proper DNS and/or WINS server addresses. There won't be any DNS name resolution if the computer

cannot contact a DNS server, or if there isn't a HOST file on the computer. A computer can talk to another computer on the local subnet via NetBIOS broadcasts, but is usually unable to talk to computers on other subnets.

- Confirm that the correct subnet mask has been entered. The subnet mask is used by the computer to determine whether a computer it is trying to communicate with is on the local subnet, or a remote network.
- Make sure that there is a gateway configured, if necessary. There must be a gateway address configured for the computer to access resources on another subnet.

After you have verified that all of the TCP/IP configuration settings are correct, use the `ping` command line utility to see how much connectivity you have.

Ping in this order:

1. The computer's loopback address, 127.0.0.1. This determines whether TCP/IP and the network card are installed and configured correctly.
2. The actual IP address of the computer you are trying to communicate with. If your IP address is not unique, you should receive an error message.
3. A computer on the same subnet. This proves that your TCP/IP settings are correctly configured. If this fails, you might have the wrong subnet configured.
4. The IP address of the default gateway. If the gateway is not operational, or you have the wrong gateway configured, you cannot communicate with anything that is not on the local subnet.
5. A computer on a subnet past the default gateway. If you can send and receive a ping through a router, the problem is not on your computer.

Internet Connection Sharing

Internet Connection Sharing (ICS) is a feature that was first used in Windows 98 and updated for Windows 2000. ICS allows a home or small business to configure a computer to share its Internet connection with other computers on the network. This shared connection can be via a network card connected to a router or cable modem, or even a dial-up connection.

ICS works by connecting to an ISP and obtaining an IP address for the server that you are running ICS on. ICS then allows other computers on your network that are configured to receive an IP address via DHCP to request an IP address from the ICS computer that acts as a DHCP server. After the client computers receive an IP address from the ICS computer, they are able to access the Internet through the ICS computer. The ICS computer uses Network Address Translation (NAT) to make it appear to sites on the Internet that all requests are coming from the single IP address that it was given by the ISP. When a client request is returned from the Internet, ICS automatically routes it to the computer that made the initial request.

There are some limitations to the version of ICS in Windows 2000:

- It can only be installed and configured by an administrator.
- It cannot be used in a network with existing DHCP or DNS servers and external gateways, because it is unpredictable whether the existing DHCP server or ICS will supply IP configuration information and name resolution to the clients.
- You cannot configure the DHCP or DNS configuration settings of ICS. This includes configuring the address range or even disabling the DHCP functions.

In the situations that were previously mentioned, when using ICS might not be practical, you can use the Remote Access and Routing Service (RRAS) with Network Address Translation (NAT) to perform the same duties as ICS. However, RRAS is somewhat harder to configure properly.

To configure ICS, you must configure the properties of the dial-up connection, or network card that is exposed to the Internet.

Always remember that the ICS configuration is performed on the interface that is connected to the Internet. This is a very important point, and as such it might appear on the exam.

To configure a dial-up connection for ICS

1. Open the Network and Dial-up Connections application by selecting Start, Programs, Accessories, Communications, and then Network and Dial-up Connections.
2. Right-click the connection that is used to connect to the ISP, and select Properties from the pop-up menu.

3. From the Properties dialog box, select the Sharing tab and select the Enable Internet Connection Sharing for this connection checkbox, as shown in Figure 7.18.

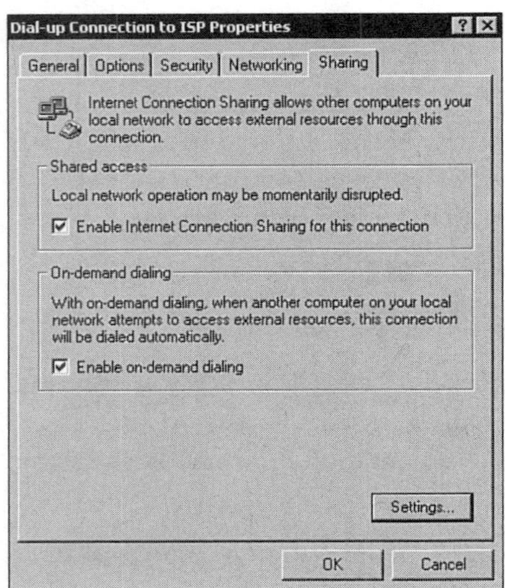

Figure 7.18 Dial-up connection Properties, showing how to enable ICS.

4. Notice that the Enable On-demand Dialing check box is selected by default. When this option is enabled, ICS automatically dials the connection when an ICS client uses an application that attempts to access the Internet.

5. Click the Settings button. This opens the ICS Settings dialog box. From the Applications tab, click the Add button. This opens the ICS Application dialog box as shown in Figure 7.19. This allows you to configure specific applications to communicate through ICS by specifying inbound and outbound ports, both UDP and TCP. If you select the Services tab, you are presented with a list of common services that are preconfigured for you to select. The Services tab enables you to allow incoming traffic to computers on your network that are hosting services such as FTP, email, or a Web site. If you have a special service that is not listed among the defaults, you can click the Add button and manually configure the server, and the ports that you need to open for inbound traffic. Click OK when finished.

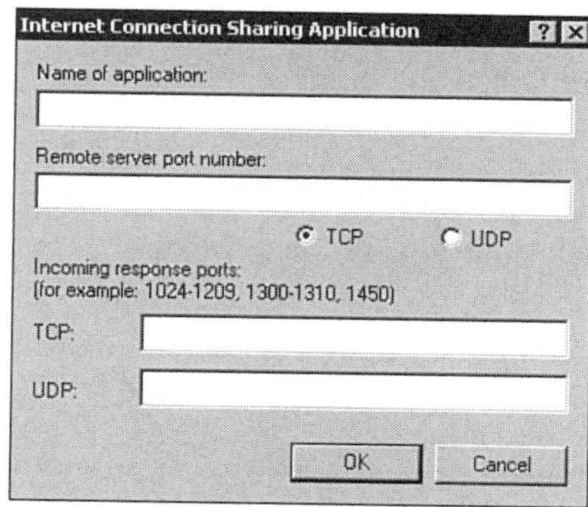

Figure 7.19 ICS Configuration, showing how to add a custom application.

6. After you have finished your ICS configuration, you receive the message shown in Figure 7.20. This message is a warning that any computers on your network that aren't configured to accept a DHCP address from your ICS-configured computer may not be able to communicate. You need to configure the DHCP client on these computers. Click Yes after you have read and understood the warning.

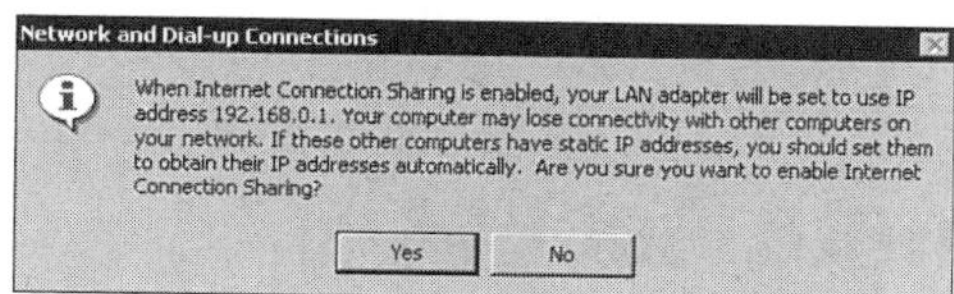

Figure 7.20 Warning message when exiting ICS configuration.

After ICS is configured, the internal network adapter has a static IP address of 192.168.0.1 with a subnet mask of 255.255.255.0. ICS now distributes IP addresses in the range of 192.168.0.2 through 192.168.0.254 and serves as a DNS proxy for your clients.

Troubleshooting Internet Connection Sharing

Although the configuration of ICS is fairly straightforward and there are few settings that you can change, occasionally you might have problems getting ICS configured. Here are some basic troubleshooting steps for ICS:

- If your network clients are having problems accessing the Internet using a custom application, test for connectivity via a Web browser first. The default configuration of ICS allows clients to access the Web via browsers. If the Web browser works, but your application does not, it's a configuration issue. Verify that you configured the correct inbound and outbound ports for your application.

- If you can't access the Web using a browser, first make sure that the ICS Internet connection is operational. Verify that you can access the Internet from the computer hosting ICS. The outside connection of the ICS computer must be configured with a public IP address, and the ISP's DNS address and gateway.
- Next, use the `ipconfig /all` command on the network client computer to verify that the IP address of the client is in the allowable IP address range of ICS, and that the gateway and DNS address is set to the IP address of the internal network card of the ICS computer.
- In addition, verify that the client has the correct subnet mask of 255.255.255.0.
- If the clients cannot automatically connect to the Internet without you manually starting the dial-up connection, verify that the Enable on-demand dialing option is turned on in the ICS properties (refer to Figure 7.18).

Routing and Remote Access Service

The Routing and Remote Access Service (RRAS) feature in Windows 2000 provides a multi-protocol router and support for remote access, including Virtual Private Networks (VPN). First introduced in Windows NT 4.0, the Windows 2000 version of RRAS combines software routing technology with remote access and authentication services.

In addition, the RRAS service in Windows 2000 supports DHCP relay and Network Address Translation. These features are covered in depth on the 70-216 exam.

The routing features in RRAS provide support for the following routing protocols:

- Routing Information Protocol (RIP) versions 1 and 2
- Open Shortest Path First (OSPF)

➤ Internet Group Management Protocol (IGMP)

➤ AppleTalk Routing

With these protocols, and other router features such as demand-dial routing, packet filtering, and Internet Control Message Protocol (ICMP) router discovery, the Windows 2000 RRAS is fully capable of replacing a hardware router in most situations.

Configuring Inbound Connections

In addition to the routing functions, RRAS is capable of being configured as a Remote Access Server. Although RRAS is included as a component of the basic install of Windows 2000, it is disabled by default. To turn on RRAS

1. Open the RRAS MMC by selecting Start, Programs, Administrative Tools, and Routing and Remote Access.

2. In the MMC, as shown in Figure 7.21, right-click on the server name in the left pane, and select Configure and Enable Routing and Remote Access from the pop-up menu. This starts the RRAS Setup Wizard. Click the Next button to get started.

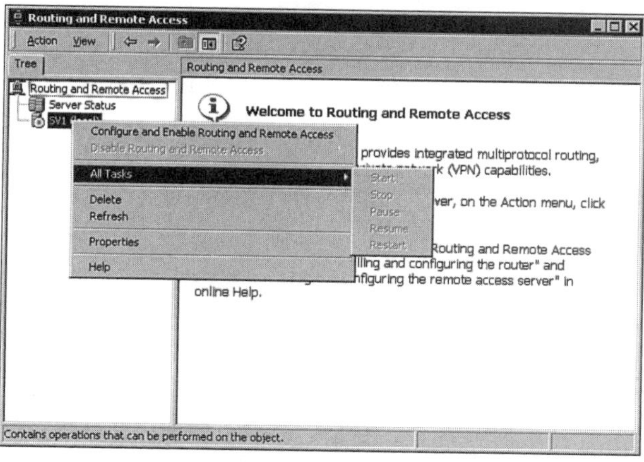

Figure 7.21 Enabling RRAS from the MMC.

3. From the common configurations dialog shown in Figure 7.22, you can configure the following options:

Figure 7.22 Configuration options available via the RRAS Setup Wizard.

- *Internet Connection Server (ICS)*—This technology was discussed in the previous section.
- *Remote Access Server*—This option allows remote clients to dial in to the network via a modem.
- *Virtual Private Network (VPN)* Server—This option allows you accept secure remote connections from clients over the Internet.
- *Network Router*—This option allows Windows 2000 to be configured as a software-based router.
- *Manually Configured Server*—This option allows the user to custom configure RRAS.

4. Select the Remote Access Server option, and then click the Next button.
5. This opens the Remote Client Protocols dialog. From here, you can verify that the protocols that you want to support, such as TCP/IP, are listed. If a protocol was not installed before you started the wizard, it will not be listed. If the necessary protocols are listed, click the Next button to continue.
6. This opens the IP Address Assignment dialog. From here you can select to assign IP addresses to the remote clients via DHCP. To let your existing DHCP server assign addresses to the remote clients, the remote access server must be a DHCP client. If it is not a DHCP client, it generates IP addresses for you. If you wish to configure a predetermined range of IP addresses, select the From a Specified Range of Addresses option. Click the Next button to continue.

7. From the Managing Multiple Remote Access Servers dialog box, you can specify whether you want the remote clients to authenticate using a Remote Authentication Dial-in User Service (RADIUS) server. RADIUS is an industry standard server that provides centralized authorization, authentication, and call accounting services for a group of remote access servers. Windows 2000 includes a RADIUS solution called the Internet Authentication Service (IAS). This optional service can be installed via the Add/Remove Programs applet in the Control Panel. Select No, then click the Next button to continue, and the Finish button to end.

Creating a Remote Access Policy and Profile

To permit a user to have dial-in access to a RRAS server, she must have permission granted via the dial-in properties of her user account and via a remote access policy. Remote access policies give the administrator more granular control over remote access. For example, the administrator is able to grant or deny access based on group membership, time of day, day of week, or type of access requested. These types of items are known as *attributes* within a remote access policy. We discuss how to add these attributes to a policy a little later. In addition, the administrator can use policies to specify the type of encryption used, the maximum session time, and callback policies.

The default remote access policy is to allow access to users who have dial-in permission enabled in their user account settings.

For the user to have authorization to connect remotely, he has to be authorized via the Dial-in Properties tab of his user account object in Active Directory. In addition, his connection properties must match at least one of the requirements that were configured in the remote access policy, such as correct time of day, and so on.

To create a remote access policy

1. From the left pane of the RRAS MMC, right-click the Remote Access Policies node under the server that you are configuring and select New Remote Access Policy from the popup.

2. In the Policy Name dialog box, enter a descriptive name for the policy, and then click the Next button.
3. From the Conditions dialog, click the Add button, and select the attribute that you want to base the policy on from the Select Attribute dialog shown in Figure 7.23. Click the Add button.

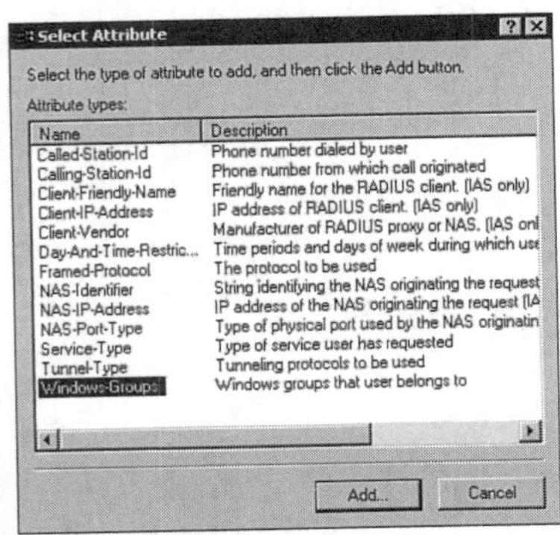

Figure 7.23 Attributes available for a remote access policy.

4. After the Add button is clicked, an additional dialog box appears where you can specify the parameters of the attribute that you selected. When finished configuring the attribute, click the OK button to return to the Conditions dialog. Click the Next button to continue.
5. In the Permissions dialog, you specify what action to take if the user matches the conditions that you configured in the previous step. Either Grant or Deny access permissions. Select an option, and then click the Next button to continue.
6. From the User Profile dialog, you can create a profile to apply to the connection. There are settings in the profile for
   - *Authentication*—This option allows you to select the types of authentication that are allowed, such as Extensible Authentication Protocol (EAP) or Challenge Handshake Authentication Protocol (CHAP).
   - *Advanced*—This option allows you to define the attributes that are sent to a RADIUS client by the Microsoft IAS server.
   - *Dial-in constraints*—This option allows you to set connection specific constraints such as idle time and maximum session length.
   - *Encryption*—This option is used to select the level of encryption to be used for this connection.

- *IP*—This option is used to set IP filtering, or whether a user can request a specific IP address.
- *Multilink*—This option is used to configure the properties of a multilink connection.

7. After configuring the profile, click the OK button to save, and then Click the Finish button on the User Profile dialog.

The combination of remote access profiles and policies allows the administrator a highly granular method of configuring remote user access.

There are a few key things to remember about remote access policies:

- Policies are applied from the top down and the first match, either allow or deny, is used.
- If the default policy is deleted, the dial-up client has to match at least one of the policy configurations that you create to be granted access.
- The user must match all properties of a policy for access to be granted.

Virtual Private Networks (VPNs)

In addition to the dial-up remote access features of RRAS covered in the previous section, RRAS supports incoming connections via *Virtual Private Network (VPN)*. A VPN uses a public medium, such as the Internet, to create a secure, encrypted tunnel to connect a client to a remote access server. After this connection is established, one of the tunneling protocols is used to encapsulate and encrypt all of the commands and data that are passed from point-to-point. This allows the data that is passed to be secure from unauthorized individuals, which is especially important when using a public medium such as the Internet. Another advantage of tunneling is that Windows 2000 supports a VPN that can encapsulate various protocols such as TCP/IP, IPX/SPX, and NetBEUI; the latter two protocols are not normally routable over the Internet.

There are two tunneling protocols available for a VPN connection are

- *Point-to-Point Tunneling Protocol (PPTP)*—PPTP is carried over from Windows NT 4.0, and is also compatible with some third-party VPN software.
- *Layer Two Tunneling Protocol (L2TP)*—L2TP is a newer protocol that uses IPSec for encryption.

A VPN works by having a remote client connect to the Internet via dial-up or some other type of connection. Then the remote client starts the VPN client software and it connects to the remote access server over the Internet. After authorization, the two computers communicate via an encrypted point to point connection.

Because a VPN is just another form of remote access, the configuration is virtually identical to the remote access connection that we previously configured. All of the same policy attributes and profiles can be configured for a VPN.

Terminal Services

Terminal Services is a Windows 2000 service that allows users to remotely access a Windows 2000 desktop and applications, even when using a computer that is not Windows 2000 capable. This allows you to reuse old hardware that cannot support current operating systems and applications.

Terminal Services consists of three separate components:

- *The Terminal Server*—The server is where the applications are running.
- *The Terminal Services Client*—The client is responsible for updating the screen, and passing the keyboard and mouse movements to the server
- *Remote Desktop Protocol (RDP)*—The RDP protocol runs on top of TCP/IP and is responsible for transmitting commands and screen updates between the client and the server.

Terminal Services operates by running the applications on the Windows 2000 Server, and transmitting the screen updates and keyboard and mouse actions between the server and the client software. This allows you to use a low-powered computer to run the client software, because all application processing is taking place on the server.

When a user logs on to a Terminal Services session, she receives a desktop that looks just like she were sitting in front of a Windows 2000 computer, as shown in Figure 7.24.

Windows 2000 Terminal service is available in two modes:

- *Remote Administration*—Remote Administration mode allows an administrator to connect remotely to a server, and manage it just like he was sitting in front of the console. Remote Administration mode only supports two concurrent connections, and does not require additional licensing.

In addition, only members of the administrators group can connect to a server using Remote Administration mode.

➤ *Application mode*—In application mode, an unlimited number of connections are supported. However each connection requires a license, called a *Terminal Server Client Access License (TSCAL)*. A special Terminal Server Licensing Server must be configured to distribute the licenses. There is a grace period of 90 days where the Terminal Server accepts client connections without a valid license.

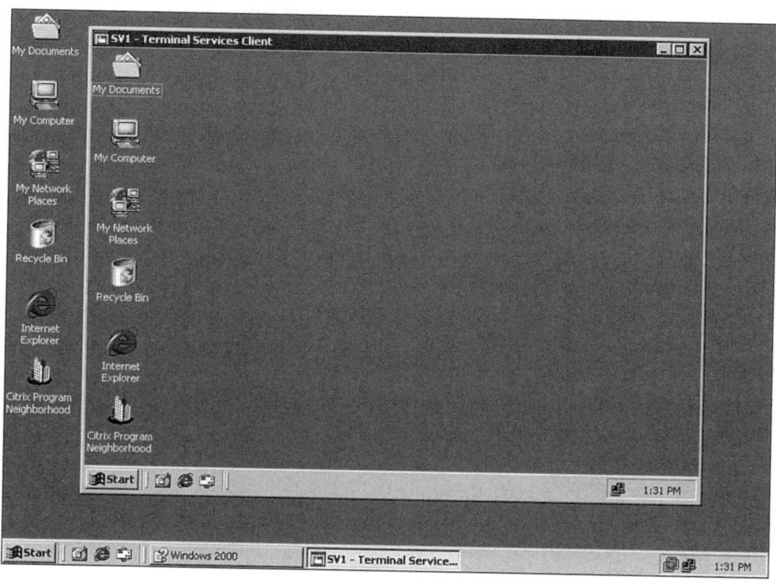

Figure 7.24 The Windows 2000 Terminal Services user experience.

To install Terminal Services

1. Select Start, Settings, Control Panel, Add/Remove Programs, Add/Remove Windows Components.
2. From the Windows Component Wizard dialog, scroll down and select Terminal Services, as shown in Figure 7.25. If you are installing Terminal Services in Application mode, make sure that you also select Terminal Services Licensing. Click the Next button.
3. This opens the Terminal Services setup dialog as shown in Figure 7.26. From here you can select either Remote or Application Server mode. Click the Next button to continue.

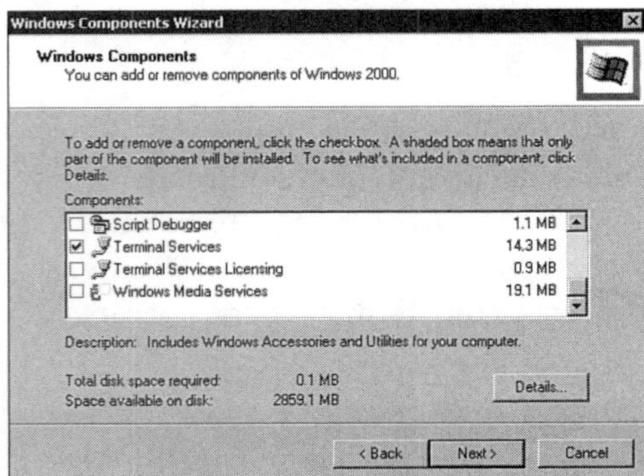

Figure 7.25 Selecting Windows 2000 Terminal Services components.

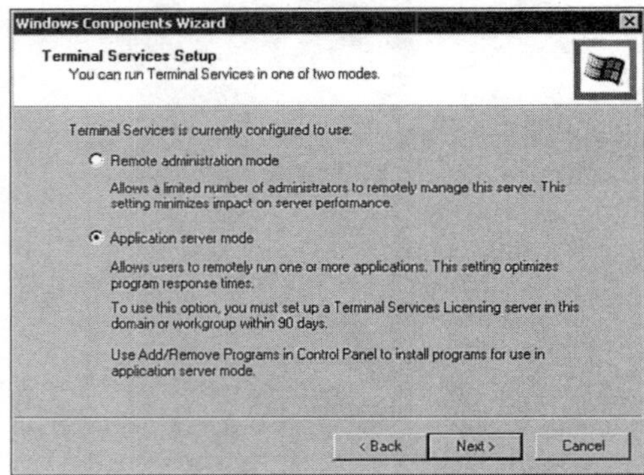

Figure 7.26 Selecting the Windows 2000 Terminal Services mode.

4. When the wizard completes, click the Finish button

After the Terminal Services server component is installed, you can install the client software on the remote client computers. The Win32 and Win16 clients are located in the following folder: %systemroot%\system32\clients\tsclient\.

Windows 2000 includes Terminal Server clients for the following platforms:

- 32-bit Windows operating systems, including Windows 9x, Me, NT, and 2000
- Windows for Workgroups running TCP/IP

Additional clients such as MS-DOS, Unix, Linux, and Macintosh, and additional protocols such as IPX/SPX are supported via a third party add-in from Citrix.

The Server-side configuration of Terminal Service is managed by two MMCs:

- *Terminal Services Configuration*—This MMC, as seen in Figure 7.27, is used to add and configure network and protocol connections to the Terminal Server, and to configure the connection settings, such as disabling desktop wallpaper and user timeout settings.
- *Terminal Services Manager*—This MMC, as shown in Figure 7.28, is used to manage and monitor users, including connecting, disconnecting, remotely controlling users, and resetting user sessions.

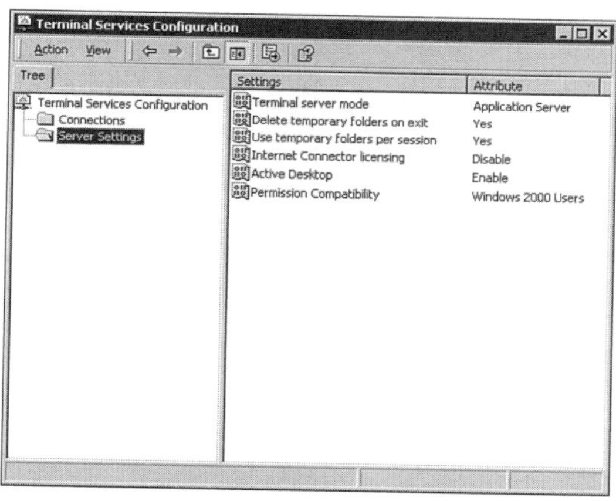

Figure 7.27 The Terminal Services Configuration MMC.

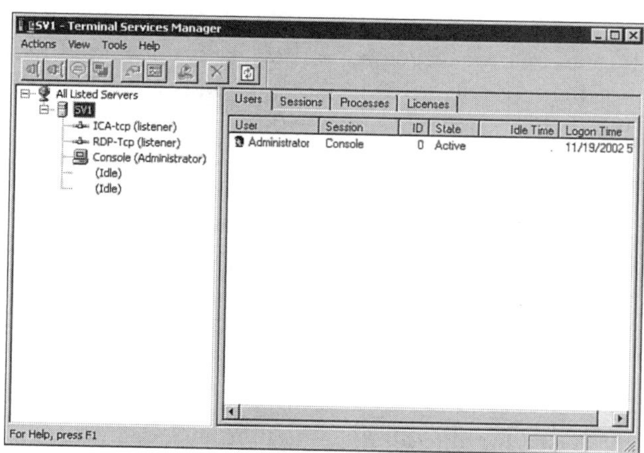

Figure 7.28 The Terminal Services Manager MMC.

Terminal Services Application Services Mode

Unlike the Remote Administrative mode of Terminal Services, in Application Services mode, by default, all users can access a Terminal Services server. This can be controlled from the Terminal Services Profile tab of the users' Properties page in the Active Directory Users and Computers MMC, as shown in Figure 7.29.

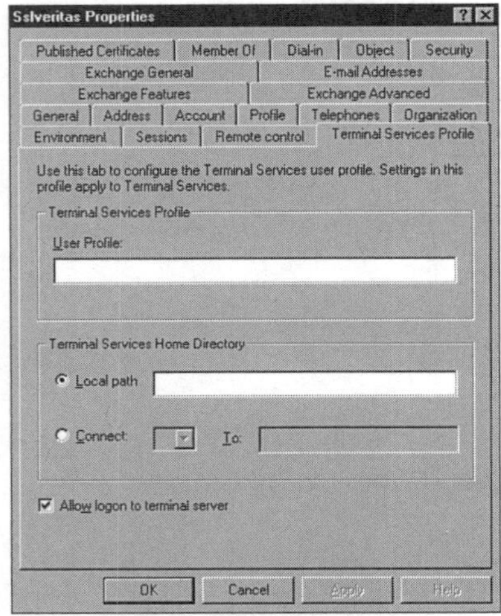

Figure 7.29 A user's Properties page, showing the Terminal Service Profile tab.

In Application Service mode, as we discussed earlier, each connected user must has a TSCAL, and the licenses must be installed and activated on the Terminal Services Licensing Server. The Licensing Server is installed using the Add/Remove Programs applet, just like other Windows 2000 Services.

The licensing rules are as follows:

- Clients have a 90-day grace period so that they can connect to the Terminal Server for testing. After 90 days, the connection is refused.
- Any Windows 2000 computer can connect to the Terminal Services server without requiring the purchase of a TSCAL.
- TSCALs must be purchased for all computers that are not running Windows 2000 that will be connecting to the Terminal Services server.
- If anonymous users will be connecting to the Terminal Services server over the Internet, you must purchase an Internet Connection license.

When Windows 2000 Terminal Services is running in Application mode, all programs must be installed using the Add/Remove Programs applet in the Control Panel.

Practice Questions

Question 1

Lee is the administrator of a Windows 2000 network consisting of 20 Windows 2000 servers and 800 Windows 2000 Professional clients. Lee needs to install and configure an additional Windows 2000 member server to support an additional mail server that is being added to support a new department. He installs and configures a copy of Windows 2000; however, his new Windows 2000 server doesn't seem to be able to communicate with other computers on the network. Which utilities would be useful in diagnosing the problem? (Choose all that apply.)

❑ A. Ipconfig

❑ B. Telnet

❑ C. Ping

❑ D. Rexec

Answers A and C are correct. Most communication problems with new installations are due to errors in configuration. Ipconfig can be used to verify the configuration, and ping can be used to see whether the computer can communicate with other computers.

Question 2

You are installing a copy of Windows 2000 Server on an older server that includes an integrated 10MB Ethernet adapter that does not appear on the HCL. You replace the integrated adapter with a new 100MB adapter that is supported in Windows 2000. However, your new Windows 2000 server doesn't seem to be able to communicate with other computers on the network. You run **Ipconfig /all** and see that the IP address is 169.254.0.9. What is the most likely cause of the problem?

❍ A. The DNS server is not available.

❍ B. The gateway address was incorrectly entered.

❍ C. The network cable is bad.

❍ D. The new network adapter is incompatible with Windows 2000.

Answer C is correct. The most likely cause of the problem is a bad network cable. If a Windows 2000 computer that is configured to use DHCP cannot contact the DHCP server to request an IP address, APIPA assigns it an address in the range 169.254.0.1 through 169.254.255.254. The other options do not accurately describe possible causes of the problem; therefore, answers A, B, and D are incorrect.

Question 3

Your network consists of 15 Windows NT 4.0 servers, 200 Windows 2000 Professional clients, and 100 Windows NT clients. You migrate all of your servers to Windows 2000 and Active Directory. Because you now have a Windows 2000 network, you decide to decommission your WINS servers. Several users call and tell you that they are having trouble logging on to the network. What is the most likely cause of the problem?

❍ A. A bad switch.

❍ B. You didn't assign their permissions correctly.

❍ C. You forgot to migrate their user accounts to the new domain.

❍ D. They are using Windows NT 4.0 clients.

Answer D is correct. Although the other options are all possibilities, the most likely cause of the problem is that the users calling you with problems are using Windows NT 4.0 clients. Pre-Windows 2000 clients require WINS to locate domain controllers to log on to a network. Therefore, answers A, B, and C are incorrect.

Question 4

To what class does the IP address 192.162.0.5 belong?

❍ A. A

❍ B. B

❍ C. C

❍ D. None of the above

Answer C is correct. Class C includes all addresses in the range 192.0.0.0–223.255.255.255. All other answers are incorrect.

Question 5

Your network consists of 15 Windows NT 4.0 servers, 200 Windows 2000 Professional clients, and 100 Windows NT clients. Your plan is to migrate all of your servers to Windows 2000 and Active Directory. However, the server that is currently hosting your WINS database does not appear on the HCL list, and is also inadequately equipped to run Windows 2000. In addition, you have had a history of WINS problems, so you are reluctant to migrate the old WINS database since it is probably corrupt. You decide to temporarily provide NetBIOS name resolution by manually mapping the new environment to the old. What is the name of the flat file that is used for NetBIOS name to IP address mapping?

❍ A. HOSTS

❍ B. HOST

❍ C. LMHOST

❍ D. LMHOSTS

Answer D is correct. LMHOSTS is the file that is used to preload NetBIOS name mappings. HOSTS is the file used for DNS mappings; therefore, answer A is incorrect. Answers B and C are incorrect because they are not valid file types.

Question 6

You are the network administrator of the examcram2.com domain. ExamCram2, Inc., has its main office in Dallas and branch offices in New York, Phoenix, and Seattle. A Windows 2000 Server computer named web1.litware.com is running Internet Information Services (IIS). This computer is located in the Dallas office. Network administrators in Dallas, New York, Phoenix, and Seattle need to be able to manage this server over the WAN. These administrators perform management tasks from their Windows NT 4.0 Workstations. The fastest WAN connection is 56K. What is the best, and cheapest way to accomplish this?

❍ A. Buy a copy of PCAnywhere for each administrator.

❍ B. Install Terminal Services in Application mode on the IIS server, and allow the administrators to connect via the Terminal Services client.

❍ C. Install Terminal Services in Remote Administration Mode on the IIS server, and allow the administrators to connect via the Terminal Services client.

❍ D. Install Terminal Services in Remote Administration mode on the IIS server, install the Terminal Services Licensing server with a TSCAL for each administrator and allow the administrators to connect via the Terminal Services client.

Answer C is correct. Although answers A and B will work, they aren't the cheapest way to accomplish the task and are therefore incorrect. A License server is only required when running Terminal Services in Application mode; therefore, answer D is incorrect.

Question 7

Your Windows 2000 network consists of various client computers, including many Windows 95 and even some Windows for Workgroups clients. You have a new application that runs only on Windows 2000, to which all of your users need access. What can you do to give all of your users access to this new application quickly are relatively cheaply?

❍ A. Upgrade all of your client machines to Windows 2000 and install the new software.

❍ B. Install a new server with Windows 2000 Terminal Services configured in Remote Administration mode, and install the application on the server.

❍ C. Install a new server with Windows 2000 Terminal Services configured in Application mode, and install the application on the server.

❍ D. None of the above.

Answer C is correct. The quickest and probably cheapest way to distribute the application is to set up a Windows 2000 Server with Terminal Services running in Application mode. In application mode, you can support multiple concurrent users, whereas Remote Administration mode limits you to two concurrent connections; therefore, answer B is incorrect. If your desktops are still running Windows 95 and Windows for Workgroups, it's unlikely that they could be upgraded to Windows 2000 quickly or cheaply; therefore, answer A is incorrect. Because answer C is correct, answer D is incorrect.

Question 8

You are the network administrator of the examcram2.com domain. ExamCram2, Inc., has its main office in Dallas and branch offices in New York, Phoenix, and Seattle. A Windows 2000 Server computer named web1.litware.com is running Internet Information Services (IIS). This computer is located in the Dallas office. Network administrators in Dallas, New York, Phoenix, and Seattle need to be able to manage this server over the WAN. These administrators perform management tasks from their Windows NT 4.0 Workstations. To help them accomplish this task, you enabled Terminal Services in Remote Administration mode on the IIS Server. Management has decided to load a new Web-based application on the same server that will be managed by a separate support group that should only be allowed limited access to your network. Which of the following user groups should you add the users in the support group to allow them to use the Remote Administration mode of Terminal Services?

- ❍ A. Domain Administrators
- ❍ B. Server Operators
- ❍ C. Power Users
- ❍ D. None of the above

Answer D is correct. Only members of the local administrators group (of which Domain Administrators are members) are allowed to access a Windows 2000 server using Remote Administration mode. Adding the users in the support group to the Domain administrators group would give them full access to your network, which is not allowed; therefore, answers A, B, and C are incorrect.

Question 9

A large multinational corporation, Backwards, Inc., has a large multiple-location Novell NetWare–based network. Its environment consists of 65 Netware 4.0 servers with NDS, and 1,000 Windows 2000 Professional clients running the Netware Client32. Bill, the new system administrator at Backwards, Inc., installs two new Windows 2000 servers in the network. When he attempts to connect to them via Terminal Services Remote Administration mode, he receives an error. What is the most likely cause?

- ❍ A. He need to install Terminal Services in Application server mode.
- ❍ B. He needs to download the Terminal Server Netware client from the Novell Web site.
- ❍ C. Terminal Services is not supported on IPX/SPX.
- ❍ D. None of the above.

Answer C is correct. Terminal Services is only supported running on TCP/IP. IPX/SPX support requires a third-party add-on. Therefore, answers A, B, and D are incorrect.

Question 10

A large multi-national corporation, Backwards, Inc., has a large multiple location Novell Netware-based network. Its environment consists of 65 Netware 6.0 servers with NDS, and 1000 Windows 2000 Professional clients running the Netware Client32. The network is pure TCP/IP and routed. All computers, including servers, receive their TCP/IP address configuration via DHCP.

Bill, the new system administrator at Backwards, Inc. installs two new Windows 2000 servers on the network on a new subnet. After he completes the installation, he opens My Network Places on one of the servers. In My Network Places, he sees the server he is logged on to, but no other computers. He then opens My Network Places on the other new server and he sees that server, and all of the other computers on the network, but not the first new server. What is the most likely cause of the problem?

❍ A. The router needs to be configured to support the new subnet.

❍ B. A DHCP Relay Agent needs to be added to the new subnet.

❍ C. An additional scope needs to be added to the DHCP server to support the new subnet.

❍ D. There is bad network cable on the first new server.

Answers D is correct. The other three answers would be valid if both servers could not browse the network. But because the second server can browse the network, the problem has to be isolated to the first server. Therefore, answers A, B, and C are incorrect.

Need to Know More?

Russel, Charlie, et al. *Windows 2000 Server Administrator's Companion, 2nd Edition*. Microsoft Press, 2002. ISBN 0735617856.

Stanek, William R. *Windows 2000 Administrator's Pocket Companion*. Microsoft Press, 2000. ISBN 0735608318.

Windows 2000 Resource Kits online at `http://www.microsoft.com/windows2000/techinfo/reskit/en-us/default.asp`. Also available in print; ISBN 1572318082 (Windows 2000 Professional) and ISBN 1572318058 (Windows 2000 Server).

Implementing, Monitoring, and Troubleshooting Security

Terms you'll need to understand

- ✓ Policy
- ✓ Local Users and Groups
- ✓ Domain Users and Groups
- ✓ Auditing
- ✓ Security Template
- ✓ User Rights
- ✓ Encrypting File System (EFS)

Techniques you'll need to master

- ✓ Creating and managing local users and groups
- ✓ Creating and managing policies
- ✓ Creating an audit policy
- ✓ Modifying a security template
- ✓ Analyzing the security settings of a computer
- ✓ Recovering an encrypted file
- ✓ Importing a security template

Introduction

Microsoft has introduced a number of new security features in the Windows 2000 operating system. New additions such as the Encrypting File System (EFS) and the security configuration tool, along with the updated auditing and policy features, allow you to configure a much more secure server. With the increased emphasis on security in the computer industry as a whole, you should expect to see a number of security related questions on the exam.

User Accounts and Groups

A Windows 2000 *user account* allows the user to log on to a computer or a domain. In addition, a user account controls what access, if any, that a user has to local or domain resources. To grant these access rights, the administrator assigns rights and permissions to the user's account.

Permissions control what a user can do with a resource, such as a file, folder, or printer. When an administrator assigns permissions, she specifies what type of access the user has. For example, a member of the accounting department may have read and write access to all folders and files related to the accounting department. Yet, this same user may well be denied all access to human resources' files and folders. Most likely this user has little to no business dealing with confidential files found in human resources.

A *group* is a collection of one or more user accounts that have at least one thing in common, such as all personnel in the sales department who will likely need access to the same resources. Assembling users into groups simplifies administration because the administrator has to configure permissions to resources only once, rather than for each user individually.

Also the administrator can add or remove users from the group at any time. This comes in especially handy when another user, not part of the group, needs access to the resources to which the group collectively has access. All the administrator has to do is to add the user to the group that has such access.

There are two types of user accounts and groups, *domain* and *local*. A local account or group can be used to assign a user or a group of users access to the resources only on the computer where the account resides. However, domain user accounts and groups can be used to grant access to any resources that are contained within the domain. You will discover each in more depth next.

Domain Accounts

A *domain* is the basic security, administrative, and replication unit of the Active Directory. Multiple domains can be connected to form a tree or forest. However, because Active Directory, forests, and trees are covered on other exams, we limit our discussion to the domain level.

Each domain has an Active Directory security database that can contain millions of objects. These objects are the users, groups, computers, and other objects that are the resources contained within the domain. Access to these resources is controlled by granting access to users and groups. To assist in sorting and categorizing these users, groups ,and resources, there is a subdomain container called an Organizational Unit (OU). Each OU can hold a large number of objects. Access to the objects in an OU can be granted at the object, OU, or domain level.

Each Active Directory domain controller contains a read/write copy of the domain database. This allows you to manage the database using any domain controller. Any changes are replicated to all of the other domain controllers.

Domain users, groups, and other objects are created and managed using the Active Directory Users and Computers snap-in, as shown in Figure 8.1. This snap-in is installed by default on Windows 2000 servers that are domain controllers, or it can be added to a Windows 2000 Professional or Windows 2000 member server by installing the Administrative Tools package. The installation file, *adminpak.msi*, is located on the Windows 2000 Server CD in the I386 folder. The snap-in is started by selecting Start, Programs, Administrative Tools, Active Directory Users and Computers.

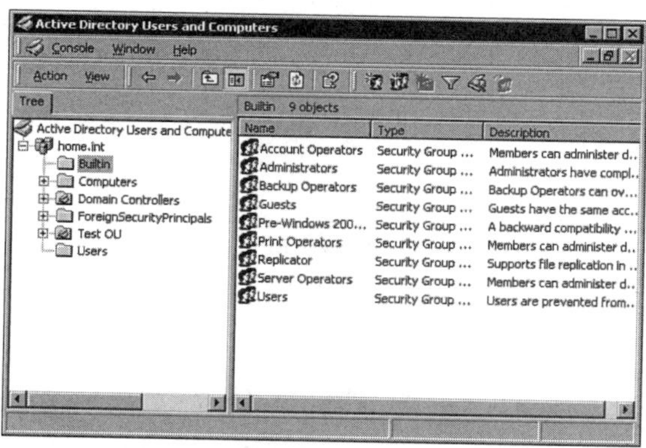

Figure 8.1 The Active Directory Users and Computers snap-in is used to create and manage users, groups, and other objects.

The Active Directory Users and Computers snap-in has five default nodes and two invisible ones:

- *Builtin*—This container holds the default groups for a Windows 2000 domain.
- *Computers*—This container is empty when Windows 2000 is first installed. As computer accounts are added to the domain, they are put here unless you specify a specific OU to put them in.
- *Domain Controllers*—This is an OU that contains the domain controllers for the domain.
- *ForeignSecurityPrincipals*—This container holds the security objects that are created when a trust is set up between domains.
- *Users*—This container holds all of the default domain and local users and groups installed by Windows 2000. You can add new users and groups to this container, or to OUs that you create.
- *LostAndFound*—This container holds orphaned objects for the domain and is not visible by default. To view it, you must turn on Advanced Features by selecting View, Advanced Features.
- *System*—This container holds the objects for policies, RAS, IP security, and other system functions, and is not visible by default. To view it, you must turn on Advanced Features by selecting View, Advanced Features.

As shown earlier in Figure 8.1, the containers are represented in Active Directory as blank file folders, whereas OUs are file folders with an open book icon. The difference between the two is that you can rename, nest, and configure the properties for OUs. You are also limited as to what objects can be created or moved to some containers. There may possibly be other containers shown if Active Directory–aware applications, such as Exchange 2000, are installed.

To create a new object, right-click the desired container in the Active Directory Users and Computers snap-in, click New, then select the type of object that you want to create (see Figure 8.2).

There could possibly be little, if any, coverage of domain accounts on the exam. On the other hand, you should be thoroughly familiar with creating and using local accounts and groups and know what accounts and groups are installed by default. Domain accounts are discussed at length in the preparation material for the 70-217 exam.

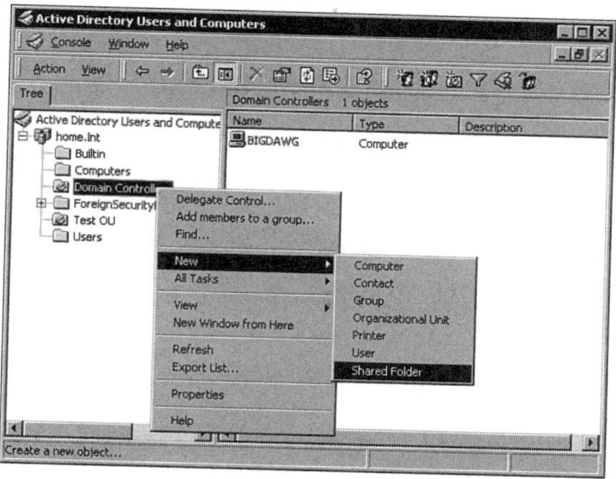

Figure 8.2 The Active Directory Users and Computers snap-in, showing how to create an object.

Local Accounts

Every member server and all workstations will have their own *local accounts*. Unlike domain accounts, in which every domain controller contains a shared database of all users, groups, and resources in the domain, these local accounts exist only on the computer where they were created. Also, these accounts can be used only to grant access to resources on the computer on which the local accounts reside.

Local users and groups are created in the local security database. Local accounts cannot be used to access any resources other than those on the local computer because other computers cannot see the local Active Directory security database in order to authenticate the users and group in the database.

There is rarely, if ever, a reason to create a local user or group on a computer that is a member of a domain.

The Local Administrator and Guest Accounts

By default, Windows 2000 Server creates two local user accounts, *Administrator* and *Guest*. The Administrator account has the following properties:

- Can be renamed
- Cannot be deleted

- Cannot be locked out
- Cannot be disabled
- Has access and control of all resources on the computer

The Administrator account is used when Windows 2000 Server is installed. This account cannot be deleted or disabled, to ensure that you never lock yourself out of your server. This is the only account that cannot be deleted or disabled.

The Guest account is disabled by default, and has the following properties:

- Can be renamed
- Cannot be deleted
- Can be disabled
- Can be locked out
- Does not save any user configuration settings between logons

The Guest account is just what the name implies, an account that has limited privileges, and is only to be used temporarily by a user who won't be around long.

Local Groups

In addition, there are several default local groups created when Windows 2000 Server is installed:

- *Administrators*—The members of this group can access and control all resources on the computer. The local Administrator account is a member of this group. When a Windows 2000 server joins a domain, the Domain Admins group (a default group that contains all administrators in the domain) is made a member of this group. This is so that all members of the Domain Admins group will have administrative control of this computer. Although the Administrator account cannot be locked out or disabled, other members of this group can be.
- *Backup Operators*—The members of this group can back up and restore files and folders, even if they don't have any access permissions for the files. In addition they can log on to the server and shut it down. However, the members of the Backup Operators group cannot change security settings on any objects that they don't own.

- *Guests*—The members of this group have limited access to resources on the server, but can log on and shut it down. The Guest account is a member of this group. When a Windows 2000 server joins a domain, the Domain Guests (a default group that contains all guests in the domain) group is made a member of this group.
- *Power Users*—The members of this group can create, modify, and delete resources such as file shares and user and group accounts. However, they have complete control only over those objects that they have created. They can remove users from the Power Users, Users, and Guests groups. They cannot modify the Administrators or Backup Operators groups, take ownership of files, perform backups or restores, load or unload device drivers, or manage the security and auditing logs. Power Users can run all Windows 2000 applications, as well as install and run most legacy applications that cannot be installed or run by members of the Users group. The Windows 2000 Power Users group has privileges roughly equivalent to that of the Users group in Windows NT 4.0.
- *Replicator*—The group is used to support file replication services in a domain. Do not add users to this group.
- *Users*—The members of the group can perform the normal user tasks such as running most Windows 2000 applications, using printers, and creating local groups. However, they cannot create local printers or share folders. Some legacy applications cannot be run by members of the users group, because the Windows 2000 Users group has fewer privileges than members of the Windows NT 4.0 Users group. By default, all local accounts created are added to the Users group. When a Windows 2000 server joins a domain, the Domain Users (a default group containing all authenticated users in the domain) group is made a member of this group.

Local groups can be used only to assign permissions to resources residing on the server where the group is created. Like local user accounts, local groups are stored in the local security database. Local groups can contain local accounts from the same computer on which they are created, and a local group can't be a member of any other group. If a server is a member of a domain, the local groups on that server can contain domain user accounts and groups.

To create a new local group, perform the following steps:

1. In the left pane of the Computer Management windows, click Local Users and Groups.

2. In the right pane, right-click the Groups folder and select New Group from the pop-up menu.
3. In the New Group dialog box, fill in the appropriate fields, then click Add.
4. When the Select Users or Groups dialog box appears, as shown in Figure 8.3, select the users to add to the group, then click Add. Click OK.
5. Click Create.
6. When the fields in the New Group dialog box have cleared, you can either create another group or click Close to quit.

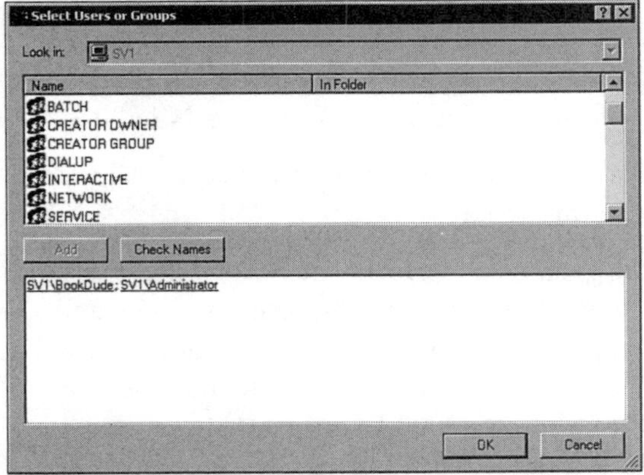

Figure 8.3 The Local Computers and Groups snap-in, showing the Select Users or Groups dialog box.

When creating and using local groups, you should always keep the following points in mind:

- A local group is visible only on the computer where it was created.
- A local group can be used only to assign permissions to resources on the computer where it was created.
- A local group can be administered only on the computer where it was created.
- A local group cannot be created on a domain controller.
- A local group cannot be a member of any other group, either local or domain.

- A local group can contain local or domain accounts domain local groups, or a global group from the domain that the computer is a member of or from any trusted domains.

Built-in System Groups

In addition to the built-in local groups, Windows 2000 also has several built-in system groups. The user cannot manipulate the membership of these groups; they are used to assign rights and permissions to resources. The Windows 2000 operating system dynamically manipulates the membership of these groups according to how the server is accessed, not by whom.

The commonly used built-in system groups are

- *Anonymous Logon*—This group contains the user account from any session that was not authenticated by the Windows 2000 security system, which occurs only when a username and password is not required to access the system.
- *Authenticated Users*—This group contains all users with a valid account in the local security database on a member server or the Active Directory domain database in a domain environment.
- *Creator Owner*—The user account that is the creator or the owner of the current object.
- *Dialup*—All users that are currently connected via a dial-up connection.
- *Everyone*—This group includes all users who access the computer, including the Guest account and anonymous logons.
- *Interactive*—This group contains the user accounts of the users that are currently logged on to the system.
- *Network*—This group contains the user accounts of the users that are connected to resources on the server over a network connection.

Assigning permissions to the Everyone group can be a huge security exposure if the Guest account is enabled. Windows 2000 will authenticate a user without a valid user account as Guest. This automatically gives this user all rights and permissions that you have assigned to the Everyone group. A better strategy would be to assign rights and permissions for resources to the Authenticated Users group instead of the Everyone Group, and never enable the Guest account, or, at a minimum, rename it.

The Local Users and Groups Snap-In

Local User accounts and groups are created and managed using the Local Users and Groups snap-in, as shown in Figure 8.4. To open the snap-in, select Start, Programs, Administrative Tools, Computer Management.

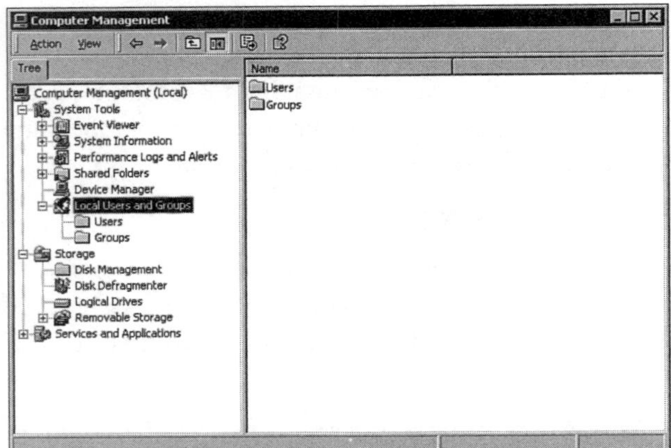

Figure 8.4 The Computer Management MMC, showing the Local Users and Groups snap-in.

The Local Users and Groups snap-in is part of the Computer Management MMC. To create a new user

1. In the left pane of the Computer Management window, click Local Users and Groups.
2. In the right pane, right-click the Users folder and select New User from the pop-up menu.
3. In the New User dialog box shown in Figure 8.5, fill in the appropriate fields, then click Create.
4. When the fields in the New User dialog box have cleared, you can either create another user or click Close to quit.

You cannot create local groups and accounts on a domain controller, because domain controllers do not have a local security database.

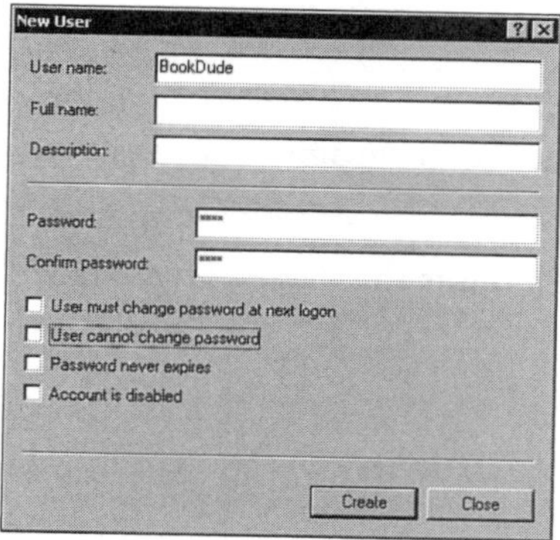

Figure 8.5 The Local Computers and Groups snap-in, showing the New User dialog box.

The rules for usernames in Windows 2000 are as follows:

- Can be up to 20 characters
- Must be unique
- Cannot contain any of the following characters: “/\[]:;|=,+*?<>
- Are not case sensitive.

The rules for passwords in Windows 2000 are:

- Can be up to 128 characters
- Are case sensitive
- Cannot contain any of the following characters: “/\[]:;|=,+*?<>

You can configure other restrictions for passwords via policies. This will be covered later in this chapter.

User Authentication

When a user logs on to a Windows 2000 computer, the user supplies a user account and a password, or possibly a Smart Card, if that technology is being used. This information is used to *authenticate* the user. In other words, these items are used to confirm that the user is who he says he is. After the user is properly authenticated, an access token is created for that user. This access token consists of

- *Security Identifier (SID)*—Each object in Windows 2000 has a unique SID that identifies it. SIDs are never reused.
- *Member of List*—This list contains the SIDs of the groups of which the user account is a member.
- *User Rights*—This list contains all the user rights that have been assigned to this user account.

After the user is logged on to the server, each process or resource that the user attempts to access will examine this access token to confirm that the user has been granted the appropriate access.

All Windows 2000 objects have security restrictions. These security restrictions are configured in the *Access Control List (ACL)*. The ACL containsa listing of the users and groups that have access to the object, and specifically what type of access.

Although the username is how we identify accounts, Windows 2000 uses the account's SID for authentication and access levels. Note that the SID will always be a unique string, such as S-1-5-25-1123561935-920026236-84092546-1000. For example, if you accidentally delete a user account and create another one using the same username and other properties, it will have a totally different SID. The new user account will not have access to the same resources as the old account unless you manually grant the permissions by assigning the user account to the same groups. The access permissions were assigned to the deleted SID. Windows 2000 never reuses a SID; they will always be unique.

If you have a user who leaves the organization and is replaced by a new employee who will be performing the same tasks, you should rename the old user account for use by the new user. This ensures that the new user has access to the same resources as the old user.

System Policies

System Policies are used to control the configuration of a machine or a users, such as whether a user can install new programs, adjust desktop settings, and so on. Windows 2000 System Policies are an updated version of the policies that were included in previous versions of Windows. Like the previous versions, in Windows 2000 you will use the System Policy Editor, poledit.exe, to configure Registry settings that control the local machine.

Normally, you should always use the Windows 2000 Group Policy to control your computers, however, there are some situations in which System Policies are useful:

- When you have to manage Windows 95, 98, or Me computers.
- When you have to manage Windows NT 4.0 Workstation or Server computers.
- When the Windows 2000 computer is a member of a Windows NT 4.0 domain.
- When you have to manage a standalone Windows 2000 computer.

In all these situations, an Active Directory based Group Policy is not available. The pre–Windows 2000 computers don't support Group Policy, so in a mixed environment, for the sake of consistency, you might want to standardize by using a common policy created using the System Policy Editor.

In addition, the Local Computer Policy is unable to create a policy that will support multiple users. So all users on a standalone computer will receive the same settings.

The System Policy Editor is not on the system menu; you must start it from the command line by entering **poledit.exe**. The editor allows you create policies that apply to single or multiple users, groups, or computers (see Figure 8.6).

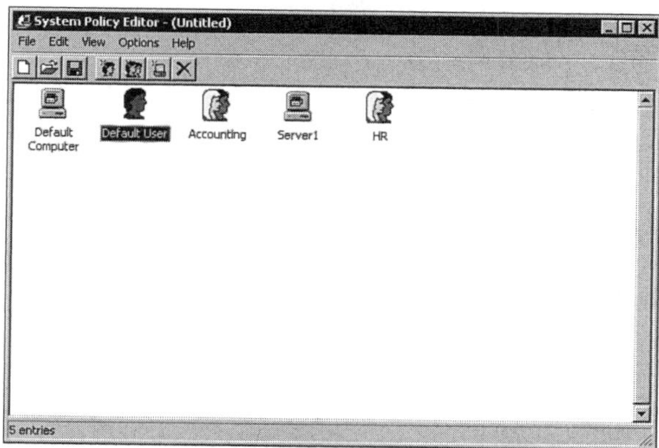

Figure 8.6 The System Policy Editor.

The System Policy Editor comes with five administrative templates:

- *Inetres.adm*—Installed by default. This template contains the settings for Internet Explorer policies.

- *System.adm*—Installed by default. This template contains the settings for Windows 2000 clients.
- *Common.adm*—This template contains user interface settings that are common to Windows 9x and Windows NT.
- *Windows.adm*—This template contains user interface settings for Windows 9x.
- *Winnt.adm*—This template contains user interface settings for Windows NT.

As shown in Figure 8.7, the editor allows you to select settings from the pre-installed templates to be applied to the selected objects.

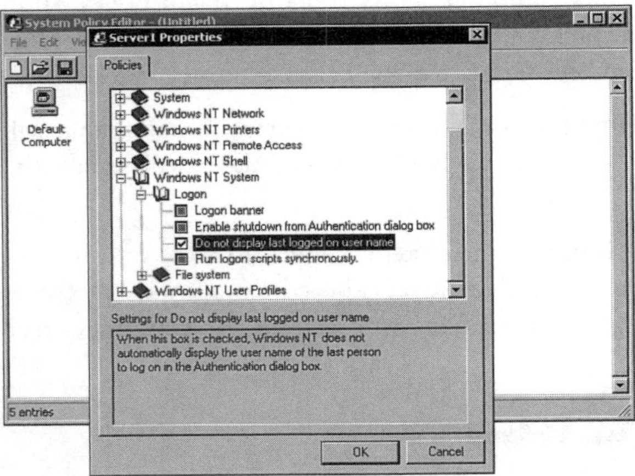

Figure 8.7 The System Policy Editor, showing configuration settings.

System policies allow you control just about everything that you can imagine on a computer. These policies can be applied to a standalone computer, or to all computers and users in a domain. To apply the policies in a domain, put the ntconfig.pol file (or config.pol for Windows 9x computers) in the NETLOGON share of the domain controller that is hosting the Primary Domain Controller (PDC) Emulator role in your domain.

Windows 2000 Group Policy

Group Policies in Windows 2000 are a set of configuration settings that the administrator can apply to one or more objects on a computer, or multiple computers, in a domain. Unlike in Windows NT where you had to use several different utilities to control security settings, Windows 2000 centralizes the control of these settings under Group Policy. Group Policies can be used to control the user experience by customizing what they can and cannot do, and what security features are enabled.

Group Policy in Windows 2000 is vastly superior to the policies that were available in Windows NT. For example, in Windows 2000 the policies are not permanent. If you decide to disable or remove a policy, the computer is restored to the state it was in before you applied the policy.

In Windows NT, when you made a change in the system policy it resulted in a physical change to the Registry of the computer. To change the settings once they were applied meant that you had to apply a different set of changes to specifically undo the first set. This tattooing of the Registry meant that even if a policy was applied at the domain level, it would still be in effect if the computer was removed from the domain.

In addition, there are far more options available via policy in Windows 2000. There are hundreds of options available via Group Policy in an Active Directory domain. Even when working with a standalone member server using Local Computer Policy, there are still many options available, including assigning startup or logoff scripts, system configuration, and password policy.

Policies can be controlled at various levels, including at the local system, domain, OU, or site level. Policies are always applied in a specific order, with the order in which they are applied governing the effective settings. For example, the policy order used in Windows 2000 is

1. Windows NT 4.0 Policies (a.k.a. System Policies)
2. Local Group Policies
3. Site Group Policies
4. Domain Group Policies
5. OU Group Policies

Because of this hierarchy, if there are conflicting settings in different policies, the policy that was applied last has precedence. A popular acronym that is used to remember this order of precedence is LSDOU, for Local, Site, Domain, and OU.

This inheritance of policy settings can be blocked by an administrator or user with the appropriate permissions, so that a policy that was configured at the site level can be prevented from being applied to a particular OU. This is called *blocking inheritance*. The administrator also has the option to prevent this from occurring by selecting the No Override option when applying the policy.

Local Computer Policy

There are two types of group policy available in a Windows 2000 environment: Local Computer Policy, which is applied to a single computer, and Domain Group Policy, which can be applied at the domain, site, or OU level. Every Windows 2000 computer has its own Local Computer Policy object, regardless of whether or not it's a member of an Active Directory domain.

There are some limitations with Local Computer Policy objects. For example:

- You can have only one Local Computer Policy object. All local users will receive the same settings.
- Fewer settings are available.
- Software installation is not available.
- Folder redirection is not available.

To access the Local Computer Policy object for a computer, key in **gpedit.msc** in the Run dialog. This opens the Group Policy MMC, shown in Figure 8.8, showing the available configuration settings for the local object.

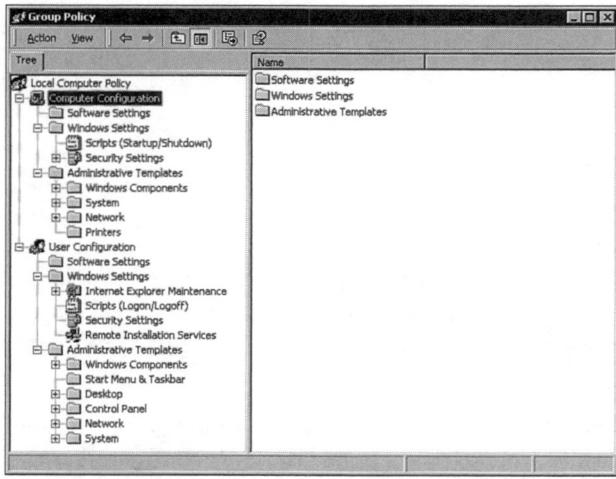

Figure 8.8 The Group Policy MMC, showing the Local Computer Policy object settings.

As you can see in Figure 8.8, group policy objects are divided into two nodes, *Computer Configuration* and *User Configuration*. In a domain, OU, or site, you can make some settings common to a machine, while other settings will vary by user. However, remember that in a local object the user settings apply to all users, so you can make your settings at either node because the result will always be the same. Computer settings are applied at startup, whereas user settings are applied at logon, with the default refresh interval for both settings set to 90 minutes.

The configuration settings listed under Administrative Templates on both nodes are similar to those settings that are available via the System Policy Editor. The other settings in the Computer Configuration and User Configuration areas are new to Windows 2000, or were only available at the domain level, such as some of the security settings that were previous configured in Windows NT 4.0 via User Manager.

The Security Settings subnode that is shown in the Group Policy MMC under the Computer Configuration node is also available from the Start menu as the Local Security Settings MMC, as shown in Figure 8.9. To open the MMC, click Start, Administrative Tools, Local Security Settings. If you are working from a domain controller, you will also see Domain Security Settings and Domain Controller Security settings.

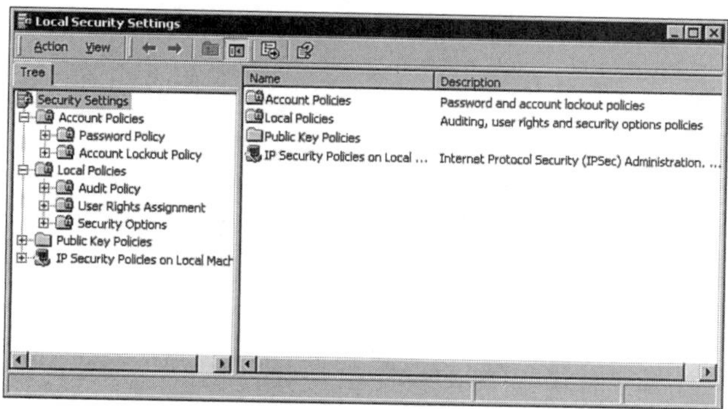

Figure 8.9 The Local Security Settings MMC, showing the available policy object settings.

The two most commonly used nodes under Security Settings are Account Policies and Local Policies.

Account Policies

Account policies are used to configure the settings for password and account lockout policy. These settings were configured in the User Manager utility in Windows NT 4.0.

The password policy settings allow you to customize the password requirements to require stronger passwords. The available settings are

- *Enforce Password History*—This setting allows you to configure a specific number of passwords that will be remembered by the computer. This prevents users from reusing passwords. The default is one password.
- *Maximum Password Age*—This sets the length of time a password can be used before the system requires the user to change to a new one. The default is 42 days.
- *Minimum Password Age*—This sets the length of time that a password must be used before a user can change it. The default is 0 days.
- *Minimum Password Length*—This sets the minimum length for a password. Seven to eight characters is typically an optimum length. The default is 0 characters.
- *Passwords Must Meet Complexity Requirements*—This invokes the requirements that are specified by the passfilt.dll file. The requirements are
    - Passwords must be at least 6 characters long.
    - Passwords may not contain your username or any part of your full name.
    - Passwords must contain characters from at least three of the following four classes: A-Z, a-z, 0-9, or punctuation marks.

  The default is disabled.
- *Store Password Using Reversible Encryption For All Users in the Domain*—Specifies whether Shiva Password Authentication Protocol (SPAP) is used. The default is disabled.

The account lockout settings allow you to lockout a user account after several sequential failed logons. The available settings are

- *Account Lockout Duration*—This setting allows you to specify the length of time that the account will be disabled. After this time period expires, the user will be able to log on again. The default is not defined.
- *Account Lockout Threshold*—This setting allows you to specify the number of times that a user can attempt to log on before the account is disabled. The default is 0, which means this setting is turned off.
- *Reset Account Lockout Counter After*—This setting allows you to specify the length of time before the lockout counter is reset. For example, say the counter is set to 10 minutes and the lockout threshold is set to 3. If

the user attempts to log on twice and fails, if they wait ten minutes, the counter will be reset and they will be able to try three times before they are locked out.

Local Policies

The Local Policies node of the Local Security Settings MMC has three subnodes: Audit Policy, User Rights Assignment, and Security Options. These items allow you to specify who has access to the computer, specify how much access, and audit specific events.

Audit Policy

The Audit Policy is used to configure which events will be recorded in the Security log. This allows you to track events, such as failed logon attempts. Auditing is not enabled by default, and must be enabled for the selected items. To turn auditing on, double-click one of the items in the right pane of the MMC as shown in Figure 8.10. Then select the desired action and click OK.

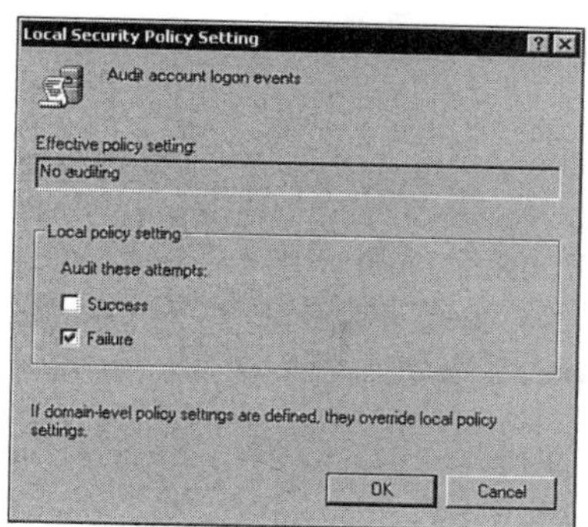

Figure 8.10 The Local Security Settings MMC, showing how to configure audit settings.

The available audit types are

- Audit Account Logon Events
- Audit Account Management
- Audit Directory Service Access
- Audit Logon Events
- Audit Object Access
- Audit Policy Change

- Audit Privilege Use
- Audit Process Tracking
- Audit System Events

Each policy can be configured to audit successes, failures, or both. Just about any activity involving a Windows 2000 object can be audited. When planning an audit policy, it's important to not only audit the accesses of resources, but also to audit user account management tasks. All entries are saved to the security log, and will provide you with a summary of the computer operations, showing which tasks were attempted and by whom. Not only does this help to detect unauthorized access, but it can also point out users who don't know what they're doing.

A typical entry in the security log will show the following items:

- The time and date that the event occurred
- The event performed
- The user account that performed the event
- The success or failure of the event

Except for the Audit Object Access selection, all of the other selections will begin recording audit events to the security log immediately after they are enabled. The Audit Object Access selection is used to allow you to audit specific objects, such as files, folders, or other resources, and needs to be specifically turned on for each object that you want to audit.

To turn auditing on for a specific object

1. From the Properties window of the desired object, select the Security tab.
2. Click the Advanced button.
3. Select the Auditing tab.
4. Click the Add button.
5. From the Add Users or Groups dialog box, select the user or group that you want to record their access of the object. Click OK.
6. From the Auditing Entry for dialog box, as shown in Figure 8.11, select the actions that you wish to audit.
7. Click OK three times when finished.

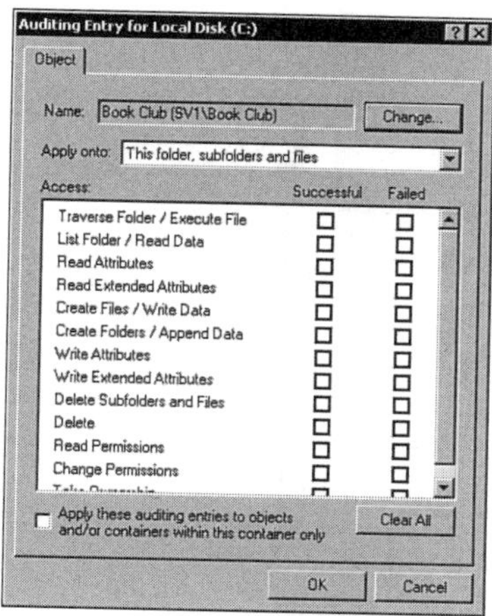

Figure 8.11 The Disk Properties dialog box, showing how to configure audit settings.

After the settings are saved, every time the specified action is taken on the object by the chosen user or group, an audit event will be written to the security log.

To audit files and folders, you must be using the NTFS file system.

User Rights

User Rights are used to assign various privileges to specific user accounts and/or groups. Some of the default user rights assignments are shown in Figure 8.12.

As you can see, several specific rights, such as the ability to back up files and directories or change the system time, are already assigned to certain groups. For example, you must be a member of the local administrators group to shut down a computer remotely.

Unlike Account policies, which are usually set at the domain level and automatically override the local settings, by default User Rights are configured at the local level. The User Rights settings in the domain Group Policy are set to Not Defined by default.

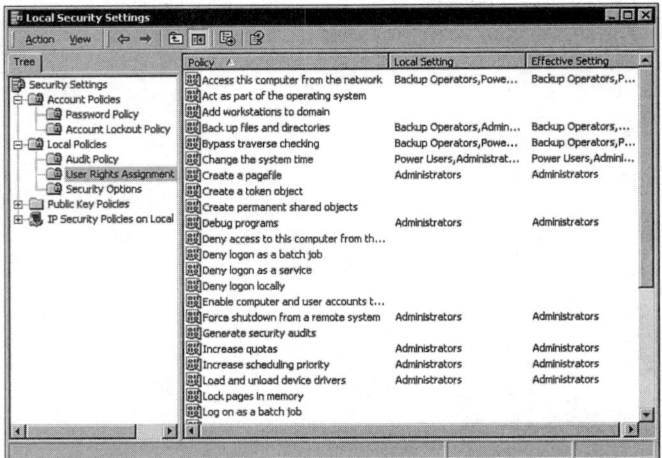

Figure 8.12 User Rights Assignment, showing some of the available settings.

Security Options

The Security Options node contains a variety of security settings, some of which are available from the Control Panel applets. Similar to User Rights, these settings are commonly set through Local Policy, because these items are set to Not Defined in the domain Group Policy.

A few of the commonly used items are

- *Allow System to Be Shut Down Without Having to Log On*—This item enables the shutdown button on the winlogon (Ctrl+Alt+Delete) dialog box.
- *Clear Virtual Memory Pagefile When System Shuts Down*—This option is important in high security environments because the pagefile contains a copy of whatever you were working on just before you shut down your system.
- *Do Not Display Last User Name in Logon Screen*—This is another good one. If the logon name is not displayed, an intruder will have to guess both the logon name and the password.
- *Message Text for Users Attempting to Log On*—This can be used to display company name, disclaimers, accepted use messages, and so on.
- *Prevent Users From Installing Printer Drivers*—This is enabled by default.

After you have configured the Local Computer Policy to your satisfaction, you can copy it to another computer. Just right-click the Security Settings node in the left pane of the Local Security Settings MMC, and select Export Policy, Local Policy, as shown in Figure 8.13.

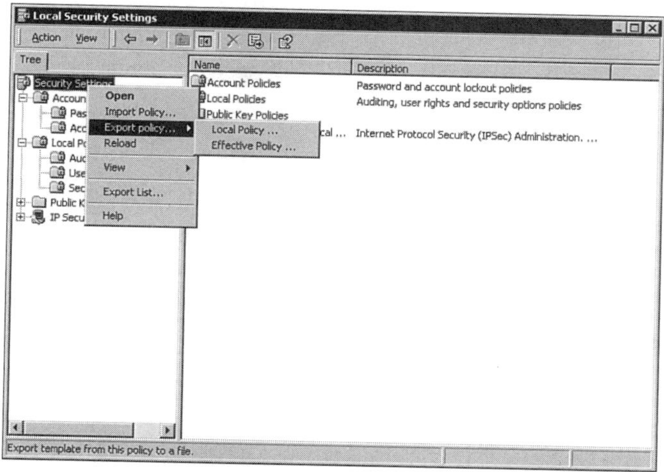

Figure 8.13 The Local Security Settings MMC, showing how to export a local policy.

After the policy is exported to a file, it can be transported to another computer. Just repeat the previous steps and select Import Policy.

When setting local security policies on a Windows 2000 computer, keep in mind that if the computer is later joined to a domain, the domain security policy will become the default security policy.

Security Configuration Tool Set

As we saw in the previous section, local policies can be exported and copied to other computers. However, trying to maintain a single policy across multiple standalone computers could potentially be a support nightmare. Fortunately, Microsoft has supplied some tools with the Security Configuration Tool Set to assist with this type of scenario. In the next few sections you will cover some of the items Microsoft provides in this set.

Security Templates

Microsoft has supplied 12 preconfigured security templates with Windows 2000 Server. These sample templates are located in the %systemroot%\security\templates folder. The supplied templates cover a variety of scenarios, from a basic low security workstation to a high security domain controller. The templates can be applied as-is using the Import Policy option from the Local Security Settings MMC, as discussed in the previous section. Or the individual settings of the template can copied, pasted, or merged with other templates.

The security templates are supplied for four different security levels:

- *Basic*—These templates contain the equivalent security settings of a fresh Windows 2000 installation. They are useful for returning a Windows 2000 installation back to the default settings.
- *Compatible*—This template sets the security level of a Windows 2000 computer to the equivalent of a Windows NT 4.0 computer. This is useful for running legacy applications that cannot run under the tighter security settings in Windows 2000.
- *Secure*—This template has more restrictive settings for password policy, auditing, and Registry access. In addition, it removes all users from the Power Users group.
- *Highly Secure*—This template can only be used in a pure Windows 2000 environment. Because of the secure settings, it will be unable to talk to any downlevel systems. All network communications will be digitally signed and encrypted.

Windows 2000 systems that were upgraded from Windows NT 4.0 or earlier will have security settings roughly equivalent to the Compatible template. The default security settings are only applied when a clean Windows 2000 installation is installed onto a NTFS partition.

Security templates are not supported if Windows 2000 is installed on a File Allocation Table (FAT) file system.

While you can import the security templates using the Local Security Policy MMC, to configure them you need to use the Security Templates snap-in. The snap-in is not available by default; you must create a new MMC, or add it to an existing MMC.

To create a new MMC to use with the Security Templates snap-in

1. Enter **MMC** in the Run dialog box.
2. From the Console Menu, select Add/Remove Snap-in.
3. Click the Add button.

4. From the Add Standalone Snap-in dialog shown in Figure 8.14, select the Security Templates snap-in. Click the Add button.
5. Click the Close button.
6. Click the OK button.

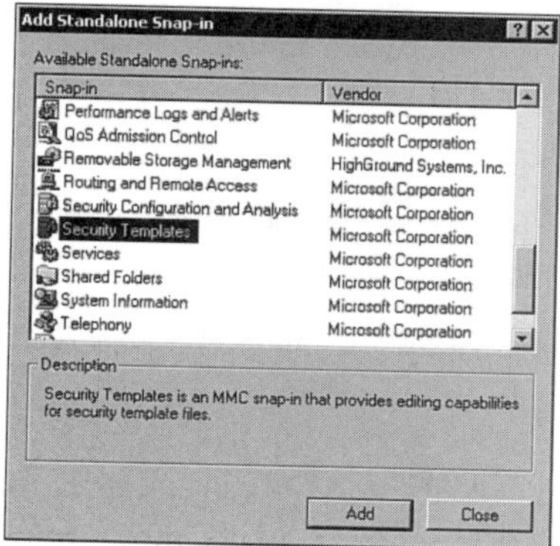

Figure 8.14 The Add Standalone Snap-in dialog box, showing how to select Security Templates.

From the Security Templates snap-in, you can

➤ Create a new security template.

➤ Customize one of the supplied security templates.

Security Configuration and Analysis Tool

The *Security Configuration and Analysis Tool* is used to compare the security settings of a computer to those of a template. It allows you to view the results and make any necessary changes to resolve the differences. The tool can also import, export or configure security settings in a Group Policy.

Like the Security Templates, the Security Configuration and Analysis Tool is a snap-in that must be added to an MMC. To create the MMC

1. Enter **MMC** in the Run dialog box.
2. From the Console Menu, select Add/Remove Snap-in.
3. Click the Add button.
4. From the Add Standalone Snap-in dialog, select the Security Configuration and Analysis snap-in. Click the Add button.

5. Click the Close button.
6. Click the OK button.

To start using the tool, you must create a database to hold the templates:

1. From the Security Configuration and Analysis tool snap-in, right-click the Security Configuration and Analysis node in the left pane of the snap-in.
2. From the pop-up menu, select Open Database.
3. From the Open Database dialog, enter the name and location of the new database that you want to create. Click the Open button.
4. When the Import Template dialog box is displayed, select the desired template. Click the Open button.

Now that the template is imported into the database, you can change the configuration, import attributes, or merge this template with other templates. After the configuration of the template is finished, you can use it to analyze your computer. The tool will compare the settings of the template in the database with those of any computer. It will flag the differences for you to examine, and allow you to make changes as desired.

To perform an analysis

1. From the Security Configuration and Analysis tool snap-in, right-click the Security Configuration and Analysis node in the left pane of the snap-in.
2. From the pop-up menu, select Open Database.
3. From the Open Database dialog, enter the name and location of the database that you want to open. Click the Open button.
4. Right-click the Security Configuration and Analysis node in the left pane of the snap-in.
5. From the pop-up menu, select Analyze Computer Now.
6. Click the OK button to save the error log in the suggested folder.
7. The Configuring Computer Security dialog box appears and displays a progress indicator. When the process is finished, right-click the Security Configuration and Analysis node in the left pane of the snap-in and select View Log File.

The log file shows all the settings encountered and whether or not they match. For a graphical view of the analysis, click each node and observe the icons for each setting. As shown in Figure 8.15, the various icons indicate the following:

➤ A green check mark means the settings were the same

➤ A red X means there was a difference

➤ No icon means that the policy was not included in the template

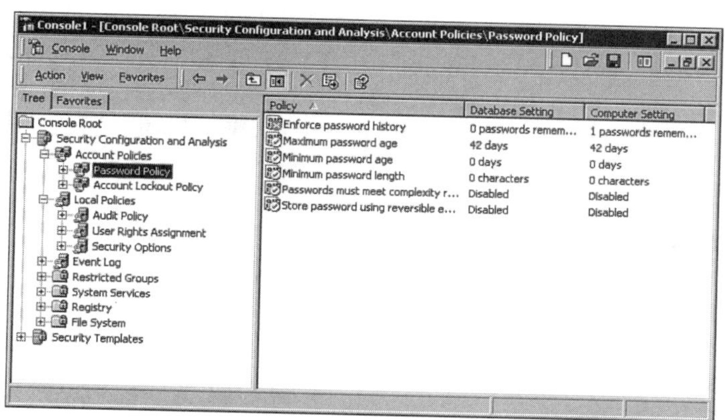

Figure 8.15 The Add Security Configuration and Analysis snap-in, showing the results of an analysis.

If you want the settings on the computer that was being analyzed to be automatically configured to match the template in the database, right-click Security Configuration and Analysis and select Configure Computer Now from the pop-up menu.

Security templates should not be applied to production systems without thorough testing to ensure that application functionality is maintained.

Encrypting File System (EFS)

The *Encrypting File System (EFS)* is a new feature in Windows 2000. EFS is an extension to NTFS version 5.0 which is included with Windows 2000, and allows the user to encrypt files and folders. EFS uses public/private key technology which makes it difficult, but not necessarily impossible to crack.

As is typical with this key technology, the public key is used to encrypt the data, and a private key is used for decryption. After encryption is configured, the encrypt/decrypt process is transparent to the user.

The file/folder encryption and compression attributes are mutually exclusive. You can apply one or the other to a file or folder, but not both.

The first time that a user selects the encryption attribute from the properties dialog of a file or folder, as shown in Figure 8.16, EFS will automatically generate a public key pair, then the private key is certified by a Certificate Authority (CA). If a CA is not available, the public key is self-signed. All of this is transparent to the user.

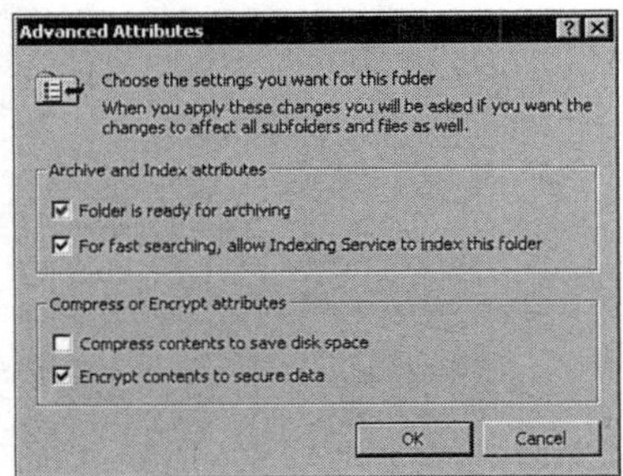

Figure 8.16 The folder properties dialog box, showing the Advanced Attributes selections.

So that the data can be recovered in case the user loses their private key, or leaves the company, the local administrator account is designated as the *Data Recovery Agent (DRA)*. This is the default, and can be changed using the Public Key Policies node of the Local Security Settings MMC as shown in Figure 8.17. Because this account is designated as the DRA, a recovery key that can be used by the local administrator to recover the encrypted data is generated and saved in the local administrators' certificate store. This recovery key can be used only to recover the data. The user's private key is never revealed.

On a standalone Windows 2000 servers and workstations, the local administrator account is designated as the Data Recovery Agent (DRA). In a domain, the domain administrators account has this role. If the DRA role is removed by a configuration error, the system assumes that no data recovery policy is in place and will refuse to encrypt any files or folders.

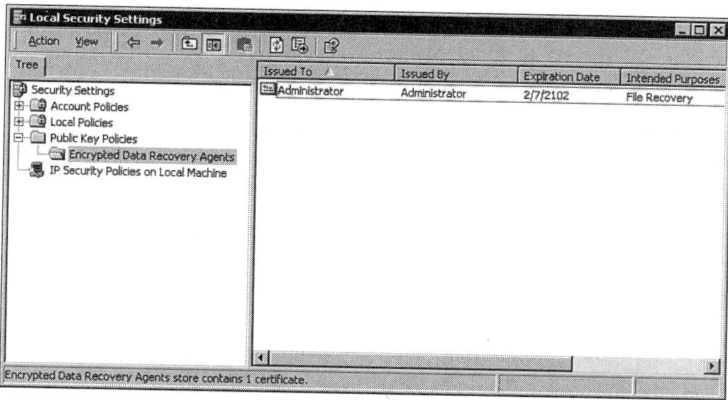

Figure 8.17 The Local Security Settings MMC, showing the Encrypted Data Recovery Agents certificate.

The following conditions apply when moving or copying encrypted files:

- If an encrypted file or folder is moved or copied to another folder on an NTFS formatted volume, it remains encrypted.
- If an encrypted file or folder is moved or copied to a FAT or FAT32 formatted volume, it is decrypted.
- If an encrypted file or folder is moved or copied to a floppy, it is decrypted.
- If a user other than the one who encrypted the file or folder attempts to copy it, they will receive the message "Access is Denied."
- If a user other than the one who encrypted the file attempts to move it to a folder that was encrypted by the original user, they will be successful.
- If a user other than the one who encrypted the file or folder attempts to move or copy it to another volume, either NTFS, FAT, or FAT32, they will receive the message "Access is Denied."

The user account with recovery agent rights will be able to copy the file to his/her computer to perform recovery operations.

Recovering an Encrypted File or Folder

To recover an encrypted file or folder, you must use the EFS recovery agent.

To recover a file or folder

1. Log on to the computer using the EFS Data Recovery Agent account.
2. Right-click the file or folder and select Properties.
3. Click the Advanced button.
4. From the Advanced Attributes dialog box, deselect the Encrypt Contents to Secure Data checkbox.
5. Click OK twice to save.

Encryption Using the Cipher Command

The *cipher command-line utility* is supplied so that you can work with encrypted files and folders from the command line. This is handy when you are encrypting or decrypting a large number of files or folders, because you can use wildcards, or run the utility from a script.

```
C:\> cipher /f
```

The cipher command options are shown in Table 8.1.

Table 8.1 Cipher Command-Line Options

Option	Meaning
No parameters	Displays the encryption state of the files in the current folder
/e	Encrypts the specified folder(s)
/d	Decrypts the specified folder(s)
/s:dir	Performs the operation on the current folder and all subfolders
/a	Encrypts/Decrypts the files in all of the folders that were specified
/I	Continues when an error occurs
/f	Forces all specified files to be encrypted
/q	Non-verbose reporting
/h	Displays hidden or system files
/k	Creates a new key. All other options are ignored

You might encounter EFS questions on the exam. You should know how to encrypt and decrypt files and folders using both the GUI and the cipher utility. In addition, you should be familiar with the key recovery process.

Practice Questions

Question 1

Which of the following utilities should be used to create and manage Windows 2000 domain accounts?

❍ A. User Manager for Domains

❍ B. User Accounts and Passwords

❍ C. Active Directory Users and Computers

❍ D. Local Users and Groups

Answer C is correct. While User Manager for Domains can create accounts if the domain hasn't been converted to native mode, it's not completely compatible. The other utilities can only be used to create local accounts.

Question 2

Which of the following utilities can be used to create and manage Windows 2000 server local accounts?

❍ A. User Manager for Domains

❍ B. User Accounts and Passwords

❍ C. Active Directory Users and Computers

❍ D. Local Users and Groups

Answer D is correct. User Manager for Domains and AD Users and Computers can only be used to create domain accounts. User Accounts and Passwords is only available on Windows 2000 Professional computers.

Question 3

Which of the following groups are created by default on a Windows 2000 member server? (Choose all that apply.)

❑ A. Builtin

❑ B. Administrators

❑ C. Computers

❑ D. Guests

Answers B and D are correct. Administrators and Guests are default accounts on a Windows 2000 member server. Builtin and Computers are not default groups; therefore, answers A and C are incorrect.

Question 4

You need to configure an account for a temporary user on your network. Which of the following accounts should you assign this user?

- ❍ A. Domain User
- ❍ B. Domain Admin
- ❍ C. Guest
- ❍ D. Local User

Answer C is correct. The Guest account should be used for any temporary user who needs limited system access. Therefore, answers A, B, and D are incorrect.

Question 5

Which Windows NT group is roughly equivalent to the Windows 2000 Power Users group?

- ❍ A. Domain Users
- ❍ B. Users
- ❍ C. Domain Admins
- ❍ D. Administrators

Answer B is correct. Security has been tightened in Windows 2000, so the Power Users group permissions are roughly equivalent to the Users group from Windows NT 4.0.

Question 6

Which of the following is not a valid password policy?

- ❍ A. Password History
- ❍ B. Maximum Password Age
- ❍ C. Minimum Password Age
- ❍ D. Minimum Password Length

Answer A is correct. The correct policy is named Enforce Password History.

Question 7

The Human Resources manager was recently terminated. Due to the sensitive nature of her files they were all encrypted. What utility can you use to decrypt her files?

- ❍ A. Cipher
- ❍ B. Decrypt
- ❍ C. Unencrypt
- ❍ D. RecoverPass

Answer A is ocrrect. Cipher is the command-line utility that can be used to decrypt files and folders. The other utilities do not exist.

Question 8

What user account(s) have the default recovery agent role in a domain?

- ❍ A. Power Users Group
- ❍ B. DRA User
- ❍ C. Domain Administrator account
- ❍ D. Domain Admins

Answer C is correct. By default the domain administrator account is granted the recovery agent role for the domain.

Question 9

What utility do you use to view audit information?

- ❍ A. Audit Log Viewer
- ❍ B. Log Viewer
- ❍ C. Event Viewer
- ❍ D. Audit Viewer

Answer C is correct. The audit information is recorded in the Security Log under Event Viewer. The other utilities do not exist.

Question 10

Which of the following items typically appear in an audit record?

- ❍ A. The time and date that the event occurred
- ❍ B. The elapsed time that the event consumed
- ❍ C. The event performed
- ❍ D. The next occurrence of the event

Answers A and C are correct. The audit record shows the event performed, the time and date that it was performed, the user account, and the success or failure of the event.

Need To Know More?

Shilmover, Barry and Stu Sjouwerman. *Windows 2000 Power Toolkit.* New Riders, Indianapolis, Indiana, 2001. ISBN 0-7357-1061-9. This book is a valuable resource for reference material on Windows security and policies.

Windows 2000 Resource Kits online at `http://www.microsoft.com/windows2000/techinfo/reskit/en-us/default.asp`. Also available in print; ISBN 1572318082.

Search TechNet on the Internet at `http://www.microsoft.com/technet` or the TechNet CD for information on Encrypting File System, Local Policy, Account Policy, auditing, Security Configuration Tool Set.

For additional information, refer to the Microsoft Windows 2000 online help. To access, select Help from the Start menu. Terms and technologies to search for include Security, Encrypting File System, and Security Configuration and Analysis Tool.

9

Practice Test #1

Question 1

Which tool(s) can be used to import and export security templates?

- ❍ A. Local Security Settings MMC
- ❍ B. Security Templates snap-in
- ❍ C. Local Policies MMC
- ❍ D. Account policies MMC

Question 2

Why would you revoke a certificate? (Choose all that apply.)

- ❑ A. Because the user can no longer be trusted.
- ❑ B. Because the certificate may be fraudulent.
- ❑ C. Because the key has been compromised.
- ❑ D. Because the network administrator needs to pare the certificate list occasionally.

Question 3

You are interviewing an applicant for an opening in your help desk group. During the course of your interview, you ask the applicant to tell you everything she knows about Windows 2000 and digitally signed drivers. Out of the four statements that the applicant makes, given below, which ones are correct? (Choose all that apply.)

- ❑ A. Digitally signed device drivers have passed rigorous testing by the Microsoft Hardware Quality Labs and therefore should provide a high degree of reliability.
- ❑ B. Digitally signed device drivers are protected against changes to the driver files since being signed by the Microsoft Hardware Quality Labs.
- ❑ C. Digitally signed device drivers are the only type of driver files that are found on the Windows Update Web site or Windows 2000 CD-ROMs.
- ❑ D. Digitally signed device drivers can't be installed unless a certificate authority has been set up on your network.

Question 4

Which of the following settings restricts users from accessing Web information on folders outside the Home Directory for a Web site?

- A. Directory browsing
- B. Index this resource
- C. Execute scripts only
- D. When connecting to this resource, the content should come from a share located on another computer.

Question 5

Which of the following VPN protocols can be used with a pre-Windows 2000 client?

- A. PPTP
- B. L2PP
- C. L2TP
- D. L1TP

Question 6

John is attempting to install a new application onto a computer, but is denied due to insufficient disk space. You check the hard disk and see that it still has 17GB of free space available. What is the most likely reason that John is not able to perform the installation?

- A. John does not have Domain Admin permissions.
- B. John has reached his disk quota limit.
- C. John is installing an incompatible version of the application.
- D. John is in Safe Mode.

Question 7

You are implementing file and folder auditing on your network file servers. What requirement must you meet to use auditing?

- ❍ A. Your network must be an Ethernet network.
- ❍ B. Your file servers must be formatted with the NTFS file system.
- ❍ C. All of your users must be using Windows 2000 Professional.
- ❍ D. Your file servers must be on the same local subnet as your users.

Question 8

Joe installed a new RAID controller in his Exchange 2000 Server. Joe plans to create a RAID 5 array using the controller. The RAID controller, however, does not appear in the Device Manager after starting the server. Joe has been assured by the hardware reseller that both the hardware and the drivers are compatible with Windows 2000. What does Joe need to do to get the new hardware installed in his computer satisfactorily?

- ❍ A. Use the Add/Remove Hardware applet in the Control Panel.
- ❍ B. Use the Phone and Modem Options applet in the Control Panel.
- ❍ C. Install the device in the computer; Windows 2000 will detect and automatically install the device the next time it is started.
- ❍ D. Use the Device Manager to install the new hardware device.

Question 9

What applications can you use to monitor your computer and network performance?

- ❍ A. Device Manager
- ❍ B. Performance Monitor
- ❍ C. Recovery Console
- ❍ D. Event Viewer

Question 10

What command is used to enable the PhysicalDisk object so that the counters can be monitored in Windows 2000?

- ❍ A. It is enabled by default
- ◉ B. Diskperf –y
- ❍ C. Diskperf –n
- ❍ D. None of the above

Question 11

You are responsible for managing the operation of an IIS 5 server that hosts two Web sites. You must meet the following performance requirements:

- ❍ You must limit the performance impact of Web sites on the server.
- ❍ You must limit the network usage of Web sites.
- ❍ You must track access to the Web sites.
- ❍ You must ensure users are allowed only to access files on the local server.

On the Properties page for each Web site, you select the Home Directory tab and select Log Visits and Directory Browsing. On the Performance tab, you select Enable process throttling, select Enforce limits, and set the Maximum CPU use setting to 15%.

Which of the following does the proposed solution provide? (Choose all that apply.)

- ☒ A. The proposed solution limits the performance impact of one Web site on the server.
- ❑ B. The proposed solution limits the network usage of two Web sites.
- ☒ C. The proposed solution tracks access to the Web sites.
- ❑ D. The proposed solution limits user access to files only on the local server.

Question 12

Chris is the network administrator of a small Windows 2000 network that has 10 servers and 125 client workstations. The network is running Active Directory and all computer configuration is controlled by Group Policy. Chris wants to include driver signing behavior in her Group Policy. Where does she need to go to configure the option for driver signing?

- ❍ A. The System applet in the Control Panel.
- ❍ B. The User Configuration, Administrative Templates, System section of the Group Policy Object.
- ❍ C. The Computer Configuration, Administrative Templates, System section of the Group Policy Object.
- ❍ D. The Computer Configuration, Windows Settings, Security Settings section of the Group Policy Object.

Question 13

The Compatible security template is used to perform what function in Windows 2000?

- ❍ A. Restores the default security configuration to the computer after application.
- ❍ B. Applies a security configuration that is approximately equivalent to a Windows NT 4.0 computer to allow legacy applications to function properly.
- ❍ C. Applies a security configuration that is more secure than the default configuration.
- ❍ D. Applies a security configuration that makes Windows 2000 computers able to share files and folders with Windows 98 computers.

Question 14

What command is used to enable the LogicalDisk object so that the counters can be monitored in Windows 2000?

- ❍ A. It is enabled by default
- ❍ B. **Diskperf –y**
- ❍ C. **Diskperf –n**
- ❍ D. None of the above

Question 15

Mary is the network administrator of a small Windows 2000 network that has 3 servers and 45 client workstations. The network is not running Active Directory. Mary wants to configure driver signing behavior for her computers. Where does she need to go to configure the option for driver signing?

❍ A. The Computer Configuration, Administrative Templates, System section of the Group Policy Object.

❍ B. The Computer Configuration, Windows Settings, Security Settings section of the Group Policy Object.

❍ C. The Computer Configuration, Administrative Templates, System section of the Group Policy Object.

❍ D. The System applet in the Control Panel.

Question 16

Jeff moves some encrypted files from his computer to a floppy disk. What is the status of the files now in regard to encryption?

❍ A. The files are encrypted if the folder that they were moved into is encrypted.

❍ B. The files are not encrypypted.

❍ C. The files are encrypted if Jeff selected this option during the move process.

❍ D. The files remain encrypted as long as Jeff's EFS certificate is on the floppy disk.

Question 17

Which of the following are advantages to using the NTFS v5 file system on your network server hard disks? (Choose all that apply.)

❑ A. Auditing of file, folder, and object access.

❑ B. Enforcement of disk space usage quotas.

❑ C. EFS encryption of files and folders.

❑ D. File and folder level security.

Question 18

If you run a normal backup on Monday, and a differential backup the other days of the week using only one tape per day, how many tapes will be needed to restore your server after a system failure on Friday?

- A. One
- B. Two
- C. Three
- D. Five

Question 19

What functions can the Routing and Remote Access Service in Windows 2000 perform? (Choose all that apply.)

- A. RAS Server
- B. VPN Server
- C. Network routing
- D. DHCP Server

Question 20

Ralph is interviewing for the position of a help desk employee. You ask him to tell you which of the following four statements about driver signing is false. Of the following statements you make, which ones are incorrect? (Choose all that apply.)

- A. Digitally signed drivers are guaranteed to have been rigorously tested by Microsoft to ensure that they will properly function in Windows 2000.
- B. Digitally signed drivers can only be obtained by calling Microsoft support directly.
- C. Digitally signed drivers do not provide any protection against tampering after they leave the Microsoft WHQL.
- D. Digitally signed drivers play an important role in Windows 2000 in keeping a computer stable and properly functioning.

Question 21

In what situation would you design your network as a workgroup instead of a domain?

- ❍ A. When the network has multiple servers.
- ❍ B. When the network is small and has no servers.
- ❍ C. When you need to use Active Directory.
- ❍ D. When you have several hundred clients spread out over multiple geographic regions.

Question 22

A user has been assigned the following permissions to the AcctInfo folder on a server:

- ❍ AcctInfo Shared folder permissions—Read (Everyone group)
- ❍ AcctInfo Shared folder permissions—Full Control (user)
- ❍ AcctInfo NTFS permissions—Read, Write, Read & Execute (user)

The user accesses the folder remotely from another computer on the network and attempts to manipulate the files in the folders. Which of the following will the user be allowed to perform? (Choose all that apply.)

- ❑ A. The user will be allowed to change the ownership for the files in the folder.
- ❑ B. The user will be able to run programs within the folder.
- ❑ C. The user will be able to view the permissions for the files in the folder.
- ❑ D. The user will be able to delete the files in the folder.

Question 23

To start in Safe Mode:

- ❍ A. Press the F7 key during system boot.
- ❍ B. Press the F8 key during system boot.
- ❍ C. Select Start, Accessories, System Tools, Safe Mode.
- ❍ D. None of the above.

Question 24

You have a striped volume on one of your Windows 2000 servers. Over the weekend, one of the disks has failed. You have a backup from Friday night. What must you do to get the server back into operation?

- ❍ A. Replace the failed disk and re-create the striped volume.
- ❍ B. Replace the failed disk, re-create the striped volume, and restore the data to the new striped volume.
- ❍ C. Replace the failed disk and restore the data to it.
- ❍ D. Re-create the striped volume and restore the data to it.

Question 25

How do you learn the status of a device? (Choose all that apply.)

- ❑ A. By looking at the icon next to the device in the Device Manager tree.
- ❑ B. By looking in the device's Properties window.
- ❑ C. By seeing if the device is in the device list.
- ❑ D. By seeing if the category of the device is in the device list.

Question 26

Christopher wants to enable NTFS compression on his local Windows 2000 Professional computer. You inform him that he cannot do so without violating the company's security policy that requires EFS to be used on all local computer hard disks. What is the cause of this problem?

- ❍ A. NTFS compression and EFS encryption cannot be implemented on local computers, only on network file servers.
- ❍ B. NTFS compression and EFS encryption are mutually exclusive, thus he will not be able to use EFS encryption.
- ❍ C. Christopher is not a member of the Domain Admins group and will not be able to configure the desired changes.
- ❍ D. Christopher does not have the required digital certificate for implementing NTFS file and folder compression.

Question 27

Rick is the administrator of a Windows 2000 network consisting of 150 Windows 2000 servers and 1,500 Windows 2000 Professional clients. His company is organized into four departments: Software, Hardware, Administration, and Support. The company manufactures and markets surveying devices that are used in the field by civil engineers. Rick wants to prevent his non-technical users from being able to install unsigned device drivers but still allow his technical users to install them as required, only after they have acknowledged the fact the drivers are unsigned. What steps should Rick perform to achieve his goals? All computer and user accounts are in one of four OUs that correspond to the four departments in the company. (Choose all that apply.)

- ❑ A. From Active Directory Users and Computers, Rick should create a GPO and link it to the Software, Hardware, Administration, and Support OUs. He should then configure the driver signing policy in the GPO for Ignore.
- ❑ B. From Active Directory Users and Computers, Rick should create a GPO and link it to the Software, Hardware, Administration, and Support OUs. He should then configure the driver signing policy in the GPO for Block.
- ❑ C. From Active Directory Users and Computers, Rick should create a GPO and link it to the Administration and Support OUs. He should then configure the driver signing policy in the GPO for Block.
- ❑ D. From Active Directory Users and Computers, Rick should create a GPO and link it to the Software and Hardware OUs. He should then configure the driver signing policy in the GPO for Warn.

Question 28

Which of the following is not a valid Safe mode option?

- ❍ A. Safe Mode
- ❍ B. Safe Mode with Networking
- ❍ C. Safe Mode with Command Prompt
- ❍ D. Safe Mode with Base Video

Question 29

Your network adapter is not on the HCL, and Plug and Play doesn't recognize it. What is your best plan of action?

- ❍ A. Manually configure the resources using Device Manager.
- ❍ B. Manually configure the resources in the server BIOS.
- ❍ C. Manually configure the resources using Computer Management.
- ❍ D. Replace the adapter with an HCL supported one.

Question 30

You are the network administrator of a large organization that is using all Windows 2000 Server computers and Windows 2000 Professional and Windows NT 4.0 Workstation computers. Users consistently seem to be using several hundred MB of hard disk space on your network's file servers. Organizational policy states that no user will use more than 50MB of disk space on any server without prior approval. What can you to prevent users from using too much disk space in the future?

- ❍ A. Create a disk quota entry for all users and limit their usage to 50MB.
- ❍ B. Upgrade the Windows NT 4.0 Workstation clients to Windows 2000 Professional.
- ❍ C. Deny the Windows NT 4.0 Workstation clients access to the Windows 2000 file servers.
- ❍ D. Establish an external trust between the root of your Windows 2000 domain and the Windows NT 4.0 domain.

Question 31

Why must you deploy service packs for Windows 2000 Server? (Choose all that apply.)

- ❑ A. So you won't be affected by security attacks over the Internet.
- ❑ B. Because Windows won't work if you don't.
- ❑ C. So you have the latest fixes and patches so Windows 2000 Server operates properly.
- ❑ D. So all other network users running Windows 2000 or XP will have the latest updates.

Question 32

Dorothy is attempting to save a large database file and is denied access due to being out of disk space. NTFS file and folder compression is in use on the disk in question, as are disk quotas. Dorothy shows that she has 15MB of space remaining and the database file is only 13MB in size. Why is she still not able to save this large file?

- ❍ A. There is not enough space for the temp file that will be created during the saving of the file.
- ◉ B. Disk quotas are based on uncompressed file sizes, not compressed file sizes.
- ❍ C. Dorothy has too many applications open, thus her paging file has grown too large.
- ❍ D. The file is too large to transmit over the network without excessive fragmentation and packet loss.

Question 33

Which of the following user groups are permitted to use the Application Server mode of Terminal Services? (Choose all that apply.)

- ☑ A. Administrators
- ☑ B. Users
- ☑ C. Power Users
- ☐ D. Anonymous

Question 34

Roger is an administrator for his company and is responsible for keeping 25 servers and 750 workstations up to date with the latest stable drivers. A driver update has been issued for the DLT backup system that is installed on three of Roger's servers. Where can Roger go to quickly install the updated device drivers on these three servers?

- ❍ A. The Services MMC snap-in
- ◉ B. Device Manager
- ❍ C. System Information
- ❍ D. The Add/Remove Programs applet in the Control Panel

Question 35

Your Windows 2000 Server is configured with both FAT32 and NTFS volumes. You must configure the server to provide the most secure access possible to all files on the server and meet the following security requirements:

- ❍ You must limit local access to change or delete files and folder all groups except Administrators and Server Operators.
- ❍ You must track all failed logon attempts.
- ❍ You must allow members of the Accounting group complete access to the files in the Accounting and Payroll folders on the NTFS volume.
- ❍ You must not allow remote access to the Everyone group to the Security Management share on the FAT volume.

The proposed solution is to change the Security Policy settings. In the Users Rights Assignments policies, change Log On Locally to include only Administrators. In the Audit Policy settings, change Audit Logon Events to Failure. On the Permissions for the shared folders Accounting and Payroll, add the Accounting group and select Allow Full Control. On the Permissions for the Security Management share, remove the Everyone group.

Which of the following does the proposed solution provide? (Choose all that apply.)

❑ A. The proposed solution limits local access to delete files and folders for all groups except Administrators and Server Operators.

❑ B. The proposed solution tracks all failed logon attempts.

❑ C. The proposed solution allows members of the Accounting group complete access to the files in the Accounting and Payroll folders.

❑ D. The proposed solution restricts remote access for Everyone to the Security Management folder.

Question 36

What is the default method of name resolution in Windows 2000?

❍ A. WINS

❍ B. NetBIOS

❍ C. NetBEUI

❍ D. DNS

Question 37

You are the administrator in your organization with the responsibility for managing all file servers. Recently, some of your users have been complaining about getting out of space errors even though they claim their individual use is within the posted guidelines for which disk quotas are configured. You open the disk quota settings window for the file server in question and see the image shown in Figure 9.1 with the red light illuminated. What is the cause of the problem?

Figure 9.1 The quota status display.

❍ A. The disk in the file server is failing and needs to be replaced.

❍ B. The disk quota service has become hung and must be restarted.

❍ C. The disk quota is disabled for this hard disk and other users have violated the usage guidelines, using all available space on the hard disk.

❍ D. The file server is disconnected from the local network.

Question 38

Austin is using the Device Manager to gather information about a particular server in his company. Which of the following items will he be able to gather information on using the Device Manager? (Choose all that apply.)

❑ A. The amount of memory installed in the server.

❑ B. A list of all interrupts currently being used on the computer.

❑ C. The status of a particular device, such as enabled or disabled.

❑ D. The size of the paging file on the server.

Question 39

What subnet mask is used for a class B address?

❍ A. 255.255.248.0

❍ B. 255.255.255.0

❍ C. 255.255.0.0

❍ D. 255.0.0.0

Question 40

You are the network administrator of your company's Windows 2000 network. All computers on the network are running Windows 2000 Server or Windows 2000 Professional. You have one central file server that all users save their documents onto. You want to be able to monitor user disk space usage without restricting it. How can you most easily accomplish this? (Choose all that apply.)

- ❑ A. Use Windows Explorer to manually examine the usage of each of your users one at a time.
- ❑ B. Enable disk quotas on the volumes of concern.
- ❑ C. Select the Do not limit disk usage option.
- ❑ D. Drag the usage statistics out of the Quota Entries window into a spreadsheet application.

Question 41

Why would you use a troubleshooter?

- ❍ A. Because you like to answer questions about devices.
- ❍ B. Because you can access Windows Help from there.
- ❍ C. So you can determine if Windows can provide a solution to your problem.
- ❍ D. So you can learn what problems you may run into.

Question 42

Where is Internet Connection Sharing configured on a Windows 2000 Server? (Choose all that apply.)

- ❑ A. In the Communications applet
- ❑ B. In the ICS applet
- ❑ C. In the RRAS MMC
- ❑ D. From the properties page of the interface that's connected to the Internet

Question 43

If you run a normal backup on Monday, and an incremental backup the other days of the week using only one tape per day, how many tapes will be needed to restore your server after a system failure on Friday?

❍ A. One

❍ B. Two

❍ C. Three

❍ D. Five

Question 44

Jeff wants to configure a RAID-5 array on his Windows 2000 Server computer. He has five hard disks installed but cannot create a RAID-5 array. What is the most likely reason for his trouble?

❍ A. Jeff is not a member of the Enterprise Admins group.

❍ B. Jeff's hard disks are basic disks instead of dynamic disks.

❍ C. Jeff's hard disks are dynamic disks instead of basic disks.

❍ D. Jeff's server does not have a hardware RAID controller installed.

Question 45

Auditing is enabled from what location?

❍ A. The Group Policy Editor

❍ B. The Event Viewer

❍ C. Windows Explorer

❍ D. The Services console

Question 46

In what two locations might permission be granted for a user to have dial-up access? (Choose all that apply.)

- ❑ A. Remote Policy
- ❑ B. Remote Access Policy
- ❑ C. User Account Properties
- ❑ D. Group Policy

Question 47

Which of the following File Replication Service functions is configured automatically?

- ❍ A. IIS virtual directory synchronization
- ❍ B. Active Directory inter-site synchronization
- ❍ C. Active Directory intra-site synchronization
- ❍ D. Dfs root replica synchronization

Question 48

Which of the following security templates requires a pure Windows 2000 environment in order to be used?

- ❍ A. Securews
- ❍ B. Ocfiless
- ❍ C. Hisecdc
- ❍ D. Securedc

Question 49

What is included in a System State backup? (Choose all that apply.)

- ❑ A. The Registry
- ❑ B. User documents
- ❑ C. Boot files
- ❑ D. Active Directory database

Question 50

Andrea recently purchased a new custom-created FAX solution for her FAX server. The solution is not Plug and Play compatible. What does Andrea need to do to get the new hardware installed in her computer satisfactorily?

❍ A. Use the Device Manager to install the new hardware device.

❍ B. Use the Phone and Modem Options applet in the Control Panel.

❍ C. Install the device in the computer. Windows 2000 will detect and automatically install the device the next time it is started.

❍ D. Use the Add/Remove Hardware applet in the Control Panel.

Question 51

What command-line switch should you use with the cipher utility if you are encrypting a folder that contains system files?

❍ A. **Cipher /h**

❍ B. **Cipher /s**

❍ C. **Cipher /e**

❍ D. **Cipher /d**

Question 52

Which of the following are required to use Internet Connection Sharing on your network? (Choose all that apply.)

❑ A. A connection to the Internet

❑ B. A computer with two network connections, one of which must be an Ethernet adapter

❑ C. Windows 2000 DHCP service

❑ D. Windows 2000 DNS service

Question 53

What type of backup would you perform if you only wanted to back up critical files such as the Registry or the Active Directory database?

❍ A. Daily

❍ B. System State

❍ C. Incremental

❍ D. Differential

Question 54

How do you create an answer file? (Choose all that apply.)

❑ A. Using the Setup Wizard

❑ B. From the CD-ROM

❑ C. From the boot disks

❑ D. Creating the file manually

Question 55

What two methods are available for the Data Recovery Agent to decrypt a file that was encrypted by a user whose user account has been deleted from Active Directory? (Choose all that apply.)

❑ A. Restore the file to a recovery server containing the DRA's recovery certificate and decrypt the file.

❑ B. Export the DRA's recovery certificate to the location of the encrypted file and decrypt the file.

❑ C. Re-create the user account with the same properties and use it to decrypt the file.

❑ D. Copy the file from the command line to a floppy disk.

Question 56

If you have a server failure and the Recovery Console was not preloaded, how can you still boot to it? (Choose all that apply.)

❑ A. From the four Windows 2000 Boot disks

❑ B. From a network share

❑ C. Using a PXE capable NIC

❑ D. From the Windows 2000 CD-ROM

Question 57

How is the Recovery Console installed on a Windows 2000 computer?

❍ A. Using the **winnt32 /reccons** command.

❍ B. Using the **winnt /cmdcons** command.

❍ C. Using the **winnt32 /cmdcons** command.

❍ D. During Windows 2000 setup.

Question 58

Andrea wants to configure NTFS file and folder compression on a folder on her Windows 2000 Professional computer from the command line. What is the required command to perform this action from the command line?

❍ A. **compress**

❍ B. **compact**

❍ C. **zip**

❍ D. **reduce**

Question 59

What is required to install an Enterprise Certificate Authority?

❍ A. An active Internet connection

❍ B. Active Directory

❍ C. A third-party digital certificate from VeriSign

❍ D. Windows 2000 Advanced Server

Question 60

Which of the following configuration limitations is true of standalone Dfs servers?

- ❍ A. They must reside on NTFS volumes.
- ❍ B. They can be configured to replicate using FRS.
- ❍ C. They are limited to one level of Dfs links.
- ❍ D. They provide fault-tolerant access to links for network users.

10

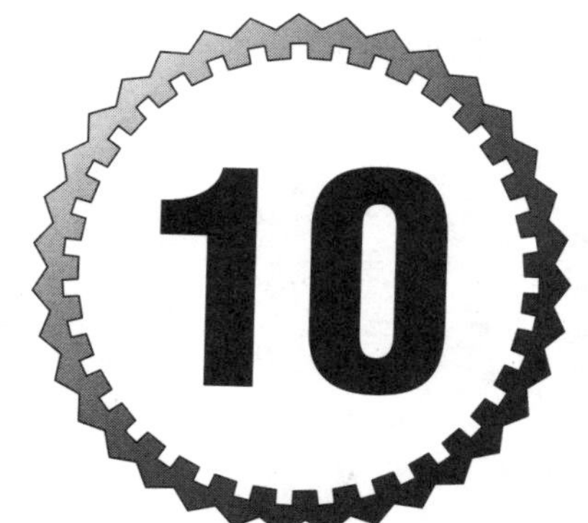

Answer Key to Practice Test #1

1. A
2. A, B, C
3. A, B, C
4. A
5. A
6. B
7. B
8. A
9. B, D
10. A
11. A, C
12. B
13. B
14. B
15. D
16. B
17. A, B, C, D
18. B
19. A, B, C
20. A, D
21. B
22. B, C
23. B
24. B
25. A, B
26. B
27. C, D
28. D
29. D
30. A
31. A, C, D
32. B
33. A, B, C
34. B
35. B, C, D
36. D
37. C
38. B, C
39. C
40. B, C, D
41. C
42. C, D
43. D
44. B
45. A
46. B, C
47. C
48. C
49. A, C, D
50. D
51. A
52. A, B
53. B
54. A, D
55. A, B
56. A, D
57. C
58. B
59. B
60. C

1. Answer A is correct. The Security Templates snap-in allows you to edit as well as cut and paste security templates, but doesn't allow you to import or export them. The Local Policies and Account policies MMCs don't exist. They are nodes in the Local Security Settings MMC.

2. Answers A, B, and C are correct. The network administrator might believe that the key is fraudulent or compromised, or the user cannot be trusted.

3. Answers A, B, and C are correct. You do not need a CA on your network to install digitally signed drivers; therefore, answer D is incorrect.

4. Answer A is correct. Directory browsing determines whether users connecting to the site are able to access information located in other folders outside the Home Directory.

5. Answer A is correct. Windows 9x and Windows NT clients can only connect to a VPN using PPTP. Therefore, answers B, C, and D are all incorrect.

6. Answer B is correct. Disk quotas are based on the ownership attribute of each file. In this case, all files that John has created, edited, or otherwise taken ownership of (including application installation) will count toward his quota usage. Most likely he does not have enough space left under his quota to allow him to install the application; therefore, answers A, C, and D are incorrect.

7. Answer B is correct. File and folder auditing can be enabled only on NTFS-formatted volumes.

8. Answer A is correct. Non–Plug and Play hardware must be added via the Add/Remove Hardware applet in the Control Panel. All drivers to be installed should be Windows 2000 compliant. The Phone and Modem Options applet of the Control Panel can be used to configure dialing rules and modem settings after a modem has been successfully installed; therefore, answer B is incorrect. Only Plug and Play hardware can be installed physically and have Windows 2000 automatically install and configure the device and drivers; therefore, answer C is incorrect. The Device Manager will not assist in installing new hardware directly; therefore, answer D is incorrect.

9. Answers B and D are correct. The Event Viewer and Performance Monitor are applications that are available in Windows 2000 Server for monitoring your computer and network performance.

10. Answer A is correct. In Windows 2000, the PhysicalDisk object is enabled by default. Diskperf with the `-y` switch turns on the LogicalDisk object; the `-n` switch turns off all disk objects.

11. Answers A and C are correct. Choosing Enable Process Throttling on the Performance tab limits the performance impact of a Web site on the server. Selecting the Log Visits selection tracks user access to the Web site. Additional configuration settings are required to limit network usage by Web sites and restrict users access to files only on the local server. Therefore, answers B and D are incorrect.

12. Answer B is correct. Driver signing in Group Policy is configured in the Computer Configuration, Administrative Templates, System section of the Group Policy Object. The System applet in the Control Panel is used for configuring a local computer's driver signing restrictions; therefore, answer A is incorrect. Driver signing restrictions are configured in Group Policy in the User Configuration section; therefore, answers C and D are incorrect.

13. Answer B is correct. The Compatible template is used to set the security settings to be roughly equivalent to those of Windows NT 4.0. The default security template is used to restore the standard Windows 2000 security settings. The secure or high secure templates can be used to increase the security of a computer. Windows 2000 and Windows 98 computers can share files and folders across the network without the need to apply a security template.

14. Answer B is correct. In Windows 2000, although the PhysicalDisk object is enabled by default, the LogicalDisk object must be turned on manually. Diskperf with the `-y` switch turns on the LogicalDisk object; the `-n` switch turns off all disk objects.

15. Answer D is correct. Driver signing behavior for a local computer is configured from the System applet of the Control Panel. Mary must visit each computer to perform the configuration because she is not running an Active Directory network. The Computer Configuration, Administrative Templates, System section of Group Policy would be used if Mary were using an Active Directory domain, which she is not. Driver signing restrictions are configured in Group Policy in the User Configuration section; therefore, answers B and C are incorrect.

16. Answer B is correct. Encryption is only supported on NTFS 5, so any files copied to a floppy will be decrypted.

17. Answers A, B, C, and D are correct. NTFS provides many benefits, including disk quotas, auditing, file and folder security, and EFS encryption.

18. Answer B is correct. A differential backup backs up the files that have changed since the last normal backup, so the backup jobs get longer everyday. But it will always only take two tapes for a restore.

19. Answers A, B, and C are correct. The Routing and Remote Access service can perform routing duties for your private network, act as a VPN (Virtual Private Network) server, or act as an RAS (Remote Access Server).

20. Answers A and D are correct. Digitally signed drivers have been tested by the WHQL to ensure that they will perform satisfactorily in Windows 2000. The advantage to having high-quality drivers is that your Windows 2000 computer will run more smoothly with fewer system instability issues. You can get digitally signed drivers from the Windows Update Web site or on any Windows 2000 Setup CD-ROM; therefore, answer B is incorrect. Digitally signed drivers, like any other digitally signed file, cannot be tampered with without changing the hash, thus rendering the signature invalid; therefore, answer C is incorrect.

21. Answer B is correct. If your network is small and has no servers, you have no choice but to configure it as a workgroup. A domain requires that you have at least one server acting as a domain controller.

22. Answers B and C are correct. Because NTFS permissions take precedence over Share permissions, the user will not be granted Full Control over the folder. However, the Read & Execute permission allows the user to run programs within the folder and view the permissions for files in the folder. Changing ownership is only available with the Full Control permission, and deleting files is only available with Modify and Full Control. Therefore, answers A and D are incorrect.

23. Answer B is correct. Press the F8 key when you see the system boot menu.

24. Answer B is correct. You must replace the failed disk, re-create the striped volume, and restore the data to the new striped volume. Simply replacing the disk and re-creating the volume will not get your data back; therefore, answer A is incorrect. Replacing the disk without re-creating the striped volume before restoring the data will not solve this problem correctly; therefore, answer C is incorrect. Re-creating the striped volume cannot be done until the failed disk has been replaced; therefore, answer D is incorrect.

25. Answers A and B are correct. From Device Manager, you can look at the icon to the left of the device name, and you can also open the Properties window for the device to see its present status.

26. Answer B is correct. NTFS compression and EFS encryption are mutually exclusive; therefore, if Christopher wants to use NTFS compression, he must disable EFS encryption. NTFS compression and EFS encryption can be configured on any Windows 2000 computer with NTFS 5.0 disks; therefore, answer A is incorrect. Membership in the Domain Admins group is not a requirement to enable NTFS

compression; therefore, answer C is incorrect. There are no digital certificates required to use NTFS compression; therefore, answer D is incorrect.

27. Answers C and D are correct. Rick needs to configure two Group Policy Objects for his network. The first one should be applied to the OUs for the Administration and Support departments with the Block setting configured. The second one should be applied to the OUs for the Software and Hardware departments with the Warn setting configured. Applying the Ignore setting to all four OUs does not accomplish any of the desired results, but instead will allow all users to install unsigned drivers without any operating system intervention; therefore, answer A is incorrect. Applying the Block setting to all four OUs will prevent his technical users from being able to install drivers as required; therefore, answer B is incorrect.

28. Answer D is correct. All Safe modes start with the base video driver.

29. Answer D is correct. The best plan of action is to replace the adapter with one that is on the HCL. Although configuring the resources from Device Manager or the BIOS might work, it isn't supported.

30. Answer A is correct. Implementing a disk quota that limits users to 50MB of disk space will solve your problem; therefore, answers B, C, and D are incorrect.

31. Answers A, C, and D are correct. Service packs can include security patches and updates. The service packs contain the latest fixes and patches for your own system and for all other computers in the network running Windows 2000 Professional or Windows XP.

32. Answer B is correct. Windows 2000 disk quotas are based on uncompressed file size, thus the 15MB of space that Dorothy sees as free may actually be something such as 8 or 10MB of free space. That is not enough room to save her 13MB file; therefore, answers A, C, and D are incorrect.

33. Answers A, B, and C are correct. Unlike the Remote Administration mode, in Application server mode, by default, any authenticated user can access Terminal Services. Therefore, anyone in the Administrators, Users, or Power Users groups is the correct answer.

34. Answers B is correct. Roger can install the new device drivers from the Device Manager. To install the new drivers, he must right-click the device to be updated and select Properties. He then needs to switch to the Driver tab and click Update Driver. The System Information utility allows you to quickly determine many facts about your computer,

but will not help you install an updated driver; therefore, answer A is incorrect. The Add/Remove Programs applet is used for installing programs and configuring Windows components, not for installing drivers; therefore, answer C is incorrect. The Services MMC snap-in is used to configure and control the services running on a computer not to install drivers; therefore, answer D is incorrect.

35. Answers B, C, and D are correct. The Security Policy settings for Audit logon events tracks failed logon attempts. Allowing Full Control to the Accounting group for the Accounting and Payroll shares gives members of that group complete access to the files and folders. Removing the Everyone group from the Security Management share ensures that only explicitly configured users or groups can access this share remotely. Because the server includes FAT and NTFS volumes, the only method for ensuring security is to limit local access to the server; however, the proposed solution does not include the Server Operators group; therefore, answer A is incorrect.

36. Answer D is correct. DNS is the default method of name resolution in Windows 2000, and is required for Active Directory.

37. Answer C is correct. In this case, the disk quotas have been disabled on the volume, allowing users to violate company hard disk space usage limits and use all free space on the hard disk.

38. Answers B and C are correct. Using the Device Manager, Austin will be able to gather information on all of the resources in use and available on his server. He will also be able to determine the status of each device in the system. The amount of memory installed in the server is not displayed in the Device Manager; therefore, answer A is incorrect. The size of the paging file is also not displayed in the Device Manager; therefore, answer D is incorrect.

39. Answer C is correct. Class A = 255.0.0.0, Class B = 255.255.0.0, Class C = 255.255.255.0

40. Answers B, C, and D are correct. By enabling disk quotas with no configured limit, you can easily monitor disk space usage from the Quota Entries window. You can drag the entries from this window into a spreadsheet application, such as Excel, for easy sorting and reporting. Manually examining each user's disk usage in Windows Explorer can get very time consuming; therefore, answer A is incorrect.

41. Answer C is correct. The troubleshooters are designed to help you find a solution to your computing and/or networking problem.

42. Answers C and D are correct. ICS can be configured using the RRAS setup Wizard, or manually by selecting the Sharing tab of the interface that is connected to the Internet. There are no Communications or ICS applets in the Control Panel; therefore, answers A and B are incorrect.

43. Answer D is correct. An incremental backup backs up the files that have changed since the last normal or incremental backup. This results in a short backup time, but it will require the normal tape plus all of the incremental tapes for a restore.

44. Answer B is correct. The most likely reason for Jeff not being able to create a RAID-5 array in this situation is that his disks are basic disks, not dynamic disks. Being a member of the Enterprise Admins group is not a requirement to create a RAID-5 array; therefore, answer A is incorrect. Dynamic disks are required to create RAID-5 arrays; therefore, answer C is incorrect. Jeff will not require a hardware RAID controller in his computer to create a RAID-5 array; therefore, answer D is incorrect.

45. Answer A is correct. Auditing is enabled from the Group Policy Editor. The Group Policy Editor is used to configure Group Policy Objects at various levels within Active Directory, such as the Domain or Organizational Unit level.

46. Answers B and C are correct. If the user account is set to allow, the access policy is ignored. If the account is set to use the policy, the policy setting is used.

47. Answer C is correct. Active Directory intra-site synchronization is configured automatically by the File Replication Service. The other functions can be handled by FRS, but must be configured manually.

48. Answer C is correct. When the Highly Secure templates are applied to a server or workstation, they can no longer communicate with down-level clients because they use encryption for all communications.

49. Answers A, C, and D are correct. System State data includes critical information about a computer, such as the Registry, the Active Directory database, and the boot files. User documents are not included in the system state backup; therefore, answer B is incorrect.

50. Answer D is correct. Non–Plug and Play hardware must be added via the Add/Remove Hardware applet of the Control Panel. All drivers to be installed should be Windows 2000 compliant. The Device Manager will not assist in installing new hardware directly; therefore, answer A

is incorrect. The Phone and Modem Options applet in the Control Panel can be used to configure dialing rules and modem settings after a modem has been successfully installed; therefore, answer B is incorrect. Only Plug and Play hardware can be installed physically and have Windows 2000 automatically install and configure the device and drivers; therefore, answer C is incorrect.

51. Answer A is correct. The `/h` switch is used when you are working with a folder that contains hidden or system files.

52. Answers A and B are correct. To use ICS, you must have a computer with two network connections (one of which must be an Ethernet adapter) that has an active connection to the Internet. You cannot have a DNS or DHCP server on your network while using ICS because ICS performs these functions for its clients; therefore, answers C and D are incorrect.

53. Answer B is correct. A System State backup backs up only critical operating system files, such as the Registry and the Active Directory database. Therefore, answers A, C, and D are incorrect.

54. Answers A and D are correct. You can use the Setup Wizard on the Windows 2000 Server CD-ROM to create the answer file automatically, or you can create the file manually by opening a text editor and entering the script code.

55. Answers A and B are correct. The supported methods of data recovery are to restore the encrypted file to a computer containing the DRA certificate and perform decryption, or to export the DRA certificate to the location of the encrypted file and perform decryption.

56. Answers A and D are correct. The Recovery console can be started via the Windows 2000 setup procedure that is available from the disks and the CD-ROM.

57. Answer C is correct. You can install the Recovery Console by using the `winnt32 /cmdcons` command after Windows 2000 has been installed.

58. Answer B is correct. The `compact` command is used to manage NTFS file and folder compression from the command line; therefore, answers A, C, and D are incorrect.

59. Answer B is correct. You must be running Windows 2000 in an Active Directory domain environment to create an Enterprise CA.

60. Answer C is correct. Standalone Dfs servers are limited to one level of Dfs links. All other answers are incorrect.

Practice Test #2

Question 1

Which of the following TCP/IP properties can be added to the DHCP scope to be distributed to clients? (Choose all that apply.)

- ❑ A. DNS Server
- ❑ B. Router
- ❑ C. Time Server Address
- ❑ D. All of the above

Question 2

The Corporate Policies and Procedures department has requested shared folders be included on all Windows 2000 servers to provide copies of the company's procedures to all employees. Policies pertaining to certain departments may be contained in individual folders on other servers. The proposed solution must meet the following requirements:

- ➤ You must provide secure read-only access to the policies documents on the server.
- ➤ You must ensure up-to-date copies of the policies are available to all users at all times.
- ➤ You must ensure departmental policies are accessible from the Policies folder.
- ➤ Members of the Policies and Procedures department should have administrator access to the documents in the folders.

The proposed solution is to implement a Policies and Procedures folder on the NTFS volume of all servers. Members of the Policies and Procedures group are assigned Full Control NTFS permission to the folders; members of the Everyone group are assigned the Read permission. Configure a Dfs root for the primary Policies folder and create root replicas for folders on all other servers. Configure the Dfs replication policy to synchronize folders on all servers. Configure the share properties for the Policies folder to allow Full Control for the Policies and Procedures group and Read access for the Everyone group.

Which of the following does the proposed solution provide? (Choose all that apply.)

- ❑ A. The proposed solution provides secure read-only access to the policies documents on the server.
- ❑ B. The proposed solution ensures copies of the policies are available to all users at all times.
- ❑ C. The proposed solution ensures departmental policies can be accessed from within the Policies folder.
- ❑ D. The proposed solution gives members of the Policies and Procedures group administrator access to the documents in the folders.

Question 3

Which of the following items is not a valid local policy?

❍ A. Audit policy

❍ B. User Policy

❍ C. User Rights Assignment

❍ D. Security Options

Question 4

How do you verify what software is currently loaded on your computer before you upgrade or install Windows 2000 Server?

❍ A. In the System Tools

❍ B. In the Start menu

❍ C. In the Add/Remove Programs applet

❍ D. In the Taskbar

Question 5

Melanie has informed you that her computer has begun to perform very slowly and that her hard disk light stays on for a very long time whenever she attempts to open one of the large database files that she is responsible for editing. What should you do to Melanie's computer to correct the problem without installing any new hardware? (Choose all that apply.)

❑ A. Defragment her hard drive.

❑ B. Renew her DHCP lease.

❑ C. Perform a disk cleanup on her hard disks.

❑ D. Move her user account to a different OU.

Question 6

What counters should be observed to diagnose a disk problem? (Choose all that apply.)

❑ A. Disk Queue Length

❑ B. Disk Bytes/transfer

❑ C. Disk Seeks/Sec

❑ D. % Disk Time

Question 7

Christopher is attempting to configure driver signing restrictions for the eight Windows 2000 Professional computers in his office running in a peer-to-peer network. After he configures the Block setting on all computers, he notices that other users can still install known unsigned drivers. What is the most likely cause of the problem?

❍ A. Christopher did not configure the setting with an administrative account, and thus the settings are not applied to all computer users.

❍ B. Christopher forget to save the newly configured settings, so they were not put into effect on the computer.

❍ C. The other users must be members of the DNS Admins group, which has the permissions required to override any configured driver signing settings.

❍ D. Christopher forgot to refresh Group Policy after applying the configuration. The changes should take effect after the computers have been restarted.

Question 8

You have recently created and configured a DHCP server for your network. Clients, however, report that they cannot obtain a DHCP lease from this new server. What is the most likely cause for this problem?

❍ A. The DHCP server is not running Windows 2000.

❍ B. You did not authorize the server in Active Directory.

❍ C. The DHCP server is not running on a domain controller.

❍ D. The DHCP server is running on a domain controller.

Question 9

How do you verify what service pack is on your system before you upgrade or install Windows 2000 Server?

❍ A. Look at the side of the Windows 2000 Server box.

❍ B. Look in the Control Panel.

❍ C. Look in the Start menu.

❍ D. Look in the System window.

Question 10

Which password would meet the complexity requirements of the password policy?

❍ A. Ay324

❍ B. 6!9280

❍ C. XxYgoGq

❍ D. Ay324!

Question 11

Ron is an administrator of his company's small Windows 2000 network. Ron's duties include managing the backup servers and keeping all hardware devices up to date with the latest drivers. As he is browsing over the Cisco Web site, he comes across a new driver for the Cisco Aironet 350 WLAN adapter that his laptop computers use. He downloads the new driver file to a file server on the network. What does Ron need to do now to ensure that all of his portable computers get the updated driver installed?

❍ A. He should manually copy the driver files into the *systemroot*\System32 folder on each portable computer. The portable computers will then automatically install the new driver files on the next restart.

❍ B. He should create a new network connection using the same Cisco Aironet 350 adapter with the new driver. Windows 2000 will automatically clean up and remove the old outdated driver and network connection upon the next restart.

❍ C. He should edit the properties of the network adapter from the Services console to ensure that it starts using the updated driver upon the next computer restart.

❍ D. He should open the Device Manager, find the applicable device, and open the Properties page for it. On the Driver tab, he should use the Update Driver button to update the installed driver with the new driver.

Question 12

Which of the following ports is automatically assigned to the Administration Web site when IIS is installed?

❍ A. 80

❍ B. 21

❍ C. 443

❍ D. None of the above

Question 13

When using Performance Logs and Alerts, what type of file should you log data to if you're low on disk space?

❍ A. Text File (CSV)

❍ B. Text File (TSV)

❍ C. Binary File

❍ D. Binary Circular File

Question 14

Why should you view the Hardware Compatibility List on the Microsoft Web site? (Choose all that apply.)

❑ A. So you know whether your hardware is compatible with Windows 2000 Server.

❑ B. Because you should become more familiar with the Microsoft Web site.

❑ C. So you can download the latest drivers for your hardware devices.

❑ D. So you know what hardware is available.

Question 15

Hannah is configuring a mirror set on her Windows 2000 Professional computer. She has two 80GB hard disks installed on her computer with the following simple volumes already created:

- C—45GB
- E—35GB
- F—45GB
- G—35GB

If Hannah creates a mirror set using volumes C and F, how much total storage capacity will she have on her computer?

- ❍ A. 90GB
- ❍ B. 160GB
- ❍ C. 80GB
- ❍ D. 115GB

Question 16

Hannah wants to find out which 3Com network adapters are certified compatible with Windows 2000 before she buys any for her 25 new computers. What is the best way for her to get this information?

- ❍ A. She should examine the Windows 2000 Readiness Analyzer.
- ❍ B. She should visit the 3Com Web site to determine which network adapters are Windows 2000 certified.
- ❍ C. She should look on the network adapter box and look for the Windows 2000 compatible logo.
- ❍ D. She should visit the HCL and search for 3Com network adapters.

Question 17

What counters should be observed to diagnose a network problem? (Choose all that apply.)

- ❑ A. Bytes Total/Sec
- ❑ B. Output Queue Length
- ❑ C. Current Bandwidth
- ❑ D. Datagrams/sec

Question 18

Where do you examine the results of auditing that you have configured on your computer?

❍ A. Performance Monitor

❍ B. Active Directory Users and Computers console

❍ C. Event Viewer

❍ D. Local Security Policy console

Question 19

Windows 2000 Terminal Services supports how many connections in Remote Administration mode?

❍ A. One

❍ B. Two

❍ C. Three

❍ D. Unlimited

Question 20

What counters should be observed to diagnose a processor problem? (Choose all that apply.)

❑ A. % Processor Time

❑ B. Processor Queue Length

❑ C. % Processor Bandwidth

❑ D. Processor Interrupts/Sec

Question 21

In Windows 2000, which of the following types of disk configurations can you create on a Windows 2000 Server? (Choose all that apply.)

❑ A. Mirrored volume

❑ B. RAID-5 array

❑ C. Spanned volume

❑ D. Primary partition

Question 22

What choices do you have in regard to configuring licensing for a new Windows 2000 Server installation? (Choose all that apply.)

❑ A. Per Seat

❑ B. Per Server

❑ C. Per Network

❑ D. Per Processor

Question 23

You are establishing an intranet site for employee access to files and important company information. All client computers are running Windows 98 or Windows 2000 Professional with Internet Explorer version 5. The proposed solution must meet the following security requirements:

- You must use an authentication method that is supported by all clients.
- You must use an encrypted authentication method.
- You must ensure all requests are authenticated.
- You must choose an authentication protocol that is part of the HTTP specification.

The proposed solution is to configure the Web site to use only Digest authentication.

Which of the following does the proposed solution provide? (Choose all that apply.)

❑ A. The proposed solution uses an authentication method supported by all clients.

❑ B. The proposed solution uses an encrypted authentication method.

❑ C. The proposed solution ensures all requests are authenticated.

❑ D. The proposed solution uses a protocol that is part of the HTTP specification.

Question 24

Andrea is the network administrator for a small software development company. She is responsible for 7 Windows 2000 servers and 58 Windows 2000 Professional clients running in an Active Directory domain. Andrea wants to provide automatic protection for the client computers used by the sales and administration departments so that they cannot install unsigned digital drivers on them under any circumstances. Andrea does not want to prevent the installation of these types of drivers on the computers used by the developers, but does want them to be queried before any unsigned driver is installed. What should Andrea do to accomplish these goals? (Choose all that apply.)

- ❑ A. Andrea should configure a Group Policy Object with the Block setting and link it to an OU that contains all of the computer accounts for the sales and administration departments.
- ❑ B. Andrea should configure a Group Policy Object with the Block setting and link it to an OU that contains all of the user accounts for the sales and administration departments.
- ❑ C. Andrea should configure a Group Policy Object with the Ignore setting and link it to an OU that contains all of the user accounts for the developers department.
- ❑ D. Andrea should configure a Group Policy Object with the Warn setting and link it to an OU that contains all of the user accounts for the developers department.

Question 25

In Windows 2000, you can have what minimum number and what maximum number of hard disks in a spanned volume?

- ❍ A. Minimum of 1, maximum of 16
- ❍ B. Minimum of 2, maximum of 32
- ❍ C. Minimum of 2, maximum of 26
- ❍ D. Minimum of 1, maximum of 26

Question 26

Which of the following statements is true concerning EFS encryption and NTFS compression?

❍ A. You can encrypt and compress a file simultaneously.

❍ B. You cannot encrypt and compress a file simultaneously.

❍ C. EFS encryption and NTFS compression require the FAT32 file system or better.

❍ D. EFS encryption and NTFS compression require a digital certificate.

Question 27

Christopher is the administrator of a Windows 2000 network consisting of 125 Windows 2000 servers and 1,750 Windows 2000 Professional clients. His company is organized into four departments: Sales, Administration, Shipping and Receiving, and Engineering. The company manufactures and markets custom medical computer solutions to several hundred medical facilities. Christopher reimages approximately 25 clients per week due to users who have installed unsigned device drivers, causing the system to become unstable and even unresponsive at times. Christopher would like to find a way to avoid having to reimage his client computers. At the same, he needs to allow a small working group in the Engineering department to test drivers that they have created for the company's solutions. What steps should Christopher perform to solve his problems without limiting the capability of the developers group? All computer and user accounts are in one of four OUs that correspond to the four departments in the company. (Choose all that apply.)

❑ A. From Active Directory Users and Computers, Christopher should create a GPO and link it to the Sales, Administration, Shipping and Receiving, and Engineering OUs. Configure the driver signing policy in the GPO for Ignore.

❑ B. From Active Directory Users and Computers, Christopher should create a GPO and link it to the Sales, Administration, Shipping and Receiving, and Engineering OUs. Configure the driver signing policy in the GPO for Block.

❑ C. From Active Directory Users and Computers, create a new OU for the developers and move their user accounts to this new OU. Create a GPO and link it to the new developers OU and configure driver signing in the GPO to Warn.

❑ D. From Active Directory Users and Computers, create a new OU for the developers and move their computer accounts to this new OU. Create a GPO and link it to the developers OU and configure driver signing in the GPO to Warn.

Question 28

How can you install Windows 2000 Server if you cannot upgrade your current installation of Windows using the upgrade version? (Choose all that apply.)

- ❑ A. You can throw the upgrade version away.
- ❑ B. You can install the upgrade version to a different hard drive or partition.
- ❑ C. You can set up a multiple-boot system and start the operating system you want when you boot the computer.
- ❑ D. You can format the hard drive that contains the current operating system, and then install the upgrade version on that formatted drive.

Question 29

You have decided to disable the default IIS Web and FTP sites and create new sites from scratch. You will be configuring multiple Web and FTP sites on a single IIS server behind a Proxy server on the local network to be accessed by employees via the Internet.

The proposed solution must meet the following requirements:

- ➤ All sites must begin with the same configuration settings.
- ➤ Each site must be limited in the amount of network capacity it is allowed to utilize, while not limiting the overall bandwidth available to the IIS server.
- ➤ Sites must be secured to the highest possible level.
- ➤ By default, all Web sites must only be managed by members of the group IIS Admins.

The proposed solution is to access the Internet Information Services snap-in and select the server object, and then select Properties from the Action menu. On the server's Properties page, select Enable Bandwidth Throttling, and then click Apply. Select the WWW Service in the Master Properties section, and then click Edit. Select the Operators tab, remove Administrators, and then add IIS Admins. Select the Directory Security tab, click Edit in the Authentication Control section, unselect Anonymous Access if selected, and then select only Digest authentication.

Which of the following does the proposed solution provide? (Choose all that apply.)

❑ A. The proposed solution lets all sites begin with the same configuration settings.

❑ B. The proposed solution limits the amount of bandwidth allowed for each site to be configured individually.

❑ C. The proposed solution is secured to the highest possible level.

❑ D. The proposed solution specifies that only members of the IIS Admins group are allowed to manage Web sites.

Question 30

What tasks can be performed from the Task Manager? (Choose all that apply.)

❑ A. Stop a running process.

❑ B. Start a new process.

❑ C. Switch the active window to a different application.

❑ D. Set the priority on a process.

Question 31

Chris reports to you that her CD-ROM is no longer functioning. You instruct her to open the Device Manager and inspect the status of the CD-ROM. When she opens Device Manager, she sees the image shown in Figure 11.1. What is the most likely solution to the problem?

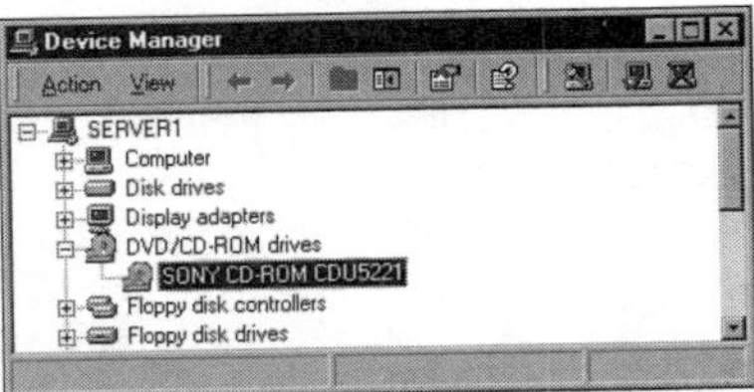

Figure 11.1 The Device Manager display.

❍ A. You should install new drivers for the CD-ROM.

❍ B. You should manually enable the CD-ROM.

❍ C. You should manually assign the resources for the CD-ROM.

❍ D. You should allow Windows 2000 to resume automatic management of the CD-ROM resources.

Question 32

Howard has implemented a RAID-5 array on one of his Windows 2000 servers that uses 11 80GB hard disks. What is the total amount of storage space that will be available to Howard in this implementation?

❍ A. 720GB

❍ B. 760GB

❍ C. 800GB

❍ D. 880GB

Question 33

The WINS database can be configured to automatically backup every:

❍ A. 3 hours

❍ B. 12 hours

❍ C. 6 hours

❍ D. 24 hours

Question 34

What options are available when a threshold is reached in Performance Logs and Alerts? (Choose all that apply.)

❑ A. Log an entry in the System Log.

❑ B. Send a network message.

❑ C. Start a performance log.

❑ D. Run a program.

Question 35

How can your network users obtain certificates?

❍ A. Through a Web site set up when Windows 2000 Server sets up certificates

❍ B. On a disk

❍ C. On a network folder

❍ D. As an attachment in an email message

Question 36

Andrea is configuring a mirror set on her Windows 2000 Professional computer using two 80GB hard disks. She has previously created a simple volume on each of the hard disks. How much storage capacity will she have after she has configured the mirror set?

❍ A. 160GB

❍ B. 80GB

❍ C. 120GB

❍ D. 140GB

Question 37

What is the name of the flat file used for host name to IP address mapping?

❍ A. LMHOSTS

❍ B. HOSTS

❍ C. LMHOST

❍ D. HOST

Question 38

Which of the following IIS 5.0 features allows recovery of interrupted file transfers?

❍ A. Virtual Directories

❍ B. Delegated Administration

❍ C. FTP Restart

❍ D. WebDAV

Question 39

You are trying to finish a database query so that you can go home for the evening. Which priority should you set for the database process in Task Manager?

❍ A. Priority 1

❍ B. Priority 4

❍ C. Priority 8

❍ D. Priority 9

Question 40

Which of the following password policies would prevent your computers from being susceptible to a dictionary attack?

❍ A. Account Threshold

❍ B. Account Lockout Counter

❍ C. Account Lockout Threshold

❍ D. Account Lockout

Question 41

What size partition is the minimum recommended on a hard drive to install Windows 2000 Server?

❍ A. 140MB

❍ B. 2GB

❍ C. 500MB

❍ D. 1GB

Question 42

Rosa has a new driver that she would like to install on her computer for her scanner. When she tries to install the driver, which she obtained from the manufacturer's Web site, she is not allowed to install it. She must have the driver installed on her computer to use some important new features from her scanner. What can you do to get the driver installed?

❍ A. Log on to Rosa's computer using your administrative account and change the driver signing behavior to Warn. Install the driver and then change the driver signing behavior back to Block.

❍ B. Change the driver signing behavior for the OU that Rosa's computer account belongs to. Install the driver and the change the driver signing behavior back to Block.

❍ C. Change the driver signing behavior for the OU that Rosa's user account belongs to. Install the driver and the change the driver signing behavior back to Block.

❍ D. Restart Rosa's computer in Safe Mode and install the driver. Restart Rosa's computer again to place it back into normal operation.

Question 43

You have applied disk quotas across all file servers in your network. You want to allow the graphic arts department to have a larger disk quota than all other departments. Additionally, you want to ensure that all departments except the graphic arts department are denied disk usage when the quota setting is exceed. What should you do?

❍ A. You should change the disk quota settings for the graphic arts department by editing the GPO that is linked to the Graphic Arts OU.

❍ B. You should change the disk quota settings for the graphic arts department from the Quota Entries window.

❍ C. You should move all of the graphic arts users to a new file server.

❍ D. You should move all of the other users to a new file server.

Question 44

Which of the following IP addresses are private addresses? (Choose all that apply.)

❑ A. 172.32.0.5

❑ B. 191.168.0.10

❑ C. 10.10.254.5

❑ D. 172.30.8.9

Question 45

Dawn reports that her computer's modem is not functioning properly. When you examine the Device Manager on Dawn's computer, you see the display shown in Figure 11.2. What is the most likely solution to this problem?

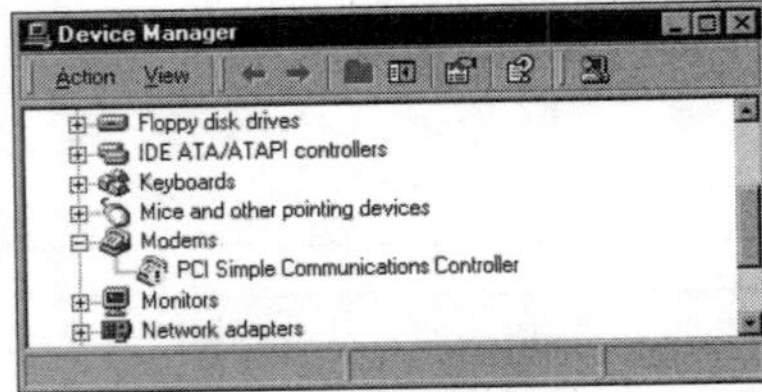

Figure 11.2 The Device Manager display.

❍ A. You should install new drivers for the modem.

❍ B. You should manually enable the modem.

❍ C. You should manually assign the resources for the modem.

❍ D. You should allow Windows 2000 to resume automatic management of the modem resources.

Question 46

Which of the following accurately describes a situation where Dfs replication will be triggered immediately?

❍ A. The administrator adds a file to the shared folder that acts as the Dfs root.

❍ B. A user is denied access to files on a Dfs link.

❍ C. The KCC identifies a change in topology that requires replication.

❍ D. There are no circumstances in Dfs that will trigger immediate replication.

Question 47

In Windows 2000, you can have what minimum number and what maximum number of hard disks in a RAID-5 array?

❍ A. Minimum of 2, maximum of 32

❍ B. Minimum of 2, maximum of 16

❍ C. Minimum of 3, maximum of 32

❍ D. Minimum of 3, maximum of 16

Question 48

Which users can decrypt an EFS encrypted file? (Choose all that apply.)

❑ A. User with DRA rights

❑ B. Enterprise Admins

❑ C. User who encrypted the file

❑ D. Domain Admins

Question 49

Bill is responsible for the six Windows 2000 Professional clients in his company's office. The company has no plans to install a Windows 2000 Server computer. To save himself extra work, Bill allows the computers to default to using APIPA. All of his computers receive an 169.254.x.x IP address. It all seems to work until they try to access the Internet. What is Bill's problem?

❍ A. Bill has some Windows 98 clients.

❍ B. Bill forgot to add the gateway IP address to the APIPA configuration.

❍ C. APIPA doesn't distribute gateway IP addresses.

❍ D. The APIPA service isn't starting.

Question 50

Bob is the only IT professional in his company. He works in a small department that has a Windows 98 workgroup. He has just received a new computer with nothing on the hard drives. He wants to install Windows 2000 Server to make it a file and print server, and he has the Windows 2000 Server CD-ROM. Due to miscommunication, the BIOS has been configured with a password, and he cannot set up the machine to boot from the CD-ROM. He needs to create a set of setup disks to begin the installation of Windows 2000. How can he accomplish this?

❍ A. Bob needs to find another Windows 2000 Server on which to run the **makebt32** program from his Windows 2000 CD.

❍ B. Bob needs to find another Windows 2000 computer (Server or Professional) on which to run **winnt32** from his Windows 2000 CD.

❍ C. Bob can use any of his Windows 98 computers and run the **makeboot** program from his Windows 2000 CD.

❍ D. Bob can use any of his Windows 98 computers and run the **makebt32** program from his Windows 2000 CD.

Question 51

How are host (A) records created in DNS for legacy (pre-Windows 2000) clients? (Choose all that apply.)

❑ A. Broadcasts, similar to WINS

❑ B. Manually by an administrator

❑ C. Dynamically by the DHCP server

❑ D. From a computer's domain account

Question 52

What counters should be observed to diagnose a memory problem? (Choose all that apply.)

- ❑ A. Pages Input/sec
- ❑ B. Page Faults/Sec
- ❑ C. Available Bytes
- ❑ D. Cache Faults/Sec

Question 53

What user account has the default recovery agent role on a standalone server?

- ❍ A. Power Users Group
- ❍ B. DRA User
- ❍ C. Domain Administrator account
- ❍ D. Local administrator

Question 54

You are working on improving the performance of a database query, and you decide to log the response time of your server that is performing the query. Which tool should you use?

- ❍ A. System Monitor
- ❍ B. Task Manager
- ❍ C. Performance Logs and Alerts
- ❍ D. Performance Monitor

Question 55

Which of the following password policies would prevent your users from selecting a blank password? (Choose all that apply.)

- ❑ A. Passwords Must Meet Complexity Requirements
- ❑ B. Password Length
- ❑ C. Minimum Password Length
- ❑ D. Require Non-Blank Password

Question 56

What is a partition?

❍ A. The blocks of data on a hard drive.

❍ B. The logical division of space on a hard drive.

❍ C. How you divide network data.

❍ D. The division of speed in your Internet connection.

Question 57

Austin has just installed a new video adapter in one of his servers. Now the video display is in 16-color 640×480 mode. What should Austin do to allow a higher screen resolution and color depth?

❍ A. Austin should remove the video adapter and install a different type of video adapter; this one must be incompatible with Windows 2000.

❍ B. Austin should update the video adapter driver from the Driver tab of the Properties page for the video adapter.

❍ C. Austin should install the default Plug and Play monitor.

❍ D. Austin should restart the computer in Safe Mode and remove the video adapter from the computer via the Device Manager.

Question 58

Milena is the administrator in your organization that is responsible for all Windows 2000 NNTP servers. All of Milena's NNTP servers have two 120GB disks installed in a mirrored set. On Monday morning, Milena comes into work and discovers that the secondary disk in one of her NNTP servers has failed. The server is still running, but she needs to restore fault tolerance to it as soon as possible. Which of the following represent steps that Milena should perform to correct the problem as quickly as possible? Note that not all steps might be listed. (Choose all that apply.)

❑ A. She must break the mirror on the server.

❑ B. She must replace the failed disk.

❑ C. She must perform a restoration of data from the most recent backup set.

❑ D. She must create a Windows 2000 boot disk and ensure that the BOOT.INI file on it points to the secondary disk.

Question 59

Windows 2000 Terminal Services supports how many connections in Application Server mode? (Choose all that apply.)

- ❑ A. 2
- ❑ B. 50
- ❑ C. Unlimited
- ❑ D. 1000

Question 60

Which of the following file systems support encryption?

- ❍ A. FAT
- ❍ B. FAT32
- ❍ C. NTFS 4
- ❍ D. NTFS 5

Answer Key to Practice Test #2

1. D

2. A, B, D

3. B

4. C

5. A, C

6. A, D

7. A

8. B

9. D

10. D

11. D

12. D

13. D

14. A, C

15. D

16. D

17. A, B

18. C

19. B

20. A, B

21. A, B, C, D

22. A, B

23. A, B, C, D

24. B, D

25. B

26. B

27. B, C

28. B, C

29. C, D

30. A, B, C, D

31. B

32. C

33. A

34. B, C, D

35. A

36. B

37. B

38. C

39. D

40. C

41. D

42. A

43. B

44. C, D

45. A

46. D

47. C

48. A, C

49. C

50. D

51. B, C

52. A, B, C

53. D

54. C

55. A, C

56. B

57. B

58. A, B

59. C

60. D

1. Answer D is correct. All the items can be added to the scope.
2. Answers A, B, and D are correct. Setting NTFS Full Control for the Policies and Procedures group gives them administrative control over the files in the folders; setting Read gives users the access they require. Utilizing Dfs to create replicas of the primary Policies folder ensure the most up-to-date files are copied to all servers automatically. However, there is no provision listed in the solution for access to folders outside the default folder; therefore, answer C is incorrect.
3. Answer B is correct. User policy does not exist. The other policies are configured from the Local Security Settings MMC.
4. Answer C is correct. The Add/Remove Programs applet, which you can access from the Control Panel, displays a list of all the software you have installed on your computer.
5. Answers A and C are correct. The most likely cause of Melanie's problems is that her hard drive is getting full and has become fragmented. In this case, running Disk Cleanup followed by Disk Defragmenter may very well correct the problem for her. Renewing her DHCP lease has nothing to do with this problem; therefore, answer B is incorrect. Moving her user account to a different OU also has nothing to do with this problem; therefore, answer D is incorrect.
6. Answers A and D are correct. If the Disk Queue Length is above 2, or the % Disk Time is a sustained 90% or better, the disk unit is too slow.
7. Answer A is correct. Christopher most likely configured the settings with his user account, without being logged in as the Administrator. Only when logged on with administrative permissions can you set the current driver signing setting as the computer default. Forgetting to close out the dialog box is possible, but not the most likely cause; therefore, answer B is incorrect. In a peer–to-peer arrangement, there is no Active Directory, thus no DNS Admins group; therefore, answer C is incorrect. These settings have been applied to the local computer because there is no Active Directory domain, thus refreshing group policy is not an issue here; therefore, answer D is incorrect.
8. Answer B is correct. Before a Windows 2000 DHCP server can begin servicing client requests, it must be authorized to do so in Active Directory. All other answers are incorrect.
9. Answer D is correct. The System window displays the version information for Windows 2000 Server, including the latest service pack installed. All other answers are incorrect.

10. Answer D is correct. The requirements are that the password is at least six characters long, may not contain your username or parts of your full name, and must contain a character from three of the following four groups: A–Z, a–z, 0–9, and punctuation characters.

11. Answer D is correct. Ron needs to manually update the driver for the WLAN adapter using the Update Driver button on the Properties page of the device. Under no circumstances will the new driver automatically install itself; therefore, answer A is incorrect. Creating a duplicate instance of the same device will most likely lead to system instability or other issues. Windows 2000 will not perform any sort of automatic clean up either; therefore, answer B is incorrect. Manually configuring the service's properties in the Service Manager will not cause the driver to become updated and will most likely result in the device not functioning properly; therefore, answer C is incorrect.

12. Answer D is correct. The Administration Web site is assigned a random port number when it is installed, to limit the chance someone would attempt unauthorized access to the site to damage the server.

13. Answer D is correct. The binary circular file will wrap around when it reaches its maximum limit, allowing you to keep recording data, but not using up all of the disk space. The two text file options are useful for importing performance data into a spreadsheet or graphing program; therefore, answers A and B are incorrect. The binary file will stop recording when the disk is full; therefore, answer C is incorrect.

14. Answers A and C are correct. You need to know whether your hardware is compatible with Windows 2000 Server before you install the operating system. The HCL also contains links to download drivers from the Windows or manufacturer's Web site.

15. Answer D is correct. Hannah will have a total of 115GB of storage capacity available to her: 45GB in the mirror set, 35GB on volume E, and 35GB on volume G; therefore, answers A, B, and C are incorrect.

16. Answer D is correct. Hannah should visit the Hardware Compatibility List (HCL) for the most up-to-date listing of hardware devices that are compatible with Windows 2000. Using the Windows 2000 Readiness Analyzer works well during the installation of Windows 2000 on a new computer, but will not help Hannah determine what hardware she should buy that is Windows 2000 compatible; therefore, answer A is incorrect. Visiting the 3Com Web site will not tell her for sure that any particular network adapter is certified for Windows 2000; therefore, answer B is incorrect. Looking at the box for a Windows 2000

logo is not a dependable way to ensure that the hardware is Windows 2000 compatible; therefore, answer C is incorrect.

17. Answers A and B are correct. The Bytes Total/sec should never be above 75% of the network interface card rating and the Output Queue Length should not be above 2.

18. Answer C is correct. You can find audit entries located in the Event Viewer's Security Log. All other answers are incorrect.

19. Answer B is correct. Windows 2000 Terminal Services supports two concurrent connections in Remote Administration mode. All other answers are incorrect.

20. Answers A and B are correct. If the Processor Queue Length is above 2, or the % Processor Time is a sustained 80% or better, the processor is a bottleneck. All other answers are incorrect.

21. Answers A, B, C, and D are correct. On a Windows 2000 Server, you can create primary, extended, and logical partitions on a basic disk. You can also create mirrored, spanned, striped, and simple volumes on a dynamic disk as well as RAID-5 arrays. RAID-5 arrays are not available for use on Windows 2000 Professional computers, only on Windows 2000 Server computers.

22. Answers A and B are correct. You can choose from either Per Seat or Per Server licensing when installing a new Windows 2000 Server computer. All other answers are incorrect.

23. Answers A, B, C, and D are correct. Digest authentication is supported by Internet Explorer 5 and later, is an encrypted authentication method, and is part of the HTTP 1.1 standard. Because Allow anonymous access is not selected, all requests must be authenticated.

24. Answers B and D are correct. Remember that driver signing in Group Policy is tied to the User configuration settings, not the computer configuration settings. By configuring Block for the sales and administration groups and Warn for the developers group, Andrea will have met the requirements of the stated problem. Configuring driver signing is done in the user configuration of a GPO, not in the computer configuration area; therefore, answer A is incorrect. Creating a policy with the Ignore setting for the developers allows them to install unsigned drivers with no warning dialogue, which is against the stated objectives of the question; therefore, answer D is incorrect.

25. Answer B is correct. In Windows 2000, you can create spanned volumes with between 2 and 32 disks; therefore, answers A, C, and D are incorrect.

26. Answer B is correct. EFS encryption and NTFS compression are mutually exclusive in Windows 2000. You can, however, use a third-party compression utility (such as WinZIP) to compress your files and folders that are EFS encrypted. EFS encryption and NTFS compression require that NTFS v5 be in use. All other answers are incorrect.

27. Answers B and C are correct. Christopher has two basic needs here: prevent the reimaging of his client computers and not prevent the developers from being able to work with the driver files they are creating. Thus, his best course of action is two create two GPOs. Create and configure one GPO to Block unsigned driver installation and link it to the Sales, Administration, Shipping and Receiving, and Engineering OUs. The Developers OU, which contains the developers' user accounts, should get a separate GPO that is configured with the Warn option, which still allows unsigned driver installation after acknowledgement of the fact the driver is unsigned. Configuring the Ignore option will allow the silent, successful installation of all driver files, signed or unsigned; therefore, answer A is incorrect. Driver signing is linked to the user configuration, not the computer configuration; therefore, answer D is incorrect.

28. Answers B and C are correct. The upgrade version of Windows 2000 Server lets you install the upgrade version onto a different hard drive or partition, and this lets you boot to multiple operating systems on your computer. All other answers are incorrect.

29. Answers C and D are correct. Digest authentication is the highest possible level of authentication available for users across the Internet. Changing the default Operators for the WWW service ensures that all Web sites are managed only by members of the IIS Admins group. Because the Master Properties for the FTP service were not changed, all sites are not configured to begin with the same configuration, only Web sites; therefore, answer A is incorrect. The default bandwidth throttling option limits the bandwidth available to the IIS server, not for each site individually; therefore, answer B is incorrect.

30. Answers A, B, C, and D are correct. You can perform many tasks with the Task Manager, such as starting and stopping processes, switching windows, setting process priority, and viewing system resource usage and network usage.

31. Answer B is correct. The CD-ROM is depicted with a red X over its icon—indicating that it has been manually disabled. Manually enabling the device will correct the problem. Installing new drivers for the

CD-ROM will not correct the problem; therefore, answer A is incorrect. Manually assigning the resources for the CD-ROM will not correct the problem; therefore, answer C is incorrect. Allowing Windows 2000 to automatically manage the CD-ROM resources is not related to this issue and will not correct the problem; therefore, answer D is incorrect.

32. Answer C is correct. RAID-5 arrays require all disks to have the same capacity. The parity information will require the capacity of one of the disks in the array; thus, if Howard uses 11 80GB disks to construct a RAID-5 array, he will have 800GB available for storage and 80GB used for the parity information; therefore, answers A, C, and D are incorrect.

33. Answer A is correct. The WINS server will perform a backup every three hours. All other answers are incorrect.

34. Answers B, C, and D are correct. The Alerts program can log an event in the Application log, not the System log; therefore, answer A is incorrect.

35. Answer A is correct. After you set up a Certification Authority and grant certificates, Windows sets up a Web site on the server so users can get those certificates. All other answers are incorrect.

36. Answer B is correct. Mirror sets require two volumes of the same size, thus her total capacity will be 80GB after the mirror set has been created; therefore, answers A, C, and D are incorrect.

37. Answer B is correct. HOSTS is the file used for DNS mappings. LMHOSTS is the file that is used to preload NetBIOS name mappings; therefore, answer A is incorrect. Answers C and D are incorrect because they are invalid terms.

38. Answer C is correct. FTP Restart allows interrupted file transfers to be recovered from the point of disconnect, rather than restarting the transfer from the beginning. The other IIS features do not control file transfer parameters; therefore, answers A, B, and D are incorrect.

39. Answer D is correct. Because the normal priority for a process is 8, only 9 would be an improvement. All other answers are incorrect.

40. Answer C is correct. The Account Lockout Threshold allows you to configure how many failed attempts will be accepted before the account is disabled. The other choices do not exist and are therefore incorrect.

41. Answer D is correct. You need 1GB of space minimum to install Windows 2000 Server. All other answers are incorrect.

42. Answer A is correct. The easiest way to allow the driver to be installed is for you to log on to Rosa's computer, change the driver signing behavior, install the driver, and then return the driver signing behavior back to Block. Driver signing applies to a user configuration, not a computer configuring; therefore, answer B is incorrect. Changing the driver signing behavior of the entire OU is not a good choice because it will allow other users to install unsigned drivers; therefore, answer C is incorrect. Installing the driver in Safe Mode is also not a good choice; therefore, answer D is incorrect.

43. Answer B is correct. Disk quota settings can be configured manually for a variety of reasons from the Quota Entries window. Disk quotas are not controlled from Group Policy; therefore, answer A is incorrect. Moving users from one file server to another will not solve this problem and will most likely cause new problems in the process; therefore, answers C and D are incorrect.

44. Answers C and D are correct. The private addresses are 10.0.0.0–10.255.255.255, 172.16.0.0–172.31.255.255, and 192.168.0.0–192.168.255.255; therefore, answers A and B are incorrect.

45. Answer A is correct. The modem is being shown with a yellow exclamation point over its icon. This indicates a device that is missing its driver. The device is not disabled, so manually enabling the modem is not the solution; therefore, answer B is incorrect. Manually assigning resources for the device is not possible because no drivers are installed; therefore, answer C is incorrect. Allowing Windows 2000 to take automatic control of the modem's properties will not be possible until the Plug and Play drivers have been installed; therefore, answer D is incorrect.

46. Answer D is correct. Dfs replication runs on a specified schedule, which cannot be triggered automatically. All other answers are incorrect.

47. Answer C is correct. In Windows 2000, your RAID-5 arrays can have between 3 and 32 disks; therefore, answers A, B, and D are incorrect.

48. Answers A and C are correct. Only the user who encrypted the file and the user account with recovery agent rights are able to decrypt an encrypted file. All other answers are incorrect.

49. Answer C is correct. APIPA only assigns private IP addresses in the 169.254.x.x range to clients—it does not distribute information, such as a default gateway, in the way that a DHCP server does. All other answers are incorrect.

50. Answer D is correct. You can create setup disks from any machine running a Microsoft operating system if it has CD-ROM support and a floppy disk. As a result, Bob does not need to go to a Windows 2000 machine; he can use his Windows 98 machines by running the `makebt32` program; therefore, answer A is incorrect. The `winnt32` program is used to install Windows 2000, not to create setup disks; therefore, answer B is incorrect. Because Windows 98 is a 32-bit operating system, he cannot use the `makeboot` program; therefore, answer C is incorrect.

51. Answers B and C are correct. Windows 2000 DNS host records are either manually created or added automatically from client registration via DHCP. All other answers are incorrect.

52. Answers A, B, and C are correct. They are all good indicators of the presence of a memory problem. Cache Faults is a processor measurement; therefore, answer D incorrect.

53. Answer D is correct. By default, the local administrator account is granted the recovery agent role for standalone workstations and servers. All other answers are incorrect.

54. Answer C is correct. Although System Monitor and Task Manager allow you to monitor performance, they don't have the logging functionality that Performance Logs and Alerts does; therefore, answers A and B are incorrect. Performance Monitor was used in previous versions of Windows; therefore, answer D is incorrect.

55. Answers A and C are correct. The complexity requirements are fairly strict, and the minimum password length can be set to at least 1. The other choices do not exist and are therefore incorrect.

56. Answer B is correct. A partition is the logical division of space on a hard drive you set when you format the hard drive. All other answers are incorrect.

57. Answer B is correct. The most likely case here is that the drivers for the new video card did not install properly or did not provide the desired resolution and color depth. Installing the most recent driver files from the Driver tab will, in most cases, correct this problem. The video adapter is most likely compatible with Windows 2000, but just needs updated drivers; therefore, answer A is incorrect. Installing the

default Plug and Play monitor will not correct the problem; therefore, answer C is incorrect. Restarting in Safe Mode and removing the video adapter is not required in this instance because the video adapter is working, just not providing full capability; therefore, answer D is incorrect.

58. Answers A and B are correct. Because the secondary mirror disk failed, Milena has it pretty easy. She must break the mirror set, replace the disk, and then re-create the mirror. No restoration of data should be required because the primary disk is still operating; therefore, answer C is incorrect. The creation of a special Windows 2000 boot disk is only required in this situation when the primary disk in the mirror set is the one that has failed; therefore, answer D is incorrect.

59. Answer C is correct. The only limitation is the number of licenses that you purchase and the horsepower of your server. All other answers are incorrect.

60. Answer D is correct. Only NTFS 5, which is included with Windows 2000, supports file and folder encryption. All other answers are incorrect.

Additional Resources

There's a lot of information out there about Windows 2000 Server and Microsoft certification. This appendix distills some of the best resources we've found on those topics.

Web Resources

- Microsoft's Training and Certification home: `http://www.microsoft.com/traincert/default.asp`
- Windows 2000 Server home from Microsoft: `http://www.microsoft.com/windows2000/server/default.asp`
- Windows 2000 Resource Kits online: `http://www.microsoft.com/windows2000/techinfo/reskit/en-us/default.asp`
- Search TechNet on the Web: `http://www.microsoft.com/technet`
- Windows 2000 Deployment Guide: `http://www.microsoft.com/windows2000/techinfo/reskit/dpg/default.asp`
- Cramsession's Windows 2000 Server Study Guide: `http://studyguides.cramsession.com/cramsession/microsoft/win2kserver/`
- Certguide.com: `http://www.certguide.com/2000/70215.asp`
- Cram4Exams free exam: `http://www.cram4exams.com/exams/w2kserbig2.shtml`
- John Savill's Frequently asked Questions on Windows 2000 Server: `http://www.windows2000faq.com/`
- A portal of MCSE information: `http://www.hardcoremcse.com/`
- CertCities MCSE certification community: `http://certcities.com/certs/microsoft/`
- TechTarget's Windows 2000 repository: `http://searchwin2000.techtarget.com/`
- Practice Exams and information on certification: `http://www.certtutor.net/`
- Paul Thurrott's SuperSite for Windows: `http://www.winsupersite.com/`
- Active Network's PC and Windows resource: `http://www.activewin.com/awin/default.asp`

Magazine Resources

- *Microsoft Certified Professional Magazine* is directly targeted at those certified by Microsoft: http://www.mcpmag.com
- *Certification Magazine* specializes in information for IT certified individuals: http://www.certmag.com
- *Windows & .NET Magazine* focuses specifically on Microsoft technologies: http://www.winnetmag.com
- *Online Learning* is a resource for professional training and development: http://onlinelearningmag.com
- *Computer* magazine is developed by the IEEE (Institute of Electrical and Electronics Engineers): http://www.computer.org/computer/
- *PC Magazine* is a staple for technology enthusiasts: http://www.pcmag.com

Book Resources

- Boswell, William. *Inside Windows 2000 Server*. New Riders, December, 1999. ISBN: 1-56205-929-7. This is an excellent guide for installation and general administration.
- *Microsoft Windows 2000 Server Resource Kit*. Microsoft Press, January, 2000. ISBN: 1-57231-805-8. This book and CD set include invaluable additional detailed documentation on Windows 2000. In addition, the CD includes many useful utilities.
- Minasi, Mark, et al. *Mastering Windows 2000 Server, fourth edition*. Sybex, February, 2000. ISBN: 0-78214-043-2. This book is written by *NT Magazine* columnist Mark Minasi and is full of excellent information.
- Russell, Charlie, et al. *Microsoft Windows 2000 Server Administrator's Companion, Second Edition*. Microsoft Press, August, 2002. ISBN: 0-73561-785-6. This book details many of the complex features and capabilities of Windows 2000 Server. It's a great handbook for any network administrator.
- Siyan, Karajit. *Windows 2000 Server Professional Reference*. New Riders, January, 2000. The book has more than 1,800 pages of detailed information on using Windows 2000 Server.

- Shilmover, Barry and Stu Sjouwerman. *Windows 2000 Power Toolkit*. New Riders, Indianapolis, Indiana, May, 2001. ISBN 0-73571-061-9. This book is a valuable resource for reference material on Windows security and policies.
- Stanek, William R. *Windows 2000 Administrator's Pocket Consultant*, Microsoft Press, January, 2000. ISBN 0-73560-831-8. This book is a detailed hands-on guide for professional Windows 2000 administrators.
- Tittel, Ed, et al. *Windows 2000 Server for Dummies*. IDG, April, 2000. ISBN: 0-76450-341-3. This is an excellent beginner's resource for Windows 2000 Server.

Glossary

Active Directory
A centralized resource and security management, administration, and control mechanism in Windows 2000, which is used to support and maintain a Windows 2000 domain. The Active Directory is hosted by domain controllers.

answer file
A text file that provides answers to questions during an unattended installation.

AppleTalk
The Apple Macintosh network protocol stack.

Application Mode
A mode of Windows Terminal Server operation in which an unlimited number of connections are supported. However each connection requires a license, called a Terminal Server Client Access License (TSCAL).

attended installation
A manual installation setup process. Typically this requires a person be at the system to install software and answer setup questions posed by the installation program.

auditing
The recording of an occurrence of a defined event or action. For example, you might want to audit a failed login attempt after four invalid tries for security purposes; such an incident could indicate someone trying to break into the system.

basic disk
A Windows definition for a standard hard disk that can contain up to four primary partitions, or three primary partitions and one extended partition, and unlimited logical drives.

binding
The OS level association of NICs, protocols, and services to maximize performance through the correlation of related components.

boot disks
A set of floppy disks used to launch Windows. These disks are sometimes used to start a failed system.

boot partition
The partition where the Windows 2000 operating system files are stored. These files are commonly found in a folder called WINNT.

certificate
A digital signature issued by a third party (called a certificate authority, or CA) that claims to have verified the identity of a server or an individual.

CHKDSK
The utility that checks the file and folder structure of your hard disk. You can also have CHKDSK check the physical structure of your hard disk. CHKDSK can perform repairs as required.

client
A computer on a network that requests resources or services from some other computer, usually referred to as a server.

Client Access License (CAL)
The number of authorized connections to a server. Options for client licensing include per seat and per server. Per server licensing is a connection-based license model. In it, you purchase one license for every connection made to a specific machine. Per seat licensing effectively licenses a user to make connections to all servers.

Client Services for NetWare (CSNW)
A Windows service that provides a Windows 2000 client computer the ability to interact with NetWare servers.

compression
The process of compacting data to save disk space.

computer account
An account representing a specific (Windows 2000) computer that is a member of a domain.

defragment
The process of reorganizing files so they are stored contiguously on the hard drive.

Device Manager
A Windows 2000 administrative tool used to install, configure, and manage hardware devices.

digital signature
An electronic certificate that verifies the identity of a client.

Disk Cleanup
A tool used to regain access to hard drive space through deleting temporary, orphaned, or downloaded files; emptying the Recycle Bin; compressing little-used files; condensing index catalog files.

Disk Defragmenter
The application built in to Windows 2000 for defragmenting hard disks. See *defragment*.

Disk Management
A tool that allows you to manage storage devices in Windows 2000.

disk quota
A configuration setting that allows you to limit the amount of storage space a user can consume.

Distributed file system (Dfs)
A Windows 2000 Server service that manages shared network resources in a single hierarchical system.

domain controller
A computer that authenticates domain logons. It also maintains a Windows 2000 domain's Active Directory, which stores all directory information and relationships about users, groups, policies, computers, and resources.

Domain Name Service (DNS)
A naming system used to translate host names to IP addresses, and to locate resources on a TCP/IP-based network.

Domain Users and Groups
This default built-in group in Active Directory contains the following groups: Account Operators, Administrators, Backup Operators, Guests, Print Operators, Replicator, Server Operators, Users.

driver
A device-specific software component used by an operating system to communicate with a device.

driver signing
A signed driver is one whose integrity is verified by Microsoft and digitally approved for installation. Windows 2000 can be configured to refuse to install any unsigned drivers. All drivers from Microsoft and approved vendors are signed.

dynamic disk
A Windows 2000 hard disk that can only house dynamic volumes created through the Disk Management administrative tool. Dynamic disks do not include partitions or logical drives, and they cannot be accessed by DOS.

Emergency Repair Disk (ERD)
A disk that can be used to repair a failed system; it is created through the Backup utility.

Encrypting File System (EFS)
A file system supported by Windows 2000 that provides encryption of data stored on NTFS volumes.

Event Viewer

A utility built in to Windows 2000 that is used to view and manage the Windows 2000 event logs. Event Viewer logs include the Application log for application-related events, Security log for security- and audit-related events, and System log for events related to hardware and software issues in Windows 2000 Server itself and any installed drivers.

File Allocation Table (FAT)

The file system originally introduced with DOS; it does not provide file system security features.

File and Print Services for NetWare

The Windows 2000 service that enables NetWare clients to access Windows 2000 file and print resources.

File Replication Service (FRS)

A service that provides multimaster file replication between designated servers running Windows of login scripts and policies stored in designated directory trees.

File Service for Macintosh

The Windows 2000 service that enables Macintosh clients to access Windows 2000 file-based resources.

File Services for Unix

The Windows 2000 service that enables Unix clients to access Windows 2000 resources.

Gateway Services for NetWare (GSNW)

A Windows 2000 service that provides a connectivity service between Windows 2000 Server and NetWare, which allows Windows 2000 clients to occasionally access NetWare resources by connecting natively to a Windows 2000 server.

Group Policy Object (GPO)

A security mechanism that provides granular control over the who, what, when, where, how, and why of configuring network settings. By using a GPO, you can easily configure security settings for each group on your network.

Hardware Compatibility List (HCL)

A list of hardware devices that are supported by Windows. A version of the HCL is found on the Windows 2000 Server distribution CD, but a Web site version is updated regularly at `http://www.microsoft.com/hwdq/hcl/`.

Internet Connection Sharing (ICS)

A basic proxy server built in to Windows 2000 that is used to grant Internet access to a small network through a single Internet connection without requiring additional hardware or applications. Network clients are automatically configured to use the shared connection by configuring the default gateway to point to the ICS server's internal NIC.

Internet Information Services (IIS)

A server platform for building and sharing distributed, dynamic Web sites.

Internetwork Packet Exchange/Sequenced Packet Exchange (IPX/SPX)

The proprietary protocol developed by Novell for communication on NetWare networks. Microsoft reverse engineered this protocol for use with Microsoft networks and called it NWLink.

Last Known Good Configuration

The system and Registry settings from the last working system configuration. Last known good configurations are loadable at boot time.

licensing

A Windows 2000 utility used to configure and manage licenses of Windows 2000 and installed applications.

Local Users and Groups

A utility in the Computer Management MMC console that enables management of users and groups on the local computer.

MAKEBOOT

The command used to create boot disks for Windows, designed to run under 16-bit operating systems, such as DOS and Windows 3.1.

MAKEBT32

The command used to create boot disks for Windows, designed to run under 32-bit operating systems, such as Windows NT and 2000.

member server

A server on a Windows network that does not participate in authenticating network users.

Microsoft Management Console (MMC)

A standardized management interface for Microsoft operating systems. The MMC enables you to create a custom console for Windows administration through the use of snap-ins.

mirrored volume

A fault tolerant disk configuration in which data is written to two hard disks, rather than one, so that if one disk fails then the data remains accessible.

NetBIOS Enhanced User Interface (NetBEUI)

A native Microsoft networking protocol that is being phased out with Windows 2000 due to its use of non-routable network broadcasts to locate resources, making it unusable for enterprise networks.

network adapter

A hardware device that enables a computer to communicate with a network.

Network Address Translation (NAT)
An Internet standard that enables a LAN to use one set of IP addresses for internal traffic and a second set of addresses for external traffic. The NAT server maintains a table and maps internal IP addresses to the external addresses used to connect them to the Internet.

Network Monitor
A Windows 2000 utility used to view and troubleshoot data packets.

NT File System (NTFS)
The preferred Windows 2000 file system, which supports file level security, encryption, compression, auditing, and more.

NTFS compression
A utility for reducing the amount of disk space data consumes on an NTFS partition.

NWLink
The Microsoft implementation of Novell's IPX/SPX protocol suite.

partition
A logical separation of space on a hard disk.

performance
The measurement of how efficiently a system runs.

Plug and Play
A technology that allows an operating system to recognize a device, install the correct driver, and enable the device automatically.

policy
A component that automatically configures user settings.

print device
The physical hardware device that produces printed output.

print server
The computer that manages print services on the network.

Print Services for Unix
The Windows 2000 service that enables Unix clients to access Windows 2000 print resources.

printer
The software component running on the print server that hosts the print service on a network.

printer driver
The piece of software that enables communication with a print device and the operating system and applications.

protocol
A defined set of rules for communication across a network. Most protocols confine themselves to one or more layers of the OSI Reference Model. Examples are the File Transfer Protocol (FTP), used to transfer files over a network, and the Hypertext Transfer Protocol (HTTP), used to deliver Web pages.

RAID-5 array
A drive configuration of three or more drives in which data is written to all drives in equal amounts

to spread the workload. For fault tolerance, parity information is added to the written data to allow for drive failure recovery.

Recovery Console

A command-line control system used in system recovery in the event of a failure of a core system component or driver. Through the Recovery Console, simple commands can be used to restore the operating system to a functional state.

Registry

The hierarchical database that stores all system information in the form of values for a Windows system.

Registry editor

The tool used to edit the Registry directly, which should be done only by seasoned administrators, and only after a full Registry backup has been performed and verified.

Remote Access Service (RAS)

Remote Access Service enables remote clients to dial in to a Windows 2000 server to access network resources as though they were physically attached to the network.

Remote Administration Mode

The Windows Terminal Server mode that allows you to connect remotely to a server and manage it just like you were sitting in front of the console.

Safe Mode

A recovery tool that allows a system to start with a minimal set of device drivers and services loaded. Safe Mode helps ease diagnosis by minimizing the number of factors that need to be considered when problems occur.

security template

A file that contains built-in guide for configuring security settings on a system.

service

Any action performed by a server, whether through the operating system or upon request of a client.

Service Pack

An executable that provides for the replacement of one set of files with another. In the case of an operating system (like Windows 2000), Service Packs have been a way to distribute bug fixes and fixes.

setup disks

A set of four disks that perform the actions carried out by booting from the Windows 2000 CD-ROM.

Setup Manager

A utility used to create an answer file for unattended installations.

simple volume

A storage volume that is essentially the same as a basic storage partition; disk space is only used from one physical disk.

slipstreaming

A process by which the most up-to-date service packs, fixes, and files are applied as part of a Windows Server installation.

spanned volume

A storage volume that can take disk space from 2 to 32 physical disks to create one large apparently contiguous volume. Spanned volumes offer you no fault tolerance, thus if one disk should fail the entire set is lost.

striped volume (with parity)

A fault-tolerant disk configuration in which parts of several physical disks are linked together in an array, and data and parity information written to all disks in this array. Should one disk fail, then the data may be reconstructed from the parity information written. A striped volume without parity is not fault-tolerant but does increase write speed to the disk.

symmetric multiprocessing (SMP)

The capability of an operating system to allow any process to be run on any processor of a multiprocessor server machine, ensuring that the operating system uses all available processor resources.

SysPrep

A utility that automates the operating system software installation process by creating a duplicate of one system and replicating it on other, identical systems.

System Monitor

An MMC snap-in that lets you view real-time performance data contained in the counters from your server or other servers or workstations on your network.

system partition

The active partition; in other words, the partition from which your computer's BIOS begins the boot process.

System State

A collection of settings for backup purposes that includes the Registry, the COM+ Class Registration database, and the system boot files. For a Windows 2000 Server that is operating as a certificate server, the System State data also includes the Certificate Services database.

Terminal Services

Windows 2000 includes native Terminal Services (previously available to Windows NT only as an add-on), which allows thin clients to be employed as network clients. Terminal Services grants remote access to applications and offers limitation controls over application access.

Transmission Control Protocol/Internet Protocol (TCP/IP)

The most popular protocol suite in use today, due to the widespread use of the global Internet. TCP/IP consists of many protocols that work together to provide communication among differing systems.

Troubleshooter

The Windows Help utility that asks questions about a device or service that isn't working properly to help you diagnose the problem.

unattended installation

A method that allows for installation of Windows 2000 Server to be performed with little or no user intervention.

Uniqueness Database File (UDF)

A file used in conjunction with an answer file during an unattended installation that provides the answers to computer-specific questions which will change from machine to machine (for example, the computer name).

User Rights

The actions that the user of a particular account is permitted to perform on a system or on network resources.

virtual private network (VPN)

An extension of a network that can be accessed securely through a public network, such as the Internet.

Windows 2000 Readiness Analyzer

A utility that can be used to determine the compatibility of hardware in an existing computer on which you want to install Windows 2000.

Windows Internet Naming Service (WINS)

A service that dynamically maps IP addresses to NetBIOS computer names used by Microsoft operating systems older than Windows 2000. Most modern operating systems use DNS rather than WINS for IP address-to-computer name translations.

WINNT

The command that launches an installation of Windows 2000 on a MS-DOS or Windows 3.x computer.

WINNT32

The command that launches an installation of Windows 2000 on a computer running a 32-bit operating system, such as Windows NT.

What's on the CD-ROM

This appendix is a brief rundown of what you'll find on the CD-ROM that comes with this book. For a more detailed description of the *PrepLogic Practice Tests, Preview Edition* exam simulation software, see Appendix D, "Using *PrepLogic, Preview Edition* Software." In addition to the *PrepLogic Practice Tests, Preview Edition*, the CD-ROM includes the electronic version of the book in Portable Document Format (PDF), several utility and application programs, and a complete listing of test objectives and where they are covered in the book. Finally, a pointer list to online pointers and references are added to this CD. You will need a computer with Internet access and a relatively recent browser installed to use this feature.

PrepLogic Practice Tests, Preview Edition

PrepLogic is a leading provider of certification training tools. Trusted by certification students worldwide, we believe PrepLogic is the best practice exam software available. In addition to providing a means of evaluating your knowledge of the Exam Cram material, *PrepLogic Practice Tests, Preview Edition* features several innovations that help you to improve your mastery of the subject matter.

For example, the practice tests allow you to check your score by exam area or domain to determine which topics you need to study more. Another feature allows you to obtain immediate feedback on your responses in the form of explanations for the correct and incorrect answers.

PrepLogic Practice Tests, Preview Edition exhibits most of the full functionality of the *Premium Edition* but offers only a fraction of the total questions. To get the complete set of practice questions and exam functionality, visit `PrepLogic.com` and order the *Premium Edition* for this and other challenging exam titles.

Again, for a more detailed description of the *PrepLogic Practice Tests, Preview Edition* features, see Appendix D.

Exclusive Electronic Version of Text

The CD-ROM also contains the electronic version of this book in Portable Document Format (PDF). The electronic version comes complete with all figures as they appear in the book. You will find that the search capabilities of the reader comes in handy for study and review purposes.

Easy Access to Online Pointers and References

The Suggested Reading section at the end of each chapter in this Exam Cram contains numerous pointers to Web sites, newsgroups, mailing lists, and other online resources. To make this material as easy to use as possible, we include all this information in an HTML document entitled "Online Pointers" on the CD. Open this document in your favorite Web browser to find links you can follow through any Internet connection to access these resources directly.

Using the *PrepLogic Practice Tests, Preview Edition* Software

This Exam Cram includes a special version of PrepLogic Practice Tests—a revolutionary test engine designed to give you the best in certification exam preparation. PrepLogic offers sample and practice exams for many of today's most in-demand and challenging technical certifications. This special *Preview Edition* is included with this book as a tool to use in assessing your knowledge of the Exam Cram material, while also providing you with the experience of taking an electronic exam.

This appendix describes in detail what *PrepLogic Practice Tests, Preview Edition* is, how it works, and what it can do to help you prepare for the exam. Note that although the *Preview Edition* includes all the test simulation functions of the complete, retail version, it contains only a single practice test. The *Premium Edition*, available at `PrepLogic.com`, contains the complete set of challenging practice exams designed to optimize your learning experience.

Exam Simulation

One of the main functions of *PrepLogic Practice Tests, Preview Edition* is exam simulation. To prepare you to take the actual vendor certification exam, PrepLogic is designed to offer the most effective exam simulation available.

Question Quality

The questions provided in the *PrepLogic Practice Tests, Preview Edition* are written to the highest standards of technical accuracy. The questions tap the content of the Exam Cram chapters and help you to review and assess your knowledge before you take the actual exam.

Interface Design

The *PrepLogic Practice Tests, Preview Edition* exam simulation interface provides you with the experience of taking an electronic exam. This enables you to effectively prepare yourself for taking the actual exam by making the test experience a familiar one. Using this test simulation can help to eliminate the sense of surprise or anxiety you might experience in the testing center because you will already be acquainted with computerized testing.

Effective Learning Environment

The *PrepLogic Practice Tests, Preview Edition* interface provides a learning environment that not only tests you through the computer, but also teaches the material you need to know to pass the certification exam. Each question comes with a detailed explanation of the correct answer and often provides reasons the other options are incorrect. This information helps to reinforce the knowledge you already have and also provides practical information you can use on the job.

Software Requirements

PrepLogic Practice Tests requires a computer with the following:

- Microsoft Windows 98, Windows Me, Windows NT 4.0, Windows 2000, or Windows XP
- A 166MHz or faster processor is recommended
- A minimum of 32MB of RAM
- As with any Windows application, the more memory, the better your performance
- 10MB of hard drive space

Installing *PrepLogic Practice Tests, Preview Edition*

Install *PrepLogic Practice Tests, Preview Edition* by running the setup program on the *PrepLogic Practice Tests, Preview Edition* CD. Follow these instructions to install the software on your computer:

1. Insert the CD into your CD-ROM drive. The Autorun feature of Windows should launch the software. If you have Autorun disabled, click the Start button and select Run. Go to the root directory of the CD and select setup.exe. Click Open, and then click OK.
2. The Installation Wizard copies the *PrepLogic Practice Tests, Preview Edition* files to your hard drive; adds *PrepLogic Practice Tests, Preview Edition* to your Desktop and Program menu; and installs test engine components to the appropriate system folders.

Removing *PrepLogic Practice Tests, Preview Edition* from Your Computer

If you elect to remove the *PrepLogic Practice Tests,, Preview Edition* product from your computer, an uninstall process has been included to ensure that it is removed from your system safely and completely. Follow these instructions to remove PrepLogic Practice Tests, Preview Edition from your computer:

1. Select Start, Settings, Control Panel.
2. Double-click the Add/Remove Programs icon.
3. You are presented with a list of software currently installed on your computer. Select the appropriate *PrepLogic Practice Tests, Preview Edition* title you wish to remove. Click the Add/Remove button. The software is then removed from you computer.

Using *PrepLogic Practice Tests, Preview Edition*

PrepLogic is designed to be user friendly and intuitive. Because the software has a smooth learning curve, your time is maximized, as you will start practicing almost immediately. *PrepLogic Practice Tests, Preview Edition* has two major modes of study: Practice Test and Flash Review.

Using Practice Test mode, you can develop your test-taking abilities, as well as your knowledge through the use of the Show Answer option. While you are taking the test, you can reveal the answers along with a detailed explanation of why the given answers are right or wrong. This gives you the ability to better understand the material presented.

Flash Review is designed to reinforce exam topics rather than quiz you. In this mode, you will be shown a series of questions, but no answer choices. Instead, you will be given a button that reveals the correct answer to the question and a full explanation for that answer.

Starting a Practice Test Mode Session

Practice Test mode enables you to control the exam experience in ways that actual certification exams do not allow:

- **Enable Show Answer Button**—Activates the Show Answer button, allowing you to view the correct answer(s) and a full explanation for each question during the exam. When not enabled, you must wait until after your exam has been graded to view the correct answer(s) and explanation(s).

- **Enable Item Review Button**—Activates the Item Review button, allowing you to view your answer choices, marked questions, and facilitating navigation between questions.
- **Randomize Choices**—Randomize answer choices from one exam session to the next; makes memorizing question choices more difficult, therefore keeping questions fresh and challenging longer.

To begin studying in Practice Test mode, click the Practice Test radio button from the main exam customization screen. This will enable the options detailed above.

To your left, you are presented with the options of selecting the pre-configured Practice Test or creating your own Custom Test. The pre-configured test has a fixed time limit and number of questions. Custom Tests allow you to configure the time limit and the number of questions in your exam.

The *Preview Edition* included with this book includes a single pre-configured Practice Test. Get the compete set of challenging PrepLogic Practice Tests at `PrepLogic.com` and make certain you're ready for the big exam.

Click the Begin Exam button to begin your exam.

Starting a Flash Review Mode Session

Flash Review mode provides you with an easy way to reinforce topics covered in the practice questions. To begin studying in Flash Review mode, click the Flash Review radio button from the main exam customization screen. Select either the pre-configured Practice Test or create your own Custom Test.

Click the Best Exam button to begin your Flash Review of the exam questions.

Standard *PrepLogic Practice Tests, Preview Edition* Options

The following list describes the function of each of the buttons you see. Depending on the options, some of the buttons will be grayed out and inaccessible or missing completely. Buttons that are accessible are active. The buttons are as follows:

- **Exhibit**—This button is visible if an exhibit is provided to support the question. An exhibit is an image that provides supplemental information necessary to answer the question.
- **Item Review**—This button leaves the question window and opens the Item Review screen. From this screen you will see all questions, your answers, and your marked items. You will also see correct answers listed here when appropriate.
- **Show Answer**—This option displays the correct answer with an explanation of why it is correct. If you select this option, the current question is not scored.
- **Mark Item**—Check this box to tag a question you need to review further. You can view and navigate your Marked Items by clicking the Item Review button (if enabled). When grading your exam, you will be notified if you have marked items remaining.
- **Previous Item**—This option allows you to view the previous question.
- **Next Item**—This option allows you to view the next question.
- **Grade Exam**—When you have completed your exam, click this button to end your exam and view your detailed score report. If you have unanswered or marked items remaining you will be asked if you would like to continue taking your exam or view your exam report.

Time Remaining

If the test is timed, the time remaining is displayed on the upper right corner of the application screen. It counts down the minutes and seconds remaining to complete the test. If you run out of time, you will be asked if you want to continue taking the test or if you want to end your exam.

Your Examination Score Report

The Examination Score Report screen appears when the Practice Test mode ends—as the result of time expiration, completion of all questions, or your decision to terminate early.

This screen provides you with a graphical display of your test score with a breakdown of scores by topic domain. The graphical display at the top of the screen compares your overall score with the PrepLogic Exam Competency Score.

The PrepLogic Exam Competency Score reflects the level of subject competency required to pass this vendor's exam. While this score does not directly translate to a passing score, consistently matching or exceeding this score does suggest you possess the knowledge to pass the actual vendor exam.

Review Your Exam

From Your Score Report screen, you can review the exam that you just completed by clicking on the View Items button. Navigate through the items viewing the questions, your answers, the correct answers, and the explanations for those answers. You can return to your score report by clicking the View Items button.

Get More Exams

Each *PrepLogic Practice Tests, Preview Edition* that accompanies your Exam Cram contains a single PrepLogic Practice Test. Certification students worldwide trust PrepLogic Practice Tests to help them pass their IT certification exams the first time. Purchase the *Premium Edition* of PrepLogic Practice Tests and get the entire set of all new challenging Practice Tests for this exam. PrepLogic Practice Tests—Because You Want to Pass the First Time.

Contacting PrepLogic

If you would like to contact PrepLogic for any reason, including information about our extensive line of certification practice tests, we invite you to do so. Please contact us online at `http://www.preplogic.com`.

Customer Service

If you have a damaged product and need a replacement or refund, please call the following phone number:

800-858-7674

Product Suggestions and Comments

We value your input! Please email your suggestions and comments to the following address:

`feedback@preplogic.com`

License Agreement

YOU MUST AGREE TO THE TERMS AND CONDITIONS OUTLINED IN THE END USER LICENSE AGREEMENT ("EULA") PRESENTED TO YOU DURING THE INSTALLATION PROCESS. IF YOU DO NOT AGREE TO THESE TERMS DO NOT INSTALL THE SOFTWARE.

Index

SYMBOLS

/a switch (winnt.exe), 49
/checkupgradeonly switch (winnt32.exe), 50
/cmd command switch (winnt32.exe), 49
/cmdcons switch (winnt32.exe), 49
/copydir folder switch (winnt32.exe), 49
/copysource folder switch (winnt32.exe), 49
/debug level file switch (winnt32.exe), 49
/e command switch (winnt.exe), 49
/i inf_file switch (winnt.exe), 49
/r folder switch (winnt.exe), 49
/rx folder switch (winnt.exe), 49
/s path switch, 49
/syspart drive switch (winnt32.exe), 50
/t drive switch (winnt.exe), 49
/tempdrive drive switch (winnt32.exe), 49
/u file switch (winnt.exe), 49
/udf file switch (winnt.exe), 49
/unattended [num] [file] switch (winnt32.exe), 49
-nosidgen (sysprep.exe switches), 52
-pnp (sysprep.exe switches), 52
-quiet (sysprep.exe switches), 52
-reboot (sysprep.exe switches), 52

A

Access Control Settings dialog box, configuring printers, 78
access tokens (user accounts) 273-274
accessing
  Disk Defragmenter, 196-197
  Disk Management, 182-183
  Disk Properties dialog box (Disk Management), 184
  files (NTFS), 80
  Local Computer Policy objects, 278
  Safe Mode, 165
  volume properties dialog box (Disk Management), 186
account policies (Local Security Settings MMC), 279-280
ACL (Access Control List), 274

Active Directory
data recovery, 166-170
DNS integration, 232
domain accounts, 265-266
Active Directory services database, System State backups, 163
Active Directory Users and Computers MMC, 254
Active Directory Users and Computers MMC snap-in, 265-266
adaptive exams, 12
fixed-length exams, 13
short-form exams, 13
strategies, 14-17
Add New Printer Wizard, 75
Add/Remove Hardware Wizard, 124-125
adding resource columns to Processes tab (Task Manager), 144
Administrators groups (local groups), 268
Advanced tab (network adapters properties page), 217
Advanced TCP/IP Settings window
DNS Properties tab, 226
IP Settings page, 225-226
Options tab, 228
WINS Properties tab, 227
alerts, creating performance alerts, 154-155
Anonymous Logon groups (built-in system groups), 271
answer files
multiple servers, installing, 40
script-based unattended installations, 38
unattended answer files, creating, 39-43, 46-48
Windows 2000, installing, 49-50
APIPA (Auto Private IP Addressing), 224
AppleTalk protocol (Macintosh), 72
Application mode (terminal services), 251, 254
Applications tab (Task Manager), 143
assigning drive letters/paths to volumes, 193
attended installations
CD-ROM based installations, 28
components, 33-34
domain names, 33
formatting partitions, 29
licensing, 31-32
passwords, 32
selecting regional settings, 30
workgroups, 33
setup disk installations, 35-36
winnt.exe, 37
winnt32.exe, 36
audit policies, 281-283
Authenticated Users groups (built-in system groups), 271
authentication, user accounts, 273-274
authoritative restores (data recovery), 167-168

B

Backup Operators groups (local groups), 268
backups, 160, 162
incremental backups, 163
normal backups, 161
System State backups, 163-164
bandwidth throttling, 96
baselines, 151, 156
Basic Authentication, 99
basic disks
dynamic disks, upgrading to, 188-189
partitions, 190-192
binary circular files, 151
binary files, 114, 151

blocking inheritance, 277
boot partitions, 26
build-list-and-reorder questions (exam formats), 6-8
built-in system groups (user accounts), 271

C

CA (Certificate Authority), 290
case studies, 12-13
- layout, 4-5
- strategies, 14-15

CAT files, 114
catalog file signing, 113-114
CD-ROM installations, 28
- components, 33-34
- domain names, 33
- licensing, 31-32
- partitions, formatting, 29
- passwords, 32
- regional settings, selecting, 30
- workgroups, 33

Certificate Services database, System State backups, 163
certification exams
- adaptive exam strategies, 16-17
- build-list-and-reorder questions, 6-8
- case studies
  - layout, 4-5
  - strategies, 14-15
- create-a-tree questions, 8-9
- drag-and-connect questions, 9-10
- fixed-length strategies, 15-16
- formats, 12-14
- multiple-choice questions, 5-6
- practice exams, taking, 18-19
- question handling strategies, 17-18
- readiness, assessing, 2
- resources, 19-20
- select-and-place questions, 10-11
- short-form strategies, 15-16
- testing centers, 3-4

changing
- hardware resource assignments, 127-128
- process priority levels, 145

Check Disk, starting, 195-196
cipher command-line utility, 292
command switches, 120
command-line switches (update.exe), 57-58
commands
- compact command, options, 199
- ipconfig/all command, troubleshooting TCP/IP protocols, 239
- ping command, troubleshooting TCP/IP protocols, 240
- Recovery Console commands, 172
- Set Affinity command (Processes tab), 146

compact command, options, 199
compatibility
- hardware compatibility
  - verifying, 120-122
  - Windows 2000 installations, 23-24
- software compatibility, Windows 2000 installation, 24-25

compressing
- files
  - compact command, 199
  - NTFS, 80
  - NTFS file/folder compression, 197-199
- folders, 197-199

Computer Configuration nodes (group policy objects), 279
Computer Management MMC, Local Users and Groups snap-in, 272-273

configuring
Dfs, 81-83
DHCP, 234-235
DNS, 226
files, 79-80
folders, 79-80
GSNW, 70-71
hardware
changing hardware resource assignments, 127-128
Device Manager, 126-127
hardware device resources, 125-126
PnP, 123-124
ICS, 241-243
IIS, 96
IP addresses, 225-226
local print devices, 76
network adapters, 216-219
network protocols, 222, 229-230
network services, 232
NTFS file/folder compression, 198-199
NWLink, 229
NWLink frame type, 69
printers, 77-78
pull partners (WINS), 238
push partners (WINS), 237
push/pull replication partners (WINS), 238
RRAS, 246
shared folders, 79-80
TCP/IP protocols, 222
DNS, 226
general properties, 225
IP address properties, 225-226
IPSec, 228
packet filtering, 228
WINS, 227-228
unsigned drivers
block option, 114
Control Panel, 118-119
Group Policy, 115-118
ignore option, 114
warn option, 114
user access, shared folders, 91
volume sharing, 187
Web sites (IIS), 95
WINS, 227
database replication, 236
pull partners, 238
push partners, 237
push/pull replication partners, 238
confirming hardware installation status, 130-131
connecting
local print devices, 75
network printers, 76
Control Panel
Add/Remove Hardware Wizard, 124-125
unsigned drivers, configuring, 118-119
controlling
file access, 79-80
folder access, 79-80
printer access, 77-78
shared folder access, 79-80
copy backups, 162
copying
databases, (WINS), 236
files (FRS), 85
NTFS files/folders, 199
servers (FRS), 86
Counter Logs (Performance Logs and Alerts MMC snap-in), 150-153
counters, 148
Memory, 156-157
Network Interface, 159
Paging File, 157
PhysicalDisk, 157-158
Processor, 158-159
System, 159

create-a-tree questions (exam formats), 8-9
Creator Owner groups (built-in system groups), 271
CSV text files, 150
customizing
- keyboard layouts, 30
- System Monitor MMC snap-in display, 148-149

D

daily backups, 162
data recovery, 204
- authoritative restores, 167-168
- Directory Services Restore Mode (Safe Mode), 168-170
- ERD, 172-174
- mirrored volumes, 204-205
- non-authoritative restores, 167
- partial authoritative restores, 169-170
- RAID-5 volumes, 205-206
- Recovery Console, 170-172
- Safe Mode, 166
  - accessing, 165
  - Directory Services Restore Mode, 168-170
- System State data, 166-170

data storage, 188-189
databases
- Active Directory services database, 163
- Certificate Services database, 163
- copying (WINS), 236

default printers, identifying, 76
defining print devices, 75
defragmenting volumes, 197
deleting
- dynamic volumes, 192
- partitions, 192

device drivers
- digital driver signing, 113
- updating, 128-129

Device Manager
- drivers, updating, 128
- hardware installation, confirming hardware installation status, 130-131
- hardware, configuring, 126-127
- network adapters properties page, 216-219

device memory blocks, 126
Dfs (Distributed file system)
- configuring, 81-83
- domain roots, 83-84
- FRS, 85-86
- links, 84
- managing, 82
- New Dfs Root Wizard, 82
- standalone roots, 83-84

DHCP (Dynamic Host Configuration Protocol), 233-236
dialog boxes
- Access Control dialog box, configuring printers, 78
- Disk Properties dialog box (Disk Management), accessing, 184
- volume properties dialog box (Disk Management), 186-187, 200-201

Dialup groups (built-in system groups), 271
differential backups, 162
Digest Authentication, 99
digital driver signing, 113
direct-attached print devices, 75
Directory Services Restore Mode (Safe Mode), 168-170
Disk Cleanup, starting, 187, 194
Disk Defragmenter, accessing, 196-197

disk drives, assigning letters/paths, 193
disk duplication, unattended installations, 51-52
Disk Management
accessing, 182-183
Check Disk, starting, 195-196
Disk Cleanup, starting, 187, 194
Disk Defragmenter, accessing, 196-197
Disk Properties dialog box, accessing, 184
dynamic disks, upgrading to, 188-189
hot swapping, 193
partitions, 190-192
physical disks, viewing properties, 184
volume properties dialog box, 186-187, 200-201
volumes
assigning drive letters, 193
assigning drive paths, 193
configuring volume sharing, 187
creating dynamic volumes, 190
deleting dynamic volumes, 192
extending dynamic volume size, 192
formatting dynamic volumes, 191
viewing health statuses, 185
viewing properties, 186-187
Disk Properties dialog box (Disk Management), accessing, 184
disk quotas, 200-203
disk subsystems, 157-158
disks
basic disks, 188-192
dynamic disks, upgrading to, 188-189
dynamic storage, 188-189
hard disks, 204-206
hot swapping, 193
MBR disks, 189
physical disks, 184
DMA (Direct Memory Access), 126
DNS (Domain Name Servers)
Active Directory integration, 232
configuring, 226
installing, 233
DNS Properties tab (Advanced TCP/IP Settings window), 226
domain accounts, 264-266
domain controllers
FRS, 85
service-oriented tasks, 75
domain groups (user accounts), 264-266
domain names, CD-ROM installations, 33
domain roots (Dfs), 83-84
domains, shared folder, 92
DRA (Data Recovery Agents), 290
drag-and-connect questions (exam formats), 9-10
Driver tab (network adapters properties page), 218
drivers
digital driver signing, 113
unsigned drivers, configuring
block option, 114
Control Panel, 118-119
Group Policy, 115-118
ignore option, 114
warn option, 114
updating, 128-129
dual-booting operating systems, 27
dynamic disks, upgrading to, 188-189
dynamic name-to-IP mapping, 236

dynamic storage, 188-189
dynamic volumes, 190-192

E

EFS (Encrypting File System), 289-291
enabling new user disk quotas, 202
encryption, cipher command-line utility, 292
ERD (Emergency Repair Disk), 172-174
Everyone groups (built-in system groups), 271
exam simulation interface (PrepLogic Practice Tests), 384
Examination Score Report, 388
exams
- adaptive exam strategies, 16-17
- build-list-and-reorder questions, 6-8
- case studies
  - layout, 4-5
  - strategies, 14-15
- create-a-tree questions, 8-9
- drag-and-connect questions, 9-10
- fixed-length exam strategies, 15-16
- formats, 12-14
- multiple-choice questions, 5-6
- practice exams, taking, 18-19
- question handling strategies, 17-18
- readiness, assessing, 2
- resources, 19-20
- select-and-place questions, 10-11
- short-form exam strategies, 15-16
- testing centers, 3-4

extending dynamic volume size, 192
extracting Setup Manager, 39

F

Fast Repair option (ERD), 174
FAT (File Allocation Table) system, 79-80
FAT16, formatting partitions, 26
FAT32, formatting partitions, 26
fault-tolerant Dfs roots. *See* domain roots (Dfs)
File and Print Services (NetWare), 72
File Server for Macintosh, 72
files
- access, controlling, 79-80
- answer files
  - installing multiple servers, 40
  - script-based unattended installations, 38
- binary circular files, 151
- binary files, 114, 151
- CAT files, 114
- catalog file signing, 113-114
- compressing
  - compact command, 199
  - NTFS, 80
- configuring, 79-80
- copying (FRS), 85
- CSV text files, 150
- EFS, 289-291
- encrypted files
  - cipher command-line utility, 292
  - recovering (EFS), 291
- FAT system, 79-80
- local files
  - assigning permissions, 88
  - NTFS permissions, 87-90
  - permissions, 89
  - user access, 86
- monitoring, 79-80
- NTFS, 79-80

NTFS file/folder compression, 197-199
security (IIS), 94
troubleshooting, 79-80
TSV text files, 151
WebDAV access, 93

fixed-length exams, 12
adaptive exams, comparisons, 13
strategies, 14-16

folders
access, controlling, 79-80
compressing, 199
configuring, 79-80
EFS, 289-291
encrypted folders, 291-292
local folders
assigning permissions, 88
NTFS permissions, 87-90
permissions, 89
user access, 86
monitoring, 79-80
NTFS file/folder compression, 197-199
security (IIS), 94
shared folders
configuring, 79-80
configuring user access, 91
controlling access, 79-80
Dfs, 81-86
domains, 92
monitoring, 79-80
permissions, 91-92
troubleshooting, 79-80
volumes, 92
WebDAV sites, 93
troubleshooting, 79-80
WebDAV access, 93

formats
adaptive exam strategies, 16-17
case study strategies, 14-15
exams, 12-14
fixed-length exam strategies, 15-16
short-form exam strategies, 15-16

formatting
dynamic volumes, 191
partitions, 26, 29, 191

Fortezza, 98

fragmentation, 196

FRS (File Replication Service), 85-86

G

General tab (network adapters properties page), 217

Group Policies, 115-118, 276-278

Group Policy MMC, 278

group policy objects, 279

groups (user accounts)
built-in system groups, 271
domain groups, 264-266
local groups, 264, 268-273

GSNW (Gateway Services for NetWare), 69-71

guests groups (local groups), 269

H

hard disks, 204-206

hardware
compatibility
verifying, 120-122
Windows 2000 installations, 23-24
configuring
Device Manager, 126-127
device resources, 125-128
PnP, 123-124
drivers, updating, 128-129
installing
Add/Remove Hardware Wizard, 124-125
confirming hardware installation status, 130-131

PnP, 122
troubleshooting, 130-132
updating, 129
Hardware tab (volume properties dialog box), 187
Hardware Troubleshooter, starting, 217
Hardware Update Wizard, 129
hashes, 114
HCL (Hardware Compatibility List), 24, 113, 120-121
health statuses, 185
hosting multiple Web sites (IIS), 100-101
hot swapping, 193

I

I/O ports, 126
IAS (Internet Authentication Service), 247
ICS (Internet Connection Sharing), 240-244
identifying default printers, 76
IIS (Internet Information Services), 92
configuring, 96
managing, 97
operators, 101
security, 94, 98-99
servers, managing, 97-100
virtual directories, 100
Web sites
administration, 98
bandwidth throttling, 96
configuring, 95
hosting multiple Web sites, 100-101
managing, 101
process throttling, 96
security, 96
WebDAV, file/folder access, 93
incremental backups, 162-163
installations, 23
troubleshooting, 58-59
unattended installations, disk duplication, 51-52
upgrades, 53-54
installing
DHCP, 234
DNS, 233
GSNW, 70
hardware
Add/Remove Hardware Wizard, 124-125
confirming hardware installation status, 130-131
PnP, 122
troubleshooting, 130-132
NetBEUI, 230
network adapters, 216
network protocols, 221
network services, 231
NWLink, 69, 229
Recovery Console, 171
Service Packs, slipstreaming, 55-57
terminal services, 251
Windows 2000, 22
answer files, 49-50
attended installations, 27-37
disk size, 25
hardware compatibility, 23-24
operating system upgradability, 27
partitions, 25-26
software compatibility, 24-25
unattended installations, 37-38
WINS, 236
Integrated Windows Authentication, 99
inter-site replication, 86
Interactive groups (built-in system groups), 271

interoperability
Macintosh, 72-73
NetWare, 68
configuring NWLink frame type, 69
File and Print Services, 72
GSNW, 69-71
installing NWLink, 69
Unix, 73
IP addresses
configuring, 225-226
DHCP, 233-236
multiple IP addresses, configuring, 225
private IP addresses, 224
public IP addresses, 222-223
WINS, 236-238
IP Security Properties page (Advanced TCP/IP Settings window), 228
IP Settings page (Advanced TCP/IP Settings window), 225-226
ipconfig/all command, troubleshooting TCP/IP protocols, 239
IPSec (IP security), 228
IRQ (Interrupt Requests), 125-126

K – L

keyboard layout, customizing, 30

L2TP (Layer Two Tunneling Protocol), 249
licensing, 31-32
local accounts, 264
creating, 272-273
local administrator accounts, 267-268
local guest accounts, 267-268
local administrator accounts, 267-268
Local backups/restores (System State backups), 163
Local Computer Policy (Windows 2000 Group Policies), 278
local files/folders, 86-90
local groups (user accounts), 264, 268-273
local guest accounts, 267-268
Local Policies node (Local Security Settings MMC), 281-285
local print devices, connecting/configuring, 75-76
local security, 86-90
Local Security Settings MMC
account policies, 279-280
Local Policies node
audit policies, 281-283
security option policies, 284-285
user rights assignment policies, 283
opening, 279
Local Users and Groups MMC snap-in, 272-273

M

Macintosh, interoperability, 72-73
managing
Dfs, 82
IIS
servers, 97-100
Web sites, 101
Manual Repair option (ERD), 174
MBR (Master Boot Record) disks, 189
memory, 126, 156-157
Microsoft certification exams
adaptive exam strategies, 16-17
build-list-and-reorder questions, 6-8

case studies
layout, 4-5
strategies, 14-15
create-a-tree questions, 8-9
drag-and-connect questions, 9-10
fixed-length exam strategies, 15-16
formats, 12-14
multiple-choice questions, 5-6
practice exams, taking, 18-19
question handling strategies, 17-18
readiness, assessing, 2
resources, 19-20
select-and-place questions, 10-11
short-form exam strategies, 15-16
testing centers, 3-4
Microsoft Certified Professional pages, 19-20
minimum hardware requirements (Windows 2000 installation), 23
mirrored volumes, 188, 204-205
MMC (Microsoft Management Console)
Active Directory Users and Computers MMC, 254
Computer Management MMC, 272-273
Group Policy MMC, 278
Local Security Settings MMC
account policies, 279-280
Local Policies node, 281-285
opening, 279
snap-ins
Active Directory Users and Computers MMC snap-in, 266
customizing System Monitor, 148-149
Local Users and Groups MMC snap-in, 272-273
Performance Logs and Alerts MMC snap-in, 150-155
Security Configuration and Analysis Tool MMC snap-in, 287-289
Security Templates MMC snap-in, 286
System Monitor MMC snap-in, 148-149
Terminal Services Manager, 253
Terminal Services Configuration, 253
monitoring
files, 79-80
folders, 79-80
printers, 77-78
moving NTFS files/folders, 199
multiple IP addresses, configuring, 225
multiple Web sites, hosting, 100-101
multiple-choice questions (exam formats), 5-6

N

NAT (Network Address Translation), 241
NetBEUI (NetBIOS Extended User Interface), installing, 230
NetBIOS (Network Basic Input/Output System) protocols, 227
NetWare, interoperability, 68-72
network adapters, 216-220
network adapters properties page (Device Manager), 216-219
Network groups (built-in system groups), 271
network interface, 159
network printers, connecting, 76

network protocols, 220
configuring, 222, 229-230
installing, 221
NetBEUI, installing, 230
NWLink, installing/configuring, 229
TCP/IP protocol
configuring, 222, 225-228
DHCP, 233-236
DNS, 232-233
private IP addresses, 224
public IP addresses, 222-223
troubleshooting, 239-240
WINS, 236-238
network services
configuring, 232
DHCP, 233
configuring, 234-235
dynamic name-to-IP mapping, 236
installing, 234
DNS, 232-233
installing, 231
Macintosh interoperability, 72-73
NetWare interoperability, 68
configuring NWLink frame type, 69
File and Print Services, 72
GSNW, 69-71
installing NWLink, 69
Unix interoperability, 72-73
WINS, 236-238
network-attached print devices, 75
New Dfs Root wizard, 82
nodes (group policy objects)
Computer Configuration nodes, 279
Local Policies node (Local Security Settings MMC), 281-285
subnodes, 279
User Configuration nodes, 279
non-authoritative restores (data recovery), 167
normal backups, 161-162
NTFS (NT File Systems), 79-80
partitions, formatting, 26
permissions, 87-90
NTFS file/folder compression, 197-199
NWLink, installing/configuring, 69, 229

O

objects
creating, Active Directory Users and Computers snap-in, 266
group policy objects, 279
Local Computer Policy objects, 278
opening
Group Policy MMC, 278
Local Security Settings MMC, 279
troubleshooting wizards, 187
operating systems
dual-booting, 27
upgradability (Windows 2000 installation), 27
operators, 101
optimizing
disk subsystem performance, 157-158
PhysicalDisk, 157-158
memory performance, 156-157
Paging File, 157
network interface performance, 159
processor performance, 158-159
Options tab (Advanced TCP/IP Settings window), 228

P

packet filtering (TCP/IP), 228
Paging File, 157
partial authoritative restores (data recovery), 169-170
partitions
  boot partitions, 26
  creating, 190
  deleting, 192
  formatting, 26, 29, 191
  system partitions, 26
  Windows 2000 installation, 25-26
passwords
  account policies (Local Security Settings MMC), 279-280
  CD-ROM installations, 32
performance alerts, creating, 154-155
Performance Logs and Alerts MMC snap-in
  Counter Logs, 150, 152-153
  creating alerts, 154-155
  recording data, 151
  saving data, 150-151
  Trace Logs, 150
Performance tab (Task Manager), 146
permissions
  assigning, 88
  Everyone groups (built-in system groups), 271
  IIS permissions, 94
  NTFS permissions, 87-90
  printer-specific permissions, 77-78
  shared folder permissions, 91-92
  special commissions, 89
  user accounts, 264
personalizing software, 30
physical disks, viewing properties, 184
PhysicalDisk, 157-158
PIC (Programmable Interrupt Controllers), 126
ping command, troubleshooting TCP/IP protocols, 240
PnP (Plug and Play) hardware, installing/configuring, 122-124
policies
  account policies (Local Security Settings MMC), 279-280
  audit policies, 281-283
  Group Policies (Windows 2000), 115-118, 276-278
  remote access policies, creating, 247-249
  security option policies, 284-285
  System Policies, 274-275
  user rights assignment policies, 283
POST (power-on self-tests), 236
Power Management tab (network adapters properties page), 219
Power Users groups (local groups), 269
PPTP (Point-to-Point Tunneling Protocol), 249
practice exams, taking, 18-19
preparing Windows 2000 installation, 22
  disk size, 25
  hardware compatibility, 23-24
  operating system upgradability, 27
  partitions, 25-26
  software compatibility, 24-25
PrepLogic, 378, 389
PrepLogic Exam Competency Score, 389

PrepLogic Practice Tests
- exam simulation interface, 384
- Examination Score Report, 388
- Flash Remove mode, starting, 387
- Flash Review mode, 386-387
- Practice Test mode, 386-387
- PrepLogic Exam Competency Score, 389
- question quality, 384
- removing from your computer, 385
- reviewing exams, 389
- software requirements, 385
- study modes, 386

PrepLogic Practice Tests, Preview Edition, 378

print devices, connecting/configuring, 74-76

print drivers, 74

print servers, 73-74

printer-specific permissions, 77-78

printers, 74
- access, controlling, 77-78
- configuring, 77-78
- default printers, identifying, 76
- monitoring, 77-78
- network printers, connecting, 76
- troubleshooting, 77-78

priority levels (processes), 145

private IP addresses, 224

private keys (CA), 290

process throttling, 96

processes, 145-146

Processes tab (Task Manager), 145-146

processors, 158-159

product keys, 31

properties
- Disk properties dialog box (Disk Management), 184
- IP Security Properties page (Advanced TCP/IP Settings window), 228
- network adapters properties page, 216-219
- physical disk properties, viewing, 184
- TCP/IP Filtering properties page (Advanced TCP/IP Settings window), 228
- TCP/IP protocols
  - general properties, 225
  - IP address properties, 225-226
- volume properties dialog box (Disk Management), 186-187, 200-201
- volume properties, viewing, 186-187

protocols
- AppleTalk (Macintosh), 72
- DHCP, 233
  - configuring, 234-235
  - dynamic name-to-IP mapping, 236
  - installing, 234
- L2TP, 249
- NetBEUI, installing, 230
- NetBIOS protocols, 227
- network protocols, 220
  - configuring, 222, 229-230
  - installing, 221
  - NetBEUI, 230
  - NWLink, 229
  - TCP/IP protocol, 222-228, 239-240
- NWLink, installing/configuring, 229

PPTP, 249
RDP, 250
TCP/IP
configuring, 222, 225-228
DHCP, 233-236
DNS, 232-233
private IP addresses, 224
public IP addresses, 222-223
troubleshooting, 239-240
WINS, 236-238
public IP addresses, 222-223
pull partners (WINS), 238
push partners (WINS), 237
push/pull replication partners (WINS), 238

Q – R

question-handling strategies (exams), 17-18
Quota tab (volume properties dialog box), 187, 200-201

RADIUS (Remote Authentication Dial-in User Service), 247
RAID-0. *See* striped volumes
RAID-5 volumes, 188, 205-206
RDP (Remote Desktop Protocol), 250
readiness, assessing (exams), 2
recording system performance data, 151
recovering data
authoritative restores, 167-168
Directory Services Restore Mode (Safe Mode), 168-170
ERD, 172-174
non-authoritative restores, 167
partial authoritative restores, 169-170
Recovery Console, 170-172
Safe Mode, 165-170
System State data, 166-170
Recovery Console, 170-171
regional settings, selecting (CD-ROM installations), 30
remote access policies, creating, 247-249
Remote Administration mode (terminal services), 250
remote print devices versus local print devices, 75
Remote restores (System State backups), 163
Replicator groups (local groups), 269
resources (exam strategies), 19-20
Resources tab (network adapters properties page), 219
RIS (Remote Installation Service), 236
roots (Dfs), 83-84
RRAS (Remote Access and Routing Service), 228, 241, 244
configuring, 246
remote access policies, creating, 247-249
starting, 245
RRAS Setup Wizard, 246

S

Safe Mode, 165-170
saving system performance data, 150-151
schedules, backup schedules, 162
script-based unattended installations, 38
security
EFS, 289-291
encryption, cipher command-line utility, 292
files
accessing, 79-80
IIS, 94

folders
controlling access, 79-80
IIS, 94
IIS, 94, 98-99
IPSec, 228
local security, 86-90
NTFS, accessing files, 80
permissions
assigning, 88
IIS permissions, 94
NTFS permissions, 87-90
shared folder permissions, 91-92
special commissions, 89
printers, controlling access/permissions, 77-78
share security, 86
shared folders, controlling access, 79-80
user accounts, user authentication, 273-274
Web sites (IIS), 94-96
Security Configuration and Analysis Tool MMC snap-in, 287-289
Security Configuration Tool Set, 285-289
security option policies, 284-285
Security Settings subnode (Computer Configuration nodes), 279
security templates, 285-287
Security Templates MMC snap-in, 286
select-and-place questions (exam formats), 10-11
selecting regional settings (CD-ROM installations), 30
servers
baselines, 151, 156
copying (FRS), 86
disk subsystems, optimizing performance, 157-158
DNS, configuring, 226
File Server for Macintosh, 72
IIS, managing, 99-100
installing, answer files, 40
managing (IIS), 97
memory, optimizing performance, 156-157
network interface, optimizing performance, 159
Print Server for Macintosh, 73
print servers, 74
processors, optimizing performance, 158-159
WINS, configuring, 227
Service Packs, 55-57
service-oriented tasks, 75
Set Affinity command (Processes tab), 146
setup disk installations, 35-36
Setup Manager, 39-43, 46-48
share security, 86
shared folders
access, controlling, 79-80
configuring, 79-80
Dfs
configuring, 81-83
domain roots, 83-84
FRS, 85-86
links, 84
managing, 82
New Dfs Root Wizard, 82
standalone roots, 83-84
domains, 92
monitoring, 79-80
permissions, 91-92
troubleshooting, 79-80
user access, configuring, 91
volumes, 92
WebDAV sites, 93
shared volumes, configuring, 187
Sharing tab (volume properties dialog box), 187

short-form exams, 12
adaptive exam comparisons, 13
strategies, 14-16
SID (Security Identifiers), 274
simple volumes, 188
slipstreaming (Service Packs), 55-57
snap-ins
Active Directory Users and Computers MMC snap-in, 266
customizing System Monitor, 148-149
Local Users and Groups MMC snap-in, 272-273
Performance Logs and Alerts MMC snap-in, 150-155
Security Configuration and Analysis Tool MMC snap-in, 287-289
Security Templates MMC snap-in, 286
System Monitor MMC snap-in, 148-149
sockets, 95
software
personalizing, 30
PrepLogic Practice Test requirements, 385
Windows 2000 installation compatibility, 24-25
sorting processes, priority levels, 145
spanned volumes, 188
SSL (Secure Sockets Layer) 3.0, 98
standalone roots (Dfs), 83-84
Start menu, 75
starting
applications, Task Manager, 143
Check Disk, 195-196
Disk Cleanup, 187, 194
Hardware Troubleshooter, 217
RRAS, 245
System Policy Editor, 275
Task Manager, 142-143
Windows 2000 Backup, 160
Status indicators (disk quotas), 201
storing data, 188-189
striped volumes, 188
subnodes, 279
switches
/a switch (winnt.exe), 49
/checkupgradeonly switch (winnt32.exe), 50
/cmd command switch (winnt32.exe), 49
/cmdcons switch (winnt32.exe), 49
/copydir folder switch (winnt32.exe), 49
/copysource folder switch (winnt32.exe), 49
/debug level file switch (winnt32.exe), 49
/e command switch (winnt.exe), 49
/i inf_file switch (winnt.exe), 49
/r folder switch (winnt.exe), 49
/rx folder switch (winnt.exe), 49
/s path switch, 49
/syspart drive switch (winnt32.exe), 50
/t drive switch (winnt.exe), 49
/tempdrive drive switch (winnt32.exe), 49
/u file switch (winnt.exe), 49
/udf file switch (winnt.exe), 49
/unattended [num] [file] switch (winnt32.exe), 49
command switches, 120
sysprep.exe switches, 51-52

update.exe command-line switches, 57-58
winnt.exe switches, 49-50
winnt32.exe switches, 49-50

sysprep.exe switches, 51-52

system memory, 126

System Monitor MMC snap-in, 148-149

system partitions, 26

System Policy Editor, 274-276

System State backups, 163-164

System State data, recovering, 166-170

SYSVOL directory, System State backups, 163

T

tabs

Advanced tab (network adapters properties page), 217
Applications tab (Task Manager), 143
DNS Properties tab (Advanced TCP/IP Settings window), 226
Driver tab (network adapters properties page), 218
General tab (network adapters properties page), 217
Hardware tab (volume properties dialog box), 187
Options tab (Advanced TCP/IP Settings window), 228
Performance tab (Task Manager), 146
Power Management tab (network adapters properties page), 219
Processes tab (Task Manager), 144-146
Quota tab (volume properties dialog box), 187, 200-201
Resources tab (network adapters properties page), 219
Sharing tab (volume properties dialog box), 187
Terminal Services Profile tab (Active Directory Users and Computers MMC), 254
Web Sharing tab (volume properties dialog box), 187
WINS Properties tab (Advanced TCP/IP Settings window), 227

Task Manager

applications, starting, 143
Applications tab, 143
Performance tab, 146
Processes tab, 144-146
starting, 142-143

TCP/IP Filtering Properties page (Advanced TCP/IP Settings window), 228

TCP/IP (Transfer Control Protocol/Internet Protocol)

configuring, 222, 225-227
DHCP, 233-236
DNS, 232-233
IP addresses, 222-224
IPSec, 228
packet filtering, 228
troubleshooting, 239-240
WINS, 236-238

templates, security templates, 285-287

Terminal Services Manager MMC, 253

terminal services

Application mode, 251, 254
installing, 251
RDP, 250
Remote Administration mode, 250
Terminal Services Configuration MMC, 253
Terminal Services Manager MMC, 253

Terminal Services Configuration MMC, 253
Terminal Services Profile tab (Active Directory Users and Computers MMC), 254
terminating processes, 146
testing center environments, 3-4
tests. *See* exams
text files, 150-151
Trace Logs (Performance Logs and Alerts MMC snap-in), 150
troubleshooting
- files, 79-80
- folders, 79-80
- hardware installation, 130-132
- ICS, 243-244
- installations, 58-59
- network adapters, 217, 219-220
- printers, 77-78
- shared folders, 79-80
- TCP/IP protocols, 239-240
- tools
  - Check Disk, 195-196
  - Disk Cleanup, 194
  - Disk Defragmenter, 196-197
  - troubleshooting wizards, 187

TSCAL (Terminal Server Client Access License), 251
TSV text files, 151

U

unattended installations
- disk duplication, 51-52
- script-based unattended installations, 37-38

unattended upgrades, 54
Unix interoperability, 73
unsigned drivers, configuring, 114-119
Update Device Driver Wizard, 129
update.exe command-line switches, 57-58
updating
- drivers, 128-129
- hardware, 129

upgrading, 27
- basic disks to dynamic disks, 188-189
- Windows NT 4.0 to Windows 2000, 53-54

user access
- local security, 86-90
- shared folders, configuring, 91

user accounts
- domain accounts, creating/managing, 264-266
- groups
  - built-in system groups, 271
  - domain groups, 264-266
  - local groups, 264, 268-273
- local accounts, 264
  - creating, 272-273
  - local administrator accounts, 267-268
  - local guest accounts, 267-268
- permissions, 264
- user authentication, 273-274

User Configuration nodes (group policy objects), 279
User groups (local groups), 269
user rights assignment policies, 283
USN (Update Sequence Numbers), 167

V

verifying hardware compatibility, 120-122
viewing
- physical disk properties, 184
- volumes
  - health statuses, 185
  - properties, 186-187

virtual directories, 100

Virtual Directory Creation Wizard, 100
volume properties dialog box (Disk Management), 186-187, 200-201
volumes
- defragmenting, 197
- disk quotas, 200-203
- drive letters, assigning, 193
- drive paths, assigning, 193
- dynamic volumes, 190-192
- health statuses, viewing, 185
- mirrored volumes, 188, 204-205
- properties, viewing, 186-187
- RAID-5 volumes, 188, 205-206
- shared folders, 92, 187
- simple volumes, 188
- spanned volumes, 188
- striped volumes, 188
- volume sharing, configuring, 187

VPN (Virtual Private Networks), 249

W

Web Sharing tab (volume properties dialog box), 187
Web sites
- administration (IIS), 98
- bandwidth throttling (IIS), 96
- configuring (IIS), 95
- HCL, 113, 120
- managing (IIS), 101
- multiple Web sites, hosting, 100-101
- process throttling (IIS), 96
- security (IIS), 94, 96
- sockets, 95
- WebDAV sites, 93
- Windows 2000 DataCenter Server HCL, 121
- Windows Update Web site, 113

Web-based resources, 19-20
WebDAV, 93
Windows 2000
- attended installations, 27
  - CD-ROM based installations, 28-34
  - setup disk installations, 35-36
  - winnt.exe, 37
  - winnt32.exe, 36
- backups, 160-164
- Group Policies, 276-278
- hardware compatibility, verifying, 120-122
- installations
  - answer file installation, 49-50
  - preparation, 22-27
  - troubleshooting, 58-59
  - unattended installations, 37-38, 51-52
- interoperability
  - Macintosh, 72-73
  - NetWare, 68-72
  - Unix, 73
- Service Packs, installing, 55-57
- Windows NT 4.0, upgrading from, 53-54

Windows 2000 DataCenter Server HCL Web site, 121
Windows 2000 Readiness Analyzer, 121-122
Windows Component Wizard, 251
Windows NT 4.0
- Service Packs, 55-57
- Windows 2000 upgrades, 53-54

Windows Services for Unix, 73
Windows Update Web site, 113
winnt.exe, 37, 49-50
winnt32.exe, 36, 49-50
WINS (Windows Internet Naming System), 227, 236-238
WINS Properties tab (Advanced TCP/IP Settings window), 227

wizards
Add New Printer Wizard, 75
Add/Remove Hardware Wizard, 124-125
Hardware Update Wizard, 129
New Dfs Root Wizard, 82
RRAS Setup Wizard, 246
troubleshooting wizards, opening, 187
Update Device Driver Wizard, 129
Virtual Directory Creation Wizard, 100
Windows Component Wizard, 251

workgroups, CD-ROM installations, 33